Foundations in Accountancy

FFA

ACCA

Paper F3

Financial Accounting

BPP Learning Media is an **ACCA Approved Content Provider** for the Foundations in Accountancy qualification. This means we work closely with ACCA to ensure this Interactive Text contains the information you need to pass your exam.

In this Interactive Text, which has been reviewed by the **ACCA examination team**, we:

- **Highlight** the **most important elements** in the syllabus and the **key skills** you need

- **Signpost** how each chapter links to the syllabus and the study guide

- **Provide** lots of **exam focus points** demonstrating what the examination team will want you to do

- **Emphasise key points** in regular **fast forward summaries**

- **Test your knowledge** in **quick quizzes**

- **Examine your understanding** in our **practice question bank**

- **Reference all the important topics** in our full index

BPP's **Practice & Revision Kit** also supports this paper.

FOR EXAMS FROM 1 SEPTEMBER 2016 TO 31 AUGUST 2017

First edition March 2011
Fifth edition January 2016

ISBN 9781 4727 4590 3
(Previous ISBN 9781 4727 3525 6)
e-ISBN 9781 4727 4631 3

British Library Cataloguing-in-Publication Data
A catalogue record for this book
is available from the British Library

Published by

BPP Learning Media Ltd
BPP House, Aldine Place
London W12 8AA

www.bpp.com/learningmedia

Printed in the United Kingdom by
Ashford Colour Press Limited.

Your learning materials, published by BPP Learning
Media Ltd, are printed on paper obtained from
traceable sustainable sources.

We are grateful to the Association of Chartered Certified
Accountants for permission to reproduce past
examination questions. The suggested solutions in the
practice answer bank have been prepared by BPP
Learning Media Ltd, except where otherwise stated.

BPP Learning Media is grateful to the IASB for
permission to reproduce extracts from the International
Financial Reporting Standards including all
International Accounting Standards, SIC and IFRIC
Interpretations (the Standards). The Standards together
with their accompanying documents are issued by:

The International Accounting Standards Board (IASB)
30 Cannon Street, London, EC4M 6XH, United
Kingdom. Email: info@ifrs.org Web: www.ifrs.org

Disclaimer: The IASB, the International Financial
Reporting Standards (IFRS) Foundation, the authors
and the publishers do not accept responsibility for any
loss caused by acting or refraining from acting in
reliance on the material in this publication, whether
such loss is caused by negligence or otherwise to the
maximum extent permitted by law.

Contents

Helping you to pass

BPP Learning Media – ACCA Approved Content Provider

As an ACCA **Approved Content Provider**, BPP Learning Media gives you the **opportunity** to use study materials reviewed by the ACCA examination team. By incorporating the examination team's comments and suggestions regarding the depth and breadth of syllabus coverage, the BPP Learning Media Interactive Text provides excellent, **ACCA-approved** support for your studies.

The PER alert!

To become a Certified Accounting Technician or qualify as an ACCA member, you have to not only pass all your exams but also fulfil a **practical experience requirement** (PER). To help you to recognise areas of the syllabus that you might be able to apply in the workplace to achieve different performance objectives, we have introduced the '**PER alert**' feature. You will find this feature throughout the Interactive Text to remind you that what you are **learning in order to pass** your Foundations in Accountancy and ACCA exams is **equally useful to the fulfilment of the PER requirement**.

Your achievement of the PER should be recorded in your online *My Experience* record.

Tackling studying

Studying can be a daunting prospect, particularly when you have lots of other commitments. The **different features** of the Interactive Text, the **purposes** of which are explained fully on the **Chapter features** page, will help you whilst studying and improve your chances of **exam success**.

Developing exam awareness

Our Interactive Texts are completely **focused** on helping you pass your exam.

Our advice on **Studying F3/FFA** outlines the **content** of the paper and the **recommended approach to studying**.

Exam focus points are included within the chapters to highlight when and how specific topics might be examined.

Using the Syllabus and Study Guide

You can find the syllabus and study guide on page ix – xxii of this Interactive Text.

Testing what you can do

Testing yourself helps you develop the skills you need to pass the exam and also confirms that you can recall what you have learnt.

We include **Questions** – lots of them – both within chapters and in the **Practice Question Bank**, as well as **Quick Quizzes** at the end of each chapter to test your knowledge of the chapter content.

Chapter features

Each chapter contains a number of helpful features to guide you through each topic.

Topic list	Tells you what you will be studying in this chapter and the relevant section numbers, together with the ACCA syllabus references.
Introduction	Puts the chapter content in the context of the syllabus as a whole.
Study Guide	Links the chapter content with ACCA guidance.
Fast Forward	Summarises the content of main chapter headings, allowing you to preview and review each section easily.
EXAMPLE	Demonstrates how to apply key knowledge and techniques.
Key Term	Definitions of important concepts that can often earn you easy marks in exams.
Exam Focus Point	Tells you how specific topics may be examined.
Formula	Formulae which have to be learnt.
PER Alert	This feature gives you a useful indication of syllabus areas that closely relate to performance objectives in your Practical Experience Requirement (PER).
Question	Gives you essential practice of techniques covered in the chapter.
Chapter Roundup	A full list of the Fast Forwards included in the chapter, providing an easy source of review.
Quick Quiz	A quick test of your knowledge of the main topics in the chapter.
Practice Question Bank	Found at the back of the Interactive Text with more exam-style chapter questions. Cross referenced for easy navigation.

Studying F3/FFA

How to Use this Interactive Text

Aim of this Interactive Text

To provide the knowledge and practice to help you succeed in the examination for Paper F3/FFA *Financial Accounting*.

To pass the examination you need a thorough understanding in all areas covered by the syllabus and teaching guide.

Recommended approach

(a) To pass you need to be able to answer questions on **everything** specified by the syllabus and teaching guide. Read the Interactive Text very carefully and do not skip any of it.

(b) Learning is an **active** process. Do **all** the questions as you work through the Interactive Text so you can be sure you really understand what you have read.

(c) After you have covered the material in the Interactive Text, work through the **Practice Question Bank**, checking your answers carefully against the **Practice Answer Bank**.

(d) Before you take the exam, check that you still remember the material using the following quick revision plan.

   (i) Read through the **chapter topic list** at the beginning of each chapter. Are there any gaps in your knowledge? If so, study the section again.

   (ii) Read and learn the **key terms**.

   (iii) Look at the **exam focus points**. These show the ways in which topics might be examined.

   (iv) Read the **chapter roundups**, which are a summary of the **fast forwards** in each chapter.

   (v) Do the **quick quizzes** again. If you know what you're doing, they shouldn't take long.

This approach is only a suggestion. You or your college may well adapt it to suit your needs. Remember this is a **practical** course.

(a) Try to relate the material to your experience in the workplace or any other work experience you may have had.

(b) Try to make as many links as you can to other papers at the Introductory and Intermediate levels.

For practice and revision use BPP Learning Media's Practice & Revision Kit and Passcards.

What F3/FFA is about

Paper F3/FFA aims to develop your knowledge and understanding of the underlying principles, concepts and regulations relating to financial accounting. You will need to demonstrate technical proficiency in the use of double entry techniques, including the preparation of basic financial statements for incorporated and unincorporated entities, as well as simple consolidated financial statements for group incorporated entities. You also need to be able to conduct a basic interpretation of financial statements. If you plan to progress through the ACCA qualification, the skills you learn at F3 will be built on in Papers F7 and P2.

Approach to examining the syllabus

Paper F3/FFA is a two-hour paper. It can be taken as a written paper or a computer based examination. The questions in the computer based examination are objective test questions – multiple choice, number entry and multiple response. (See page xxiii for frequently asked questions about computer based examinations.)

Both the written and computer based examinations are structured as follows.

		Number of marks
Section A	35 compulsory objective test questions of two marks each	70
Section B	2 compulsory multi-task questions of fifteen marks each	30
		100

Multi-task questions are a series of short questions relating to one scenario. These short questions can take a number of formats, eg drop down lists, multiple choice, number entry and multiple response.

In paper exams, multi-task questions will require longer answers and workings need to be shown to ensure that an error is only penalised once.

Syllabus and Study Guide

Financial Accounting (F3/FFA) September 2016 to August 2017

This syllabus and study guide are designed to help with teaching and learning and is intended to provide detailed information on what could be assessed in any examination session.

THE STRUCTURE OF THE SYLLABUS AND STUDY GUIDE

Relational diagram with other papers

This diagram shows direct and indirect links between this examination and other examinations which precede or follow it. Some examinations are directly underpinned by others. These links are shown as solid line arrows. The indirect links are shown as dotted line arrows. The relational diagram therefore indicates where learners are expected to have underpinning knowledge and where it would be useful to review previous learning before undertaking study.

Overall aim of the syllabus

This explains briefly the overall objective of the examination and indicates in the broadest sense the capabilities to be developed within the examination.

Main capabilities

This syllabus's aim is broken down into several main capabilities which divide the syllabus and study guide into discrete sections.

Relational diagram of main capabilities

This diagram illustrates the flows and links between the main capabilities (sections) of the syllabus and should be used as an aid to planning teaching and learning in a structured way.

Syllabus rationale

This is a narrative explaining how the syllabus is structured and how the main capabilities or sections of the syllabus are linked. The rationale also explains in further detail what the examination intends to assess and how.

Detailed syllabus

This shows the breakdown of the main capabilities (sections) of the syllabus into subject areas. This is the blueprint for the detailed study guide.

Approach to examining the syllabus

This section briefly explains the structure of the examination and how it is assessed.

Study Guide

This is the main document that students and learning and content providers should use as the basis of their studies, instruction and materials respectively.

Examinations will be based on the detail of the study guide which comprehensively identifies what could be assessed within any examination session. The study guide is a precise reflection and breakdown of the syllabus. It is divided into sections based on the main capabilities identified in the syllabus. These sections are divided into subject areas which relate to the sub-capabilities included in the detailed syllabus. Subject areas are broken down into sub-headings which describe the detailed outcomes that could be assessed in examinations. These outcomes indicate what exams may require students to demonstrate, and the broad intellectual level at which these may need to be demonstrated (*see intellectual levels below).

LEVEL OF ASSESSMENTS – INTELLECTUAL DEMAND

ACCA qualifications are designed to progressively broaden and deepen the knowledge and skills demonstrated by the student at a range of levels through each qualification.

Throughout, the study guides assess both knowledge and skills. Therefore a clear distinction is drawn, within each subject area, between assessing knowledge and skills and in assessing their application within an accounting or business context. The assessment of knowledge is denoted by a superscript [K] and the assessment of skills is denoted by the superscript [S].

VALUE OF ASSESSMENTS – GUIDED LEARNING HOURS AND EDUCATION RECOGNITION

As a member of the International Federation of Accountants, ACCA seeks to enhance the education recognition of its qualification on both national and international education frameworks, and with educational authorities and partners globally. In doing so, ACCA aims to ensure that its qualifications are recognized and valued by governments, regulatory authorities and employers across all sectors. To this end, ACCA qualifications are currently recognized on the education frameworks in several countries. Please refer to your national education framework regulator for further information about recognition.

GUIDE TO EXAM STRUCTURE

The structure of examinations varies within and between modules and levels.
The Foundations examinations contain 100% compulsory questions to encourage candidates to study across the breadth of each syllabus.
All Foundations examinations are assessed by two-hour paper based and computer based examinations.
The pass mark for all FIA examination papers is 50%.

GUIDE TO EXAMINATION ASSESSMENT

ACCA reserves the right to examine anything contained within any study guide within any examination session. This includes knowledge, techniques, principles, theories, and concepts as specified.

For specified financial accounting, audit and tax papers, except where indicated otherwise, ACCA will publish *examinable documents* once a year to indicate exactly what regulations and legislation could potentially be assessed within identified examination sessions.

For this examination regulation *issued* or legislation *passed* on or before 1st September 2015, will be assessed from September 2016 to August 31st 2017. Please refer to the examinable documents for the paper (where relevant) for further information.

Regulation issued or legislation passed in accordance with the above dates may be examinable even if the *effective* date is in the future.

The term issued or passed relates to when regulation or legislation has been formally approved.

The term effective relates to when regulation or legislation must be applied to entity transactions and business practices.

The study guide offers more detailed guidance on the depth and level at which the examinable documents will be examined. The study guide should therefore be read in conjunction with the examinable documents list.

Qualification Structure

The qualification structure requires candidates who wish to be awarded the Diploma in Accounting and Business to pass the F1/FAB, F2/FMA and the F3/FFA examinations and successfully complete the Foundations in Professionalism module

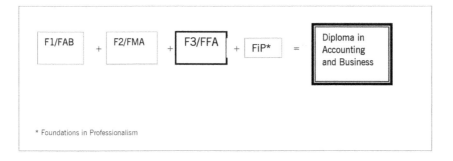

* Foundations in Professionalism

Syllabus Structure

The Foundations in Accountancy suite of qualifications is designed so that a student can progress through three discrete levels; Introductory Certificate level, Intermediate Certificate level and the Diploma level.

Students are recommended to enter Foundations in Accountancy at the level which is most appropriate to their needs and to take examinations in order, but this is not a mandatory requirement

Syllabus

AIM

To develop knowledge and understanding of the underlying principles and concepts relating to financial accounting and technical proficiency in the use of double-entry accounting techniques including the preparation of basic financial statements.

RATIONALE

The syllabus for Paper FFA/F3, *Financial Accounting*, introduces the candidate to the fundamentals of the regulatory framework relating to accounts preparation and to the qualitative characteristics of useful information. The syllabus then covers drafting financial statements and the principles of accounts preparation. The syllabus then concentrates in depth on recording, processing, and reporting business transactions and events. The syllabus then covers the use of the trial balance and how to identify and correct errors, and then the preparation of financial statements for incorporated and unincorporated entities. The syllabus then moves in two directions, firstly requiring candidates to be able to conduct a basic interpretation of financial statements; and secondly requiring the preparation of simple consolidated

financial statements from the individual financial statements of group incorporated entities.

MAIN CAPABILITIES

On successful completion of this paper, candidates should be able to:

A. Explain the context and purpose of financial reporting

B. Define the qualitative characteristics of financial information

C. Demonstrate the use of double-entry and accounting systems

D. Record transactions and events

E. Prepare a trial balance (including identifying and correcting errors)

F. Prepare basic financial statements for incorporated and unincorporated entities.

G. Prepare simple consolidated financial statements

H. Interpretation of financial statements

RELATIONAL DIAGRAM OF MAIN CAPABILITIES

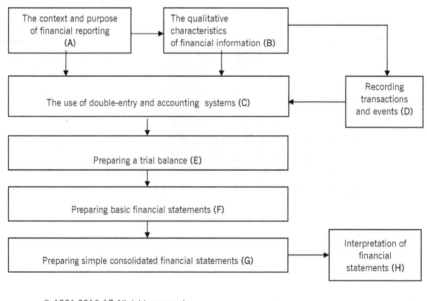

DETAILED SYLLABUS

A   The context and purpose of financial reporting

1.   The scope and purpose of financial statements for external reporting

2.   Users' and stakeholders' needs

3.   The main elements of financial reports

4.   The regulatory framework (legislation and regulation, reasons and limitations, relevance of accounting standards)

5.   Duties and responsibilities of those charged with governance.

B   The qualitative characteristics of financial information

1.   The qualitative characteristics of financial information

C   The use of double-entry and accounting systems

1.   Double-entry book-keeping principles including the maintenance of accounting records and sources of accounting information

2.   Ledger accounts, books of prime entry, and journals

D   Recording transactions and events

1.   Sales and purchases

2.   Cash

3.   Inventory

4.   Tangible non-current assets

5.   Depreciation

6.   Intangible non-current assets and amortisation

7.   Accruals and prepayments

8.   Receivables and payables

9.   Provisions and contingencies

10. Capital structure and finance costs

E   Preparing a trial balance

1.   Trial balance

2.   Correction of errors

3.   Control accounts and reconciliations

4.   Bank reconciliations

5.   Suspense accounts

F   Preparing basic financial statements

1.   Statements of financial position

2.   Statements of profit or loss and other comprehensive income

3.   Disclosure notes

4   Events after the reporting period

5.   Statements of cash flows
6.   Incomplete records

G   Preparing simple consolidated financial statements

1.   Subsidiaries

2.   Associates

H   Interpretation of financial statements

1.   Importance and purpose of analysis of financial statements

2.   Ratios

3.   Analysis of financial statements

5

APPROACH TO EXAMINING THE SYLLABUS

THE SYLLABUS IS ASSESSED BY A TWO HOUR PAPER-BASED OR COMPUTER-BASED EXAMINATION.

The syllabus is assessed by a two hour paper-based or computer-based examination. Questions will assess all parts of the syllabus and will test knowledge and some comprehension or application of this knowledge. The examination will consist of two sections. Section A will contain 35 two mark objective questions. Section B will contain 2 fifteen mark multi-task questions. These will test consolidations and accounts preparation. The consolidation question could include a small amount of interpretation and the accounts preparation question could be set in the context of a sole trader or a limited company.

Study Guide

A THE CONTEXT AND PURPOSE OF FINANCIAL REPORTING

1. The scope and purpose of, financial statements for external reporting

a) Define financial reporting – recording, analysing and summarising financial data.[K]

b) Identify and define types of business entity – sole trader, partnership, limited liability company.[K]

c) Recognise the legal differences between a sole trader, partnership and a limited liability company.[K]

d) Identify the advantages and disadvantages of operating as a limited liability company, sole trader or partnership.[K]

e) Understand the nature, principles and scope of financial reporting.[K]

2. Users' and stakeholders' needs

a) Identify the users of financial statements and state and differentiate between their information needs.[K]

3. The main elements of financial reports

a) Understand and identify the purpose of each of the main financial statements.[K]

b) Define and identify assets, liabilities, equity, revenue and expenses.[K]

4. The regulatory framework

a) Understand the role of the regulatory system including the roles of the IFRS Foundation (IFRSF), the International Accounting Standards Board (IASB), the IFRS Advisory Council (IFRS AC) and the IFRS Interpretations Committee (IFRS IC).[K]

b) Understand the role of International Financial Reporting Standards.[K]

5. Duties and responsibilities of those charged with governance

a) Explain what is meant by governance specifically in the context of the preparation of financial statements[K]

b) Describe the duties and responsibilities of directors and other parties covering the preparation of the financial statements.[K]

B THE QUALITATIVE CHARACTERISTICS OF FINANCIAL INFORMATION

1. The qualitative characteristics of financial information

a) Define, understand and apply qualitative characteristics:[K]
   i) Relevance
   ii) Faithful representation
   iii) Comparability
   iv) Verifiability
   v) Timeliness
   vi) Understandability

b) Define, understand and apply accounting concepts:[K]
   i) Materiality
   ii) Substance over form
   iii) Going concern
   iv) Business entity concept
   v) Accruals
   vi) Fair presentation
   vii) Consistency

C THE USE OF DOUBLE-ENTRY AND ACCOUNTING SYSTEMS

1. Double-entry book-keeping principles including the maintenance of accounting records

a) Identify and explain the function of the main data sources in an accounting system.[K]

b) Outline the contents and purpose of different types of business documentation, including: quotation, sales order, purchase order, goods received note, goods despatched note, invoice,

7

statement, credit note, debit note, remittance advice, receipt.[K]

c) Understand and apply the concept of double-entry accounting and the duality concept.[K]

d) Understand and apply the accounting equation.[S]

e) Understand how the accounting system contributes to providing useful accounting information and complies with organisational policies and deadlines.[K]

f) Identify the main types of business transactions e.g. sales, purchases, payments, receipts.[K]

2. **Ledger accounts, books of prime entry and journals**

a) Identify the main types of ledger accounts and books of prime entry, and understand their nature and function.[K]

b) Understand and illustrate the uses of journals and the posting of journal entries into ledger accounts.[S]

c) Identify correct journals from given narrative.[S]

d) Illustrate how to balance and close a ledger account.[S]

D **RECORDING TRANSACTIONS AND EVENTS**

1. **Sales and purchases**

a) Record sale and purchase transactions in ledger accounts.[S]

b) Understand and record sales and purchase returns.[S]

c) Understand the general principles of the operation of a sales tax.[K]

d) Calculate sales tax on transactions and record the consequent accounting entries.[S]

e) Account for discounts allowed and discounts received.[S]

2. **Cash**

a) Record cash transactions in ledger accounts.[S]

b) Understand the need for a record of petty cash transactions.[K]

3. **Inventory**

a) Recognise the need for adjustments for inventory in preparing financial statements.[K]

b) Record opening and closing inventory.[S]

c) Identify the alternative methods of valuing inventory.[K]

d) Understand and apply the IASB requirements for valuing inventories.[S]

e) Recognise which costs should be included in valuing inventories.[S]

f) Understand the use of continuous and period end inventory records.[K]

g) Calculate the value of closing inventory using FIFO (first in, first out) and AVCO (average cost) – both periodic weighted average and continuous weighted average.[S]

h) Understand the impact of accounting concepts on the valuation of inventory.[K]

i) Identify the impact of inventory valuation methods on profit and on assets.[S]

4. **Tangible non-current assets**

a) Define non-current assets.[K]

b) Recognise the difference between current and non-current assets.[K]

c) Explain the difference between capital and revenue items.[K]

d) Classify expenditure as capital or revenue expenditure.[S]

e) Prepare ledger entries to record the acquisition and disposal of non-current assets.[S]

8

f) Calculate and record profits or losses on disposal of non-current assets in the statement of profit or loss including part exchange transactions.[S]

g) Record the revaluation of a non-current asset in ledger accounts, the statement of profit or loss and other comprehensive income and in the statement of financial position.[S]

h) Calculate the profit or loss on disposal of a revalued asset.[S]

i) Illustrate how non-current asset balances and movements are disclosed in financial statements.[S]

j) Explain the purpose and function of an asset register.[K]

5. Depreciation

a) Understand and explain the purpose of depreciation.[K]

b) Calculate the charge for depreciation using straight line and reducing balance methods.[S]

c) Identify the circumstances where different methods of depreciation would be appropriate.[K]

d) Illustrate how depreciation expense and accumulated depreciation are recorded in ledger accounts.[S]

e) Calculate depreciation on a revalued non-current asset including the transfer of excess depreciation between the revaluation surplus and retained earnings.[S]

f) Calculate the adjustments to depreciation necessary if changes are made in the estimated useful life and/or residual value of a non-current asset.[S]

g) Record depreciation in the statement of profit or loss and statement of financial position.[S]

6. Intangible non-current assets and amortisation

a) Recognise the difference between tangible and intangible non-current assets.[K]

b) Identify types of intangible assets.[K]

c) Identify the definition and treatment of "research costs" and "development costs" in accordance with International Financial Reporting Standards.[K]

d) Calculate amounts to be capitalised as development expenditure or to be expensed from given information.[S]

e) Explain the purpose of amortisation.[K]

f) Calculate and account for the charge for amortisation.[S]

7. Accruals and prepayments

a) Understand how the matching concept applies to accruals and prepayments.[K]

b) Identify and calculate the adjustments needed for accruals and prepayments in preparing financial statements.[S]

c) Illustrate the process of adjusting for accruals and prepayments in preparing financial statements.[S]

d) Prepare the journal entries and ledger entries for the creation of an accrual or prepayment.[S]

e) Understand and identify the impact on profit and net assets of accruals and prepayments.[S]

8. Receivables and payables

a) Explain and identify examples of receivables and payables.[K]

b) Identify the benefits and costs of offering credit facilities to customers.[K]

c) Understand the purpose of an aged receivables analysis.[K]

d) Understand the purpose of credit limits.[K]

9

e) Prepare the bookkeeping entries to write off an irrecoverable debt.[S]

f) Record an irrecoverable debt recovered.[S]

g) Identify the impact of irrecoverable debts on the statement of profit or loss and on the statement of financial position.[S]

h) Prepare the bookkeeping entries to create and adjust an allowance for receivables.[S]

i) Illustrate how to include movements in the allowance for receivables in the statement of profit or loss and how the closing balance of the allowance should appear in the statement of financial position.[S]

j) Account for contras between trade receivables and payables.[S]

k) Prepare, reconcile and understand the purpose of supplier statements.[S]

l) Classify items as current or non-current liabilities in the statement of financial position.[S]

9. Provisions and contingencies

a) Understand the definition of "provision", "contingent liability" and "contingent asset".[K]

b) Distinguish between and classify items as provisions, contingent liabilities or contingent assets.[K]

c) Identify and illustrate the different methods of accounting for provisions, contingent liabilities and contingent assets.[K]

d) Calculate provisions and changes in provisions.[S]

e) Account for the movement in provisions.[S]

f) Report provisions in the final accounts.[S]

10. Capital structure and finance costs

a) Understand the capital structure of a limited liability company including: [K]
i) Ordinary shares

ii) Preference shares (redeemable and irredeemable)
iii) Loan notes.

b) Record movements in the share capital and share premium accounts.[S]

c) Identify and record the other reserves which may appear in the company statement of financial position.[S]

d) Define a bonus (capitalisation) issue and its advantages and disadvantages.[K]

e) Define a rights issue and its advantages and disadvantages.[K]

f) Record and show the effects of a bonus (capitalisation) issue in the statement of financial position.[S]

g) Record and show the effects of a rights issue in the statement of financial position.[S]

h) Record dividends in ledger accounts and the financial statements.[S]

i) Calculate and record finance costs in ledger accounts and the financial statements.[S]

j) Identify the components of the statement of changes in equity.[K]

E PREPARING A TRIAL BALANCE

1. Trial balance

a) Identify the purpose of a trial balance.[K]

b) Extract ledger balances into a trial balance.[S]

c) Prepare extracts of an opening trial balance.[S]

d) Identify and understand the limitations of a trial balance.[K]

2. Correction of errors

a) Identify the types of error which may occur in bookkeeping systems.[K]

b) Identify errors which would be highlighted by the extraction of a trial balance.[K]

10

c) Prepare journal entries to correct errors.[S]

d) Calculate and understand the impact of errors on the statement of profit or loss and other comprehensive income and statement of financial position.[S]

3. Control accounts and reconciliations

a) Understand the purpose of control accounts for accounts receivable and accounts payable.[K]
b) Understand how control accounts relate to the double-entry system.[K]

c) Prepare ledger control accounts from given information.[S]

d) Perform control account reconciliations for accounts receivable and accounts payable.[S]

e) Identify errors which would be highlighted by performing a control account reconciliation.[K]

f) Identify and correct errors in control accounts and ledger accounts.[S]

4. Bank reconciliations

a) Understand the purpose of bank reconciliations.[K]

b) Identify the main reasons for differences between the cash book and the bank statement.[K]

c) Correct cash book errors and/or omissions.[S]

d) Prepare bank reconciliation statements.[S]

e) Derive bank statement and cash book balances from given information.[S]

f) Identify the bank balance to be reported in the final accounts.[S]

5. Suspense accounts

a) Understand the purpose of a suspense account.[K]

b) Identify errors leading to the creation of a suspense account.[K]

c) Record entries in a suspense account.[S]

d) Make journal entries to clear a suspense account.[S]

F PREPARING BASIC FINANCIAL STATEMENTS

1. Statements of financial position

a) Recognise how the accounting equation, accounting treatments (as stipulated within sections D, E and examinable documents) and business entity convention underlie the statement of financial position.[K]

b) Understand the nature of reserves.[K]

c) Identify and report reserves in a company statement of financial position.[S]

d) Prepare a statement of financial position or extracts as applicable from given information using accounting treatments as stipulated within sections D, E and examinable documents.[S]

e) Understand why the heading retained earnings appears in a company statement of financial position.[K]

2. Statements of profit or loss and other comprehensive income

a) Prepare a statement of profit or loss and other comprehensive income or extracts as applicable from given information using accounting treatments as stipulated within section D, E and examinable documents.[S]

b) Understand how accounting concepts apply to revenue and expenses.[K]

c) Calculate revenue, cost of sales, gross profit, profit for the year, and total comprehensive income from given information.[S]

d) Disclose items of income and expenditure in the statement of profit or loss. [S]

e) Record income tax in the statement of profit or loss of a company including the under and overprovision of tax in the prior year.[S]

11

f) Understand the interrelationship between the statement of financial position and the statement of profit or loss and other comprehensive income. [K]

g) Identify items requiring separate disclosure on the face of the statement of profit or loss.[K]

3. **Disclosure notes**

a) Explain the purpose of disclosure notes[K]

b) Draft the following disclosure notes[S]
   i) Non current assets including tangible and in tangible assets
   ii) Provisions
   iii) Events after the reporting period
   iv) Inventory

4. **Events after the reporting period**

a) Define an event after the reporting period in accordance with International Financial Reporting Standards.[K]

b) Classify events as adjusting or non-adjusting.[S]

c) Distinguish between how adjusting and non-adjusting events are reported in the financial statements.[K]

5 **Statements of cash flows (excluding partnerships)**

a) Differentiate between profit and cash flow.[K]

b) Understand the need for management to control cash flow.[K]

c) Recognise the benefits and drawbacks to users of the financial statements of a statement of cash flows. [K]

d) Classify the effect of transactions on cash flows.[S]

e) Calculate the figures needed for the statement of cash flows including:[S]
   i) Cash flows from operating activities
   ii) Cash flows from investing activities
   iii) Cash flows from financing activities

f) Calculate the cash flow from operating activities using the indirect and direct method.[S]

g) Prepare statements of cash flows and extracts from statements of cash flows from given information.[S]

h) Identify the treatment of given transactions in a company's statement of cash flows.[K]

6. **Incomplete records**

a) Understand and apply techniques used in incomplete record situations: [S]
   i) Use of accounting equation
   ii) Use of ledger accounts to calculate missing figures
   iii) Use of cash and/or bank summaries
   iv) Use of profit percentages to calculate missing figures.

G **PREPARING SIMPLE CONSOLIDATED FINANCIAL STATEMENTS**

1. **Subsidiaries**

a) Define and describe the following terms in the context of group accounting: [K]
   i) Parent
   ii) Subsidiary
   iii) Control
   iv) Consolidated or group financial statements
   v) Non-controlling interest
   vi) Trade / simple investment

b) Identify subsidiaries within a group structure. [K]

c) Describe the components of and prepare a consolidated statement of financial position or extracts thereof including: [S]
   i) Fair value adjustments at acquisition on land and buildings (excluding depreciation adjustments)
   ii) Fair value of consideration transferred from cash and shares (excluding deferred and contingent consideration)
   iii) Elimination of intra-group trading balances (excluding cash and goods in transit)
   iv) Removal of unrealised profit arising on intra-group trading
   v) Acquisition of subsidiaries part way through the financial year

d) Calculate goodwill (excluding impairment of goodwill) using the full goodwill method only as follows: [S]

Fair value of consideration	X
Fair value of non-controlling interest	X
Less fair value of net assets at acquisition	(X)
Goodwill at acquisition	X

e) Describe the components of and prepare a consolidated statement of profit or loss or extracts thereof including: [S]
   i) Elimination of intra-group trading balances (excluding cash and goods in transit)
   ii) Removal of unrealised profit arising on intra-group trading
   iii) Acquisition of subsidiaries part way through the financial year

2. Associates

a) Define and identify an associate and significant influence and identify the situations where significant influence or participating interest exists. [K]

b) Describe the key features of a parent-associate relationship and be able to identify an associate within a group structure. [K]

c) Describe the principle of equity accounting [K]

H INTERPRETATION OF FINANCIAL STATEMENTS

1. Importance and purpose of analysis of financial statements

a) Describe how the interpretation and analysis of financial statements is used in a business environment. [K]

b) Explain the purpose of interpretation of ratios [K].

2. Ratios

a) Calculate key accounting ratios [S]
   i) Profitability
   ii) Liquidity
   iii) Efficiency
   iv) Position
b) Explain the interrelationships between ratios [K]

3. Analysis of financial statements

a) Calculate and interpret the relationship between the elements of the financial statements with regard to profitability, liquidity, efficient use of resources and financial position [S].

b) Draw valid conclusions from the information contained within the financial statements and present these to the appropriate user of the financial statements. [S]

SUMMARY OF CHANGES TO F3/FFA

13

BPP
LEARNING MEDIA

ACCA periodically reviews its qualification syllabuses so that they fully meet the needs of stakeholders including employers, students, regulatory and advisory bodies and learning providers. These syllabus changes take effect from 1st September each year.

The detailed changes to the syllabus are summarised in the table below.

Section and subject area	Syllabus content

Describe the components of and prepare a consolidated statement of profit or loss or extracts thereof including: [S]
  i) Elimination of intra-group trading balances (excluding cash and goods in transit)
  ii) Removal of unrealised profit arising on intra-group trading
  iii) Acquisition of subsidiaries part way through the financial year.
	This learning outcome has been amended so that "other comprehensive income" is no longer assessed within the section of this syllabus relating to consolidated financial statements.

14

The Computer Based Examination

Computer based examinations (CBEs) are available for the first seven Foundations in Accountancy papers (not papers FAU, FTX or FFM) and ACCA papers F1, F2 and F3, in addition to the conventional paper based examination.

CBEs must be taken at an ACCA CBE Licensed Centre.

How does CBE work?

- Questions are displayed on a monitor.
- Candidates enter their answer directly onto the computer.
- Candidates have two hours to complete the examination.
- When the candidate has completed their examination, the final percentage score is calculated and displayed on screen.
- Candidates are provided with a Provisional Result Notification showing their results before leaving the examination room.
- The CBE Licensed Centre uploads the results to the ACCA (as proof of the candidate's performance) within 72 hours.
- Candidates can check their exam status on the ACCA website by logging into myACCA.

Benefits

- **Flexibility**, as a CBE can be sat at any time.
- **Resits** can also be taken at any time and there is no restriction on the number of times a candidate can sit a CBE.
- **Instant feedback** is provided, as the computer displays the results at the end of the CBE.
- Results are notified to ACCA within 72 hours.

CBE question types

- Multiple choice – choose one answer from four options
- Multiple response – select more than one response by clicking the appropriate tick boxes
- Multiple response matching – select a response to a number of related statements by choosing one option from a number of drop-down menus
- Number entry – key in a numerical response to a question
- Multiple task questions – a series of short questions related to one scenario. Question formats could include number entry, drop-down lists, multiple choice, multiple response and hotspot

For more information on CBEs, visit the ACCA website.

www.accaglobal.com/en/student/Exams/Computer-based-exams.html

Tackling Multiple Choice Questions

MCQs are part of all Foundations in Accountancy exams and ACCA papers F1, F2 and F3.

The MCQs in your exam contain four possible answers. You have to **choose the option that best answers the question**. The three incorrect options are called distracters. There is a skill in answering MCQs quickly and correctly. By practising MCQs you can develop this skill, giving you a better chance of passing the exam.

You may wish to follow the approach outlined below, or you may prefer to adapt it.

Step 1	Skim read all the MCQs and identify what appear to be the easier questions.
Step 2	Attempt each question – **starting with the easier questions** identified in Step 1. Read the question **thoroughly**. You may prefer to work out the answer before looking at the options, or you may prefer to look at the options at the beginning. Adopt the method that works best for you.
Step 3	Read the four options and see if one matches your own answer. Be careful with numerical questions, as the distracters are designed to match answers that incorporate common errors. Check that your calculation is correct. Have you followed the requirement exactly? Have you included every stage of the calculation?
Step 4	You may find that none of the options matches your answer.
	• Re-read the question to ensure that you understand it and are answering the requirement
	• Eliminate any obviously wrong answers
	• Consider which of the remaining answers is the most likely to be correct and select the option
Step 5	If you are still unsure make a note and continue to the next question.
Step 6	Revisit unanswered questions. When you come back to a question after a break you often find you are able to answer it correctly straight away. If you are still unsure have a guess. You are not penalised for incorrect answers, so **never leave a question unanswered!**

After extensive practice and revision of MCQs, you may find that you recognise a question when you sit the exam. Be aware that the detail and/or requirement may be different. If the question seems familiar read the requirement and options carefully – do not assume that it is identical.

A

The context and purpose of financial reporting

Introduction to accounting

We will begin by looking at the aim of F3/FFA, as laid out in ACCA's syllabus and Study Guide and discussed already in the introductory pages to this Text (if you haven't read through the introductory pages, do so now – the information in there is extremely important).

'Aim

To develop knowledge and understanding of the underlying principles and concepts relating to financial accounting and technical proficiency in the use of double-entry accounting techniques including the preparation of basic financial statements.'

Before you learn **how** to prepare financial reports, it is important to understand **why** they are prepared. Sections 1 to 3 of this chapter introduce some basic ideas about financial reports and give an indication of their purpose. You will also be introduced to the **functions** which accountants carry out: financial accounting and management accounting. These functions will be developed in detail in your later studies.

Section 4 identifies the main **users** of financial statements and their **needs**. Section 5 considers the responsibilities for financial reporting of those charged with governance.

Finally, in Section 6, we will look at the **main financial statements**: the **statement of financial position** and the **statement of profit or loss**; as well as the main elements of assets, liabilities, equity, revenue and expense.

TOPIC LIST	SYLLABUS REFERENCE
1 The purpose of financial reporting	A1(a)
2 Types of business entity	A1(b)–(d)
3 Nature, principles and scope of financial reporting	A1(e)
4 Users' and stakeholders' needs	A2(a)
5 Governance	A5(a),(b)
6 The main elements of financial reports	A3(a),(b)

Study Guide	Intellectual level
A **The context and purpose of financial reporting**	
1 **The scope and purpose of financial statements for external reporting**	
(a) Define financial reporting – recording, analysing and summarising financial data.	K
(b) Identify and define types of business entity – sole trader, partnership, limited liability company.	K
(c) Recognise the legal differences between a sole trader, partnership and a limited liability company.	K
(d) Identify the advantages and disadvantages of operating as a limited liability company, sole trader or partnership.	K
(e) Understand the nature, principles and scope of financial reporting.	K
2 **Users' and stakeholders' needs**	
(a) Identify the users of financial statements and state and differentiate between their information needs.	K
3 **The main elements of financial reports**	
(a) Understand and identify the purpose of each of the main financial statements.	K
(b) Define and identify assets, liabilities, equity, revenue and expenses.	K
5 **Duties and responsibilities of those charged with governance**	
(a) Explain what is meant by governance specifically in the context of the preparation of financial statements.	K
(b) Describe the duties and responsibilities of directors and other parties covering the preparation of the financial statements.	K

1 The purpose of financial reporting

1.1 What is financial reporting?

> **Financial reporting** is a way of recording, analysing and summarising financial data.

Financial data is the name given to the actual transactions carried out by a business eg sales of goods, purchases of goods, payment of expenses. These transactions are **recorded** in **books of prime entry**.

The transactions are **analysed** in the books of prime entry and the totals are posted to the ledger accounts.

Finally, the transactions are **summarised** in the financial statements.

QUESTION

Financial reporting

Financial reporting is only carried out by large quoted companies.

Is this statement correct?

A   Yes
B   No

ANSWER

The correct answer is B. Financial reporting is carried out by all businesses, no matter what their size or structure.

 ## 2 Types of business entity

2.1 What is a business?

Businesses of whatever size or nature exist to make a **profit**.

There are a number of different ways of looking at a business. Some ideas are listed below.

- A business is a **commercial or industrial concern** which exists to deal in the manufacture, resale or supply of goods and services.
- A business is an **organisation which uses economic resources** to create goods or services which customers will buy.
- A business is an **organisation providing jobs** for people.
- A business invests **money in resources** (for example buildings, machinery, employees) in order to make even more money for its owners.

This last definition introduces the important idea of profit. Businesses vary from very small businesses (the local shopkeeper or plumber) to very large ones (Vodafone, IKEA, Corus). However, all of them want to earn profits.

Profit is the excess of income over expenditure. When expenditure exceeds revenue, the business is running at a loss.

One of the jobs of an accountant is to measure income and expenditure, and so profit. It is not as straightforward a task as it may seem.

2.2 Types of business entity

There are three main types of business entity.

Sole traders. A sole tradership is a business owned and run by one individual, perhaps employing one or two assistants and controlling their work. The individual's business and personal affairs are, for legal and tax purposes, identical.

Limited liability companies. Limited liability status means that the business's debts and the personal debts of the business's owners (shareholders) are legally separate. The shareholders cannot be sued for the debts of the business unless they have given some personal guarantee. This is called limited liability.

Partnerships. These are arrangements between individuals to carry on business in common with a view to profit. A partnership, however, involves obligations to others, and so a partnership is usually governed by a partnership agreement. Unless it is a limited liability partnership (LLP), partners will be fully liable for debts and liabilities, for example if the partnership is sued.

In law, sole traders and partnerships are not separate entities from their owners. However, a limited liability company is **legally a separate entity** from its owners. Contracts can therefore be issued in the company's name.

For **accounting purposes**, all three entities are treated as separate from their owners. This is called the **business entity concept**.

2.3 Sole traders

This is the oldest and most straightforward structure for a business. Sole traders are people who work for themselves. Of course, it doesn't necessarily mean that the business has only one worker. The sole trader can employ others to do any or all of the work in the business. A sole trader owns and runs a business, contributes the capital to start the enterprise, runs it with or without employees, and earns the profits or stands the loss of the venture. Typical sole trading organisations include small local shops, hairdressers, plumbers and IT repair services. Sole traders tend to operate in industries where the barriers to entry are low and where limited capital is required on start up.

In law, a sole trader is **not legally separate** from the business they operate. The owner is legally responsible for the business.

A sole trader must maintain financial records and produce financial accounts. However, there is no legal requirement to make these accounts publicly available; they are usually only used to calculate the tax due to the tax authorities on the profits of the business. Banks and other financiers may request to see the financial accounts of the business when considering applications for loans and overdraft facilities.

2.3.1 Advantages of being a sole trader

This type of structure is ideal if the business is not complicated, and especially if it does not require a great deal of outside capital. Advantages include:

(a)   Limited paperwork and therefore cost in establishing this type of structure

(b)   Owner has complete control over the business

(c)   Owner is entitled to profits and the ownership of assets

(d)   Less stringent reporting obligations compared with other business structures – no requirement to make financial accounts publicly available, no audit requirement

(e)   Can be highly flexible

2.3.2 Disadvantages of being a sole trader

(a)   Owner is personally liable for all debts (unlimited liability)

(b)   Personal property may be vulnerable for debts and other business liabilities

(c)   Large sums of capital are less likely to be available to a sole trader, leading to reliance on overdrafts and personal savings

(d)   May lead to long working hours without the normal employee recreation leave and other benefits

(e)   May be issues of continuity of business in the event of death or illness of the owner

2.4 Partnerships

Partnerships occur when two or more people decide to run a business together. Examples include an accountancy practice, a medical practice and a legal practice. Partnerships are generally formed by contract. Partnership agreements are legally binding and are designed to outline the proportionate amount of capital invested, allocation of profits between parties, the responsibilities of each of the parties, allocation of salary and procedures for dissolving the partnership. Some countries have specific legislation for partnerships. In the UK, the provisions of the Partnership Act 1890 apply where no partnership agreement exists.

Like sole traders, partnerships are not separate legal entities from their owners. To overcome the problematic risk factors associated with unlimited personal liability for the debts of the business a new form of **LLP** has been created in some countries.

As with sole traders, partnerships must maintain financial records and produce financial accounts. However, there is no legal requirement to make these accounts publicly available, unless the partnership has LLP status.

2.4.1 Advantages of partnerships

(a)   Less stringent reporting obligations – no requirement to make financial accounts publicly available, no audit requirement, unless the partnership has LLP status

(b)   Additional capital can be raised because more people are investing in the business

(c)   Division of roles and responsibilities and an increased skill set

(d)   Sharing of risk and losses between more people

(e)   No company tax on the business (profits are distributed to partners and then subject to personal tax)

2.4.2 Disadvantages of partnerships

(a)   Partners are jointly personally liable for all debts (unlimited liability) unless they have formed an LLP

(b)   There are costs associated with setting up partnership agreements

(c)   There may be issues of continuity of business in the event of death or illness of the partners

(d)   Slower decision making due to the need for consensus between partners

(e)   Unless a clause is written into the original agreement, when one partner leaves, the partnership is automatically dissolved and another agreement is required between existing partners

2.5 Limited liability companies

Limited liability companies are incorporated to take advantage of '**limited liability**' for their owners (shareholders). This means that, while sole traders and partners are personally responsible for the amounts owed by their businesses, the shareholders of a limited liability company are **only responsible for the amount paid for their shares**. They are not responsible for the company's debts unless they have given personal guarantees (of a bank loan, for example). However, they may lose the money they have invested in the company if it fails.

Shareholders may be individuals or other companies.

Limited liability companies are formed under specific legislation (eg in the UK, the Companies Act 2006). A limited liability company is **legally a separate entity** from its owners, and can confer various rights and duties.

There is a clear distinction between **shareholders** and **directors** of limited companies.

(a)   **Shareholders** are the **owners**, but have limited rights as shareholders over the day to day running of the company. They provide capital and receive a return (dividend).

(b)   The **board of directors** are appointed to run the company on behalf of shareholders. In practice, they have a great deal of autonomy. Directors are often shareholders.

The reporting requirements for limited liability companies are much more stringent than for sole traders or partnerships. In the UK, there is a legal requirement for a company to:

•   Be registered at Companies House

•   Complete a Memorandum of Association and Articles of Association to be deposited with the Registrar of Companies

- Have at least one director (two for a public limited company (PLC)) who may also be a shareholder
- Prepare financial accounts for submission to Companies House
- Have its financial accounts audited (larger companies only)
- Distribute the financial accounts to all shareholders

2.5.1 Advantages of trading as a limited liability company

(a)   **Limited liability** makes investment less risky than being a sole trader or investing in a partnership. However, lenders to a small company may ask for a shareholder's personal guarantee to secure any loans.

(b)   Limited liability makes raising finance easier (eg through the sale of shares) and there is no limit on the number of shareholders.

(c)   A limited liability company has a **separate legal identity** from its shareholders. So a company continues to exist regardless of the identity of its owners.

(d)   There are **tax advantages** to being a limited liability company. The company is taxed as a separate entity from its owners and the tax rate on companies may be lower than the tax rate for individuals.

(e)   It is relatively easy to **transfer shares** from one owner to another. In contrast, it may be difficult to find someone to buy a sole trader's business or to buy a share in a partnership.

2.5.2 Disadvantages of trading as a limited liability company

(a)   Limited liability companies have to **publish annual financial statements**. This means that anyone (including competitors) can see how well (or badly) they are doing. In contrast, sole traders and partnerships do not have to publish their financial statements.

(b)   Limited liability company financial statements have to comply with **legal and accounting requirements**. In particular, the financial statements have to comply with accounting standards. Sole traders and partnerships may comply with accounting standards, eg for tax purposes.

(c)   The financial statements of larger limited liability companies have to be **audited**. This means that the statements are subject to an independent review to ensure that they comply with legal requirements and accounting standards. This can be inconvenient, time consuming and expensive.

(d)   **Share issues** are regulated by law. For example, it is difficult to reduce share capital. Sole traders and partnerships can increase or decrease capital as and when the owners wish.

QUESTION

Financial accounts

Mark the following statements as true or false.

A   Shareholders receive annual accounts, prepared in accordance with legal and professional requirements

B   The accounts of limited liability companies are sometimes filed with the Registrar of Companies

C   Employees always receive the company's accounts and an employee report

D   The tax authorities will receive the published accounts and as much supplementary detail as they need to assess the tax payable on profits

E   Banks frequently require more information than is supplied in the published accounts when considering applications for loans and overdraft facilities

ANSWER

True

A   Yes, and in addition, companies listed on the stock exchange have to comply with the regulations in the stock exchange's Listing Rules.

D   Yes.

E   Yes, banks may require cash flow and profit forecasts and budgets prepared to show management's estimates of future activity in the business.

False

B   The accounts of limited liability companies **must always** be filed with the Registrar of Companies and be available for public inspection. In addition, the company itself will often distribute these accounts on request to potential shareholders, the bank and financial analysts. These accounts are all that is usually available to suppliers and customers.

C   Employees will not necessarily receive company accounts (unless they are shareholders for example), but many companies do distribute the accounts to employees as a matter of policy. Some companies produce employee reports which summarise and expand on matters which are covered in the annual accounts and are of particular interest to them.

 ## 3 Nature, principles and scope of financial reporting

Financial accounting and management accounting are different. The F3/FFA syllabus focuses on financial accounting.

You may have a wide understanding of what accounting and financial reporting is about. Your job may be in one area or type of accounting, but you must understand the breadth of work which an accountant undertakes.

3.1 Financial accounting

So far we have dealt with **financial** accounts. Financial accounting is mainly a method of reporting the financial performance and financial position of a business. It is not primarily concerned with providing information towards the more efficient running of the business. Although financial accounts are of interest to management, their principal function is to satisfy the information needs of persons not involved in running the business. They provide **historical** information.

3.2 Management accounting

The information needs of management go far beyond those of other account users. Managers have the responsibility of planning and controlling the resources of the business. Therefore they need much more detailed information. They also need to **plan for the future** (eg budgets, which predict future revenue and expenditure).

 Management (or cost) accounting is a management information system which analyses data to provide information as a basis for managerial action. The concern of a management accountant is to present accounting information in the form most helpful to management.

You need to understand this distinction between management accounting and financial accounting.

The principles of financial reporting will be dealt with in Chapter 3.

4 Users' and stakeholders' needs

4.1 The need for financial statements

There are various groups of people who need information about the activities of a business.

Why do businesses need to produce financial statements? If a business is being run efficiently, why should it have to go through all the bother of accounting procedures in order to produce financial information?

The International Accounting Standards Board (IASB) states in its document *Conceptual framework for financial reporting*:

'The objective of financial statements is to provide information about the **financial position, performance** and **changes in financial position** of an entity that is useful to a wide range of users in making economic decisions.'

In other words, a business should produce information about its activities because there are various groups of people who want, or need, to know that information. This sounds rather vague: to make it clearer, we will study the classes of people who need information about a business. We also need to think about what information in particular is of interest to the members of each class.

Large businesses are of interest to a greater variety of people and so we will consider the case of a large public company, whose shares can be purchased and sold on a stock exchange.

4.2 Users of financial statements and accounting information

The following people are likely to be interested in financial information about a large company with shares that are listed on a stock exchange.

(a) **Managers of the company** are appointed by the company's owners to supervise the day to day activities of the company. They need information about the company's financial situation as it is currently and as it is expected to be in the future. This is to enable them to manage the business efficiently and to make effective decisions.

(b) **Shareholders of the company**, ie the company's owners, want to assess how well its management is performing. They want to know how profitable the company's operations are and how much profit they can afford to withdraw from the business for their own use.

(c) **Trade contacts** include suppliers who provide goods for the company on credit and customers who purchase the goods or services provided by the company. **Suppliers** want to know about the company's ability to pay its debts; **customers** need to know that the company is a secure source of supply and is in no danger of having to close down.

(d) **Providers of finance to the company** might include a bank which allows the company to operate an overdraft, or provides longer-term finance by granting a loan. The bank wants to ensure that the company is able to keep up interest payments, and eventually to repay the amounts advanced.

(e) **The taxation authorities** want to know about business profits in order to assess the tax payable by the company, including sales taxes.

(f) **Employees of the company** should have a right to information about the company's financial situation, because their future careers and the size of their wages and salaries depend on it.

(g) **Financial analysts and advisers** need information for their clients or audience. For example, stockbrokers need information to advise investors. Credit agencies want information to advise potential suppliers of goods to the company. Journalists need information for their reading public.

(h) **Government and their agencies** are interested in the allocation of resources and therefore in the activities of business entities. They also require information in order to provide a basis for national statistics.

(i)   **The public**. Entities affect members of the public in a variety of ways. For example, they may make a substantial contribution to a local economy by providing employment and using local suppliers. Another important factor is the effect of an entity on the environment, for example as regards pollution.

Accounting information is summarised in financial statements to satisfy the **information needs** of these different groups. Not all will be equally satisfied.

4.3 Needs of different users

Managers of a business need the most information, to help them make their planning and control decisions. They obviously have 'special' access to information about the business, because they are able to demand whatever internally produced statements they require. When managers want a large amount of information about the costs and profitability of individual products, or different parts of their business, they can obtain it through a system of cost and management accounting.

QUESTION   Information for managers

Which of the following is most useful for managers?

A   Financial statements for the last financial year
B   Tax records for the past five years
C   Budgets for the coming financial year
D   Bank statements for the past year

ANSWER

The correct answer is C. Managers need to look forward and make plans to keep the business profitable. Therefore the most useful information for them would be the budgets for the coming financial year.

In addition to management information, financial statements are prepared (and perhaps published) for the benefit of other user groups, which may demand certain information.

(a)   The **national laws** of a country may provide for the provision of some accounting information for shareholders and the public.

(b)   **National taxation authorities** will receive the information they need to make tax assessments.

(c)   A **bank** might demand a forecast of a company's expected future cash flows as a precondition of granting an overdraft.

(d)   The **IASB** is responsible for issuing **International Financial Reporting Standards (IFRSs)**. These require companies to publish certain additional information. Accountants, as members of professional bodies, are placed under a strong obligation to ensure that company financial statements conform to the requirements of IFRSs.

(e)   Some companies voluntarily provide specially prepared financial information for issue to their employees. These statements are known as '**employee reports**'.

EXAM FOCUS POINT

The needs of users can easily be examined. For example, you could be given a list of types of information and asked which user group would be most interested in this information.

5 Governance

Those charged with **governance** of a company are responsible for the preparation of the financial statements.

EXAM FOCUS POINT

The ACCA examining team reported that questions on governance were particularly badly answered in the 2011 assessment round. Make sure you read this section carefully and be prepared to answer questions on it in your exam.

Corporate governance is the system by which companies and other entities are directed and controlled. Good corporate governance is important because the owners of a company and the people who manage the company are not always the same, which can lead to conflicts of interest.

The board of directors of a company are usually the top management and are those who are **charged with governance** of that company. The responsibilities and duties of directors are usually laid down in law and are wide ranging.

5.1 Legal responsibilities of directors

Directors have a **duty of care** to show **reasonable competence** and may have to **indemnify the company** against loss caused by their negligence. Directors are also said to be in a **fiduciary position** in relation to the company, which means that they must act honestly in what they consider to be the best interest of the company and in good faith.

In the UK, the Companies Act 2006 sets out seven statutory duties of directors. Directors should:

- Act within their powers
- Promote the success of the company
- Exercise independent judgement
- Exercise reasonable skill, care and diligence
- Avoid conflicts of interest
- Not accept benefits from third parties
- Declare an interest in a proposed transaction or arrangement

An overriding theme of the Companies Act 2006 is the principle that the **purpose of the legal framework** surrounding companies should be **to help companies do business**. A director's main aim should be to **create wealth for the shareholders**.

In essence, this principle means that the law should encourage **long-termism** and **regard for all stakeholders** by directors and that **stakeholder interests** should be **pursued** in an **enlightened** and **inclusive** way.

When exercising this duty directors should consider:

- The **consequences of decisions** in the long term
- The **interests of** their **employees**
- The need to **develop good relationships** with **customers** and **suppliers**
- The **impact of the company** on the **local community** and the **environment**
- The desirability of **maintaining high standards of business conduct** and a **good reputation**
- The need to **act fairly as between all members** of the company

This list identifies areas of **particular importance** and **modern day expectations** of **responsible business behaviour**, for example the interests of the company's employees and the impact of the company's operations on the community and the environment.

5.2 Responsibility for the financial statements

Directors are responsible for the **preparation of the financial statements** of the company. Specifically, directors are responsible for:

- The preparation of the financial statements of the company in accordance with the applicable financial reporting framework (eg IFRSs)

- The internal controls necessary to enable the preparation of financial statements that are free from material misstatement, whether due to error or fraud

- The prevention and detection of fraud

It is the directors' responsibility to ensure that the entity complies with the **relevant laws** and **regulations**.

Directors should **explain** their **responsibility for preparing accounts** in the financial statements. They should also report that the business is a **going concern**, with supporting assumptions and qualifications as necessary.

Directors should present a **balanced and understandable assessment** of the **company's position and prospects** in the annual accounts and other reports, such as interim reports and reports to regulators. The directors should also explain the basis on which the company **generates or preserves value** and the **strategy for delivering the company's longer-term objectives**.

Companies over a certain size limit are subjected to an **annual audit** of their financial statements. An audit is an independent examination of the accounts to ensure that they comply with legal requirements and accounting standards. Note that the auditors are **not** responsible for preparing the financial statements. The findings of an audit are reported to the **shareholders** of the company. An audit gives the shareholders assurance that the accounts, which are the responsibility of the directors, fairly present the financial performance and position of the company. An audit therefore goes some way in helping the shareholders assess how well management have carried out their responsibility for stewardship of the company's assets.

6 The main elements of financial reports

The principal financial statements of a business are the **statement of financial position** and the **statement of profit or loss**.

6.1 Statement of financial position

The statement of financial position is simply a **list** of all the **assets owned** and all the **liabilities owed** by a business as at a particular date.

It is a snapshot of the financial position of the business at a particular moment. Monetary amounts are attributed to each of the assets and liabilities.

6.1.1 Assets

An **asset** is something valuable which a business owns or can use. The IASB's *Conceptual framework for financial reporting* defines an asset as follows.

An asset is a resource controlled by an entity as a result of past events and from which future economic benefits are expected to flow to the entity.

Examples of assets are factories, office buildings, warehouses, delivery vans, lorries, plant and machinery, computer equipment, office furniture, cash and goods held in store awaiting sale to customers.

Some assets are held and used in operations for a long time. An office building is occupied by staff for years. Similarly, a machine has a productive life of many years before it wears out.

Other assets are held for only a short time. The owner of a newsagent shop, for example, has to sell their newspapers on the same day that they get them. The more quickly a business can sell the goods it has in store, the more profit it is likely to make; provided, of course, that the goods are sold at a higher price than what it cost the business to acquire them.

6.1.2 Liabilities

A **liability** is something which is owed to somebody else. 'Liabilities' is the accounting term for the debts of a business. The IASB's *Conceptual framework for financial reporting* defines a liability as follows.

A liability is a present obligation of the entity arising from past events, the settlement of which is expected to result in an outflow from the entity of resources embodying economic benefits.

Examples of liabilities are amounts owed to a supplier for goods bought on credit, amounts owed to a bank (or other lender), a bank overdraft and amounts owed to tax authorities (eg in respect of sales tax).

Some liabilities are due to be repaid fairly quickly eg suppliers. Other liabilities may take some years to repay (eg a bank loan).

QUESTION

Assets and liabilities

Which of the following is an asset according to the definition in the *Conceptual framework*?

A   Bank overdraft
B   Factory buildings
C   Payables
D   Amounts owed to tax authorities

ANSWER

The correct answer is B, Factory buildings. It is the only one which the business owns rather than owes.

6.1.3 Capital or equity

The amounts invested in a business by the owner are amounts that the business owes to the owner. This is a special kind of liability, called **capital**. In a limited liability company, capital usually takes the form of shares. Share capital is also known as **equity**. The IASB's *Conceptual framework for financial reporting* defines equity as follows.

Equity is the residual interest in the assets of the entity after deducting all its liabilities.

6.1.4 Form of the statement of financial position

A statement of financial position used to be called a **balance sheet**. The former name is apt because assets will always be equal to liabilities plus capital (or equity). An example of a very simple statement of financial position for a sole trader is shown below.

A TRADER
STATEMENT OF FINANCIAL POSITION AS AT 30 APRIL 20X7

	$	$
Assets		
Plant and machinery		55,000
Inventory	5,000	
Receivables (from customers)	1,500	
Bank	500	
		7,000
Total assets		62,000
Capital		
Balance brought forward		25,000
Profit for the year		10,400
Balance carried forward		35,400
Liabilities		
Bank loan		25,000
Payables (to suppliers)		1,600
Total capital plus liabilities		62,000

6.2 Statement of profit or loss

A statement of profit or loss is a **record** of **income generated** and **expenditure incurred** over a given period. The statement shows whether the business has had more revenue than expenditure (a profit) or vice versa (loss).

6.2.1 Revenue and expenses

Revenue is the income generated by the operations of a business for a period.

Expenses are the costs of running the business for the same period.

The IASB's *Conceptual framework* defines income, revenue and expenses as follows.

Income is increases in economic benefits during the accounting period in the form of inflows or enhancements of assets or decreases of liabilities that result in increases in equity, other than those relating to contributions from equity participants.

Revenue is the gross inflow of economic benefits (cash, receivables, other assets) arising from the ordinary operating activities of an enterprise (such as sales of goods, sales of services, interest, royalties and dividends).

Expenses are decreases in economic benefits during the accounting period in the form of outflows or depletions of assets or incurrences of liabilities that result in decreases in equity, other than those relating to distributions to equity participants.

6.2.2 Form of the statement of profit or loss

The period chosen will depend on the purpose for which the statement is produced. The statement of profit or loss which forms part of the published annual financial statements of a **limited liability company** will usually be for the period of a **year**, commencing from the date of the previous year's statements. On the other hand, **management** might want to keep a closer eye on a company's profitability by making up **quarterly or monthly** statements.

A simple statement of profit or loss for a sole trader is shown below.

A TRADER
STATEMENT OF PROFIT OR LOSS FOR THE YEAR ENDED 30 APRIL 20X7

	$
Revenue	150,000
Cost of sales	75,000
Gross profit	75,000
Other expenses	64,600
Profit for the year	10,400

Once again, this example is given purely for illustrative purposes.

6.3 Purpose of financial statements

Both the statement of financial position and the statement of profit or loss are **summaries of accumulated data**. For example, the statement of profit or loss shows a figure for revenue earned from selling goods to customers. This is the total amount of revenue earned from all the individual sales made during the period. One of the jobs of an accountant is to devise methods of recording such individual transactions, so as to produce summarised financial statements from them.

The statement of financial position and the statement of profit or loss form the basis of the financial statements of most businesses. For limited liability companies, other information by way of statements and notes may be required by national legislation and/or accounting standards, for example a **statement of profit or loss and other comprehensive income** and a **statement of cash flows** (which will be dealt with in detail in Chapters 20 and 22 respectively).

QUESTION

The financial statements of a limited liability company will consist solely of the statement of financial position and statement of profit or loss.

Is this statement true or false?

A   True
B   False

ANSWER

The correct answer is B, False. As shown above, other statements, such as a statement of cash flows, are usually needed.

One of the competences you require to fulfil performance objective PO5 Leadership and management of the PER is the ability to manage time and tasks effectively to meet business needs and professional commitments, and be capable of working under pressure. In the course of your F3/FFA studies, you will be demonstrating this competence.

CHAPTER ROUNDUP

ᔔ **Financial reporting** is a way of recording, analysing and summarising financial data.

ᔔ Businesses of whatever size or nature exist to make a **profit**.

ᔔ Financial accounting and management accounting are different. The F3/FFA syllabus focuses on financial accounting.

ᔔ There are various groups of people who need information about the activities of a business.

ᔔ Those charged with **governance** of a company are responsible for the preparation of the financial statements.

ᔔ The principal financial statements of a business are the **statement of financial position** and the **statement of profit or loss**.

QUICK QUIZ

1 Fill in the blanks.

   Financial reporting is a way of ...., ... and .... financial data.

2 A business entity is owned and run by Alpha, Beta and Gamma.

   What type of business is this an example of?
   A   Sole trader
   B   Partnership
   C   Limited liability company
   D   None of the above

3 Identify seven user groups who need accounting information.

4 What are the two main financial statements drawn up by accountants?

5 The directors of a company are responsible for the preparation of the financial statements of a company.

   True or false?

6 Which of the following is an example of a liability?

   A   Inventory
   B   Receivables
   C   Plant and machinery
   D   Loan

ANSWERS TO QUICK QUIZ

1   Financial reporting is a way of **recording**, **analysing** and **summarising** financial data.

2   B   A partnership, as it is owned and run by three people

3   See Paragraph 4.2.

4   The statement of profit or loss and the statement of financial position

5   True. Those charged with governance of that company, ie the directors, are responsible for the preparation of the financial statements.

6   D   A loan. The rest are all assets.

Now try ...

Attempt the questions below from the **Practice Question Bank**

Number

Qs 1 – 5

02

In this chapter, we introduce the regulatory system run by the International Accounting Standards Board (IASB). We are concerned with the **IASB's relationship with other bodies**, and with the way the IASB operates.

You must try to understand and appreciate the contents of this chapter. The ACCA examining team is not only interested in whether you can add up; they want to know whether you can think about a subject which, after all, is your future career. This chapter can and **will be examined**.

The regulatory framework

1   The regulatory system

A number of factors have shaped the **development** of financial accounting.

1.1 Introduction

Although new to the subject, you will be aware from your reading of the press that there have been some considerable upheavals in financial reporting, mainly in response to criticism. The **details** of the regulatory framework of accounting, and the technical aspects of the changes made, will be covered later in this chapter and in your more advanced studies. The purpose of this section is to give a **general picture** of some of the factors which have shaped financial accounting. We will concentrate on the accounts of limited liability companies, as these are the accounts most closely regulated by statute or otherwise.

The following factors that have shaped financial accounting can be identified.

- National/local legislation
- Accounting concepts and individual judgement
- Accounting standards
- Other international influences
- Generally accepted accounting principles (GAAP)
- Fair presentation

1.2 National/local legislation

In most countries, limited liability companies are required by law to prepare and publish accounts annually. The form and content of the accounts is regulated primarily by national legislation.

1.3 Accounting concepts and individual judgement

Many figures in financial statements are derived from the **application of judgement** in applying fundamental accounting assumptions and conventions. This can lead to subjectivity. Accounting standards were developed to try to address this subjectivity.

Financial statements are prepared on the basis of a number of **fundamental accounting assumptions and conventions**. Many figures in financial statements are derived from the application of judgement in putting these assumptions into practice.

It is clear that different people exercising their judgement on the same facts can arrive at very different conclusions.

CASE STUDY

An accountancy training firm has an excellent **reputation** among students and employers. How would you value this? The firm may have relatively little in the form of assets that you can touch; perhaps a building, desks and chairs. If you simply drew up a statement of financial position showing the cost of the assets owned, then the business would not seem to be worth much, yet its income earning potential might be high. This is true of many service organisations where the people are among the most valuable assets.

Other examples of areas where the judgement of different people may vary are as follows.

(a)   Valuation of buildings in times of rising property prices

(b)   Research and development: is it right to treat this only as an expense? In a sense it is an investment to generate future revenue

(c)   Accounting for inflation

(d)   Brands such as 'Dr Pepper' and 'Cadbury Dairy Milk'. Are they assets in the same way that a fork lift truck is an asset?

Working from the same data, different groups of people produce very different financial statements. If the exercise of judgement is completely unfettered, there will be no comparability between the accounts of different organisations. This will be all the more significant in cases where deliberate manipulation occurs, in order to present accounts in the most favourable light.

1.4 Accounting standards

In an attempt to deal with some of the subjectivity, and to achieve comparability between different organisations, **accounting standards** were developed. These are developed at both a national level (in most countries) and an international level. The F3/FFA syllabus is concerned with **International Financial Reporting Standards** (IFRSs).

IFRSs are produced by the **International Accounting Standards Board (IASB)**.

2 The International Accounting Standards Board (IASB)

 The IASB develops IFRSs. The main objectives of the IFRS Foundation are to raise the standard of financial reporting and eventually bring about global harmonisation of accounting standards.

The International Accounting Standards Board (IASB) is an independent, privately funded body that develops and approves IFRSs.

Prior to 2003, standards were issued as International Accounting Standards (IASs). In 2003 IFRS 1 was issued and all new standards are now designated as IFRSs.

IMPORTANT

Throughout this Text, we will use the abbreviation IFRSs to include both IFRSs and IASs.

The members of the IASB come from several countries and have a variety of backgrounds, with a mix of auditors, preparers of financial statements, users of financial statements and academics.

The IASB operates under the oversight of the **IFRS Foundation**.

2.1 The IFRS Foundation

The IFRS Foundation (formally called the International Accounting Standards Committee Foundation or IASCF) is a not for profit, private sector body that oversees the IASB.

The objectives of the IFRS Foundation are to:

- Develop a single set of high quality, understandable, enforceable and globally accepted IFRSs through its standard-setting body, the IASB

- Promote the use and rigorous application of those standards

- Take account of the financial reporting needs of emerging economies and small and medium-sized entities (SMEs)

- Bring about convergence of national accounting standards and IFRSs to high quality solutions

The IFRS Foundation is made up of several trustees, who essentially monitor and fund the IASB, the IFRS Advisory Council and the IFRS Interpretations Committee. The Trustees are appointed from a variety of geographical and functional backgrounds.

The structure of the IFRS Foundation and related bodies is shown below.

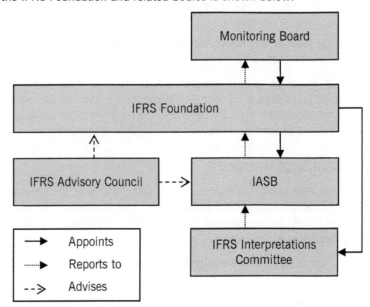

2.1.1 IFRS Advisory Council

The IFRS Advisory Council (formerly called the Standards Advisory Council or SAC) is essentially a forum used by the IASB to consult with the outside world. It consults with national standard setters, academics, user groups and a host of other interested parties to advise the IASB on a range of issues, from the IASB's work programme for developing new IFRSs to giving practical advice on the implementation of particular standards.

The IFRS Advisory Council meets the IASB at least three times a year and puts forward the views of its members on current standard-setting projects.

2.1.2 IFRS Interpretations Committee

The IFRS Interpretations Committee (formerly called the International Financial Reporting Interpretations Committee or IFRIC) was set up in March 2002 and provides guidance on specific practical issues in the interpretation of IFRSs. Note that despite the name change, interpretations issued by the IFRS Interpretations Committee are still known as IFRIC Interpretations. In your exam, you may see the IFRS Interpretations Committee referred to as the IFRS IC.

The IFRS Interpretations Committee has two main responsibilities.

- To review, on a timely basis, newly identified financial reporting issues not specifically addressed in IFRSs

- To clarify issues where unsatisfactory or conflicting interpretations have developed, or seem likely to develop in the absence of authoritative guidance, with a view to reaching a consensus on the appropriate treatment

3 International Financial Reporting Standards (IFRSs)

IFRSs are created in accordance with due process. There are currently 28 IASs and 15 IFRSs in issue.

3.1 The use and application of IFRSs

IFRSs have helped to both improve and harmonise financial reporting around the world. The standards are used in the following ways.

- As **national requirements**
- As the **basis** for all or some **national requirements**
- As an **international benchmark** for those countries which develop their own requirements
- By **regulatory authorities** for domestic and foreign companies
- **By companies** themselves

In the UK, the consolidated accounts of listed companies have had to be produced in accordance with IFRSs since January 2005.

3.2 Standard-setting process

The IASB prepares IFRSs in accordance with **due process**. You do not need to know this for your exam, but the following diagram may be of interest.

The procedure can be summarised as follows.

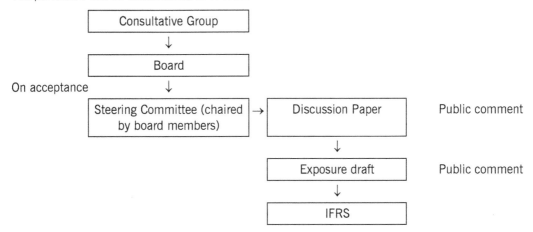

3.2.1 Current IFRSs

The current list is as follows. Those examinable in F3/FFA are marked with a *. IAS 18 *Revenue* has been replaced by IFRS 15 *Revenue from contracts with customers* for reporting periods beginning on or after 1 January 2018. However, **IAS 18 will continue to be examined for this syllabus period September 2016 to August 2017**, and not IFRS 15.

Conceptual Framework for Financial Reporting *

IFRS 1	First-time adoption of International Financial Reporting Standards
IFRS 2	Share-based payment
IFRS 3*	Business combinations
IFRS 4	Insurance contracts
IFRS 5	Non-current assets held for sale and discontinued operations
IFRS 6	Exploration for the evaluation of mineral resources
IFRS 7	Financial instruments: disclosures
IFRS 8	Operating segments
IFRS 9	Financial instruments
IFRS 10*	Consolidated financial statements
IFRS 11	Joint arrangements
IFRS 12	Disclosure of interests in other entities
IFRS 13	Fair value measurement
IFRS 14	Regulatory deferral accounts
IFRS 15	Revenue from contracts with customers
IAS 1*	Presentation of financial statements
IAS 2*	Inventories
IAS 7*	Statement of cash flows
IAS 8	Accounting policies, changes in accounting estimates and errors
IAS 10*	Events after the reporting period
IAS 11	Construction contracts
IAS 12	Income taxes
IAS 16*	Property, plant and equipment
IAS 17	Leases
IAS 18*	Revenue
IAS 19	Employee benefits
IAS 20	Accounting for government grants and disclosure of government assistance
IAS 21	The effects of changes in foreign exchange rates
IAS 23	Borrowing costs
IAS 24	Related party disclosures
IAS 26	Accounting and reporting by retirement benefit plans
IAS 27*	Separate financial statements
IAS 28*	Investments in associates and joint ventures
IAS 29	Financial reporting in hyperinflationary economies
IAS 32	Financial instruments: presentation
IAS 33	Earnings per share
IAS 34	Interim financial reporting
IAS 36	Impairment of assets
IAS 37*	Provisions, contingent liabilities and contingent assets
IAS 38*	Intangible assets
IAS 39	Financial instruments: recognition and measurement
IAS 40	Investment property
IAS 41	Agriculture

Various exposure drafts and discussion papers are currently at different stages within the IFRS process, but these are not of concern to you at this stage.

3.3 Scope and application of IFRSs

3.3.1 Scope

Any limitation of the applicability of a specific IFRS is made clear within that standard. IFRSs are **not intended to be applied to immaterial items, nor are they retrospective**. Each individual standard lays out its scope at the beginning of the standard.

3.3.2 Application

Within each individual country **local regulations** govern, to a greater or lesser degree, the issue of financial statements. These local regulations include accounting standards issued by the national regulatory bodies and/or professional accountancy bodies in the country concerned.

QUESTION

Standards

How far do the accounting standards in force in your country diverge from the IFRSs you will cover in this Interactive Text?

If you have the time, perhaps you could find out.

CHAPTER ROUNDUP

↳ A number of factors have shaped the **development** of financial accounting.

↳ Many figures in financial statements are derived from the **application of judgement** in applying fundamental accounting assumptions and conventions. This can lead to subjectivity. Accounting standards were developed to try to address this subjectivity.

↳ The IASB develops IFRSs. The main objectives of the IASB are to raise the standard of financial reporting and eventually bring about global harmonisation of accounting standards.

↳ IFRSs are created in accordance with due process. There are currently 28 IASs and 15 IFRSs in issue.

QUICK QUIZ

1   Which of the following is **not** an objective of the IFRS Foundation?

   A   To enforce IFRSs in most countries
   B   To develop IFRSs through the IASB
   C   To bring about convergence of accounting standards and IFRSs
   D   To take account of the financial reporting needs of SMEs

2   Fill in the blanks.

   The IFRS .... issues .... which aid users' interpretation of

   IFRSs.

3   How many IASs and IFRSs are currently in issue?

4   What happened in 2005 for listed companies in the UK?

   A   IFRSs to be used for all financial statements
   B   IFRSs to be used for consolidated financial statements

5   The IASB is responsible for the standard-setting process. True or false?

1   A   The IFRS Foundation has no powers of enforcement.

2   The IFRS **Interpretations Committee** issues **IFRIC interpretations** which aid users' interpretation of IFRSs.

3   43. 28 IASs and 15 IFRSs

4   B   IFRSs to be used for consolidated financial statements

5   True

Now try ...

Attempt the questions below from the **Practice Question Bank**

Number

Qs 6 – 7

part

B

The qualitative characteristics of financial information

03

The purpose of this chapter is to encourage you to think more deeply about the **assumptions** on which financial statements are prepared.

This chapter deals with the accounting conventions which lie behind accounts preparation and which you will meet in Part C in the chapters on bookkeeping.

In Part D, you will see how conventions and assumptions are **put into practice**. You will also deal with certain items which are the subject of accounting standards.

The qualitative characteristics of financial information

TOPIC LIST	SYLLABUS REFERENCE
1 Background	B1(a)
2 The IASB's *Conceptual framework*	B1(a),(b)
3 The qualitative characteristics of financial information	B1(a),(b)
4 Other accounting concepts	B1(b)

Study Guide	Intellectual level
B **The qualitative characteristics of financial information**	
1 **The qualitative characteristics of financial information**	
(a) Define, understand and apply qualitative characteristics:	K

(i)   Relevance
    (ii)   Faithful representation
    (iii)   Comparability
    (iv)   Verifiability
    (v)   Timeliness
    (vi) Understandability	

(b) Define, understand and apply accounting concepts:	K

(i)   Materiality
    (ii)   Substance over form
    (iii)   Going concern
    (iv)   Business entity concept
    (v)   Accruals
    (vi)   Fair presentation
    (vii) Consistency	

EXAM FOCUS POINT

Always **read the question carefully** before answering. Make sure that you understand the requirement and have picked out the main points of the question. This may sound obvious but the ACCA examining team regularly comments that students have failed to read the question.

1 Background

In preparing financial statements, accountants follow certain **fundamental assumptions**.

Accounting practice has developed gradually over time. Many of its procedures are operated automatically by people who have never questioned whether alternative methods exist which have equal validity. However, the procedures in common use imply the acceptance of certain concepts which are by no means self-evident; nor are they the only possible concepts which could be used to build up an accounting framework.

Our next step is to look at some of the more important concepts which are taken for granted in preparing accounts. In this chapter we shall single out the important assumptions and concepts for discussion.

2 The IASB's *Conceptual Framework*

- The **IASB's** *Conceptual Framework* is the basis on which IFRSs are formulated.
- The main **underlying assumption** for financial statements is **going concern**.

2.1 Introduction to the *Conceptual Framework*

The *Conceptual Framework for Financial Reporting* ('*Conceptual Framework*') is a set of principles which underpin the foundations of financial accounting. It is a **conceptual** framework on which all IFRSs are based and hence determines how financial statements are prepared and the information they contain. The *Conceptual Framework* is not an accounting standard in itself.

The *Conceptual Framework* is currently as follows.

Chapter 1: The objective of general purpose financial reporting

Chapter 2: The reporting entity (to be issued)

Chapter 3: Qualitative characteristics of useful financial information

Chapter 4: Remaining text of the 1989 *Framework*:

- Underlying assumption
- The elements of financial statements
- Recognition of the elements of financial statements
- Measurement of the elements of financial statements
- Concepts of capital and capital maintenance

We are only concerned with Chapter 3 and parts of Chapter 4 for the F3/FFA syllabus.

2.2 Underlying assumption

The *Conceptual Framework* sets out one important underlying assumption for financial statements, the **going concern concept**.

2.2.1 Going concern

Going concern. The financial statements are normally prepared on the assumption that an entity is a **going concern** and will continue in operation for the foreseeable future. Hence, it is assumed that the entity has neither the intention nor the need to liquidate or curtail materially the scale of its operations.

This concept assumes that, when preparing a normal set of accounts, the business will **continue to operate** in approximately the same manner for the foreseeable future (at least the next 12 months). In particular, the entity will not go into liquidation or scale down its operations in a material way.

The main significance of the going concern concept is that the assets **should not be values at their 'break-up' value** (the amount they would sell for if they were sold off piecemeal and the business were broken up).

QUESTION
Going concern

A retailer commences business on 1 January and buys inventory of 20 washing machines, each costing $100. During the year they sell 17 machines at $150 each. How should the remaining machines be valued at 31 December in the following circumstances?

A   They are forced to close down their business at the end of the year and the remaining machines will realise only $60 each in a forced sale

B   They intend to continue their business into the next year

ANSWER

A   If the business is to be closed down, the remaining three machines must be valued at the amount they will realise in a forced sale, ie 3 × $60 = $180.

B   If the business is regarded as a going concern, the inventory unsold at 31 December will be carried forward into the following year, when the cost of the three machines will be matched against the eventual sale proceeds in computing that year's profits. The three machines will therefore be valued at cost, 3 × $100 = $300.

If the going concern assumption is not followed, that fact must be disclosed, together with the following information.

(a)   The basis on which the financial statements have been prepared

(b)   The reasons why the entity is not considered to be a going concern

2.2.2 Accruals basis

Accruals basis. The effects of transactions and other events are recognised when they occur (and not as cash or its equivalent is received or paid) and they are recorded in the accounting records and reported in the financial statements of the periods to which they relate.

The accruals basis is not an underlying assumption but Chapter 1 of the *Conceptual Framework* makes it clear that financial statements should be prepared on an accruals basis.

Entities should prepare their financial statements on the basis that transactions are recorded in them, not as the cash is paid or received, but as the revenues or expenses are **earned or incurred** in the accounting period to which they relate.

According to the accruals assumption, in computing profit revenue earned must be **matched against** the expenditure incurred in earning it. This is also known as the **matching convention**.

Example: accruals basis

Emma purchases 20 T-shirts in her first month of trading (May) at a cost of $5 each. She then sells all of them for $10 each. Emma has therefore made a profit of $100, by matching the revenue ($200) earned against the cost ($100) of acquiring them.

If, however, Emma only sells 18 T-shirts, it is incorrect to charge her statement of profit or loss with the cost of 20 T-shirts, as she still has two T-shirts in inventory. Therefore, only the purchase cost of 18 T-shirts (18 × $5 = $90) should be matched with her sales revenue (18 × $10 = $180), leaving her with a profit of $90.

Her statement of financial position will look like this.

	$
Assets	
Inventory (at cost, ie 2 × $5)	10
Accounts receivable (18 × $10)	180
	190
Capital and liabilities	
Proprietor's capital (profit for the period)	90
Accounts payable (20 × $5)	100
	190

However, if Emma had decided to give up selling T-shirts, then the going concern assumption no longer applies and the value of the two T-shirts in the statement of financial position is break-up valuation not cost.

Similarly, if the two unsold T-shirts are unlikely to be sold at more than their cost of $5 each (say, because of damage or a fall in demand) then they should be recorded on the statement of financial position at their **net realisable value** (ie the likely eventual sales price less any expenses incurred to

make them saleable) rather than cost. This shows the application of the **prudence concept**. Prudence, however is no longer defined in the *Conceptual Framework*. It is defined in the pre-2010 Conceptual Framework as 'the inclusion of a degree of caution in the exercise of the judgements needed in making the estimates required under conditions of uncertainty, such that assets or income are not overstated and liabilities or expenses are not understated'. Although the 2010 *Conceptual Framework* no longer refers to prudence (this has been replaced by neutrality (see Section 3.2 below)) prudence is sometimes referred to in this Interactive Text because as an accountant, it is still important to exercise caution when making accounting estimates.

In this example, the concepts of going concern and accruals are linked. Since the business is assumed to be a going concern, it is possible to carry forward the cost of the unsold T-shirts as a charge against profits of the next period.

EXAM FOCUS POINT

The ACCA examining team commented that questions on the *Conceptual Framework* have been particularly well answered in recent exams.

3 The qualitative characteristics of financial information

- The *Conceptual Framework* states that qualitative characteristics are the attributes that make the information provided in financial statements useful to users.
- The two fundamental qualitative characteristics are **relevance and faithful representation**.
- Enhancing qualitative characteristics are **comparability, verifiability, timeliness** and **understandability**.

3.1 Relevance

Only relevant information can be useful. Information should be released on a timely basis to be relevant to users.

Relevance. Relevant information is capable of making a difference in the decisions made by users. Financial information is capable of making a difference in decisions if it has **predictive value, confirmatory value** or both.   *(Conceptual Framework)*

The predictive and confirmatory roles of information are interrelated. Information on financial position and performance is often used to predict future position and performance and other things of interest to the user, eg likely dividend, wage rises. The **manner of showing information** will enhance the ability to make predictions, eg by highlighting unusual items.

The relevance of information is affected by its nature and **materiality**.

3.1.1 Materiality

Materiality. Information is material if omitting it or misstating it could influence decisions that users make on the basis of financial information about a specific reporting entity.   *(Conceptual Framework)*

Information may be judged relevant simply because of its nature. In other cases, both the nature and materiality of the information are important.

An error which is too trivial to affect anyone's understanding of the accounts is referred to as **immaterial**. In preparing accounts it is important to assess what is material and what is not, so that time and money are not wasted in the pursuit of excessive detail.

Determining whether or not an item is material is a very **subjective exercise**. There is no absolute measure of materiality. It is common to apply a convenient rule of thumb (for example, material items are those with a value greater than 5% of net profits). However, some items disclosed in the accounts are regarded as particularly sensitive and even a very small misstatement of such an item is taken as a material error. An example, in the accounts of a limited liability company, is the amount of remuneration (salaries and other rewards) paid to directors of the company.

The assessment of an item as material or immaterial may **affect its treatment in the accounts**. For example, the statement of profit or loss of a business shows the expenses incurred grouped under suitable captions (administrative expenses, distribution expenses etc); but in the case of very small expenses it may be appropriate to lump them together as 'sundry expenses', because a more detailed breakdown is inappropriate for such immaterial amounts.

In assessing whether or not an item is material, it is not only the value of the item which needs to be considered. The **context** is also important.

(a) If a statement of financial position shows non-current assets of $2m and inventories of $30,000, an error of $20,000 in the depreciation calculations might not be regarded as material. However, an error of $20,000 in the inventory valuation would be material. In other words, the total of which the error forms part must be considered.

(b) If a business has a bank loan of $50,000 and a $55,000 balance on bank deposit account, it will be a material misstatement if these two amounts are netted off on the statement of financial position as 'cash at bank $5,000'. In other words, incorrect presentation may amount to material misstatement even if there is no monetary error.

QUESTION   Materiality

Would you treat the following items as assets in the accounts of a company?

A   A box file
B   A computer
C   A plastic display stand

ANSWER

A   No. You would write it off to the statement of profit or loss as an expense.

B   Yes. You would capitalise the computer and charge depreciation on it.

C   Your answer depends on the size of the company and whether writing off the item has a material effect on its profits. A larger organisation might well write this item off under the heading of advertising expenses, while a small one might capitalise it and depreciate it over time. This is because the item is material to the small company, but not to the large company.

3.2 Faithful representation

Faithful representation. Financial reports represent **economic phenomena** in words and numbers. To be useful, financial information must not only represent relevant phenomena but must **faithfully represent** the phenomena that it purports to represent.   *(Conceptual Framework)*

To be a faithful representation information must be **complete, neutral** and **free from error**.

A **complete** depiction includes all information necessary for a user to understand the phenomenon being depicted, including all necessary descriptions and explanations.

A **neutral** depiction is without bias in the selection or presentation of financial information. This means that information must not be manipulated in any way in order to influence the decisions of users.

Free from error means there are no errors or omissions in the description of the phenomenon and no errors made in the process by which the financial information was produced. It does not mean that no inaccuracies can arise, particularly where estimates have to be made.

3.2.1 Substance over form

This is **not a separate qualitative characteristic** under the *Conceptual Framework*. The IASB says that to so include it would be redundant because it is **implied in faithful representation**. Faithful representation of a transaction is only possible if it is accounted for according to its **substance and economic reality**.

For example, a business may have entered into a leasing agreement for some equipment. However, the terms are such that the business is really buying the equipment. The equipment should therefore be included in the statement of financial position as an asset of the business and the leasing agreement should be treated as a financing arrangement.

3.3 Enhancing qualitative characteristics

3.3.1 Comparability

Comparability. Comparability is the qualitative characteristic that enables users to identify and understand similarities in, and differences among, items. Information about a reporting entity is more useful if it can be compared with similar information about other entities and with similar information about the same entity for another period or date. *(Conceptual Framework)*

Consistency, although related to comparability, **is not the same**. It refers to the use of the same methods for the same items (ie consistency of treatment) either from period to period within a reporting entity or in a single period across entities.

The **disclosure of accounting policies** is particularly important here. Users must be able to distinguish between different accounting policies in order to be able to make a valid comparison of similar items in the accounts of different entities.

Comparability is **not the same as uniformity**. Entities should change accounting policies if those policies become inappropriate.

Corresponding information for preceding periods should be shown to enable comparison to be made over time.

3.3.2 Verifiability

Verifiability. Verifiability helps assure users that information faithfully represents the economic phenomena it purports to represent. It means that different knowledgeable and independent observers could reach consensus that a particular depiction is a faithful representation. *(Conceptual Framework)*

Information that can be independently verified is generally more decision-useful than information that cannot.

3.3.3 Timeliness

Timeliness. Timeliness means having information available to decision-makers in time to be capable of influencing their decisions. Generally, the older information is the less useful it is.
(Conceptual Framework)

Information may become less useful if there is a delay in reporting it. There is a **balance between timeliness and the provision of reliable information**.

If information is reported on a timely basis when not all aspects of the transaction are known, it may not be complete or free from error.

Conversely, if every detail of a transaction is known, it may be too late to publish the information because it has become irrelevant. The overriding consideration is how best to satisfy the economic decision-making needs of the users.

3.3.4 Understandability

Understandability. Classifying, characterising and presenting information clearly and concisely makes it understandable. *(Conceptual Framework)*

Financial reports are prepared for users who have a **reasonable knowledge of business and economic activities** and who review and analyse the information diligently. Some phenomena are inherently complex and cannot be made easy to understand. Excluding information on those phenomena might make the information easier to understand, but without it those reports would be incomplete and therefore misleading. Therefore matters should not be left out of financial statements simply due to their difficulty, as even well-informed and diligent users may sometimes need the aid of an adviser to understand information about complex economic phenomena.

4 Other accounting concepts

There are other accounting concepts which are useful in the preparation of financial statements.

4.1 Fair presentation

Financial statements are required to give a **fair presentation** or **present fairly in all material respects** the financial results of the entity. **Compliance with IFRSs** will almost always achieve this.

The following points made by IAS 1 *Presentation of financial statements* expand on this principle.

(a) **Compliance with IFRSs** should be disclosed

(b) **All relevant IFRSs** must be followed if compliance with IFRSs is disclosed

(c) Use of an **inappropriate accounting treatment** cannot be rectified either by disclosure of accounting policies or notes / explanatory material

There may be (very rare) circumstances when management decides that compliance with a requirement of an IFRS would be misleading. **Departure from the IFRS** is therefore required to achieve a fair presentation.

IAS 1 states what is required for a fair presentation.

(a) Selection and application of **accounting policies**

(b) **Presentation of information** in a manner which provides relevant, reliable, comparable and understandable information

(c) Additional disclosures where required

4.2 Consistency

To maintain consistency, the presentation and classification of items in the financial statements should **stay the same from one period to the next**, except as follows.

(a) There is a significant change in the **nature of the operations** or a review of the financial statements indicates a **more appropriate presentation**

(b) A change in presentation is **required by an IFRS**

4.3 The business entity concept

Financial statements always treat the business as a **separate entity**.

It is crucial that you understand that the convention adopted in preparing accounts (the **business entity concept**) is **always** to treat a business as a separate entity from its owner(s). This means the transactions of the owner should never be mixed with the business's transactions. This applies whether or not the business is recognised in law as a separate legal entity.

QUESTION
Revision of qualitative characteristics

See if you can write a short sentence explaining each of the following characteristics.

A   Relevance
B   Faithful representation
C   Comparability
D   Understandability

ANSWER

A   **Relevance**. The information provided satisfies the needs of users, helping them to evaluate past, present or future events and confirming or correcting their past evaluations.

B   **Faithful representation**. The information gives full details of its effects on the financial statements and is only recognised if its financial effects are certain.

C   **Comparability**. The information should be produced on a consistent basis so that valid comparisons can be made with previous periods and with other entities.

D   **Understandability**. Information may be difficult to understand if it is incomplete, but too much detail can also confuse the issue.

QUESTION
Consistency

Which of the following statements **best** describes the consistency concept?

A   Only material items are disclosed.

B   The way an item is presented always remains the same.

C   Presentation and classification of items should remain the same unless a change is required by an IFRS.

ANSWER

The correct answer is C; presentation and classification of items should remain the same unless a change is required by an IFRS.

EXAM FOCUS POINT

The syllabus shows that you must understand and be able to apply both qualitative characteristics and accounting concepts. Do not neglect this section.

CHAPTER ROUNDUP

- ↳ In preparing financial statements, accountants follow certain **fundamental assumptions**.

- ↳ The **IASB's** *Conceptual Framework* is the basis on which IFRSs are formulated.

- ↳ The main **underlying assumption** for financial statements is **going concern**.

- ↳ The *Conceptual Framework* states that qualitative characteristics are the attributes that make the information provided in financial statements useful to users.

- ↳ The two fundamental qualitative characteristics are **relevance and faithful representation**.

- ↳ Enhancing qualitative characteristics are **comparability, verifiability, timeliness** and **understandability**.

- ↳ There are other accounting concepts which are useful in the preparation of financial statements.

- ↳ Financial statements always treat the business as a **separate entity**.

QUICK QUIZ

1 Define 'going concern' in no more than 25 words.

2 Fill in the blanks.

    .... helps assure users that information faithfully represents the .... it purports to represent. It means that different knowledgeable and independent observers could reach consensus that a particular depiction is a ....*(Conceptual Framework)*

3 Making an allowance for receivables is an example of which concept?

    A   Accruals
    B   Going concern
    C   Materiality
    D   Fair presentation

4 What does 'relevance' mean in the context of financial statements?

5 What are the four enhancing qualitative characteristics of financial statements identified in the *Conceptual Framework*?

ANSWERS TO QUICK QUIZ

1   The assumption that a business will continue in operation for the foreseeable future, without going into liquidation or materially scaling down its operations.

2   **Verifiability** helps assure users that information faithfully represents the **economic phenomena** it purports to represent. It means that different knowledgeable and independent observers could reach consensus that a particular depiction is a **faithful representation** *(Conceptual Framework)*.

3   D   Fair presentation, as it shows the likely recoverability of receivables

4   Relevant information is capable of making a difference in the decisions made by users, by having **predictive value**, **confirmatory value** or both.

5   Comparability, verifiability, timeliness and understandability

Now try ...

Attempt the questions below from the **Practice Question Bank**

Number

Qs 8 – 10

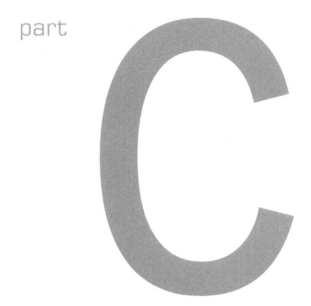

part

The use of double entry and accounting systems

The use of double entry and accounting systems

04

From your studies of the first three chapters you should have grasped some important points about the nature and purpose of accounting.

- Most organisations provide products and services in the hope of making a profit for their owners, by receiving payment in money for those goods and services.

- The role of the accounting system is to record these monetary effects and create information about them.

You should also, by now, understand the basic principles underlying the statement of financial position and statement of profit or loss.

We now turn our attention to the process by which a business transaction works its way through to the financial statements.

It is usual to record a business transaction on a **document**. Such documents include invoices, orders, credit notes and goods received notes, all of which will be discussed in Section 1 of this chapter. In terms of the accounting system these are known as **source documents**. The information on them is processed by the system by, for example, aggregating (adding together) or classifying.

Records of source documents are kept in 'books of prime entry' which, as the name suggests, is the first stage at which a business transaction enters the accounting system. The various types of books of prime entry are discussed in Sections 2 to 4 and petty cash is considered briefly in Section 5.

In the next chapter we consider what happens to transactions after the books of prime entry stage.

Sources, records and books of prime entry

TOPIC LIST	SYLLABUS REFERENCE
1 The role of source documents	C1(a),(b),(f)
2 The need for books of prime entry	C2(a)
3 Sales and purchase day books	C2(a), D1(b)
4 Cash book	C2(a)
5 Petty cash	D2(b)

1 The role of source documents

> Business transactions are recorded on **source documents**. Examples include sales and purchase orders, invoices and credit notes.

1.1 Types of source documents

Whenever a business transaction takes place, involving sales or purchases, receiving or paying money, or owing or being owed money, it is usual for the transaction to be recorded on a document. These documents are the source of all the information recorded by a business.

Documents used to record the business transactions in the 'books of account' of the business include the following.

(a) **Quotation**. A document sent to a customer by a company stating the fixed price that would be charged to produce or deliver goods or services. Quotations tend to be used when businesses do not have a standard listing of prices for products, for example when the time, materials and skills required for each job vary according to the customer's needs. Quotations can't be changed once they have been accepted by the customer.

(b) **Purchase order**. A document of the company that details goods or services which the company wishes to purchase from another company. Two copies of a purchase order are often made, one is sent to the company from which the goods or services will be purchased, and the other is kept internally so the company can keep track of its orders. Purchase orders are often sequentially numbered.

(c)   **Sales order**. A document of the company that details an order placed by a customer for goods or services. The customer may have sent a purchase order to the company from which the company will then generate a sales order. Sales orders are usually sequentially numbered so that the company can keep track of orders placed by customers.

(d)   **Goods received note**. A document of the company that lists the goods that a business has received from a supplier. A goods received note is usually prepared by the business's own warehouse or goods receiving area. This is discussed further below.

(e)   **Goods despatched note**. A document of the company that lists the goods that the company has sent out to a customer. The company will keep a record of goods despatched notes in case of any queries by customers about the goods sent. The customer will compare the goods despatched note to what they receive to make sure all the items listed have been delivered and are the right specification.

(f)   **Invoice**. This is discussed further below.

(g)   **Statement**. A document sent out by a supplier to a customer listing the transactions on the customer's account, including all invoices and credit notes issued and all payments received from the customer. The statement is useful, as it allows the customer to reconcile the amount that they believe they owe the supplier to the amount the supplier believes they are owed. Any differences can then be queried.

(h)   **Credit note**. A document sent by a supplier to a customer in respect of goods returned or overpayments made by the customer. It is a 'negative' invoice. This is discussed further below.

(i)   **Debit note**. A document sent by a customer to a supplier in respect of goods returned or an overpayment made. It is a formal request for the supplier to issue a credit note.

(j)   **Remittance advice**. A document sent to a supplier with a payment, detailing which invoices are being paid and which credit notes offset. A remittance advice allows the supplier to update the customer's records to show which invoices have been paid and which are still outstanding. It also confirms the amount being paid, so that any discrepancies can be easily identified and investigated.

(k)   **Receipt**. A document confirming confirmation that a payment has been received. This is usually in respect of cash sales, eg a till receipt from a cash register. This is discussed further below.

1.2 Invoices

An invoice relates to a sales order or a purchase order.

(a)   When a business sells goods or services on credit to a customer, it sends out an invoice. The details on the invoice should match the details on the sales order. The invoice is a request for the customer to pay what they owe.

(b)   When a business buys goods or services on credit it receives an invoice from the supplier. The details on the invoice should match the details on the purchase order.

The invoice is primarily a demand for payment, but it is used for other purposes as well, as we shall see. Most accounting software packages can generate invoices; however, in smaller businesses with paper based systems, the invoice is often produced on multi-part stationery, or photocopied, or carbon-copied. The top copy will go to the customer and other copies will be used by various people within the business.

1.2.1 What does an invoice show?

Invoices should be numbered, so that the business can keep track of all the invoices it sends out. Information usually shown on an invoice includes the following.

(a)   Name and address of the seller and the purchaser
(b)   Date of the sale
(c)   Description of what is being sold
(d)   Quantity and unit price of what has been sold (eg 20 pairs of shoes at $25 a pair)

(e)   Details of trade discount, if any (eg 10% reduction in cost if buying over 100 pairs of shoes)

(f)   Total amount of the invoice including (usually) details any of sales tax

(g)   Sometimes, the date by which payment is due, and other terms of sale

1.2.2 Uses of invoices

As stated above, invoices may be used for different purposes.

- Copy to customer as a request for payment
- Copy to accounts department to match to eventual payment
- Copy to warehouse to generate a despatch of goods, as evidenced by a goods despatched note
- Copy matched to sales order and kept in sales department as a record of sales

1.3 The credit note

China Supplies sent out an invoice for 20 dinner plates, but the typist accidentally typed in a total of $162.10, instead of $62.10. The china shop has been **overcharged** by $100. What is China Supplies to do?

Alternatively, when the china shop received the plates it found that they had all been broken in the post and that it was going to send them back. Although the china shop has received an invoice for $62.10, it has no intention of paying it because the plates were useless. Again, what is China Supplies to do?

The answer is that China Supplies sends out a **credit note**. A credit note is sometimes printed in red to distinguish it from an invoice. Otherwise, it will be made out in much the same way as an invoice, but with less detail and 'Credit Note Number' instead of 'Invoice Number'.

A credit note is a document relating to returned goods or refunds when a customer has been overcharged. It can be regarded as a **negative invoice**.

1.4 Other documents

The following documents are sometimes used in connection with sales and purchases.

(a)   Debit notes

(b)   Goods received notes

A **debit note** might be issued to **adjust an invoice** already issued. This is also commonly achieved by issuing a revised invoice after raising a credit or debit note purely for internal purposes (ie to keep the records straight).

More commonly, a debit note is issued to a supplier as a means of formally requesting a credit note.

Goods received notes (GRNs) record a receipt of goods, most commonly in a warehouse. They may be used in addition to suppliers' advice notes.

Note. Although referred to as 'goods' received notes, GRNs can be used as a record that a **service** has been carried out. This is especially the case in electronic purchase order systems where a fundamental step in the purchase order process is for the accounts department to match a GRN to a purchase order for goods and services received, before paying a supplier's invoice. This is a key control to ensure that invoices are not paid if the goods or services have not been received (although there are exceptions to this, as some suppliers may require payment in advance).

Even where GRNs are not routinely used, the details of a consignment from a supplier which arrives without an advice note must always be recorded.

GRNs are also key documents in estimating a company's figure for accrued purchases (accruals) that needs to go into the financial statements. This is because they are evidence of liabilities to pay for goods or services received, that have not yet been invoiced by the suppliers. The figure goes into the accruals account or sometimes more specifically a 'GRNI' account (Good Received Not Invoiced) which forms part of the overall accruals figure. Accruals are discussed in more detail in Chapter 10.

QUESTION

Documentation

Fill in the blanks.

'China Supplies sends out a . . . . to a credit customer in order to correct an error where a customer has been overcharged on an . . . .'

ANSWER

Credit note; invoice.

2 The need for books of prime entry

In the course of business, source documents are created. The details on these source documents need to be summarised, as otherwise the business might forget to ask for some money, or forget to pay some, or even accidentally pay something twice. It needs to keep records of source documents – of transactions – so that it knows what is going on. Such records are made in **books of prime entry**.

Books of prime entry are books in which we first record transactions.

The main **books of prime entry** are as follows.

(a)   Sales day book
(b)   Purchase day book
(c)   Sales returns day book
(d)   Purchase returns day book
(e)   Journal (described in the next chapter)
(f)   Cash book
(g)   Petty cash book

It is worth bearing in mind that, for convenience, this chapter describes books of prime entry as if they are actual books written by hand. However, books of prime entry are often not books at all, but rather files stored on a computer or within accounting software. However, the principles remain the same whether they are manual or computerised.

EXAM FOCUS POINT

The ACCA examining team commented that this topic has been particularly well answered in recent exams.

3 Sales and purchase day books

Invoices and credit notes are recorded in **day books**.

3.1 The sales day book

The sales day book is the book of prime entry for credit sales.

The sales day book is used to keep a list of all invoices sent out to customers each day. An extract from a sales day book might look like this.

SALES DAY BOOK

Date	Invoice	Customer	Total amount invoiced $
Jan 10 20X0	247	Jones & Co	105.00
	248	Smith Co	86.40
	249	Alex & Co	31.80
	250	Enor College	1,264.60
			1,487.80

Most businesses 'analyse' their sales. For example, this business sells boots and shoes. The sale to Smith was entirely boots, the sale to Alex was entirely shoes, and the other two sales were a mixture of both.

Then the sales day book might look like this.

SALES DAY BOOK

Date	Invoice	Customer	Total amount invoiced $	Boot sales $	Shoe sales $
Jan 10 20X0	247	Jones & Co	105.00	60.00	45.00
	248	Smith Co	86.40	86.40	
	249	Alex & Co	31.80		31.80
	250	Enor College	1,264.60	800.30	464.30
			1,487.80	946.70	541.10

The analysis gives the managers of the business useful information which helps them to decide how best to run the business.

Most accounting software allows you to raise sales invoices, and automatically generate sales day book reports of the invoices raised.

3.2 The purchase day book

A business also keeps a record in the purchase day book of all the invoices it receives.

The purchase day book is the book of prime entry for credit purchases.

An extract from a purchase day book might look like this.

PURCHASE DAY BOOK

Date	Internal inv no.	Supplier inv. no.	Supplier	Total amount invoiced $	Purchases $	Electricity etc $
Mar 15	654	YH000939	Cook & Co	315.00	315.00	
20X0	655	A00167	W Butler	29.40	29.40	
	656	1267	EEB	116.80		116.80
	657	GB17789	Show Fair Co	100.00	100.00	
				561.20	444.40	116.80

The purchase day book records **other people's invoices**, which have all sorts of different numbers. For ease of reference, the business may assign its own sequential internal invoice number to each purchase invoice.

Like the sales day book, the purchase day book analyses the invoices which have been sent in. In this example, three of the invoices related to goods which the business intends to resell (called simply 'purchases') and the other invoice was an electricity bill.

Most accounting software allows you to enter details of the purchase invoices onto the system, and automatically generate Purchases Day Book reports of the invoices entered.

3.3 The sales returns day book

When customers return goods for some reason, a credit note is raised. All credit notes are recorded in the sales returns day book. An extract from the sales returns day book follows.

SALES RETURNS DAY BOOK

Date	Credit note	Customer and goods	Amount $
30 April 20X8	CR008	Owen Plenty Three pairs 'Texas' boots	135.00

The sales returns day book is the book of prime entry for credit notes raised.

Not all sales returns day books analyse what goods were returned, but it makes sense to keep as complete a record as possible. Where a business has very few sales returns, it may record a credit note as a negative entry in the sales day book.

3.4 The purchase returns day book

Not surprisingly, the purchase returns day book records credit notes received in respect of goods which the business sends back to its suppliers.

An extract from the purchase returns day book follows.

PURCHASE RETURNS DAY BOOK

Date	Supplier and goods	Amount $
29 April 20X8	Boxes Co 300 cardboard boxes	46.60

The purchase returns day book is the book of prime entry for credit notes received from suppliers.

Once again, a business with very few purchase returns may record a credit note received as a negative entry in the purchase day book.

4 Cash book

The **cash book** may be a manual record or a computer file. It records all transactions that go through the bank account.

4.1 The cash book

The cash book is also a day book, used to keep a record of money received and money paid out by the business. The cash book deals with money paid into and out of the business **bank account**. This could be money received on the business premises in notes, coins and cheques, subsequently paid into the bank. There are also receipts and payments made by bank transfer, standing order, direct debit and bank interest and charges, directly by the bank.

Some cash, in notes and coins, is usually kept on the business premises in order to make occasional payments for odd items of expense. This cash is usually accounted for separately in a **petty cash book**.

One side (the left) of the cash book is used to record receipts of cash, and the other side (the right) is used to record payments. The best way to see how the cash book works is to follow through an example. For convenience, we are showing the cash receipts and cash payments sides separately, but they are part of the same book.

The cash book is the book of prime entry for cash receipts and payments.

4.2 Example: cash book

At the beginning of 1 September, Robin Plenty had $900 in the bank.

During 1 September 20X7, Robin Plenty had the following receipts and payments.

(a)   Cash sale: receipt of $80
(b)   Payment from credit customer Hay $400 less discount allowed $20
(c)   Payment from credit customer Been $720
(d)   Payment from credit customer Seed $150 less discount allowed $10
(e)   Cheque received from Len Dinger $1,800 to provide a short-term loan
(f)   Second cash sale: receipt of $150
(g)   Cash received for sale of machine $200
(h)   Payment to supplier Kew $120
(i)   Payment to supplier Hare $310
(j)   Payment of telephone bill $400
(k)   Payment of gas bill $280
(l) $100 in cash withdrawn from bank for petty cash
(m)   Payment of $1,500 to Hess for new plant and machinery

If you look through these transactions, you will see that seven of them are receipts and six of them are payments.

The receipts part of the cash book for 1 September would look like this.

CASH BOOK (RECEIPTS)

Date	Narrative	Total $
1 Sep 20X7	Balance b/d*	900
	Cash sale	80
	Accounts receivable: Hay	380
	Accounts receivable: Been	720
	Accounts receivable: Seed	140
	Loan: Len Dinger	1,800
	Cash sale	150
	Sale of non-current asset	200
		4,370

* 'b/d' = brought down (ie brought forward)

Notes

1   There is a space on the right-hand side of the cash book so that the receipts can be analysed under various headings – for example, 'cash from receivables', 'cash sales' and 'other receipts'.

2   The cash received in the day amounted to $3,470. Added to the $900 at the start of the day, this comes to $4,370. This is not the amount to be carried forward to the next day, because first we have to subtract all the payments made during 1 September.

The payments part of the cash book for 1 September would look like this.

CASH BOOK (PAYMENTS)

Date	Narrative	Total $
1 Sep 20X7	Accounts payable: Kew	120
	Accounts payable: Hare	310
	Telephone	400
	Gas bill	280
	Petty cash	100
	Machinery purchase	1,500
	Balance c/d (balancing figure)	1,660
		4,370

As you can see, this is very similar to the receipts part of the cash book. The only points to note are as follows.

(a)   The analysis on the right would be under headings like 'payments to payables', 'payments into petty cash', 'wages' and 'other payments'.

(b)   Payments during 1 September totalled $2,710. We know that the total of receipts was $4,370. That means that there is a balance of $4,370 – $2,710 = $1,660 to be 'carried down' to the start of the next day. As you can see, this 'balance carried down' is noted at the end of the payments column, so that the receipts and payments totals show the same figure of $4,370 at the end of 1 September.

With analysis columns completed, the cash book given in the examples above might look as follows.

CASH BOOK (RECEIPTS)

Date	Narrative	Total $	Accounts receivable $	Cash sales $	Other $
1 Sep 20X7	Balance b/d	900			
	Cash sale	80		80	
	Accounts receivable: Hay	380	380		
	Accounts receivable: Been	720	720		
	Accounts receivable: Seed	140	140		
	Loan: Len Dinger	1,800			1,800
	Cash sale	150		150	
	Sale of non-current asset	200			200
		4,370	1,240	230	2,000

CASH BOOK (PAYMENTS)

Date	Narrative	Total $	Accounts payable $	Petty cash $	Wages $	Other $
1 Sep 20X7	Accounts payable: Kew	120	120			
	Accounts payable: Hare	310	310			
	Telephone	400				400
	Gas bill	280				280
	Petty cash	100		100		
	Machinery purchase	1,500				1,500
	Balance c/d	1,660				
		4,370	430	100	–	2,180

4.3 Bank statements

Weekly or monthly, a business will receive a **bank statement**. Bank statements should be used to check that the amount shown as a balance in the cash book agrees with the amount on the bank statement, and that no cash has 'gone missing'. This agreement or 'reconciliation' of the cash book with a bank statement is the subject of a later chapter.

5 | Petty cash

Most businesses keep **petty cash** on the premises, which is topped up from the main bank account. Under the **imprest system**, the petty cash is kept at an agreed sum, so that each topping up is equal to the amount paid out in the period.

5.1 What is petty cash?

Most businesses keep a small amount of cash on the premises to make occasional small payments in cash, eg staff refreshments, postage stamps, to pay the office cleaner, taxi fares, etc. This is often called the cash float or **petty cash** account. The cash float can also be the resting place for occasional small receipts, eg cash paid by a visitor to make a phone call.

5.2 The petty cash book

A petty cash book is a cash book for small payments.

Although the amounts involved are small, petty cash transactions still need to be recorded; otherwise the cash float could be abused for personal expenses or even stolen.

There are usually more payments than receipts, and petty cash must be 'topped up' from time to time with cash from the business bank account. A typical layout follows.

PETTY CASH BOOK

Receipts $	Date	Narrative	Total $	Milk $	Postage $	Travel $	Other $
250	1 Sep 20X7	Bal b/d					
		Milk bill	25	25			
		Postage stamps	5		5		
		Taxi fare	10			10	
		Flowers for sick staff	15				15
		Bal c/d	195				
250			250	25	5	10	15

5.3 Imprest system

Under what is called the **imprest system**, the amount of money in petty cash is kept at an agreed sum or 'float' (say, $250). This is called the **imprest amount**. Expense items are recorded on vouchers as they occur, so that at any time:

	$
Cash still held in petty cash	195
Plus voucher payments (25+5+10+15)	55
Must equal the imprest amount	250

The total float is replenished regularly (to $250, or whatever the imprest amount is) by means of a cash payment from the bank account into petty cash. The amount of the 'top-up' into petty cash will be the total of the voucher payments since the previous top-up.

5.4 Example: petty cash and the imprest system

DEF operates an imprest system for petty cash. During February 20X9, the following petty cash transactions took place.

		$
2.2.X9	Stamps	12.00
3.2.X9	Milk	25.00
8.2.X9	Taxi fare	15.00
17.2.X9	Stamps	5.00
18.2.X9	Received from staff for photocopying	8.00
28.2.X9	Stationery	7.50

The amount remaining in petty cash at the end of the month was $93.50. What is the imprest amount?

A $166.00
B $150.00
C $72.50
D $56.50

The solution is B.

	$	
Opening balance (imprest amount)	150.00	(balancing figure)
Add amount received from staff	8.00	
	158.00	
Less expenditure	(64.50)	(12 + 25 + 15 + 5 + 7.50)
Cash in hand at end of month	93.50	

EXAM FOCUS POINT

You will not get numerical questions on the imprest system in your exam. However, you do need to be aware of how the imprest system works, so make sure you work through the above example carefully.

QUESTION

Books of prime entry

State which books of prime entry the following transactions would be entered into.

A Your business pays A Brown (a supplier) $450.00
B You send D Smith (a customer) an invoice for $650
C Your accounts manager asks you for $12 urgently in order to buy some envelopes
D You receive an invoice from A Brown for $300
E You pay D Smith $500
F F Jones (a customer) returns goods to the value of $250
G You return goods to J Green to the value of $504
H F Jones pays you $500

ANSWER

A Cash book
B Sales day book
C Petty cash book
D Purchases day book
E Cash book
F Sales returns day book
G Purchase returns day book
H Cash book

Two of the requirements of performance objective PO6, 'Record and process transactions and events' are:

• Implement or effectively operate appropriate systems to record accounting data and ensure effective credit and vendor management and control;

• Verify, input, and process routine financial accounting data within the accounting system

This chapter of the Text will help you fulfil these requirements.

CHAPTER ROUNDUP

- ↳ Business transactions are recorded on **source documents**. Examples include sales and purchase orders, invoices and credit notes.

- ↳ The main **books of prime entry** are as follows.
  - – Sales day book
  - – Purchase day book
  - – Sales returns day book
  - – Purchase returns day book
  - – Journal (described in the next chapter)
  - – Cash book
  - – Petty cash book

- ↳ Invoices and credit notes are recorded in **day books**.

- ↳ The **cash book** may be a manual record or a computer file. It records all transactions that go through the bank account.

- ↳ Most businesses keep **petty cash** on the premises, which is topped up from the main bank account. Under the **imprest system**, the petty cash is kept at an agreed sum, so that each topping up is equal to the amount paid out in the period.

QUICK QUIZ

1 Name four pieces of information normally shown on an invoice.

2 Which of the following is not a book of prime entry?

  A Sales invoice
  B Purchase day book
  C Sales day book
  D Journal

3 What is the purchase returns day book used to record?

  A Suppliers' invoices
  B Customers' invoices
  C Details of goods returned to suppliers
  D Details of goods returned by customers

4 The petty cash book records payments into and out of the bank account. True or false?

5 Fill in the blank.

  Cash still held in petty cash + ... = the imprest amount.

ANSWERS TO QUICK QUIZ

1   **Four** from the following:
- Invoice number
- Seller's name and address
- Purchaser's name and address
- Date of sale
- Description of goods or services
- Quantity and unit price
- Trade discount (if any)
- Total amount, including sales tax (if any)
- Any special terms

2   A   Sales invoice is a source document.

3   C   Suppliers' invoices (A) are recorded in the purchase day book, customers' invoices (B) are recorded in the sales day book and goods returned by customers (D) are recorded in the sales returns day book.

4   False. The cash book records amounts paid into or out of the bank account. The petty cash book records payments of small amounts of cash.

5   Cash still held in petty cash + **voucher payments** = the imprest amount.

Now try ...

Attempt the questions below from the **Practice Question Bank**

Number

Qs 11 – 15

Ledger accounts and double entry

In the previous chapter we saw how to organise transactions into lists (ie entered into books of prime entry). It is not easy, however, to see how a business is doing from the information scattered throughout these books of prime entry. The lists need to be summarised. This is **ledger accounting**, which we look at in Sections 1 and 2.

The summary is produced in the nominal ledger by a process known as **double entry bookkeeping**. This is the cornerstone of accounts preparation and is surprisingly simple, once you have grasped the rules. We will look at the essentials in Sections 3 and 4.

In Section 5, we will deal with the final book of prime entry: **the journal**.

We will then look in detail at **posting transactions** from the day books to the ledgers in Section 6.

Finally, we will consider how to deal with **credit transactions** in Section 7.

Study Guide	Intellectual level
C **The use of double entry and accounting systems**	
1 **Double entry bookkeeping principles including the maintenance of accounting records**	
(c) Understand and apply the concept of double entry accounting and the duality concept.	K
(d) Understand and apply the accounting equation.	S
(e) Understand how the accounting system contributes to providing useful accounting information and complies with organisational policies and deadlines.	K
2 **Ledger accounts, books of prime entry and journals**	
(a) Identify the main types of ledger accounts and books of prime entry, and understand their nature and function.	K
(b) Understand and illustrate the uses of journals and the posting of journal entries into ledger accounts.	S
(c) Identify correct journals from given narrative.	S
D **Recording transactions and events**	
1 **Sales purchases**	
(a) Record sale and purchase transactions in ledger accounts.	S
(b) Understand and record sales and purchase returns.	S
2 **Cash**	
(a) Record cash transactions in ledger accounts.	S
8 **Receivables and payables**	
(a) Explain and identify examples of receivables and payables.	K

1   Why do we need ledger accounts?

> Ledger accounts **summarise** all the individual transactions listed in the books of prime entry.

A business is continually making transactions, eg buying and selling. It does not prepare a statement of profit or loss and a statement of financial position on completion of every individual transaction. To do so would be a time-consuming and cumbersome administrative task.

However, a business should keep a record of the transactions that it makes, the assets it acquires and liabilities it incurs. When the time comes to prepare a statement of profit or loss and a statement of financial position, the relevant information can be taken from those records.

The **records of transactions, assets and liabilities** should be kept in the following ways.

(a)   In **chronological order**, and **dated** so that transactions can be related to a particular period of time.

(b)   Built up in **cumulative totals**.

    (i)   Day by day (eg total sales on Monday, total sales on Tuesday)
    (ii)   Week by week

(iii)   Month by month
(iv)   Year by year

We have already seen the first step in this process, which is to list all the transactions in various books of prime entry. Now we will look at the method used to summarise these records: **ledger accounting** and **double entry**.

This system of summarising information speeds up the provision of useful information to managers and so helps managers to keep to organisational deadlines (eg provision of monthly profit figures for management purposes). This system also provides useful accounting information to other parts of the organisation. For example:

(a)   The credit control department monitors the receivables balances. The accounting system will provide valuable information to the credit control department by summarising all the sales made on credit. This will enable the credit control department to monitor receivables balances and make sure they are paid within the company's allowed credit period. The accounting information produced can also help with cash planning, as the credit control department can provide management with predicted timings of cash receipts based on outstanding receivables balances.

(b)   Summarised information relating to sales will be very useful to the sales department. The information provided could be used to work out which products are best sellers and which are not selling very well, whether products sell better at different times of the year and so on. The sales department could also liaise with the credit control department to make sure that sales are not made to customers who have a history of not paying their bills.

(c)   Summarised information on sales and purchases can also help the company manage its inventory levels. The purchasing department can use the summarised accounting information to spot trends in the use of raw materials to help it predict demand levels and avoid stock outs.

2   The nominal ledger

The principal accounts are contained in a ledger called the **general** or **nominal ledger**.

The nominal ledger is an accounting record which summarises the financial affairs of a business.

The nominal ledger is sometimes called the '**general ledger**'. The information contained in the books of prime entry (eg the sales and purchases day books) is **summarised** and **posted** to accounts in the nominal ledger. Accounting software operates in the same way; however, it is more common for the information in the sales and purchases day books to be posted to the nominal ledger as individual transactions rather than summaries.

The nominal ledger contains details of all accounts including assets, liabilities, capital, income and expenditure, and so profit and loss. Each account has an account name and an account code. Access to certain accounts in the nominal ledger may be restricted to certain accounting staff, as a control against fraud, or for confidentiality reasons (eg salary accounts).

Examples of accounts in the nominal ledger include the following.

(a)   Plant and machinery at cost (non-current asset)
(b)   Motor vehicles at cost (non-current asset)
(c)   Plant and machinery, provision for depreciation (liability)
(d)   Motor vehicles, provision for depreciation (liability)
(e)   Proprietor's capital (liability)
(f)   Inventories – raw materials (current asset)
(g)   Inventories – finished goods (current asset)
(h)   Total trade accounts receivable (current asset)
(i)   Total trade accounts payable (current liability)
(j)   Wages and salaries (expense item)
(k)   Rent and local taxes (expense item)

(l)   Advertising expenses (expense item)
(m)   Bank charges (expense item)
(n)   Motor expenses (expense item)
(o)   Telephone expenses (expense item)
(p)   Sales (revenue item)
(q)   Total cash or bank overdraft (current asset or liability)

When it comes to drawing up the financial statements, the revenue and expense accounts will help to form the statement of profit or loss, while the asset and liability accounts go into the statement of financial position.

2.1 The format of a ledger account

If a ledger account were to be kept as a manual system in an actual book, rather than as a file in a computerised system, it might look like this:

ADVERTISING EXPENSES

Date	Narrative	Ref.	$	Date	Narrative	Ref.	$
15 April 20X6	JFK Agency for quarter to 31 March	PL 348	2,500				

For the rest of this chapter, we will assume that a manual system is being used, in order to illustrate fully the working of the ledger accounts. Remember that a computerised system performs the same functions, although the actual ledger accounts will be stored as computer files and so may be hidden away within the system.

There are two sides to a ledger account, and an account heading on top, and so they are often referred to as T-accounts.

(a)   On top of the account is its name.
(b)   There is a left-hand side, or debit side.
(c)   There is a right-hand side, or credit side.

NAME OF ACCOUNT

DEBIT SIDE	$	CREDIT SIDE	$

We will look at 'debits' and 'credits' in detail in Section 4, but first we shall consider the accounting equation.

EXAM FOCUS POINT

The ACCA examining team commented that processing of ledger accounts has been particularly well answered in recent exams.

3 The accounting equation

The **accounting equation** is ASSETS = CAPITAL + LIABILITIES.

We will start by showing how to account for a business's transactions from the time that trading first begins. We will use an example to illustrate the 'accounting equation', ie the rule that the assets of a business will at all times equal its liabilities. This is also known as the **statement of financial position equation**.

3.1 Example: the accounting equation

Business entity concept. Regardless of how a business is legally set up, for accounting purposes, a business is always treated separately from its owner(s).

Liza Doolittle starts a business. The business begins by owning the cash that Liza has put into it, $2,500. The business is a separate entity in accounting terms and so it owes the money to Liza as **capital**.

In accounting, capital is an investment of money (funds) with the intention of earning a return. A business proprietor invests capital with the intention of earning profit. As long as that money is invested, accountants will treat the capital as money owed to the proprietor by the business.

When Liza Doolittle sets up her business:

Capital invested   = $2,500
Cash   = $2,500

Capital invested is a form of liability, because it is an amount owed by the business to its owner(s). Adapting this to the idea that assets and liabilities are always equal amounts, we can state the accounting equation as follows.

FORMULA TO LEARN

The accounting equation is:

$$ASSETS = CAPITAL + LIABILITIES$$

For Liza Doolittle, as at 1 July 20X6:

Assets	=	*Capital*	+	*Liabilities*
$2,500 (cash)	=	$2,500	+	$0

3.2 Example continued

Liza Doolittle purchases a market stall from Len Turnip, who is retiring from his fruit and vegetables business. The cost of the stall is $1,800.

She also purchases some flowers and potted plants from a trader in the wholesale market, at a cost of $650. This leaves $50 in cash, after paying for the stall and goods for resale, out of the original $2,500.

The assets and liabilities of the business have now altered and, at 3 July before trading begins, the state of her business is as follows.

Assets		=	*Capital*	+	*Liabilities*
	$				
Stall	1,800	=	$2,500	+	$0
Flower and plants	650				
Cash	50				
	2,500				

The stall and the flowers and plants are physical items, but they must be given a monetary value. This monetary value is usually what they cost the business (called **historical cost** in accounting terms).

3.3 Profit introduced into the accounting equation

On 3 July Liza has a very successful day. She sells all of her flowers and plants for $900 cash.

Since Liza has sold goods costing $650 to earn revenue of $900, we can say that she has **earned a profit of $250 on the day's trading**.

Profits belong to the owners of a business. In this case, the $250 belongs to Liza Doolittle. However, so long as the business retains the profits and does not pay anything out to its owners, the **retained profits** are accounted for as an addition to the proprietor's capital.

Assets		=	Capital		+	Liabilities
	$			$		
Stall	1,800		Original investment	2,500		
Flowers and plants	0		Retained profit			
Cash (50 + 900)	950		(900 – 650)	250		
	2,750			2,750	+	$0

We can rearrange the accounting equation to help us to calculate the capital balance.

Assets – liabilities = Capital, which is the same as
Net assets = Capital

At the beginning and end of 3 July 20X6, Liza Doolittle's financial position was as follows.

		Net assets	Capital
(a)	At the beginning of the day:	$(2,500 – 0) = $2,500 =	$2,500
(b)	At the end of the day:	$(2,750 – 0) = $2,750 =	$2,750

There has been an increase of $250 in net assets, which is the amount of profits earned during the day.

3.4 Drawings

Drawings are amounts of money taken out of a business by its owner. **Note**. Drawings are relevant in sole traderships and partnerships. In limited companies, the owners, ie shareholders, are paid dividends. If the owner of a limited company is also a director of that company, they may opt to pay themselves a salary as an employee. If they withdraw any other money from the company for their personal use, this should be accounted for as a director's loan, which they must repay in accordance with an agreed repayment schedule.

Since Liza Doolittle has made a profit of $250 from her first day's work, she might want to withdraw some money from the business. After all, business owners, like everyone else, need income for living expenses. Liza decides to pay herself $180 in 'wages'. However, the $180 is not an expense to be deducted in arriving at the figure of net profit. In other words, it is **incorrect** to calculate the net profit earned by the business as follows.

	$
Profit on sale of flowers etc	250
Less 'wages' paid to Liza	180
Net profit earned by business (incorrect)	70

This is because any amounts paid by a business to its proprietor are treated by accountants as withdrawals of profit (the usual term is **drawings**) and not as expenses incurred by the business. In the case of Liza's business, the true position is that the net profit earned is the $250 surplus on sale of flowers.

	$
Net profit earned by business	250
Less profit withdrawn by Liza	180
Net profit retained in the business	70

Profits are capital as long as they are retained in the business. Once they are **withdrawn**, the business suffers a reduction in capital.

The withdrawals of profit are taken in cash, and so the business loses $180 of its cash assets. After the withdrawals have been made, the accounting equation would be restated.

(a)

Assets		=	*Capital*		+	*Liabilities*
	$			$		
Stall	1,800		Original investment	2,500		
Flowers and plants	0		Retained profit			
Cash (950 – 180)	770		(250 – 180)	70		
	2,570			2,570	+	$0

(b)   Alternatively   Net assets   Capital
                      $(2,570 – 0)   = $2,570

The increase in net assets since trading operations began is now only $(2,570 – 2,500) = $70, which is the amount of the retained profits.

QUESTION

Capital

Which of the following is correct?

A   Capital = assets + liabilities
B   Capital = liabilities – assets
C   Capital = assets – liabilities
D   Capital + assets = liabilities

ANSWER

The correct answer is C. As assets = liabilities + capital, then capital = assets – liabilities.

3.5 Example continued

When business transactions are accounted for, it should be possible to **restate the assets and liabilities** of the business after the transactions have taken place.

The next market day is on 10 July and Liza purchases more flowers and plants for cash, at a cost of $740. She is not feeling well because of a heavy cold, and so she decides to accept help for the day from her cousin Ethel. Ethel is to be paid a wage of $40 at the end of the day.

Trading on 10 July was again very brisk, and Liza and Ethel sold all their goods for $1,100 cash. Liza paid Ethel her wage of $40 and drew out $200 for herself.

Required

(a)   State the accounting equation before trading began on 10 July.
(b)   State the accounting equation at the end of 10 July, after paying Ethel:
    (i)   But before drawings are made
    (ii)   After drawings have been made

Solution

(a)   After the purchase of the goods for $740:

Assets		=	*Capital*	+	*Liabilities*
	$				
Stall	1,800				
Flowers and plants	740				
Cash (770 – 740)	30				
	2,570	=	$ 2,570	+	$0

(b) (i) On 10 July, all the goods are sold for $1,100 cash, and Ethel is paid $40. The profit for the day is $320.

	$	$
Sales		1,100
Less cost of goods sold	740	
Ethel's wage	40	
		780
Profit		320

Assets	$	= Capital	$	+	Liabilities
Stall	1,800	At beginning of 10 July	2,570		
Flowers and plants	0	Profits earned on 10 July	320		
Cash (30 + 1,100 – 40)	1,090				
	2,890		2,890	+	$0

(ii) After Liza has withdrawn $200 in cash, retained profits will be only $(320 – 200) = $120.

Assets	$	= Capital	$	+	Liabilities
Stall	1,800	At beginning of 10 July	2,570		
Flowers and plants	0	Retained profits for 10 July	120		
Cash (1,090 – 200)	890				
	2,690		2,690	+	$0

IMPORTANT

It is very important that you understand the principles described so far. Do not read on until you are confident that you understand the solution to this example.

3.6 Payables and receivables

Trade accounts payable are liabilities. Trade accounts receivable are assets.

3.6.1 Trade accounts payable and trade accounts receivable

A payable is a person or organisation to whom a business owes money.

A **trade payable** is a person or organisation to whom a business owes money for debts incurred in the course of trading operations. In the accounts of a business, debts still outstanding which arise from the purchase of materials, components or goods for resale are called **trade accounts payable**, sometimes abbreviated to 'accounts payable' or 'payables'. In some businesses, you may see trade accounts payable referred to as **trade creditors**.

A business does not always pay immediately for goods or services it buys. It is a common business practice to make purchases on credit, with a promise to pay, typically within 30 days of the date of the invoice for the goods. For example, A buys goods costing $2,000 on credit from B, B sends A an invoice for $2,000, dated 1 March, with credit terms that payment must be made within 30 days. If A then delays payment until 31 March, B will be a payable of A between 1 and 31 March for $2,000. From A's point of view, the amount owed to B is a **trade account payable**.

A trade account payable is a **liability** of a business.

Just as a business might buy goods on credit, so too might it sell goods to customers on credit. A customer who buys goods without paying cash for them straightaway is a receivable.

For example, suppose that C sells goods on credit to D for $6,000 on terms that the debt must be settled within two months of the invoice date 1 October. If D does not pay the $6,000 until 30 November, D will be a receivable of C for $6,000 from 1 October until 30 November. In the accounts of the business, amounts owed by receivables are called **trade accounts receivable**, sometimes abbreviated to 'accounts receivable' or 'receivables'. Some businesses refer to trade accounts receivable as **trade debtors**.

A trade account receivable is an **asset** of a business. When the debt is finally paid, the trade account receivable 'disappears' as an asset, to be replaced by 'cash at bank and in hand' as an asset.

3.6.2 Example continued

The example of Liza Doolittle's market stall is continued, by looking at the consequences of the following transactions in the week to 17 July 20X6. (See Section 3.5 for the situation as at the end of 10 July.)

(a) Liza Doolittle realises that she is going to need more money in the business and so she makes the following arrangements.

   (i) She immediately invests a further $250 of her own capital.

   (ii) She persuades her Uncle Henry to lend her $500 immediately. Uncle Henry tells her that she can repay the loan whenever she likes but, in the meantime, she must pay him interest of $5 each week at the end of the market day. They agree that it will probably be quite a long time before the loan is eventually repaid.

(b) She decides to buy a secondhand van to pick up flowers and plants from her supplier and bring them to her stall in the market. She finds a car dealer, Laurie Loader, who agrees to sell her a van on credit for $700. Liza agrees to pay for the van after 30 days' trial use.

(c) During the week, Liza's Uncle George telephones her to ask whether she would sell him some garden gnomes and furniture for his garden. Liza tells him that she will look for a supplier. After some investigations, she buys what Uncle George has asked for, paying $300 in cash to the supplier. Uncle George accepts delivery of the goods and agrees to pay $350, but he asks if she can wait until the end of the month for payment. Liza agrees.

(d) Liza buys flowers and plants costing $800. Of these purchases, $750 are paid in cash, with the remaining $50 on 7 days' credit. Liza decides to use Ethel's services again as an assistant on market day, at an agreed wage of $40.

(e) On 17 July, Liza succeeds in selling all her goods earning revenue of $1,250 (all in cash). She decides to withdraw $240 for her week's work. She also pays Ethel $40 in cash. She decides to make the interest payment to her Uncle Henry the next time she sees him.

(f) We shall ignore any van expenses for the week, for the sake of relative simplicity.

Required

State the accounting equation:

(i) After Liza and Uncle Henry have put more money into the business and after the purchase of the van

(ii) After the sale of goods to Uncle George

(iii) After the purchase of goods for the weekly market

(iv) At the end of the day's market trading on 17 July, and after withdrawals have been appropriated out of profit

Solution

There are a number of different transactions to account for here. This solution deals with them one at a time in chronological order. (In practice, it is possible to do one set of calculations which combines the results of all the transactions.)

(i) *The addition of Liza's extra capital and Uncle Henry's loan*

An investment analyst might call Uncle Henry's loan a capital investment on the grounds that it will probably be for the long term. Uncle Henry is not the owner of the business, however, even though he has made a loan to it. He would only become an owner if Liza offered him a partnership in the business, and she has not done so. To the business, Uncle Henry is a long-term payable, and it is more appropriate to define his investment as a liability of the business and not as business capital.

The accounting equation after $(250 + 500) = $750 cash is put into the business will be:

Assets		= Capital		+ Liabilities	
	$		$		$
Stall	1,800	As at end of 10 July	2,690	Loan	500
Flowers and plants	0	Additional capital put in	250		
Cash (890 + 750)	1,640				
	3,440 =		2,940 +		500

The purchase of the van (cost $700) on credit

Assets		= Capital		+ Liabilities	
	$		$		$
Stall	1,800	As at end of 10 July	2,690	Loan	500
Van	700	Additional capital	250	Payables	700
Cash	1,640				
	4,140 =		2,940 +		1,200

(ii) *The sale of goods to Uncle George on credit ($350) which cost the business $300 (cash paid)*

Assets		= Capital		+ Liabilities	
	$		$		$
Stall	1,800	As at end of 10 July	2,690	Loan	500
Van	700	Additional capital	250	Payables	700
Receivable	350	Profit on sale to			
Cash		Uncle George			
		(350 – 300)	50		
(1,640 – 300)	1,340				
	4,190 =		2,990 +		1,200

(iii) *After the purchase of goods for the weekly market ($750 paid in cash and $50 of purchases on credit)*

Assets		= Capital		+ Liabilities	
	$			$	$
Stall	1,800	As at end of 10 July	2,690	Loan	500
Van	700	Additional capital	250	Payables	
Flowers and plants	800	Profit on sale to		(van)	700
Receivables	350	Uncle George	50	Payables	
Cash				(goods)	50
(1,340 – 750)	590				
	4,240 =		2,990 +		1,250

(iv) *After market trading on 17 July*

Sales of goods costing $800 earned revenues of $1,250. Ethel's wages were $40 (paid), Uncle Henry's interest charge is $5 (not paid yet) and withdrawals on account of profits were $240 (paid). The profit for market trading on 17 July may be calculated as follows, taking the full $5 of interest as a cost on that day.

BPP
LEARNING MEDIA

	$	$
Sales		1,250
Cost of goods sold	800	
Wages	40	
Interest	5	
		845
Profit earned on 17 July		405
Drawings		240
Retained profit		165

Assets		= **Capital**		+ **Liabilities**	
	$		$		$
Stall	1,800	As at end of 10 July	2,690	Loan	500
Van	700	Additional capital	250	Payable for	
Flowers and plants	0	Profit on sale to		van	700
(800 – 800)		Uncle George	50		
Receivables	350			Payable for	
Cash (590 +		Profits retained	165	goods	50
1,250 – 40 – 240)	1,560			Payable for	
				interest	
				payment	5
	4,410		3,155		1,255

3.7 Matching

The **matching convention** requires that revenue earned is matched with the expenses incurred in earning it.

The matching convention comes from the **accruals assumption**. In the example above, we have 'matched' the revenue earned with the expenses incurred in earning it. So in part (iv), we included all the costs of the goods sold of $800, even though $50 had not yet been paid in cash. Also, the interest of $5 was deducted from revenue, even though it had not yet been paid. This is an example of the **matching convention**.

QUESTION   The accounting equation

How would each of these transactions affect the accounting equation?

A   Purchasing $800 worth of inventory on credit
B   Paying the telephone bill $25
C   Selling $450 worth of inventory for $650
D   Paying $800 to the supplier

ANSWER

A	Increase in liabilities (payables)	$800
	Increase in assets (inventory)	$800
B	Decrease in assets (cash)	$25
	Decrease in capital (profit)	$25
C	Decrease in assets (inventory)	$450
	Increase in assets (cash)	$650
	Increase in capital (profit)	$200
D	Decrease in liabilities (payables)	$800
	Decrease in assets (cash)	$800

4 Double entry bookkeeping

Double entry bookkeeping is based on the idea that each transaction has an equal but opposite effect. Every accounting event must be entered in ledger accounts both as a debit and as an equal but opposite credit.

4.1 Dual effect (duality concept)

Double entry bookkeeping is the method used to transfer the weekly/monthly totals from the books of prime entry into the nominal ledger.

Double entry bookkeeping is the method by which a business records financial transactions. An account is maintained for every asset, liability, income and expense. Every transaction is recorded twice so that every **debit** is balanced by a **credit**.

Central to this process is the idea that every transaction has two effects, the **dual effect**. This feature is not something peculiar to businesses. If you were to purchase a car for $1,000 cash, for instance, you would be affected in two ways.

(a)   You own a car worth $1,000
(b)   You have $1,000 less cash

If instead you got a bank loan to make the purchase:

(a)   You own a car worth $1,000
(b)   You owe the bank $1,000

A month later if you pay a garage $50 to have the exhaust replaced:

(a)   You have $50 less cash
(b)   You have incurred a repairs expense of $50

Ledger accounts, with their debit and credit sides, are kept in a way which allows the two-sided nature of every transaction to be recorded. This is known as the **'double entry'** system of bookkeeping, because **every transaction is recorded twice** in the accounts.

4.2 The rules of double entry bookkeeping

A debit entry will:

- Increase an asset
- Decrease a liability
- Increase an expense

A credit entry will:

- Decrease an asset
- Increase a liability
- Increase income

The basic rule, which must always be observed, is that **every financial transaction gives rise to two accounting entries, one a debit and the other a credit**. The total value of debit entries in the nominal ledger is therefore always equal at any time to the total value of credit entries. Which account receives the credit entry and which receives the debit depends on the nature of the transaction.

- An **increase** in an **expense** (eg a purchase of stationery) or an **increase in an asset** (eg a purchase of office furniture) is a debit.

- An **increase** in **revenue** (eg a sale) or an **increase in a liability** (eg buying goods on credit) is a credit.

- A **decrease** in an **asset** (eg making a cash payment) is a credit.

- A **decrease** in a **liability** (eg paying a creditor) is a debit.

In terms of T-accounts:

ASSET			LIABILITY			CAPITAL		
DEBIT	$	CREDIT $	DEBIT	$	CREDIT $	DEBIT	$	CREDIT $
Increase		Decrease	Decrease		Increase	Decrease		Increase

For income and expenses, think about profit. Profit retained in the business increases capital. Income increases profit and expenses decrease profit.

INCOME			EXPENSE		
DEBIT	$	CREDIT $	DEBIT	$	CREDIT $
Decrease		Increase	Increase		Decrease

Have a go at the question below before you learn about this topic in detail.

QUESTION

Debits and credits

Complete the following table relating to the transactions of a bookshop. (The first two are done for you.)

A   Purchase of books on credit

(i)	accounts payable increase	CREDIT	accounts payable	(increase in liability)
(ii)	purchases expense increases	DEBIT	purchases	(item of expense)

B   Purchase of cash register

(i)	own a cash register	DEBIT	cash register	(increase in asset)
(ii)	cash at bank decreases	CREDIT	cash at bank	(decrease in asset)

C   Payment received from a credit customer

(i)   accounts receivable decrease
(ii)   cash at bank increases

D   Purchase of van

(i)   own a van
(ii)   cash at bank decreases

ANSWER

C   Payment received from a credit customer

(i)	accounts receivable decrease	CREDIT	accounts receivable	decrease in asset
(ii)	cash at bank increases	DEBIT	cash at bank	increase in asset

D   Purchase of van

(i)	own a van	DEBIT	van	increase in asset
(ii)	cash at bank decreases	CREDIT	cash at bank	decrease in asset

How did you get on? Students coming to the subject for the first time often have difficulty in knowing where to begin. A good starting point is the cash account, ie the nominal ledger account in which receipts and payments of cash are recorded. The rule to remember about the cash account is as follows.

(a)   A cash **payment** is a **credit** entry in the cash account. Here the **asset is decreasing**. Cash may be paid out, for example, to pay an expense (such as tax) or to purchase an asset (such as a

machine). The matching debit entry is therefore made in the appropriate expense or asset account.

(b)   A cash **receipt** is a **debit** entry in the cash account. Here the **asset is increasing**. Cash might be received, for example, by a retailer who makes a cash sale. The credit entry would then be made in the sales account.

This can be confusing since **bank statements** refer to a receipt as a credit, and a payment as a debit. Think of accounting entries for cash in the opposite way to how they are referred to on a bank statement.

Furthermore, although we use the term 'cash', this term covers all money going in and out of the bank account, eg payments and receipts of physical cash, electronic transfers of money, credit card transactions and cheques. Cheques are still used in smaller businesses; however, in larger businesses, electronic payment methods are more common, such as electronic transfers, direct debit and credit cards. For the purposes of this Interactive Text, we will give examples using the term 'cash', but the same principles apply to the other forms of payment and receipt mentioned above.

4.3 Example: double entry for cash transactions

In the cash book of a business, the following transactions have been recorded.

(a)   A cash sale (ie a receipt) of $250
(b)   Payment of a rent bill totalling $150
(c)   Buying some goods for cash at $100
(d)   Buying some shelves for cash at $200

How would these four transactions be posted to the ledger accounts and to which ledger accounts should they be posted? Don't forget that each transaction will be posted twice, in accordance with the rule of double entry.

Solution

(a)   The two sides of the transaction are:

(i)   Cash is received (debit entry in the cash at bank account).
(ii)   Sales increase by $250 (credit entry in the sales account).

CASH AT BANK ACCOUNT

	$		$
Sales a/c	250		

SALES ACCOUNT

	$		$
		Cash a/c	250

(Note how the entry in the cash at bank account is cross-referenced to the sales account and vice versa. This enables a person looking at one of the accounts to trace where the other half of the double entry can be found.)

(b)   The two sides of the transaction are:

(i)   Cash is paid (credit entry in the cash at bank account).
(ii)   Rent expense increases by $150 (debit entry in the rent account).

CASH AT BANK ACCOUNT

	$		$
		Rent a/c	150

RENT ACCOUNT

	$		$
Cash at bank a/c	150		

(c) The two sides of the transaction are:

(i) Cash is paid (credit entry in the cash at bank account).

(ii) Purchases increase by $100 (debit entry in the purchases account).

CASH AT BANK ACCOUNT

	$		$
		Purchases a/c	100

PURCHASES ACCOUNT

	$		$
Cash at bank a/c	100		

(d) The two sides of the transaction are:

(i) Cash is paid (credit entry in the cash at bank account).

(ii) Assets – in this case, shelves – increase by $200 (debit entry in shelves account).

CASH AT BANK ACCOUNT

	$		$
		Shelves a/c	200

SHELVES (ASSET) ACCOUNT

	$		$
Cash at bank a/c	200		

4.4 Credit transactions

Some accounts in the nominal ledger represent the total of very many smaller balances. For example, the **trade accounts receivable** account represents all the balances owed by individual customers of the business while the **trade accounts payable account** represents all money owed by the business to its suppliers.

As we have seen already, not all transactions are settled immediately in cash or by cheque or credit card. A business can purchase goods or non-current assets on credit terms, so that the suppliers would be trade accounts payable until settlement was made in cash. Equally, the business might grant credit terms to its customers who would then be trade accounts receivable of the business. Clearly no entries can be made in the cash book when a credit transaction occurs, because no cash has been received or paid, so where can the details of the transactions be entered?

The solution to this problem is to use **trade accounts receivable and trade accounts payable accounts**. When a business acquires goods or services on credit, the credit entry is made in an account designated 'trade accounts payable' instead of in the cash at bank account. The debit entry is made in the appropriate expense or asset account, exactly as in the case of cash transactions. Similarly, when a sale is made to a credit customer the entries made are a debit to the total trade accounts receivable account (instead of cash at bank account) and a credit to sales account.

4.5 Example: credit transactions

Recorded in the sales day book and the purchase day book are the following transactions.

(a) The business sells goods on credit to a customer Mr A for $2,000

(b) The business buys goods on credit from a supplier B Inc for $100

How and where are these transactions posted in the ledger accounts?

Solution

(a)

TRADE ACCOUNTS RECEIVABLE

	$		$
Sales a/c	2,000		

SALES ACCOUNT

	$		$
		Trade accounts receivable a/c	2,000

(b)

TRADE ACCOUNTS PAYABLE

	$		$
		Purchases a/c	100

PURCHASES ACCOUNT

	$		$
Trade accounts payable a/c	100		

4.5.1 When cash is paid to suppliers or by customers

What happens when a credit transaction is eventually settled? Suppose that, in the example above, the business paid $100 to B Inc one month after the goods were acquired. The two sides of this new transaction are:

(a) Cash is paid (credit entry in the cash at bank account).

(b) The amount owing to trade accounts payable is reduced (debit entry in the trade accounts payable account).

CASH AT BANK ACCOUNT

	$		$
		Trade accounts payable a/c	100

TRADE ACCOUNTS PAYABLE

	$		$
Cash a/c	100		

If we now bring together the two parts of this example, the original purchase of goods on credit and the eventual settlement in cash, we find that the accounts appear as follows.

CASH AT BANK ACCOUNT

	$		$
		Trade accounts payable a/c	100

PURCHASES ACCOUNT

	$		$
Trade accounts payable a/c	100		

TRADE ACCOUNTS PAYABLE

	$		$
Cash at bank a/c	100	Purchases a/c	100

The two entries in trade accounts payable cancel each other out, indicating that no money is owing to suppliers any more. We are left with a credit entry of $100 in the cash at bank account and a debit entry of $100 in the purchases account. These are exactly the same as the entries used to record a **cash** purchase of $100 (compare example above). This is what we would expect: after the business has paid off its trade accounts payable, it is in exactly the same position as if it had made a cash purchase, and the accounting records reflect this similarity.

Similar reasoning applies when a customer settles their debt. In the example above, when Mr A pays his debt of $2,000 the two sides of the transaction are:

(a)   Cash is received (debit entry in the cash at bank account)

(b)   The amount owed by trade accounts receivable is reduced (credit entry in the trade accounts receivable account)

CASH AT BANK ACCOUNT

	$		$
Trade accounts receivable a/c	2,000		

TRADE ACCOUNTS RECEIVABLE

	$		$
		Cash at bank a/c	2,000

The accounts recording this sale to, and payment by, Mr A now appear as follows.

CASH AT BANK ACCOUNT

	$		$
Trade accounts receivable a/c	2,000		

SALES ACCOUNT

	$		$
		Trade accounts receivable a/c	2,000

TRADE ACCOUNTS RECEIVABLE

	$		$
Sales a/c	2,000	Cash at bank a/c	2,000

The two entries in trade accounts receivable cancel each other out, while the entries in the cash at bank account and sales account reflect the same position as if the sale had been made for cash (see above).

Now try the following questions.

QUESTION

Debit and credit

See if you can identify the debit and credit entries in the following transactions.

A   Bought a machine on credit from A, cost $8,000
B   Bought goods on credit from B, cost $500
C   Sold goods on credit to C, value $1,200
D   Paid D (a credit supplier) $300
E   Collected $180 from E, a credit customer

F   Paid wages $4,000
G   Received rent bill of $700 from landlord G
H   Paid rent of $700 to landlord G
I   Paid insurance premium $90
J   Received a credit note for $450 from supplier H
K   Sent out a credit note for $200 to customer I

ANSWER

			$	$
A	DEBIT	Machine account (non-current asset)	8,000	
	CREDIT	Sundry* accounts payable		8,000
B	DEBIT	Purchases account	500	
	CREDIT	Trade accounts payable		500
C	DEBIT	Trade accounts receivable	1,200	
	CREDIT	Sales		1,200
D	DEBIT	Trade accounts payable	300	
	CREDIT	Cash at bank		300
E	DEBIT	Cash at bank	180	
	CREDIT	Trade accounts receivable		180
F	DEBIT	Wages account	4,000	
	CREDIT	Cash at bank		4,000
G	DEBIT	Rent account	700	
	CREDIT	Trade accounts payable		700
H	DEBIT	Trade accounts payable	700	
	CREDIT	Cash at bank		700
I	DEBIT	Insurance costs	90	
	CREDIT	Cash at bank		90
J	DEBIT	Trade accounts payable	450	
	CREDIT	Purchase returns		450
K	DEBIT	Sales returns	200	
	CREDIT	Trade accounts receivable		200

* **Note**. Suppliers who have supplied non-current assets are included among sundry accounts payable, as distinct from trade suppliers (who have supplied raw materials or goods for resale) who are trade accounts payable. It is quite common to have separate 'total accounts payable' accounts, one for trade accounts payable and another for sundry other accounts payable.

QUESTION   Ledger entries

See now whether you can record the ledger entries for the following transactions. Ron Knuckle set up a business selling keep fit equipment, trading under the name of Buy Your Biceps Shop. He put $7,000 of his own money into a business bank account (transaction A) and in his first period of trading, the following transactions occurred.

Transaction		$
B	Paid rent of shop for the period	3,500
C	Purchased equipment (inventories) on credit	5,000
D	Raised loan from bank	1,000
E	Purchase of shop fittings (for cash)	2,000
F	Sales of equipment: cash	10,000
G	Sales of equipment: on credit	2,500
H	Payments for trade accounts payable	5,000
I	Payments from trade accounts receivable	2,500
J	Interest on loan (paid)	100
K	Other expenses (all paid in cash)	1,900
L	Drawings	1,500

Try to do as much of this question as you can by yourself before reading the solution.

ANSWER

Clearly, there should be an account for cash at bank, trade accounts receivable, trade accounts payable, purchases, a shop fittings account, sales, a loan account and a proprietor's capital account. It is also useful to keep a separate account for **drawings** until the end of each accounting period. Other accounts should be set up as they seem appropriate. In this exercise, accounts for rent, bank interest and other expenses would seem appropriate.

It has been suggested to you that the cash at bank account is a good place to start, if possible. You should notice that cash transactions include the initial input of capital by Ron Knuckle, subsequent drawings, the payment of rent, the loan from the bank, the interest, some cash sales and cash purchases, and payments for trade accounts payable and from trade accounts receivable. (The transactions are identified below by their reference, to help you to find them.)

CASH AT BANK

	$		$
Capital – Ron Knuckle (A)	7,000	Rent (B)	3,500
Bank loan (D)	1,000	Shop fittings (E)	2,000
Sales (F)	10,000	Trade accounts payable (H)	5,000
Trade accounts receivable (I)	2,500	Bank loan interest (J)	100
		Other expenses (K)	1,900
		Drawings (L)	1,500

CAPITAL (RON KNUCKLE)

	$		$
		Cash at bank (A)	7,000

BANK LOAN

	$		$
		Cash at bank (D)	1,000

PURCHASES

	$		$
Trade accounts payable (C)	5,000		

TRADE ACCOUNTS PAYABLE

	$		$
Cash at bank (H)	5,000	Purchases (C)	5,000

RENT

	$		$
Cash at bank (B)	3,500		

NON-CURRENT ASSETS (SHOP FITTINGS)

	$		$
Cash at bank (E)	2,000		

SALES

	$		$
		Cash at bank (F)	10,000
		Trade accounts receivable (G)	2,500

TRADE ACCOUNTS RECEIVABLE

	$		$
Sales (G)	2,500	Cash at bank (I)	2,500

BANK LOAN INTEREST

	$		$
Cash at bank (J)	100		

OTHER EXPENSES

	$		$
Cash at bank (K)	1,900		

DRAWINGS ACCOUNT

	$		$
Cash at bank (L)	1,500		

(a) If you want to make sure that this solution is complete, you should go through the transactions A to L and tick off each of them twice in the ledger accounts, once as a debit and once as a credit. When you have finished, all transactions in the T-account should be ticked.

(b) In fact, there is an easier way to check that the solution to this sort of problem does 'balance' properly, which we will meet in the next chapter.

(c) On asset and liability accounts, the debit or credit balance represents the amount of the asset or liability outstanding at the period end. For example, on the cash at bank account, debits exceed credits by $6,500 and so there is a debit balance of cash in hand of $6,500. On the capital account, there is a credit balance of $7,000 and so the business owes Ron $7,000.

(d) The balances on the revenue and expense accounts represent the total of each revenue or expense for the period. For example, sales for the period total $12,500.

5 The journal

The **journal** is the record of prime entry for transactions which are not recorded in any of the other books of prime entry.

You should remember that one of the books of prime entry is the **journal**.

The journal keeps a record of unusual movement between accounts. It is used to record any double entries made which do not arise from the other books of prime entry, ie non-routine transactions. For example, journal entries are made when errors are discovered and need to be corrected.

Whatever type of transaction is being recorded, the **format of a journal entry** is:

Date		Debit	Credit
		$	$
Account to be debited		X	
Account to be credited			X
(Narrative to explain the transaction)			

Remember: in due course, the ledger accounts will be written up to include the transactions listed in the journal.

A **narrative explanation** must accompany each journal entry. It is required for audit and control, to indicate the purpose and authority of every transaction which is not first recorded in a book of original entry. Some larger organisations require that the above information is entered on a manual journal form (sometimes called a journal voucher form) and authorised by an appropriate member of staff, such as the Financial Controller. The form is usually attached to documentation to support the reason for the journal.

EXAM FOCUS POINT

An examination question might ask you to 'journalise' transactions which would not in practice be recorded in the journal at all. If you are faced with such a problem, you should simply record the debit and credit entries for every transaction.

5.1 Examples: journal entries

The following is a summary of the transactions of Hair by Fiona Middleton hairdressing business, of which Fiona is the sole proprietor.

1 January	Put in cash of $2,000 as capital
	Purchased brushes and combs for cash $50
	Purchased hairdriers from Gilroy Ltd on credit $150
30 January	Paid three months' rent to 31 March $300
	Collected and paid in takings $600
31 January	Gave Mrs Sullivan a perm, highlights etc on credit $80

Show the transactions by means of journal entries.

Solution

JOURNAL

			$	$
1 January	DEBIT	Cash at bank	2,000	
	CREDIT	Fiona Middleton – capital account		2,000
	Initial capital introduced			
1 January	DEBIT	Brushes and combs account	50	
	CREDIT	Cash at bank		50
	The purchase for cash of brushes and combs as non-current assets			
1 January	DEBIT	Hairdryer account	150	
	CREDIT	Sundry accounts payable*		150
	The purchase on credit of hairdryers as non-current assets			
30 January	DEBIT	Rent account	300	
	CREDIT	Cash at bank		300
	The payment of rent to 31 March			
30 January	DEBIT	Cash at bank	600	
	CREDIT	Sales account		600
	Cash takings			

31 January   DEBIT   Trade accounts receivable   80
                          CREDIT   Sales account   80
                          The provision of a hair-do on credit

* Note. Suppliers who have supplied non-current assets are included among sundry accounts payable, as distinct from trade suppliers (who have supplied raw materials or goods for resale) who are trade accounts payable. It is quite common to have separate 'total accounts payable' accounts, one for trade accounts payable and another for sundry other accounts payable.

In order to see how the journal is posted to the ledger accounts, we will look at the first two entries.

CASH AT BANK ACCOUNT

	$		$
Capital a/c (jnl)	2,000	Brushes and combs account (jnl)	50

CAPITAL ACCOUNT

	$		$
		Cash a/c (jnl)	2,000

BRUSHES AND COMBS ACCOUNT

	$		$
Cash a/c (jnl)	50		

5.2 The correction of errors

The journal is most commonly used to record corrections to errors that have been made in writing up the nominal ledger accounts. Errors corrected by the journal must be **capable of correction by means of a double entry** in the ledger accounts. In other words, the error must not have caused total debits and total credits to be unequal.

Special rules apply when errors are made which break the rule of double entry.

We will deal with errors later in your studies.

QUESTION
The journal

In business, the journal is used to post what types of transactions?

A   Unusual movements
B   Cash day book
C   Purchases
D   Sales

ANSWER

A   In business (as opposed to exams!) the journal is used to record unusual movements on the accounts.

6   Day book analysis

Entries in the day books (books of prime entry) are totalled and analysed before posting to the nominal ledger.

6.1 Sales day book

In the previous chapter, we used the following example of four transactions entered into the sales day book.

SALES DAY BOOK

Date	Invoice	Customer	Total amount invoiced	Boot sales	Shoe sales
20X0			$	$	
Jan 10	247	Jones & Co	105.00	60.00	45.00
	248	Smith Ltd	86.40	86.40	
	249	Alex & Co	31.80		31.80
	250	Enor College	1,264.60	800.30	464.30
			1,487.80	946.70	541.10

We have already seen that in theory these transactions are posted to the ledger accounts as follows.

DEBIT	Trade accounts receivable	$1,487.80	
CREDIT	Sales account		$1,487.80

However, a total sales account is not very informative, particularly if the business sells lots of different products. So, using our example, the business might open up a 'sale of shoes' account and a 'sale of boots' account. Then the ledger account postings are:

		$	$
DEBIT	Trade accounts receivable	1,487.80	
CREDIT	Sale of shoes account		541.10
	Sale of boots account		946.70

That is why the analysis of sales is kept. Exactly the same reasoning lies behind the analyses kept in the other books of prime entry.

6.2 Sales returns day book

We will now look at the sales returns day book.

SALES RETURNS DAY BOOK

Date	Credit note	Customer and goods	Amount
20X8			$
30 April	CR008	Owen Plenty	
		3 pairs 'Texas' boots	135.00

This will be posted as follows.

		$	$
DEBIT	Sales returns book	135.00	
CREDIT	Trade accounts receivable		135.00

6.3 Purchase day book and purchases returns day book

The purchase day book and purchases returns day book can be posted in a similar way.

6.3.1 Purchases

		$	$
DEBIT	Purchases	444.40	
	Electricity	116.80	
CREDIT	Trade accounts payable		561.20

6.3.2 Purchase returns

		$	$
DEBIT	Trade accounts payable	46.60	
CREDIT	Purchases returns		46.60

7 The receivables and payables ledgers

> The receivables and payables ledgers contain the **personal accounts** of individual customers and suppliers. They do not normally form part of the double entry system.

7.1 Impersonal accounts and personal accounts

The accounts in the nominal ledger (ledger accounts) relate to types of income, expense, asset, liability – rent, sales, trade receivables, payables etc – rather than to the person to whom the money is paid or from whom it is received. They are therefore called **impersonal** accounts. However, there is also a need for **personal** accounts, most commonly for receivables and payables, and these are contained in the receivables ledger and payables ledger.

7.2 The receivables ledger

The sales day book provides a chronological record of invoices sent out by a business to credit customers. For many businesses, this might involve very large numbers of invoices per day or per week. The same customer might appear in several different places in the sales day book, for sales made on credit at different times. So a customer may owe money on several unpaid invoices.

In addition to keeping a chronological record of invoices, a business should also keep a record of how much money each individual credit customer owes, and the makeup of this total debt. The need for a **personal account for each customer** is a practical one.

(a) A customer might telephone, and ask how much they currently owe. Staff must be able to tell them.

(b) It is a common practice to send out statements to credit customers at the end of each month, showing how much they still owe, and itemising new invoices sent out and payments received during the month.

(c) The managers of the business will want to keep a check on the credit position of an individual customer, and to ensure that no customer is exceeding their credit limit by purchasing more goods.

(d) Most important is the need to match payments received against debts owed. If a customer makes a payment, the business must be able to set off the payment against the customer's debt and establish how much they still owe on balance.

The receivables ledger is a ledger for customers' personal accounts.

Receivables ledger accounts are written up as follows.

(a) When entries are made in the sales day book (invoices sent out), they are subsequently also made in the **debit side** of the relevant customer account in the receivables ledger.

(b) Similarly, when entries are made in the cash book (payments received), or in the sales returns day book, they are also made in the **credit side** of the relevant customer account.

Each customer account is given a reference or code number, and it is that reference which appears in the **sales day book**. We say that amounts are **posted** from the sales day book to the receivables ledger.

Here is an example of how a receivables ledger account is laid out.

ENOR COLLEGE

A/c no: RL 9

	$		$
Balance b/f	250.00		
10.1.X0 Sales – SDB 48			
(invoice no. 250)	1,264.60	Balance c/d	1,514.60
	1,514.60		1,514.60
11.1.X0 Balance b/d	1,514.60		

The debit side of this personal account, then, shows amounts owed by Enor College. When Enor pays some of the money it owes it will be entered into the cash book (receipts) and subsequently 'posted' to the credit side of the personal account. For example, if the college paid $250 on 10.1.20X0, it would appear as follows.

ENOR COLLEGE

A/c no: RL 9

	$			$
Balance b/f	250.00	10.1.X0	Cash	250.00
10.1.X0 Sales – SDB 48				
(invoice no. 250)	1,264.60		Balance c/d	1,264.60
	1,514.60			1,514.60
11.1.X0 Balance b/d	1,264.60			

The opening balance owed by Enor College on 11.1.X0 is now $1,264.60 instead of $1,514.60, because of the $250 receipt which came in on 10.1.X0.

7.3 The payables ledger

The payables ledger, like the receivables ledger, consists of a number of personal accounts. These are separate accounts for **each individual supplier**, and they enable a business to keep a continuous record of how much it owes each supplier at any time.

The payables ledger is a ledger for suppliers' personal accounts.

After entries are made in the purchase day book, cash book, or purchase returns day book – ie after entries are made in the books of prime entry – they are also made in the relevant supplier account in the payables ledger. Again we say that the entries in the purchase day book are **posted** to the suppliers' personal accounts in the payables ledger.

Here is an example of how a payables ledger account is laid out.

COOK & CO

A/c no: PL 31

	$		$
Balance c/d	515.00	Balance b/f	200.00
		15 Mar 20X8	
		Invoice received	
		PDB 37	315.00
	515.00		515.00
		16 March 20X8	
		Balance b/d	515.00

The credit side of this personal account, then, shows amounts owing to Cook & Co. If the business paid Cook & Co some money, it would be entered into the cash book (payments) and subsequently be posted to the debit side of the personal account. For example, if the business paid Cook & Co $100 on 15 March 20X8, it would appear as follows.

COOK & CO

A/c no: PL 31

		$			$
15.3.X8	Cash	100.00		Balance b/f	200.00
			15.3.X8	Invoice received	
	Balance c/d	415.00	PDB 37		315.00
		515.00			515.00
			16.3.X8	Balance b/d	415.00

The opening balance owed to Cook & Co on 16 March 20X8 is now $415.00 instead of $515.00 because of the $100 payment made during 15 March 20X8.

The remainder of the balance brought forward of $100.00 ($200.00 brought forward less payment of $100.00) is in dispute and Cook & Co sends the business a credit note for $100.00 on 17 March 20X8.

COOK & CO

A/c no: PL 31

		$			$
17.3.X8	Credit note received	100.00	16.3.X8	Balance b/f	415.00
	Balance c/d	315.00			
		415.00			415.00
			12.3.X8	Balance b/d	315.00

The business now owes Cook & Co the amount of the invoice received on 15 March 20X8.

Note that in a manual system, the account is not 'balanced off' after each transaction. It is more likely to be done once a month. However, we have done this to show the effect of the transactions.

Two of the requirements of performance objective PO6, 'Record and process transactions and events' are:

- Implement or effectively operate appropriate systems to record accounting data and ensure effective credit and vendor management and control;

- Verify, input, and process routine financial accounting data within the accounting system

This chapter of the Text will help you fulfil these requirements.

CHAPTER ROUNDUP

↳ Ledger accounts **summarise** all the individual transactions listed in the books of prime entry.

↳ The principal accounts are contained in a ledger called the **general** or **nominal ledger**.

↳ The **accounting equation** is ASSETS = CAPITAL + LIABILITIES.

↳ When business transactions are accounted for it should be possible to **restate the assets and liabilities** of the business after the transactions have taken place.

↳ **Trade accounts payable** are **liabilities. Trade accounts receivable** are **assets**.

↳ The **matching convention** requires that revenue earned is matched with the expenses incurred in earning it.

↳ **Double entry bookkeeping** is based on the idea that each transaction has an equal but opposite effect. Every accounting event must be entered in ledger accounts both as a debit and as an equal but opposite credit.

↳ A debit entry will:

- Increase an asset
- Decrease a liability
- Increase an expense

A credit entry will:

- Decrease an asset
- Increase a liability
- Increase income

↳ Some accounts in the nominal ledger represent the total of very many smaller balances. For example, the **trade accounts receivable** account represents all the balances owed by individual customers of the business, while the **trade accounts payable account** represents all money owed by the business to its suppliers.

↳ The **journal** is the record of prime entry for transactions which are not recorded in any of the other books of prime entry.

↳ Entries in the day books (books of prime entry) are totalled and analysed before posting to the nominal ledger.

↳ The receivables and payables ledgers contain the **personal accounts** of individual customers and suppliers. They do not normally form part of the double entry system.

1   What is the double entry to record a cash sale of $50?

2   What is the double entry to record a credit sale of $50?

A   DEBIT cash $50, CREDIT sales $50
B   DEBIT receivables $50, CREDIT sales $50
C   DEBIT sales $50, CREDIT receivables $50
D   DEBIT sales $50, CREDIT cash $50

3   The double entry to record a purchase of office chairs for $1,000 is:

DEBIT non-current assets $1,000, CREDIT cash $1,000. True or false?

4   A debit/credit* will increase a liability and decrease an asset, whereas a debit/credit* will decrease a liability and increase an asset.

* Select one item to complete the sentence.

5   Name one reason for making a journal entry.

6   Individual customer accounts are kept in the ....

ANSWERS TO QUICK QUIZ

1
		$	$
DEBIT	Cash a/c	50	
CREDIT	Sales a/c		50

2   B   DEBIT receivables $50, CREDIT sales $50

3   True

4   A **credit** will increase a liability and decrease an asset, whereas a **debit** will decrease a liability and increase an asset.

5   Most commonly to correct an error, although it can be used to make any entry that is not recorded in a book of prime entry (eg prepayments, accrued expenses, depreciation)

6   Individual customer accounts are kept in the **receivables ledger**.

Now try ...

Attempt the questions below from the **Practice Question Bank**

Number

Qs 16 – 19

From trial balance to financial statements

In the previous chapter you learned the principles of double entry and how to post to the ledger accounts. The next step in our progress towards the financial statements is the **trial balance**.

Before transferring the relevant balances at the end of the period to the statement of profit or loss and putting closing balances carried forward into the statement of financial position, it is usual to test the accuracy of double entry bookkeeping records by preparing **a list of account balances**. This is done by taking all the balances on every account; because of the self-balancing nature of the system of double entry, **the total of the debit balances will be exactly equal to the total of the credit balances**.

In very straightforward circumstances, where no complications arise and where the records are complete, it is possible to prepare accounts directly from a trial balance.

TOPIC LIST	SYLLABUS REFERENCE
1 The trial balance	C2(d), E1(a)–(d)
2 The statement of profit or loss	A3(a)
3 The statement of financial position	A3(a)
4 Balancing accounts and preparing financial statements	C2(d), A3(a)

1   The trial balance

At suitable intervals, the entries in each ledger account are totalled and a **balance** is struck. Balances are usually collected in a **trial balance** which is then used as a basis for preparing a statement of profit or loss and a statement of financial position.

You have a list of transactions, and have been asked to post them to the relevant ledger accounts. You do it as quickly as possible and find that you have a little time left over at the end of the day. How do you check that you have posted all the debit and credit entries properly? There is no foolproof method, but a technique which shows up the more obvious mistakes is to prepare a **trial balance**.

A trial balance is a list of ledger balances shown in debit and credit columns.

1.1 The first step

Before you draw up a list of account balances, you must have a collection of ledger accounts. For the sake of convenience, we will use the accounts of Ron Knuckle, which we drew up in the previous chapter.

CASH AT BANK

	$		$
Capital: Ron Knuckle	7,000	Rent	3,500
Bank loan	1,000	Shop fittings	2,000
Sales	10,000	Trade accounts payable	5,000
Trade accounts receivable	2,500	Bank loan interest	100
		Other expenses	1,900
		Drawings	1,500

CAPITAL (RON KNUCKLE)

	$		$
		Cash at bank	7,000

BANK LOAN

	$		$
		Cash at bank	1,000

PURCHASES

	$		$
Trade accounts payable	5,000		

TRADE ACCOUNTS PAYABLE

	$		$
Cash at bank	5,000	Purchases	5,000

RENT

	$		$
Cash at bank	3,500		

SHOP FITTINGS

	$		$
Cash at bank	2,000		

SALES

	$		$
		Cash at bank	10,000
		Trade accounts receivable	2,500

TRADE ACCOUNTS RECEIVABLE

	$		$
Sales	2,500	Cash at bank	2,500

BANK LOAN INTEREST

	$		$
Cash at bank	100		

OTHER EXPENSES

	$		$
Cash at bank	1,900		

DRAWINGS

	$		$
Cash at bank	1,500		

The next step is to 'balance' each account.

1.2 Balancing ledger accounts

At the end of an accounting period, a balance is struck on each account in turn. This means that all the debits on the account are totalled and so are all the credits. **If the total debits exceed the total credits there is said to be a debit balance on the account; if the credits exceed the debits then the account has a credit balance**.

In our simple example, there is very little balancing to do.

(a) Both the trade accounts payable and the trade accounts receivable balance off to zero.

(b) The cash at bank account has a debit balance of $6,500.

(c) The total on the sales account is $12,500, which is a credit balance.

CASH AT BANK

	$		$
Capital: Ron Knuckle	7,000	Rent	3,500
Bank loan	1,000	Shop fittings	2,000
Sales	10,000	Trade accounts payable	5,000
Trade accounts receivable	2,500	Bank loan interest	100
		Other expenses	1,900
		Drawings	1,500
			14,000
		Balancing figure – the amount of cash left over after payments have been made	6,500
	20,500		20,500

TRADE ACCOUNTS PAYABLE

	$		$
Cash at bank	5,000	Purchases	5,000

SALES

	$		$
		Cash at bank	10,000
		Trade accounts receivable	2,500
			12,500

TRADE ACCOUNTS RECEIVABLE

	$		$
Sales	2,500	Cash at bank	2,500

Otherwise, the accounts have only one entry each, so there is no totalling to do to arrive at the balance on each account.

1.3 Collecting the balances

If the basic principle of double entry has been correctly applied throughout the period it will be found that the credit balances equal the debit balances in total. This can be illustrated by collecting together the balances on Ron Knuckle's accounts.

	Dr	Cr
	$	$
Cash at bank	6,500	
Capital		7,000
Bank loan		1,000
Purchases	5,000	
Trade accounts payable	–	–
Rent	3,500	
Shop fittings	2,000	
Sales		12,500
Trade accounts receivable	–	–
Bank loan interest	100	
Other expenses	1,900	
Drawings	1,500	
	20,500	20,500

This is called a **trial balance**. It does not matter in what order the various accounts are listed. It is just a method used to test the accuracy of the double entry bookkeeping.

1.4 What if the trial balance shows unequal debit and credit balances?

A trial balance can be used to **test the accuracy of the double entry accounting records**. It works by listing the balances on ledger accounts, some of which are debits and some credits. Total debits should equal total credits.

If the two columns of the list are not equal, there must be an error in recording the transactions in the accounts. A list of account balances, however, will **not** disclose the following types of errors.

(a) The **complete omission** of a transaction, because neither a debit nor a credit is made

(b) The posting of a debit or credit to the correct side of the ledger, but to a **wrong account**

(c) **Compensating errors** (eg an error of $100 is exactly cancelled by another $100 error elsewhere)

(d) **Errors of principle** (eg cash from receivables being debited to trade accounts receivable and credited to cash at bank instead of the other way round)

The trial balance should reveal errors where the rules of double entry have been broken, such as:

(a) One-sided entries

(b) Where an entry has been posted as a credit to one account and a credit to a second account and no debit entry has been made (or two debits and no credits)

1.5 Example: trial balance

As at 30.3.20X7, your business has the following balances on its ledger accounts.

Accounts	Balance
	$
Bank loan	12,000
Cash at bank	11,700
Capital	13,000
Local business taxes	1,880
Trade accounts payable	11,200
Purchases	12,400
Sales	14,600
Sundry payables	1,620
Trade accounts receivable	12,000
Bank loan interest	1,400
Other expenses	11,020
Vehicles	2,020

During 31.3.20X7, the business made the following transactions.

(a) Bought materials for $1,000, half for cash and half on credit
(b) Made $1,040 sales, $800 of which was for credit
(c) Paid wages to shop assistants of $260 in cash

You are required to draw up a trial balance showing the balances as at the end of 31.3.20X7.

Solution

First it is necessary to decide which of the original balances are debits and which are credits.

Account	Dr	Cr
	$	$
Bank loan (liability)		12,000
Cash at bank (asset; overdraft = liability)	11,700	
Capital (liability)		13,000
Local taxes (expense)	1,880	
Trade accounts payable (liability)		11,200
Purchases (expense)	12,400	
Sales (revenue)		14,600
Sundry payables (liability)		1,620
Trade accounts receivable (asset)	12,000	

Account	Dr $	Cr $
Bank loan interest (expenses)	1,400	
Other expenses	11,020	
Vehicles (non-current asset)	2,020	
	52,420	52,420

Now we must take account of the effects of the three transactions which took place on 31.3.20X7.

			$	$
(a)	DEBIT	Purchases	1,000	
	CREDIT	Cash at bank		500
		Trade accounts payable		500
(b)	DEBIT	Cash at bank	240	
		Trade accounts receivable	800	
	CREDIT	Sales		1,040
(c)	DEBIT	Other expenses	260	
	CREDIT	Cash at bank		260

When these figures are included in the trial balance, it becomes:

Account	Dr $	Cr $
Bank loan		12,000
Cash at bank (11,700 + 240 − 500 − 260)	11,180	
Capital		13,000
Local taxes	1,880	
Trade accounts payable (11,200 + 500)		11,700
Purchases (12,400 + 1,000)	13,400	
Sales (14,600 + 1,040)		15,640
Sundry payables		1,620
Trade accounts receivable (12,000 + 800)	12,800	
Bank loan interest	1,400	
Other expenses (11,020 + 260)	11,280	
Vehicles	2,020	
	53,960	53,960

---

2 The statement of profit or loss

A **profit or loss** ledger account is opened up to gather all items relating to income and expenses. When rearranged, these items make up the **statement of profit or loss**.

The first step in the process of preparing the financial statements is to open up another ledger account, called the **profit or loss account**. In it a business summarises its results for the period by gathering together all the ledger account balances relating to the statement of profit or loss. This account is still part of the double entry system, so the basic rule of double entry still applies: every debit must have an equal and opposite credit entry.

This profit or loss account contains the same information as the financial statement we are aiming for, ie the statement of profit or loss, and in fact there are very few differences between the two. However, the statement of profit or loss lays the information out differently and it may be much less detailed.

So what do we do with this new ledger account? The first step is to **look through the ledger accounts** and identify which ones relate to income and expenses. In the case of Ron Knuckle, these accounts consist of purchases, rent, sales, bank loan interest and other expenses.

The balances on these accounts are transferred to the new profit or loss account. For example, the balance on the purchases account is $5,000 DR. To balance this to zero, we write in $5,000 CR. But to comply with the rule of double entry, there has to be a debit entry somewhere, so we write $5,000

DR in the profit or loss (P/L) account. Now the balance on the purchases account has been moved to the P/L account.

If we do the same thing with all the separate accounts of Ron Knuckle dealing with income and expenses, the result is as follows.

PURCHASES

	$		$
Trade account payables	5,000	P/L a/c	5,000

RENT

	$		$
Cash at bank	3,500	P/L a/c	3,500

SALES

	$		$
P/L a/c	12,500	Cash at bank	10,000
		Trade accounts receivable	2,500
	12,500		12,500

BANK LOAN INTEREST

	$		$
Cash at bank	100	P/L a/c	100

OTHER EXPENSES

	$		$
Cash at bank	1,900	P/L a/c	1,900

PROFIT OR LOSS ACCOUNT

	$		$
Purchases	5,000	Sales	12,500
Rent	3,500		
Bank loan interest	100		
Other expenses	1,900		

(Note that the P/L account has not yet been balanced off but we will return to that later.)

If you look at the items we have gathered together in the P/L account, they should strike a chord in your memory. They are the same items that we need to draw up the statement of profit or loss.

QUESTION

Statement of profit or loss

Draw up Ron Knuckle's statement of profit or loss.

ANSWER

RON KNUCKLE: STATEMENT OF PROFIT OR LOSS

	$	$
Revenue		12,500
Cost of sales (= purchases in this case)		(5,000)
Gross profit		7,500
Expenses		
Rent	3,500	
Bank loan interest	100	
Other expenses	1,900	
		(5,500)
Profit for the year		2,000

3 The statement of financial position

The balances on all **remaining ledger accounts** (including the profit or loss account) can be listed and rearranged to form the **statement of financial position**.

Look back at the ledger accounts of Ron Knuckle. Now that we have dealt with those relating to income and expenses, which ones are left? The answer is that we still have to find out what to do with the cash, capital, bank loan, trade accounts payable, shop fittings, trade accounts receivable and the drawings accounts.

Are these the only ledger accounts left? No: don't forget there is still the last one we opened up, called the **profit or loss account**. The balance on this account represents the profit earned by the business and, if you go through the arithmetic, you will find that it has a credit balance – a profit – of $2,000. (Not surprisingly, this is the figure that is shown in the statement of profit or loss.)

These remaining accounts must also be **balanced and ruled off**, but since they represent assets and liabilities of the business (not income and expenses) their balances are not transferred to the P/L account. Instead they are **carried down** in the books of the business. This means that they become opening balances for the next accounting period and indicate the value of the assets and liabilities at the end of one period and the beginning of the next.

The conventional method of ruling off a ledger account at the end of an accounting period is illustrated by the bank loan account in Ron Knuckle's books.

BANK LOAN ACCOUNT

	$		$
Balance carried down (c/d)	1,000	Cash (D)	1,000
		Balance brought down (b/d)	1,000

Ron Knuckle therefore begins the new accounting period with a credit balance of $1,000 on this account. A **credit balance brought down** denotes a liability. An asset would be represented by a **debit balance brought down**.

One further point is worth noting before we move on to complete this example. You will remember that a proprietor's capital comprises any cash introduced by them, plus any profits made by the business, less any drawings made by them. At the stage we have now reached, these three elements are contained in different ledger accounts. Cash introduced of $7,000 appears in the capital account. Drawings of $1,500 appear in drawings. The profit made by the business is represented by the $2,000 credit balance on the P/L account.

It is convenient to gather together all these amounts into one **capital account**, in the same way as we earlier gathered together income and expense accounts into one P/L account.

If we go ahead and gather the three amounts together, the results are as follows.

DRAWINGS

	$		$
Cash at bank	1,500	Capital a/c	1,500

PROFIT OR LOSS ACCOUNT

	$		$
Purchases	5,000	Sales	12,500
Rent	3,500		
Bank loan interest	100		
Other expenses	1,900		
Capital a/c	2,000		
	12,500		12,500

CAPITAL

	$		$
Drawings	1,500	Cash at bank	7,000
Balance c/d	7,500	P/L a/c	2,000
	9,000		9,000
		Balance b/d	7,500

QUESTION

Statement of financial position

You can now complete Ron Knuckle's simple statement of financial position.

ANSWER

RON KNUCKLE
STATEMENT OF FINANCIAL POSITION AT END OF FIRST TRADING PERIOD

	$
Assets	
Non-current assets	
Shop fittings	2,000
Current assets	
Cash at bank	6,500
Total assets	8,500
Capital and liabilities	
Proprietor's capital	7,500
Non-current liabilities	
Bank loan	1,000
Total capital and liabilities	8,500

When a statement of financial position is drawn up for an accounting period which is not the first one, then it ought to show the capital at the start of the accounting period and the capital at the end of the accounting period. This will be illustrated in the next example.

In an examination question, you might not be given the ledger accounts – you might have to draw them up in the first place. That is the case with the following exercise – see if you can do it by yourself before looking at the solution.

The opening trial balance for the next period is the closing statement of financial position for the previous period. So the opening trial balance for Ron Knuckle at the beginning of the second trading period will be:

Account	Dr $	Cr $
Shop fittings	2,000	
Cash at bank	6,500	
Capital		7,500
Bank loan		1,000
Totals	8,500	8,500

4 | Balancing accounts and preparing financial statements

The exercise which follows is by far the most important in this Text so far. It uses all the accounting steps, from entering up ledger accounts to preparing the financial statements. It is **very important that you try to complete the question by yourself**: if you do not, you will be missing out a vital part of this Text.

QUESTION

Financial statements

A business is established with capital of $2,000, and this amount is paid into a business bank account by the proprietor. During the first year's trading, the following transactions occurred.

	$
Purchases of goods for resale, on credit	4,300
Payments to trade accounts payable	3,600
Sales, all on credit	5,800
Payments from trade accounts receivable	3,200
Non-current assets purchased for cash	1,500
Other expenses, all paid in cash	900

The bank has provided an overdraft facility of up to $3,000.

Required

Prepare the ledger accounts, a statement of profit or loss for the year and a statement of financial position as at the end of the year.

ANSWER

The first thing to do is to open ledger accounts so that the transactions can be entered. The relevant accounts which we need for this example are: cash at bank; capital; trade accounts payable; purchases; non-current assets; sales; trade accounts receivable; and other expenses.

The next step is to work out the double entry bookkeeping for each transaction. Normally you would write them straight into the accounts but, to make this example easier to follow, they are first listed below.

		Debit	*Credit*
(a)	Establishing business ($2,000)	Cash at bank	Capital
(b)	Purchases ($4,300)	Purchases	Trade accounts payable
(c)	Payments to trade accounts payable ($3,600)	Trade accounts payable	Cash at bank
(d)	Sales ($5,800)	Trade accounts receivable	Sales
(e)	Payments from trade accounts receivable ($3,200)	Cash at bank	Trade accounts receivable
(f)	Non-current assets ($1,500)	Non-current assets	Cash at bank
(g)	Other (cash) expenses ($900)	Other expenses	Cash at bank

So far, the ledger accounts will look like this.

CASH AT BANK

	$		$
Capital	2,000	Trade accounts payable	3,600
Trade account receivables	3,200	Non-current assets	1,500
		Other expenses	900

CAPITAL

	$		$
		Cash at bank	2,000

TRADE ACCOUNTS PAYABLE

	$		$
Cash at bank	3,600	Purchases	4,300

PURCHASES

	$		$
Trade accounts payable	4,300		

NON-CURRENT ASSETS

	$		$
Cash at bank	1,500		

SALES

	$		$
		Trade accounts receivable	5,800

TRADE ACCOUNTS RECEIVABLE

	$		$
Sales	5,800	Cash at bank	3,200

OTHER EXPENSES

	$		$
Cash at bank	900		

The next thing to do is to balance all these accounts. After balancing the accounts, the profit or loss account should be opened. Into it should be transferred all the balances relating to income and expense (ie purchases, other expenses and sales). At this point, the ledger accounts will be as follows.

CASH AT BANK

	$		$
Capital	2,000	Trade accounts payable	3,600
Trade accounts receivable	3,200	Non-current assets	1,500
Balance c/d	800	Other expenses	900
	6,000		6,000
		Balance b/d	800*

* A credit balance b/d means that this cash item is a liability, not an asset. This indicates a bank overdraft of $800, with cash income of $5,200 falling short of payments of $6,000 by this amount.

CAPITAL

	$		$
Balance c/d	2,600	Cash at bank	2,000
		P/L a/c	600
	2,600		2,600
		Balance b/d	2,600

TRADE ACCOUNTS PAYABLE

	$		$
Cash at bank	3,600	Purchases	4,300
Balance c/d	700		
	4,300		4,300
		Balance b/d	700

PURCHASES

	$		$
Trade accounts payable	4,300	P/L a/c	4,300

NON-CURRENT ASSETS

	$		$
Cash at bank	1,500	Balance c/d	1,500
Balance b/d	1,500		

SALES

	$		$
P/L a/c	5,800		5,800

TRADE ACCOUNTS RECEIVABLE

	$		$
Sales	5,800	Cash at bank	3,200
		Balance c/d	2,600
	5,800		5,800
Balance b/d	2,600		

OTHER EXPENSES

	$		$
Cash at bank	900	P/L a/c	900

PROFIT OR LOSS ACCOUNT

	$		$
Purchases	4,300	Sales	5,800
Gross profit c/d	1,500		
	5,800		5,800
Other expenses	900	Gross profit b/d	1,500
Profit for the year (transferred to capital account)	600		
	1,500		1,500

So the statement of profit or loss will be:

STATEMENT OF PROFIT OR LOSS FOR THE ACCOUNTING PERIOD

	$
Revenue	5,800
Cost of sales (purchases)	4,300
Gross profit	1,500
Expenses	900
Profit for the year	600

Listing and then rearranging the balances on the ledger accounts gives the statement of financial position as:

STATEMENT OF FINANCIAL POSITION AS AT THE END OF THE PERIOD

	$	$
Assets		
Non-current assets		1,500
Current assets		
Trade accounts receivable		2,600
Total assets		4,100
Capital and liabilities		
Capital		
At start of period	2,000	
Profit for the year for period	600	
At end of period		2,600
Current liabilities		
Bank overdraft	800	
Trade accounts payable	700	
		1,500
Total capital and liabilities		4,100

EXAM FOCUS POINT

The above example is highly detailed. This detail is given to help you to work through the example properly. You may wish to do things this way yourself until you get more practised in accounting techniques and are confident enough to take short cuts.

The techniques are worth practising, as you are highly likely to get a question requiring you to calculate a figure for the statement of profit or loss or statement of financial position from a trial balance, particularly in one of the 15 mark questions.

QUESTION

Opening trial balance

Alpha has the following opening balances on its ledger accounts.

	$
Fixtures	5,000
Trade accounts receivable	2,000
Bank account	1,000
Loan	3,000

A What is the total assets figure?

    (a) $6,000
    (b) $5,000
    (c) $8,000
    (d) $3,000

B What is the opening figure for capital?

    (a) $6,000
    (b) $5,000
    (c) $8,000
    (d) $3,000

ANSWER

A   (c)   Assets = 5,000 + 2,000 + 1,000
                      = 8,000
B   (b)   Capital= assets – liabilities
                      = (5,000 + 2,000 + 1,000) – 3,000
                      = 5,000

Two of the requirements of performance objective PO6, 'Record and process transactions and events' are:

- Implement or effectively operate appropriate systems to record accounting data and ensure effective credit and vendor management and control;

- Verify, input, and process routine financial accounting data within the accounting system

This chapter of the Text will help you fulfil these requirements.

CHAPTER ROUNDUP

↳ At suitable intervals, the entries in each ledger account are totalled and a **balance** is struck. Balances are usually collected in a **trial balance** which is then used as a basis for preparing a statement of profit or loss and a statement of financial position.

↳ A trial balance can be used to **test the accuracy of the double entry accounting** records. It works by listing the balances on ledger accounts, some of which will be debits and some credits. The total debits should equal total credits.

↳ A **profit or loss** ledger account is opened up to gather all items relating to income and expenses. When rearranged, these items make up the **statement of profit or loss**.

↳ The balances on all **remaining ledger accounts** (including the profit or loss account) can be listed and rearranged to form the **statement of financial position**.

QUICK QUIZ

1 What is the purpose of a trial balance?

2 A trial balance may still balance if some of the balances are wrong. True or false?

3 In a period, sales are $140,000, purchases $75,000 and other expenses $25,000. What is the figure for profit for the year to be transferred to the capital account?

A $40,000
B $65,000
C $75,000
D $140,000

4 The balance on an expense account will go to the P/L account. However, the balance on a liability account is written off to capital.

Is this statement correct?

A Yes
B No

5 Fill in the blank.

The balance brought forward on the bank account is a credit figure. This means that the balance is
....

6 Which of the following would not be identified by extracting a trial balance?

A Two credit entries and no debit
B One-sided entry
C Transaction omitted completely
D Two debit entries and no credit

1   To test the accuracy of the double entry bookkeeping

2   True. See Section 1.4.

3   A

PROFIT OR LOSS ACCOUNT

	$		$
Purchases	75,000	Sales	140,000
Gross profit c/d	65,000		
	140,000		140,000
Other expenses	25,000	Gross profit b/d	65,000
Profit for the year – to capital a/c	40,000		
	65,000		65,000

B is the **gross** profit figure, while C is the figure for purchases and D sales.

4   B   When an expense account is balanced off, the balance is transferred to the profit or loss account. When a liability account is balanced off, the balance is carried forward to the next accounting period.

5   The balance brought forward on the bank account is a credit figure. This means that the balance is **overdrawn**.

6   C   As no entries have been made at all, the trial balance will still balance.

Now try ...

Attempt the questions below from the **Practice Question Bank**

Number

Qs 20 – 24

---

part

D

Recording transactions and events

Recording transactions and events

07

Inventory

Inventory is one of the most important assets in a company's statement of financial position. As we will see, it also affects the statement of profit or loss, having a direct impact on gross profit.

So far you have come across inventories in the preparation of a simple statement of financial position. Here we will look at inventories in the calculation of the cost of goods sold. This chapter also explores the **difficulties of valuing inventories**.

This is the first time that you will be required to consider the impact of the relevant IFRS on the valuation and presentation of an item in the accounts: IAS 2 *Inventories*.

Study Guide	Intellectual level
D **Recording transactions and events**	
3 **Inventory**	
(a) Recognise the need for adjustments for inventory in preparing financial statements.	K
(b) Record opening and closing inventory.	S
(c) Identify the alternative methods of valuing inventory.	K
(d) Understand and apply the International Accounting Standards Board (IASB) requirements for valuing inventories.	S
(e) Recognise which costs should be included in valuing inventories.	S
(f) Understand the use of continuous and period-end inventory records.	K
(g) Calculate the value of closing inventory using first in, first out (FIFO) and average cost (AVCO) – both periodic weighted average and continuous weighted average.	S
(h) Understand the impact of accounting concepts on the valuation of inventory.	K
(i) Identify the impact of inventory valuation methods on profit and on assets.	S
F **Preparing basic financial statements**	
3 **Disclosure notes**	
(b) Draft the following disclosure notes:	S
(iv) Inventory	

1   Cost of goods sold

The **cost of goods sold** is calculated as:

Opening inventory + purchases – closing inventory.

1.1 Unsold goods in inventory at the end of an accounting period

Goods might be unsold at the end of an accounting period and so still be **held in inventory**. The purchase cost of these goods should therefore not be included in the cost of sales of the period.

1.2 The cost of goods sold

The cost of goods sold is found by applying the following formula.

FORMULA TO LEARN

	$
Opening inventory value	X
Add cost of purchases (or, in the case of a manufacturing company, the cost of production)	X
	X
Less closing inventory value	(X)
Cost of goods sold	X

In other words, to match 'sales' and the 'cost of goods sold', it is necessary to adjust the cost of goods manufactured or purchased to allow for increases or reduction in inventory levels during the period.

The 'formula' above is based on a logical idea. You should learn it, because it is a fundamental principle of accounting.

1.3 Example: cost of goods sold

Perry P Louis, trading as the Umbrella Shop, ends his financial year on 30 September each year. On 1 October 20X4 he had no goods in inventory. During the year to 30 September 20X5, he purchased 30,000 umbrellas costing $60,000 from umbrella wholesalers and suppliers. He resold the umbrellas for $5 each, and sales for the year amounted to $100,000 (20,000 umbrellas). At 30 September there were 10,000 unsold umbrellas left in inventory, valued at $2 each.

What was Perry P Louis's gross profit for the year?

Solution

Perry P Louis purchased 30,000 umbrellas, but only sold 20,000. Purchase costs of $60,000 and sales of $100,000 do not represent the same quantity of goods.

The gross profit for the year should be calculated by 'matching' the sales value of the 20,000 umbrellas sold with the cost of those 20,000 umbrellas. The cost of sales in this example is therefore the cost of purchases minus the cost of goods in inventory at the year end.

	$	$
Sales (20,000 units)		100,000
Purchases (30,000 units)	60,000	
Less closing inventory (10,000 units @ $2)	20,000	
Cost of sales (20,000 units)		40,000
Gross profit		60,000

1.4 Example continued

We shall continue the example of the Umbrella Shop into its next accounting year, 1 October 20X5 to 30 September 20X6. During the course of this year, Perry P Louis purchased 40,000 umbrellas at a total cost of $95,000. During the year he sold 45,000 umbrellas for $230,000. At 30 September 20X6 he had 5,000 umbrellas left in inventory, which had cost $12,000.

What was his gross profit for the year?

Solution

In this accounting year, he purchased 40,000 umbrellas to add to the 10,000 he already had in inventory at the start of the year. He sold 45,000, leaving 5,000 umbrellas in inventory at the year end. Once again, gross profit should be calculated by matching the value of 45,000 units of sales with the cost of those 45,000 units.

The cost of sales is the value of the 10,000 umbrellas in inventory at the beginning of the year, plus the cost of the 40,000 umbrellas purchased, less the value of the 5,000 umbrellas in inventory at the year end.

	$	$
Sales (45,000 units)		230,000
Opening inventory (10,000 units)*	20,000	
Add purchases (40,000 units)	95,000	
	115,000	
Less closing inventory (5,000 units)	12,000	
Cost of sales (45,000 units)		103,000
Gross profit		127,000

* Taken from the closing inventory value of the previous accounting year

QUESTION

Costs of goods sold

On 1 January 20X6, the Grand Union Food Stores had goods in inventory valued at $6,000. During 20X6 its proprietor purchased supplies costing $50,000. Sales for the year to 31 December 20X6 amounted to $80,000. The cost of goods in inventory at 31 December 20X6 was $12,500.

What is the gross profit for the year?

ANSWER

	$	$
Sales		80,000
Opening inventories	6,000	
Add purchases	50,000	
	56,000	
Less closing inventories	12,500	
Cost of goods sold		43,500
Gross profit		36,500

1.5 The cost of carriage inwards and outwards

Carriage inwards is included in the cost of purchases. **Carriage outwards** is a selling expense.

'Carriage' refers to the **cost of transporting purchased goods** (ie delivery costs) from the supplier to the premises of the business which has bought them. Someone has to pay for these delivery costs: sometimes the supplier pays, and sometimes the purchaser pays. When the purchaser pays, the cost to the purchaser is carriage inwards (**into** the business). When the supplier pays, the cost to the supplier is known as carriage outwards (**out** of the business).

IMPORTANT

The **cost of carriage inwards** is usually added to the **cost of purchases**.

The **cost of carriage outwards** is a **selling and distribution expense** in the **statement of profit or loss**.

1.6 Example: carriage inwards and carriage outwards

Gwyn Tring, trading as Clickety Clocks, imports and resells clocks. He pays for the costs of delivering the clocks from his supplier in Switzerland to his shop in Wales.

He resells the clocks to other traders throughout the country, paying the costs of carriage for the consignments from his business premises to his customers.

On 1 July 20X5, he had clocks in inventory valued at $17,000. During the year to 30 June 20X6 he purchased more clocks at a cost of $75,000. Carriage inwards amounted to $2,000. Sales for the year were $162,100. Other expenses of the business amounted to $56,000 excluding carriage outwards which cost $2,500. The value of the goods in inventory at the year end was $15,400.

Required

Prepare the statement of profit or loss of Clickety Clocks for the year ended 30 June 20X6.

Solution

CLICKETY CLOCKS
STATEMENT OF PROFIT OR LOSS FOR THE YEAR ENDED 30 JUNE 20X6

	$	$
Revenue		162,100
Opening inventory	17,000	
Purchases	75,000	
Carriage inwards	2,000	
	94,000	
Less closing inventory	15,400	
Cost of goods sold		78,600
Gross profit		83,500
Carriage outwards	2,500	
Other expenses	56,000	
		58,500
Profit for the year		25,000

1.7 Goods written off or written down

A trader might be unable to sell all the goods that they purchase, because a number of things might happen to the goods before they can be sold. For example:

(a) Goods might be lost or stolen.

(b) Goods might be damaged, become worthless and so be thrown away.

(c) Goods might become obsolete or out of fashion. These might be thrown away, or sold off at a very low price in a clearance sale.

When goods are **lost, stolen or thrown away** as worthless, the business will make a loss on those goods because their **'sales value' will be nil**.

Similarly, when goods lose value because they have become **obsolete** or out of fashion, the business will **make a loss** if their clearance sales value is less than their cost. For example, if goods which originally cost $500 are now obsolete and could only be sold for $150, the business would suffer a loss of $350.

If, at the end of an accounting period, a business still has goods in inventory which are either worthless or worth less than their original cost, the value of the inventories should be **written down** to:

(a) Nothing, if they are worthless
(b) Their net realisable value, if this is less than their original cost

This means that the loss will be reported as soon as the loss is foreseen, even if the goods have not yet been thrown away or sold off at a cheap price. This is an example of prudence, referred to in Chapter 3.

The costs of inventory written off or written down should not usually cause any problems when calculating the gross profit of a business, because the cost of goods sold will include the cost of inventories written off or written down, as the following example shows.

1.8 Example: inventories written off and written down

Lucas Wagg, trading as Fairlock Fashions, ends his financial year on 31 March. At 1 April 20X5 he had goods in inventory valued at $8,800. During the year to 31 March 20X6, he purchased goods costing $48,000. Fashion goods which cost $2,100 were still held in inventory at 31 March 20X6, and Lucas Wagg believes that these could only now be sold at a sale price of $400. The goods still held in inventory at 31 March 20X6 (including the fashion goods) had an original purchase cost of $7,600. Sales for the year were $81,400.

Required

Calculate the gross profit of Fairlock Fashions for the year ended 31 March 20X6.

Solution

Initial calculation of closing inventory values:

INVENTORY COUNT

	At cost $	Realisable value $	Amount written down $
Fashion goods	2,100	400	1,700
Other goods (balancing figure)	5,500	5,500	
	7,600	5,900	1,700

GROSS PROFIT CALCULATION

	$	$
Sales		81,400
Value of opening inventory	8,800	
Purchases	48,000	
	56,800	
Less closing inventory	5,900	
Cost of goods sold		50,900
Gross profit		30,500

By using the figure of $5,900 for closing inventories, the cost of goods sold automatically includes the inventory written down of $1,700.

QUESTION

Gross profit

Gross profit for 20X7 can be calculated from:

A   Purchases for 20X7, plus inventory at 31 December 20X7, less inventory at 1 January 20X7
B   Purchases for 20X7, less inventory at 31 December 20X7, plus inventory at 1 January 20X7
C   Cost of goods sold during 20X7, plus sales during 20X7
D   Profit for the year for 20X7, plus expenses for 20X7

ANSWER

The correct answer is D. Gross profit less expenses = profit for the year. Therefore profit for the year plus expenses = gross profit.

---

2   Accounting for opening and closing inventories

Opening inventories brought forward in the inventory account are transferred to the profit or loss account, and so at the end of the accounting year the balance on the inventory account ceases to be the opening inventory value b/f and becomes instead the closing inventory value c/f.

2.1 Recap

In Section 1, we saw that in order to calculate **gross profit** it is necessary to work out the **cost of goods** sold. In order to calculate the cost of goods sold it is necessary to have values for the **opening inventory** (ie inventory in hand at the beginning of the accounting period) and **closing inventory** (ie inventory in hand at the end of the accounting period).

You should remember that the trading part of a statement of profit or loss includes:

	$
Opening inventory	X
Plus purchases	X
Less closing inventory	(X)
Cost of goods sold	X

However, there are three basic problems with this formula.

(a)   How do you manage to get a **precise count** of inventory in hand at any one time?

(b)   Even once it has been counted, how do you **value** the inventory?

(c)   Assuming the inventory is given a value, how does the **double entry bookkeeping** for inventory work?

The purpose of this chapter is to answer all three of these questions. In order to make the content easier to follow, it is convenient to take the last one first.

2.2 Ledger accounting for inventories

The value of **closing inventories** is accounted for in the **nominal ledger** by debiting an inventory account and crediting the profit or loss account at the end of an accounting period. Inventory will therefore have a debit balance at the end of a period, and this balance will be shown in the statement of financial position as a current asset.

It has already been shown that purchases are introduced to the statement of profit or loss by means of the double entry.

DEBIT	Profit or loss account	$X
CREDIT	Purchases account	$X

But what about opening and closing inventories? How are their values accounted for in the double entry bookkeeping system? The answer is that a inventory account must be kept. This inventory account is only ever used **at the end of an accounting period**, when the business counts up and values the inventory in hand, in a inventory count.

(a)   When a inventory count is made, the business will have a value for its closing inventory, and the double entry is:

DEBIT	Inventory account (closing inventory value)	$X
CREDIT	Profit or loss account	$X

However, rather than show the closing inventory as a 'plus' value in the profit or loss account (by adding it to sales) it is usual to show it as a 'minus' figure in arriving at cost of sales. This is illustrated in Section 2.1 above. The debit balance on inventory account represents an asset, which will be shown as part of current assets in the statement of financial position.

(b)   Closing inventory at the end of one period becomes opening inventory at the start of the next period. The inventory account remains unchanged until the end of the next period, when the value of opening inventory is taken to the profit or loss account.

DEBIT	Profit or loss account	$X
CREDIT	Inventory account (value of opening inventory)	$X

Partly as an example of how this ledger accounting for inventories works, and partly as revision on ledger accounting in general, try the following exercise.

QUESTION

Inventories

A business is established with capital of $2,000 and this amount is paid into a business bank account by the proprietor. During the first year's trading, the following transactions occurred.

	$
Purchases of goods for resale, on credit	4,300
Payments for trade accounts payable	3,600
Sales, all on credit	4,000
Payments from trade accounts receivable	3,200
Non-current assets purchased for cash	1,500
Other expenses, all paid in cash	900

The bank has provided an overdraft facility of up to $3,000.

All 'other expenses' relate to the current year.

Closing inventory is valued at $1,800. (Because this is the first year of the business, there are no opening inventories.)

Required

Prepare the ledger accounts, a profit or loss account for the year and a statement of financial position as at the end of the year.

ANSWER

CASH

	$		$
Capital	2,000	Trade payables	3,600
Trade receivables	3,200	Non-current assets	1,500
Balance c/d	800	Other expenses	900
	6,000		6,000
		Balance b/d	800

CAPITAL

	$		$
Balance c/d	2,600	Cash	2,000
		P/L a/c	600
	2,600		2,600
		Balance b/d	2,600

TRADE PAYABLES

	$		$
Cash	3,600	Purchases	4,300
Balance c/d	700		
	4,300		4,300
		Balance b/d	700

PURCHASES ACCOUNT

	$		$
Trade payables	4,300	P/L a/c	4,300

NON-CURRENT ASSETS

	$		$
Cash	1,500	Balance c/d	1,500
Balance b/d	1,500		

SALES

	$		$
P/L a/c	4,000	Trade receivables	4,000

TRADE RECEIVABLES

	$		$
Sales	4,000	Cash	3,200
		Balance c/d	800
	4,000		4,000
Balance b/d	800		

OTHER EXPENSES

	$		$
Cash	900	P/L a/c	900

PROFIT OR LOSS ACCOUNT

	$		$
Purchases account	4,300	Sales	4,000
Gross profit c/d	1,500	Closing inventory (inventory a/c)	1,800
	5,800		5,800
Other expenses	900	Gross profit b/d	1,500
Profit for the year (transferred to			
capital account)	600		
	1,500		1,500

Alternatively, closing inventory could be shown as a minus value on the debit side of the profit or loss account, instead of a credit entry, giving purchases $4,300 less closing inventory $1,800 equals cost of goods sold $2,500.

INVENTORY ACCOUNT

	$		$
a/c (closing inventory)	1,800	Balance c/d	1,800
Balance b/d (opening inventory)	1,800		

STATEMENT OF FINANCIAL POSITION AS AT THE END OF THE PERIOD

	$	$
Assets		
Non-current assets		1,500
Current assets		
Goods in inventory	1,800	
Trade accounts receivable	800	
		2,600
Total assets		4,100
Capital and liabilities		
Capital		
At start of period	2,000	
Profit for period	600	
At end of period		2,600
Current liabilities		
Bank overdraft	800	
Trade accounts payable	700	
		1,500
Total capital and liabilities		4,100

Make sure you can see what has happened here. The balance on the inventory account was $1,800, which appears in the statement of financial position as a current asset. As it happens, the $1,800 closing inventory was the only entry in the inventory account – there was no figure for opening inventory.

If there had been, it would have been eliminated by transferring it as a debit balance to the income and expenditure account, ie:

DEBIT   P/L account (with value of opening inventory)
CREDIT   Inventory account (with value of opening inventory)

The debit in the profit or loss account would then have increased the cost of sales, ie opening inventory is added to purchases in calculating cost of sales. Again, this is illustrated in Section 2.1 above.

So if we can establish the value of inventories on hand, the above paragraphs and exercise show us how to account for that value. That takes care of one of the problems noted at the beginning of this chapter. But now another of those problems becomes apparent – how do we establish the **value** of inventories on hand? The first step must be to establish **how much inventory is held**.

3 Counting inventories

The **quantity** of inventories held at the year end is established by means of a **physical count** of inventory in an annual counting exercise, or by a '**continuous**' inventory count.

Business trading is a continuous activity, but accounting statements must be drawn up at a particular date. In preparing a statement of financial position it is necessary to '**freeze**' the activity of a business to determine its assets and liabilities at a given moment. This includes establishing the quantities of inventories on hand, which can create problems.

In simple cases, usually when a business holds easily counted and relatively small amounts of inventory, quantities of inventories on hand at the reporting date can be determined by physically counting them in an **inventory count** at that date.

In more complicated cases, where a business holds considerable quantities of varied inventory, an alternative approach to establishing quantities is to maintain **continuous inventory records**. This means that a card, or a computerised record, is kept for every item of inventory, showing receipts and issues from the stores, and a running total. A few inventory items are counted each day to make sure their record cards are correct – this is called a 'continuous' count because it is spread out over the year rather than completed in one count at a designated time.

One obstacle is overcome once a business has established how much inventory is on hand. But another of the problems noted in the introduction immediately raises its head. What value should the business place on those inventories?

4 Valuing inventories

The value of inventories is calculated at the lower of **cost** and **net realisable value** for each separate item or group of items. **Cost** can be arrived at by using **FIFO** (first in, first out) or **AVCO** (weighted average costing).

4.1 The basic rule

There are **several methods** which, in theory, might be used for the valuation of inventory.

(a)   Inventories might be valued at their **expected selling price**.

(b)   Inventories might be valued at their expected selling price, less any costs still to be incurred in getting them ready for sale and then selling them. This amount is referred to as the **net realisable value** (NRV) of the inventories.

(c)   Inventories might be valued at their **historical cost** (ie the cost at which they were originally bought).

(d)   Inventories might be valued at the amount it would cost to replace them. This amount is referred to as the **current replacement cost** of inventories.

Current replacement costs are not used in the type of accounts dealt with in this syllabus.

The use of selling prices in inventory valuation is ruled out because this would create a profit for the business before the inventory has been sold.

A simple example might help to explain this. A trader buys two items of inventory, each costing $100. They can sell them for $140 each but, in the accounting period we shall consider, they have only sold one of them. The other is closing inventory in hand.

Since only one item has been sold, you might think it is common sense that profit ought to be $40. But if closing inventory is valued at selling price, profit would be $80, ie profit would be taken on the closing inventory as well.

	$	$
Sales		140
Opening inventory	–	
Purchases (2 × $100)	200	
	200	
Less closing inventory (at selling price)	140	
Cost of sales		60
Profit		80

The same objection **usually** applies to the use of NRV in inventory valuation. The item purchased for $100 requires $5 of further expenditure in getting it ready for sale and then selling it (eg $5 of processing costs and distribution costs). If its expected selling price is $140, its NRV is $(140 – 5) = $135. To value it at $135 in the statement of financial position would still be to anticipate a $35 profit.

We are left with **historical cost** as the normal basis of inventory valuation. **The only time when historical cost is not used is where it is prudent to use a lower value.**

Staying with the example above, suppose that the market in this kind of product suddenly slumps and the item's expected selling price is only $90. The item's NRV is then $(90 – 5) = $85 and the business has in effect made a loss of $15 ($100 – $85). Losses should be recognised as soon as they are foreseen. This can be achieved by valuing the inventory item in the statement of financial position at its NRV of $85.

The argument developed above suggests that the rule to follow is that inventories should be valued at cost or, if lower, NRV. The accounting treatment of inventory is governed by an accounting standard, IAS 2 *Inventories*. IAS 2 states that **inventory should be valued at the lower of cost and NRV**, as we will see below. This is an important rule and one which you should learn by heart.

IMPORTANT

Inventory should be valued at the lower of cost and net realisable value.

4.2 Applying the basic valuation rule

If a business has many inventory items on hand, the comparison of cost and NRV should theoretically be carried out for each item separately. It is not sufficient to compare the total cost of all inventory items with their total NRV. An example will show why.

Suppose a company has four items of inventory on hand at the end of its accounting period. Their cost and NRVs are as follows.

Inventory item	Cost	NRV	Lower of cost/NRV
	$	$	$
1	27	32	27
2	14	8	8
3	43	55	43
4	29	40	29
	113	135	107

It would be incorrect to compare total costs ($113) with total NRV ($135) and to state inventories at $113 in the statement of financial position. The company can foresee a loss of $6 on item 2 and this should be recognised. If the four items are taken together in total, the loss on item 2 is masked by the anticipated profits on the other items. By performing the cost/NRV comparison for each item separately the prudent valuation of $107 can be derived. This is the value which should appear in the statement of financial position.

However, for a company with large amounts of inventory, this procedure may be impracticable. In this case it is acceptable to group similar items into categories and perform the comparison of cost and NRV category by category, rather than item by item.

QUESTION
Valuation

The following figures relate to inventory held at the year end.

	A	B	C
	$	$	$
Cost	20	9	12
Selling price	30	12	22
Modification cost to enable sale	–	2	8
Marketing costs	7	2	2
Units held	200	150	300

Required

Calculate the value of inventory held.

ANSWER

Item	Cost	NRV	Valuation	Quantity	Total value
	$	$	$	Units	$
A	20	23	20	200	4,000
B	9	8	8	150	1,200
C	12	12	12	300	3,600
					8,800

So have we now solved the problem of how a business should value its inventories? It seems that all the business has to do is choose the lower of cost and NRV. This is true as far as it goes, but there is one further problem, perhaps not so easy to foresee: for a given type of inventory, **what was the cost**?

4.3 Determining the purchase cost

Inventories may be **raw materials** or components bought from suppliers, **finished goods** which have been made by the business but not yet sold, or work in the process of production, but only part-completed (this type of inventory is called **work in progress** or WIP). It will simplify matters, however, if we think about the historical cost of purchased raw materials and components, which ought to be their purchase price.

A business may be continually purchasing consignments of a particular component. As each consignment is received from suppliers the components are stored in the appropriate bin or on the appropriate shelf or pallet, where they will be mingled with previous consignments. When the storekeeper issues components to production they will simply pull out from the bin the nearest components to hand, which may have arrived in the latest consignment, in an earlier consignment or in several different consignments. Our concern is to devise a pricing technique, which we can use to attribute a cost to each of the components issued from stores.

There are several techniques which are used in practice.

- FIFO (first in, first out). Using this technique, we assume that components are used in the order in which they are received from suppliers. The components issued are deemed to have formed part of the oldest consignment still unused and are costed accordingly.

- AVCO (average cost). As purchase prices change with each new consignment, the average price of components held is constantly changed. Each component held at any moment is assumed to have been purchased at the average price of all components held at that moment.

- LIFO (last in, first out). We assume that components used formed part of the most recent delivery, and inventories are the oldest receipts.

If you are preparing **financial accounts** you would normally expect to use FIFO or AVCO for the valuation of inventory. **IAS 2 *Inventories* does not permit the use of LIFO**. Furthermore, you should note that terms such as AVCO and FIFO refer to **pricing techniques** only. The **actual** components can be used in any order.

To illustrate FIFO and AVCO, the following transactions will be used in each case.

TRANSACTIONS DURING MAY 20X7

	Quantity Units	Unit cost $	Total cost $	Market value per unit on date of transactions $
Opening balance 1 May	100	2.00	200	
Receipts 3 May	400	2.10	840	2.11
Issues 4 May	200			2.11
Receipts 9 May	300	2.12	636	2.15
Issues 11 May	400			2.20
Receipts 18 May	100	2.40	240	2.35
Issues 20 May	100			2.35
Closing balance 31 May	200			2.38
			1,916	

Receipts mean goods are received into store and issues represent the issue of goods from store. The problem is to put a valuation on the following.

(a) The issues of materials
(b) The closing inventory

How would issues and closing inventory be valued using FIFO and AVCO?

4.4 FIFO

FIFO assumes that materials are **issued out of inventory in the order in which they were delivered into inventory**, ie issues are priced at the cost of the earliest delivery remaining in inventory.

The cost of issues and closing inventory value in the example, using FIFO, would be as follows.

Date of issue	Quantity Units	Value issued	Cost of issues $	$
4 May	200	100 OI* at $2	200	
		100 at $2.10	210	
				410
11 May	400	300 at $2.10	630	
		100 at $2.12	212	
				842
20 May	100	100 at $2.12		212
				1,464
Closing inventory value	200	100 at $2.12	212	
		100 at $2.40	240	
				452
				1,916

* OI = opening inventory

Note that the cost of materials issued plus the value of closing inventory equals the cost of purchases plus the value of opening inventory ($1,916).

4.5 AVCO

There are various ways in which average costs may be used in pricing inventory issues. The most common (cumulative or continuous weighted average pricing) is illustrated below.

The **cumulative or continuous weighted average pricing method** calculates a weighted average price for all units in inventory. Issues are priced at this average cost, and the balance of inventory remaining would have the same unit valuation.

A new weighted average price is calculated whenever a new delivery of materials into store is received. This is the key feature of cumulative weighted average pricing.

In our example, issue costs and closing inventory values would be as follows.

Date	Received Units	Issued Units	Balance Units	Total inventory value $	Unit cost $	Price of issue $
Opening inventory			100	200	2.00	
3 May	400			840	2.10	
			500	1,040	2.08 *	
4 May		200		(416)	2.08 **	416
			300	624	2.08	
9 May	300			636	2.12	
			600	1,260	2.10 *	
11 May		400		(840)	2.10 **	840
			200	420	2.10	
18 May	100			240	2.40	
			300	660	2.20 *	
20 May		100		(220)	2.20 **	220
						1,476
Closing inventory value			200	440	2.20	440
						1,916

* A new unit cost of inventory is calculated whenever a new receipt of materials occurs.

** Whenever inventories are issued, the unit value of the items issued is the current weighted average cost per unit at the time of the issue.

For this method too, the cost of materials issued plus the value of closing inventory equals the cost of purchases plus the value of opening inventory ($1,916).

The **periodic weighted average pricing method** is similar to the continuous weighted average pricing method; however, the unit price is calculated at the end of the period.

This is a simpler approach; however, it means that values are not known until the end of the period.

In our example above in Section 4.3, the weighted average price under the periodic method for May is:

= Total cost/(Opening quantity + Total quantity received)
= 1,916/(100 + 400 + 300 + 100)
= $2.13 per unit

This gives a valuation of 200 × $2.13 = $426.00

4.6 Inventory valuations and profit

In the previous descriptions of FIFO and AVCO the example used raw materials as an illustration. Each method of valuation produced different costs both of closing inventories and also of material issues. Since raw material costs affect the cost of production, and the cost of production works through eventually into the cost of sales, it follows that different methods of inventory valuation will provide different profit figures. An example may help to illustrate this point.

4.7 Example: inventory valuations and profit

On 1 November 20X2 a company held 300 units of finished goods item No 9639 in inventory. These were valued at $12 each. During November 20X2 three batches of finished goods were received into store from the production department, as follows.

Date	Units received	Production cost per unit
10 November	400	$12.50
20 November	400	$14
25 November	400	$15

Goods sold out of inventory during November were as follows.

Date	Units sold	Sale price per unit
14 November	500	$20
21 November	500	$20
28 November	100	$20

What was the profit from selling inventory item 9639 in November 20X2, applying the following principles of inventory valuation?

(a)   FIFO
(b)   AVCO (using cumulative weighted average costing)

Ignore administration, sales and distribution costs.

Solution

(a)   *FIFO*

		Issue cost total $	Closing inventory $
Date	Issue costs		
14 November	300 units × $12 plus		
	200 units × $12.50	6,100	
21 November	200 units × $12.50 plus		
	300 units × $14	6,700	
28 November	100 units × $14	1,400	
Closing inventory	400 units × $15		6,000
		14,200	6,000

(b)   *AVCO (cumulative weighted average cost)*

			Unit cost $	Balance in inventory $	Total cost of issues $	Closing inventory $
1 November	Opening inventory	300	12.000	3,600		
10 November	400		12.500	5,000		
	700		12.286	8,600		
14 November	500		12.286	6,143	6,143	
	200		12.286	2,457		
20 November	400		14.000	5,600		
	600		13.428	8,057		
21 November	500		13.428	6,714	6,714	
	100		13.428	1,343		
25 November	400		15.000	6,000		
	500		14.686	7,343		
28 November	100		14.686	1,469	1,469	
30 November	400		14.686	5,874	14,326	5,874

Summary: profit

	FIFO $	AVCO $
Opening inventory	3,600	3,600
Cost of production	16,600	16,600
	20,200	20,200
Closing inventory	6,000	5,874
Cost of sales	14,200	14,326
Sales (1,100 × $20)	22,000	22,000
Profit	7,800	7,674

Different inventory valuations have produced different cost of sales figures, and therefore different profits. In our example, opening inventory values are the same, therefore the difference in the amount of profit under each method is the same as the difference in the valuations of closing inventory.

The profit differences are only temporary. In our example, the opening inventory in December 20X2 will be $6,000 or $5,874, depending on the inventory valuation used. Different opening inventory values will affect the cost of sales and profits in December, so that in the long run inequalities in cost of sales each month will even themselves out.

QUESTION

A firm has the following transactions with its product R.

Year 1
Opening inventory: nil
Buys 10 units at $300 per unit
Buys 12 units at $250 per unit
Sells 8 units at $400 per unit
Buys 6 units at $200 per unit
Sells 12 units at $400 per unit

Year 2
Buys 10 units at $200 per unit
Sells 5 units at $400 per unit
Buys 12 units at $150 per unit
Sells 25 units at $400 per unit

Required

Using FIFO, calculate the following on an item by item basis for both year 1 and year 2.

(i)   The closing inventory
(ii)   The sales
(iii)   The cost of sales
(iv)   The gross profit

ANSWER

Year 1

Purchases Units	Sales Units	Balance Units	Inventory value $	Unit cost $	Cost of sales $	Sales $
10		10	3,000	300		
12			3,000	250		
		22	6,000			
	8		(2,400)		2,400	3,200
		14	3,600			
6			1,200	200		
		20	4,800			
	12		(3,100)*		3,100	4,800
		8	1,700		5,500	8,000

* 2 @ $300 + 10 @ $250 = $3,100

Year 2

Purchases Units	Sales Units	Balance Units	Inventory value $	Unit cost $	Cost of sales $	Sales $
B/f		8	1,700			
10			2,000	200		
		18	3,700			
	5		(1,100)*		1,100	2,000
		13	2,600			
12		25	1,800	150		
			4,400			
	25		(4,400)**		4,400	10,000
		0	0		5,500	12,000

* 2 @ $250 + 3 @ $200 = $1,100
** 13 @ $200 + 12 @ $150 = $4,400

PROFIT OR LOSS ACCOUNT

		FIFO
	$	$
Year 1		
Sales		8,000
Opening inventory		
Purchases (3,000 + 3,000 + 1,200)	7,200	
	7,200	
Closing inventory	1,700	
Cost of sales		5,500
Gross profit		2,500
Year 2		
Sales		12,000
Opening inventory	1,700	
Purchases (2,000 + 1,800)	3,800	
	5,500	
Closing inventory	0	
Cost of sales		5,500
Gross profit		6,500

5 IAS 2 *Inventories*

> IAS 2 *Inventories* lays out the required accounting treatment for inventories under International Financial Reporting Standards.

5.1 Scope

The following items are **excluded** from the scope of the standard.

- Work in progress under **construction contracts** (covered by IAS 11 *Construction contracts,* which you will study in later financial accounting papers)

- **Financial instruments** (ie shares, bonds)

- **Livestock**, agricultural and forest products, and mineral ores

5.2 Definitions

The standard gives the following important definitions.

- Inventories are assets:

    – Held for sale in the ordinary course of business

    – In the process of production for such sale

    – In the form of materials or supplies to be consumed in the production process or in the rendering of services

- Net realisable value is the estimated selling price in the ordinary course of business less the estimated costs of completion and the estimated costs necessary to make the sale. (*IAS 2*)

Inventories can **include** any of the following.

- **Goods purchased and held for resale**, eg goods held for sale by a retailer, or land and buildings held for resale

- **Finished goods** produced

- Work in progress (WIP) being produced

- Materials and supplies awaiting use in the production process (**raw materials**)

5.3 Measurement of inventories

The standard states that 'Inventories should be measured at the lower of cost and net realisable value.'

5.4 Cost of inventories

The cost of inventories will consist of all the following costs.

(a)   **Purchase**
(b)   **Costs of conversion**
(c)   Other costs incurred in bringing the inventories to their **present location and condition**

5.4.1 Costs of purchase

The standard lists the following as comprising the costs of purchase of inventories.

(a)   **Purchase price**

(b)   **Import duties** and other taxes

(c)   Transport, handling and any other cost **directly attributable** to the acquisition of finished goods, services and materials

(d)   **Less any trade discounts**, rebates and other similar amounts

5.4.2 Costs of conversion

Costs of conversion of inventories consist of two main parts.

(a)   Costs **directly related** to the units of production, eg direct materials, direct labour

(b)   Fixed and variable **production overheads** that are incurred in converting materials into finished goods, allocated on a systematic basis

You may have come across the terms 'fixed production overheads' or 'variable production overheads' elsewhere in your studies. The standard defines them as follows.

- Fixed production overheads are those indirect costs of production that remain relatively constant regardless of the volume of production, eg the cost of factory management and administration.

- Variable production overheads are those indirect costs of production that vary directly, or nearly directly, with the volume of production, eg indirect materials and labour.   *(IAS 2)*

The standard emphasises that fixed production overheads must be allocated to items of inventory on the basis of the **normal capacity of the production facilities**. This is an important point.

(a)   **Normal capacity** is the expected achievable production based on the average over several periods/seasons, under normal circumstances

(b)   The above figure should take account of the capacity lost through **planned maintenance**

(c)   If it approximates to the normal level of activity then the **actual level of production** can be used

(d)   **Low production** or **idle plant** will **not** result in a higher fixed overhead allocation to each unit

(e)   **Unallocated overheads** must be recognised as an expense in the period in which they were incurred

(f) When production is **abnormally high**, the fixed production overhead allocated to each unit will be reduced, so avoiding inventories being stated at more than cost

(g) The allocation of variable production overheads to each unit is based on the **actual use** of production facilities

5.4.3 Other costs

Any other costs should only be recognised if they are incurred in bringing the inventories to their **present location and condition**.

The standard lists types of cost which **would not be included** in cost of inventories. Instead, they should be recognised as an **expense** in the period they are incurred.

- **Abnormal amounts** of wasted materials, labour or other production costs

- **Storage costs** (except costs which are necessary in the production process before a further production stage)

- **Administrative overheads** not incurred to bring inventories to their present location and conditions

- **Selling costs**

5.5 Determining cost

Cost of inventories should be assigned by **specific identification** of their individual costs for items that are not ordinarily interchangeable (ie identical or very similar) and for goods or services produced and segregated for **specific projects**. Specific identification of cost means that specific costs are attributed to identified items of inventory. However, calculating costs on an individual item basis could be onerous. For convenience, IAS 2 allows the use of cost estimation techniques, such as the **standard cost method** or the **retail method**, provided that the results approximate cost.

(a) **Standard costs** take into account **normal** levels of materials and supplies, labour, efficiency and capacity utilisation. They are regularly reviewed and revised if necessary to ensure that they appropriately resemble actual costs.

(b) The **retail method** is often used in the retail industry for measuring inventories of large numbers of rapidly changing items with similar margins for which it is impracticable to use other costing methods. The cost of the inventory is determined by reducing the sales value of the inventory by the percentage gross margin.

5.5.1 Interchangeable items

Where inventories consist of a large number of interchangeable (ie identical or very similar) items, it will be virtually impossible to determine costs on an individual item basis. Therefore IAS 2 allows the following cost estimation techniques.

(a) **FIFO**. Using this technique, we assume that components are used in the order in which they are received from suppliers. The components issued are deemed to have formed part of the oldest consignment still unused and are costed accordingly.

(b) **Weighted average cost (AVCO)**. As purchase prices change with each new consignment, the average price of components in inventory is constantly changed. Each component in inventory at any moment is assumed to have been purchased at the average price of all components in inventory at that moment. Under the AVCO method, a recalculation can be made after each purchase, **or alternatively only at the period end**.

The same technique should be used by the entity for all inventories that have a similar nature and use.

Note that the LIFO formula is **not permitted** by IAS 2.

QUESTION

You are the accountant at Water Pumps Co, and you have been asked to calculate the valuation of the company's inventory at cost at its year end of 30 April 20X5.

Water Pumps manufactures a range of pumps. The pumps are assembled from components bought by Water Pumps (the company does not manufacture any parts).

The company does not use a standard costing system, and WIP and finished goods are valued as follows.

(a) Material costs are determined from the product specification, which lists the components required to make a pump.

(b) The company produces a range of pumps. Employees record the hours spent on assembling each type of pump; this information is input into the payroll system which prints the total hours spent each week assembling each type of pump. All employees assembling pumps are paid at the same rate and there is no overtime.

(c) Overheads are added to the inventory value in accordance with IAS 2 *Inventories.* The financial accounting records are used to determine the overhead cost, and this is applied as a percentage based on the direct labour cost.

For direct labour costs, you have agreed that the labour expended for a unit in WIP is half that of a completed unit.

The draft accounts show the following materials and direct labour costs in inventory.

	Raw materials	WIP	Finished goods
	$	$	$
Materials	74,786	85,692	152,693
Direct labour		13,072	46,584

The costs incurred in April, as recorded in the financial accounting records, were as follows.

	$
Direct labour	61,320
Selling costs	43,550
Depreciation and finance costs of production machines	4,490
Distribution costs	6,570
Factory manager's wage	2,560
Other production overheads	24,820
Purchasing and accounting costs relating to production	5,450
Other accounting costs	7,130
Other administration overheads	24,770

For your calculations assume that all WIP and finished goods were produced in April 20X5 and that the company was operating at a normal level of activity.

Required

Calculate the value of overheads which should be added to WIP and finished goods in accordance with IAS 2 *Inventories.*

Note. You should include details and a description of your workings and all figures should be calculated to the nearest $.

ANSWER

Calculation of overheads for inventory

Production overheads are as follows.

	$
Depreciation/finance costs	4,490
Factory manager's wage	2,560
Other production overheads	24,820
Accounting/purchase costs	5,450
	37,320

Direct labour = $61,320

$\therefore$ Production overhead rate $= \dfrac{37,320}{61,320} = 60.86\%$

Inventory valuation

	Raw materials $	WIP $	Finished goods $	Total $
Materials	74,786	85,692	152,693	313,171
Direct labour	–	13,072	46,584	59,656
Production overhead (at 60.86% of labour)	–	7,956	28,351	36,307
	74,786	106,720	227,628	409,134

Variable overheads will be included in the cost of inventory.

5.6 Net realisable value (NRV)

As a general rule, assets should not be carried at amounts greater than those expected to be realised from their sale or use. In the case of inventories this amount could fall below cost when items are **damaged or become obsolete**, or where the **costs to completion have increased** in order to make the sale.

In fact, we can identify the principal situations in which **NRV is likely to be less than cost**.

(a)   An **increase in costs** or a **fall in selling price**
(b)   A **physical deterioration** in the condition of inventory
(c)   **Obsolescence** of products
(d)   A decision as part of the company's marketing strategy to manufacture and sell products at a **loss**
(e)   **Errors in production or purchasing**

A write down of inventories would normally take place on an item by item basis, but similar or related items may be **grouped together**. This grouping together is acceptable for, say, items in the same product line, but it is not acceptable to write down inventories based on a whole classification (eg finished goods) or a whole business.

The assessment of NRV should take place **at the same time** as estimates are made of selling price, using the most reliable information available. Fluctuations of price or cost should be taken into account if they relate directly to **events after the reporting period**, which confirm conditions existing at the end of the period.

The reasons why inventory is held must also be taken into account. Some inventory, for example, may be held to satisfy a firm contract and its NRV will therefore be the **contract price**. Any additional inventory of the same type held at the period end will, in contrast, be assessed according to general sales prices when NRV is estimated.

NRV must be reassessed at the end of each period and compared again with cost. If the NRV has risen for inventories held over the end of more than one period, then the previous write down must be **reversed** to the extent that the inventory is then valued at the lower of cost and the new NRV. This may be possible when selling prices have fallen in the past and then risen again.

On occasion a write down to NRV may be of such size, incidence or nature that it must be **disclosed separately**.

5.7 Recognition as an expense

The following treatment is required **when inventories are sold**.

(a)   The **carrying amount** is recognised as an expense in the period in which the related revenue is recognised.
(b)   The amount of any **write down of inventories** to NRV and all losses of inventories are recognised as an expense in the period the write down or loss occurs.

(c) The amount of any **reversal of any write down of inventories**, arising from an increase in NRV, is recognised as a reduction in the amount of inventories recognised as an expense in the period in which the reversal occurs.

5.8 Disclosure

The financial statements should disclose the following.

(a) **Accounting policies** adopted in measuring inventories, including the cost formula used

(b) **Total carrying amount of inventories** and the carrying amount in classifications appropriate to the entity

(c) **Carrying amount** of inventories carried at NRV

Example disclosure

An example of disclosure for inventories is given below.

Accounting policies

Inventories

Inventories are valued at the lower of cost and net realisable value. Cost is determined using the FIFO method. Net realisable value is the estimated selling price in the ordinary course of business, less the costs estimated to make the sale.

Note X   **Inventories**

	20X1	20X0
	$'000	$'000
Raw materials	31	28
Work in progress	23	25
Finished goods	25	15
	79	68

Included in the carrying value presented above was $8,000 (20X0: $10,000) of inventories held at net realisable value.

EXAM FOCUS POINT

The ACCA examining team commented recently that inventory is one of the areas usually well answered in the exam.

This chapter, in addition to Chapters 8 to 12, will help you fulfil the following requirement of performance objective PO6, 'Record and process transactions and events':

• Apply the appropriate requirements of relevant accounting standards and policies to economic transactions and events.

CHAPTER ROUNDUP

⮡ The **cost of goods sold** is calculated as:

Opening inventory + purchases – closing inventory.

⮡ **Carriage inwards** is included in the cost of purchases. **Carriage outwards** is a selling expense.

⮡ **Opening inventories** brought forward in the inventory account are transferred to the profit or loss account, and so at the end of the accounting year the balance on the inventory account ceases to be the opening inventory value b/f and becomes instead the closing inventory value c/f.

⮡ The value of **closing inventories** is accounted for in the **nominal ledger** by debiting an inventory account and crediting the profit or loss account at the end of an accounting period. Inventory will therefore have a debit balance at the end of a period, and this balance will be shown in the statement of financial position as a current asset.

⮡ The **quantity** of inventories held at the year end is established by means of a **physical count** of inventory in an annual counting exercise, or by a '**continuous**' inventory count.

⮡ The value of inventories is calculated at the lower of **cost** and **net realisable value (NRV)** for each separate item or group of items. **Cost** can be arrived at by using first in, first out (**FIFO**) or weighted average costing (**AVCO**).

⮡ IAS 2 *Inventories* lays out the required accounting treatment for inventories under International Financial Reporting Standards.

1 When is an inventory account used?

2 How is closing inventory incorporated in the financial statements?

A DEBIT: statement of profit or loss   CREDIT: statement of financial position

B DEBIT: statement of financial position   CREDIT: statement of profit or loss

3 What is 'continuous' inventory counting?

4 An item of inventory was purchased for $10. However, due to a fall in demand, its selling price will be only $8. In addition, further costs will be incurred prior to sale of $1. What is the NRV?

A $7
B $8
C $10
D $11

5 Why is inventory not valued at expected selling price?

6 When valuing inventory, the following methods are available.

1 FIFO
2 AVCO
3 LIFO
4 Standard cost

Which methods are allowable under IAS 2 *Inventories*?

A 1, 2, 3
B 1, 2, 3, 4
C 1 only
D 1, 2

7 What is included in the cost of purchase of inventories according to IAS 2?

A Purchase price less trade discount
B Purchase price plus transport costs less trade discount
C Purchase price less import duties less trade discount
D Purchase price plus import duties plus transport costs less trade discount

8 What type of costs should be recognised as an expense, not as part of the cost of inventory?

9 What are the most likely situations when the NRV of inventories falls below cost?

ANSWERS TO QUICK QUIZ

1 Only at the end of an accounting period

2 B DEBIT: Inventory in hand (statement of financial position)

   CREDIT: Closing inventory (income and expense account)

3 A card is kept for every item of inventory. It shows receipts and issues, with a running total. A few inventory items are counted each day to test that the cards are correct.

4 A NRV is selling price ($8) less further costs to sale ($1), ie $7.

5 Mainly because this would result in the business taking a profit before the goods have been sold.

6 D Only FIFO and AVCO are allowed.

7 D Purchase price **plus** import duties (and other taxes) **plus** transport costs **less** trade discount.

8 See Section 5.4.3.

9 • Increase in costs or a fall in selling price
   • Physical deterioration of inventory
   • Obsolescence
   • Marketing strategy
   • Errors in production or purchasing

Now try ...

Attempt the questions below from the **Practice Question Bank**

Number

Qs 29 – 33

Tangible non-current assets

Non-current assets can be expensive items and so can have a big impact on a business's financial statements. It is therefore crucial that expenditure on non-current assets is accounted for correctly.

In this chapter, we focus on **tangible non-current assets**, ie those with physical form.

The main categories of tangible non-current assets are governed by **IAS 16 *Property, plant and equipment***, which is the main focus of this chapter.

Study Guide	Intellectual level
D **Recording transactions and events**	
4 **Tangible non-current assets**	
(a) Define non-current assets.	K
(b) Recognise the difference between current and non-current assets.	K
(c) Explain the difference between capital and revenue items.	K
(d) Classify expenditure as capital or revenue expenditure.	S
(e) Prepare ledger entries to record the acquisition and disposal of non-current assets.	S
(f) Calculate and record profits or losses on disposal of non-current assets in the statement of profit or loss, including part-exchange transactions.	S
(g) Record the revaluation of a non-current asset in ledger accounts, the statement of profit or loss and other comprehensive income and in the statement of financial position.	S
(h) Calculate the profit or loss on disposal of a revalued asset.	S
(i) Illustrate how non-current asset balances and movements are disclosed in financial statements.	S
(j) Explain the purpose and function of an asset register.	K
5 **Depreciation**	
(a) Understand and explain the purpose of depreciation.	K
(b) Calculate the charge for depreciation using straight line and reducing balance methods.	S
(c) Identify the circumstances where different methods of depreciation would be appropriate.	S
(d) Illustrate how depreciation expense and accumulated depreciation are recorded in ledger accounts.	S
(e) Calculate depreciation on a revalued non-current asset, including the transfer of excess depreciation between the revaluation surplus and retained earnings.	S
(f) Calculate the adjustments to depreciation necessary if changes are made in the estimated useful life and/or residual value of a non-current asset.	S
(g) Record depreciation in the statement of profit or loss and statement of financial position.	S
F **Preparing basic financial statements**	
3 **Disclosure notes**	
(b) Draft the following disclosure notes:	S
(i) Non-current assets including tangible and intangible assets	

1 Non-current and current assets

> **Non-current assets** are assets which are bought by the business for **continuing use**. **Tangible non-current assets** are those with **physical form**.

A statement of financial position contains both non-current assets and current assets. But what is the difference between the two?

TERM

Non-current assets are assets which are intended to be used by the business on a continuing basis and include both tangible and intangible assets.

Non-current assets are assets that are bought by the business for use in the **long term**. Non-current assets include **tangible** assets (those with physical form, that are the subject of this chapter) and **intangible** assets (which we will look at in the next chapter). **Current assets** are assets that will be realised, consumed or sold in the normal **operating cycle** of the business or are assets held primarily for trading. Current assets include trade receivables and inventories.

2 Capital and revenue expenditure

> **Capital expenditure** is expenditure which forms part of the cost **of non-current assets**. **Revenue expenditure** is expenditure incurred for the **purpose of the trade** or to **maintain non-current assets**.

2.1 The distinction between capital and revenue expenditure

In order to tackle the subject of non-current assets, you need to be familiar with an important distinction, the distinction between **capital** and **revenue expenditure**.

TERM

Capital expenditure is expenditure which results in the acquisition of non-current assets, or improvements to existing non-current assets.

(a)   Capital expenditure is not charged as an expense in the statement of profit or loss, although a depreciation or amortisation charge will usually be made to write off the capital expenditure gradually over time. Depreciation and amortisation charges are expenses in the statement of profit or loss.

(b)   Capital expenditure on non-current assets results in the recognition of a non-current asset in the statement of financial position of the business.

Revenue expenditure is expenditure which is incurred for either of the following reasons.

(a)   For the purpose of the trade of the business. This includes expenditure classified as selling and distribution expenses, administration expenses and finance charges.

(b)   To maintain the existing earning capacity of non-current assets.

These definitions sound a bit confusing, but the principle behind them is fairly straightforward. Think of capital expenditure as expenditure that provides long-term benefits (eg a building, item of machinery) and revenue expenditure as trading costs relating to the short-term (eg electricity, wages).

Also, the term 'capital' in capital expenditure should not be confused with the capital invested in a business.

IMPORTANT

Capital expenditure is expenditure that can be **capitalised** as part of the cost of a non-current asset. **Revenue expenditure** cannot be capitalised as part of the cost of a non-current asset and must be expensed in the statement of profit or loss.

2.2 Example: capital and revenue expenditure

A business purchases a building for $30,000. It then adds an extension to the building at a cost of $10,000. The building needs to have a few broken windows mended, its floors polished and some missing roof tiles replaced. These cleaning and maintenance jobs cost $900.

In this example, the original purchase ($30,000) and the cost of the extension ($10,000) are capital expenditure, because they are incurred to **acquire** and then **improve** a non-current asset and so can be capitalised as part of it. The other costs of $900 are revenue expenditure, because these merely **maintain** the building and thus the 'earning capacity' of the building.

2.3 Capital income and revenue income

Capital income is the proceeds from the sale of non-trading assets (ie proceeds from the sale of non-current assets, including long-term investments). The profits (or losses) from the sale of non-current assets are included in the statement of profit or loss of a business, for the accounting period in which the sale takes place. For instance, the business may sell vehicles or machinery which it no longer needs – the proceeds will be capital income.

Revenue income is income derived from the following sources.

(a)   The sale of trading assets, such as goods held in inventory
(b)   The provision of services
(c)   Interest and dividends received from investments held by the business

2.4 Capital transactions

The categorisation of capital and revenue items given above does not mention raising additional capital from the owner(s) of the business, or raising and repaying loans.

(a)   These transactions add to the cash assets of the business, thereby creating a corresponding liability (capital or loan)

(b)   When a loan is repaid, it reduces the liabilities (loan) and the assets (cash)

None of these transactions would be reported through the statement of profit or loss.

2.5 Why is the distinction between capital and revenue items important?

Revenue expenditure results from the purchase of goods and services for one of the following reasons.

(a)   To be used fully in the accounting period in which they are purchased, and so be a cost or expense in the statement of profit or loss.

(b)   To result in a current asset as at the end of the accounting period because the goods or services have not yet been consumed or used. The current asset would be shown in the statement of financial position and is not yet a cost or expense in the statement of profit or loss.

For instance, inventory which is purchased for resale will either be sold during the period as per (a) or still be in inventory as per (b).

Capital expenditure results in the **purchase or improvement of non-current assets**, which are assets that will provide benefits to the business in more than one accounting period, and which are not acquired with a view to being resold in the normal course of trade. The cost of purchased non-current assets is not charged in full to the statement of profit or loss of the period in which the purchase occurs. Instead, the non-current asset is gradually depreciated over a number of accounting periods in accordance with the accruals concept.

Since revenue items and capital items are accounted for in different ways, the correct and consistent calculation of profit for any accounting period depends on the correct and consistent classification of items as revenue or capital.

This may seem rather confusing at the moment, but things will become clearer in the next few chapters. You must get used to the terminology used, as these words appear in the accounting standards themselves, as we will see.

QUESTION

Capital or revenue

State whether each of the following items should be classified as 'capital' or 'revenue' expenditure or income for the purpose of preparing the statement of profit or loss and the statement of financial position of the business.

A   The purchase of a property (eg an office building)

B   The annual depreciation of such a property

C   Solicitors' fees in connection with the purchase of such a property

D   The costs of adding extra storage capacity to a computer used by the business

E   Computer repairs and maintenance costs

F   Profit on the sale of an office building

G   Revenue from sales by credit card

H   The cost of new plant

I   Customs duty charged on the plant when imported into the country

J   The 'carriage' costs of transporting the new plant from the supplier's factory to the premises of the business purchasing the plant

K   The cost of installing the new plant in the premises of the business

L   The wages of the machine operators

ANSWER

A   Capital expenditure

B   Depreciation of a non-current asset is revenue expenditure

C   The legal fees associated with the purchase of a property may be added to the purchase price and classified as capital expenditure. The cost of the property in the statement of financial position of the business will then include the legal fees

D   Capital expenditure (enhancing an existing non-current asset)

E   Revenue expenditure

F   Capital income (net of the costs of sale)

G   Revenue income

H   Capital expenditure

I   If customs duties are borne by the purchaser of the non-current asset, they may be added to the cost of the machinery and classified as capital expenditure

J   Similarly, if carriage costs are paid for by the purchaser of the non-current asset, they may be included in the cost of the non-current asset and classified as capital expenditure

K   Installation costs of a non-current asset are also added to the non-current asset's cost and classified as capital expenditure

L   Revenue expenditure

EXAM FOCUS POINT

Exam questions on the distinction between capital and revenue expenditure are highly likely.

3 IAS *16 Property, plant and equipment*

The accounting treatment of tangible non-current assets is covered by IAS 16 *Property, plant and equipment*.

3.1 Definitions

IAS 16 *Property, plant and equipment* is the International Financial Reporting Standard that should be followed when accounting for tangible non-current assets. The key concepts that we will cover in the next few sections come from IAS 16 and are very important.

IAS 16 gives a large number of definitions that you need to be aware of.

- **Property, plant and equipment** are tangible assets that:

    - Are held by an entity for **use** in the production or supply of goods or services, for rental to others, or for administrative purposes

    - Are expected to be used during more than one period

- **Cost** is the amount of cash or cash equivalents paid or the fair value of the other consideration given to acquire an asset at the time of its acquisition or construction.

- **Fair value** is the price that would be received to sell an asset or paid to transfer a liability in an orderly transaction between market participants at the measurement date.

- **Carrying amount** is the amount at which an asset is recognised after deducting any accumulated depreciation and impairment losses.   *(IAS 16)*

3.2 Recognition in the accounts

Recognition simply means incorporation of the asset in the business's accounts. The recognition of property, plant and equipment depends on two criteria.

(a)   It is probable that **future economic benefits** associated with the asset will flow to the entity.
(b)   The cost of the asset to the entity can be **measured reliably**.

Property, plant and equipment can amount to **substantial amounts** in financial statements, affecting both the presentation of the company's statement of financial position and the profitability of the entity as shown in the statement of profit or loss. Smaller items such as tools are often written off as expenses of the period. Most companies have their own policy on this – items below a certain value are charged as expenses instead of being capitalised.

3.3 Initial measurement

Once an item of property, plant and equipment qualifies for recognition as an asset, it will initially be **measured at cost**.

3.4 Components of cost

IAS 16 lists the components that make up the cost of an item of property, plant and equipment as follows.

- **Purchase price**, **including** any import duties paid, but **excluding** any trade discount and sales tax paid

- Initial estimate of the **costs of dismantling and removing** the item and **restoring the site** on which it is located

- **Directly attributable costs** of bringing the asset to **working condition** for its intended use, eg:

    - The cost of site preparation, eg levelling the floor of the factory so the machine can be installed

    - Initial delivery and handling costs

    - Installation and assembly costs

    - Professional fees (lawyers, architects, engineers)

    - Costs of testing whether the asset is working properly, after deducting the net proceeds from selling samples produced when testing equipment

    - Staff costs arising directly from the construction or acquisition of the asset

EXAM FOCUS POINT

Only staff costs arising **directly** from the construction or acquisition of the asset can be capitalised as part of the cost of the asset.

The **costs of training staff** to use a new asset cannot be capitalised because it is not probable that economic benefits will be generated from training the staff, as we can't guarantee that those staff will stay and use the asset. The costs of training staff should be expensed. Watch out for this in your exam!

The following costs **will not be part of the cost** of property, plant or equipment unless they can be attributed directly to the asset's acquisition, or bringing it into its working condition.

- Expenses of operations that are incidental to the construction or development of the item
- Administration and other general overhead costs
- Start-up and similar pre-production costs
- Initial operating losses before the asset reaches planned performances
- Staff training costs
- Maintenance contracts purchased with the asset

All of these will be recognised as an **expense** rather than as part of the cost of the asset.

3.5 Subsequent expenditure

Subsequent expenditure is added to the carrying amount of the asset, but only when it is probable that future economic benefits, in excess of the originally assessed standard of performance of the existing

asset, will flow to the enterprise. All other subsequent expenditure is simply recognised as an expense in the period in which it is incurred.

The important point here is whether any subsequent expenditure on an asset **improves** the condition of the asset beyond the previous performance. The following are examples of such improvements.

(a) **Modification** of an item of plant to extend its useful life, including increased capacity
(b) **Upgrade** of machine parts to improve the quality of output
(c) Adoption of a **new production process** leading to large reductions in operating costs

Normal repairs and maintenance on property, plant and equipment items merely maintain or restore value; they do **not** improve or increase it, so such costs are recognised as an expense when incurred.

4 Depreciation accounting

The **cost** of a non-current asset, less its **estimated residual value**, is allocated fairly between accounting periods by means of **depreciation**. Depreciation is both of the following.

- Charged against profit
- Deducted from the value of the non-current asset in the statement of financial position

Two methods of depreciation are specified in your syllabus.

- The straight line method
- The reducing balance method

4.1 What is depreciation?

The need to depreciate non-current assets arises from the **accruals assumption**. If money is expended in purchasing an asset then the amount expended must at some time be charged against profits. If the asset consumes economic benefits over a number of accounting periods it would be inappropriate to charge any single period (eg the period in which the asset was acquired) with the whole of the expenditure. Instead, some method must be found of spreading the cost of the asset over its useful life.

This view of depreciation as a process of allocation of the cost of an asset over several accounting periods is the view adopted by IAS 16. It is worth mentioning here two **common misconceptions** about the purpose and effects of depreciation.

(a) It is sometimes thought that the carrying amount of an asset is equal to its net realisable value (ie the amount the asset could be sold for less the selling costs) and that the reason for charging depreciation is to reflect the fall in value of an asset over its life. This misconception is the basis of a common, but incorrect, argument which says that freehold properties (say) need not be depreciated in times when property values are rising. It is true that historical cost often gives a misleading impression when a property's carrying amount is much below its market value, but in such a case the business can choose to revalue the property. This is a separate problem from that of allocating the property's cost over successive accounting periods.

(b) Another misconception is that depreciation is provided so that an asset can be replaced at the end of its useful life. This is not the case.

   (i) If there is no intention of replacing the asset, it could then be argued that there is no need to provide for any depreciation at all.

   (ii) If prices are rising, the replacement cost of the asset will exceed the amount of depreciation provided.

4.2 Requirements of IAS 16 for depreciation

Depreciation accounting is governed by IAS 16. Below are some of the important definitions you need to be aware of.

- Depreciation is the allocation of the depreciable amount of an asset over its estimated useful life. Depreciation for the accounting period is charged to net profit or loss for the period either directly or indirectly.

- Depreciable assets are assets which:

  – Are expected to be used during more than one accounting period

  – Have a limited useful life

  – Are held by an enterprise for use in the production or supply of goods and service, for rental to others, or for administrative purposes

- Depreciable amount of a depreciable asset is the historical cost or other amount substituted for historical cost in the financial statements, less the estimated residual value.   *(IAS 16)*

An 'amount substituted for historical cost' will normally be a **current market value** after a revaluation has taken place.

4.3 Useful life

IAS 16 requires the depreciable amount to be allocated on a **systematic basis** to each accounting period during the **useful life** of the asset.

Useful life is either:

- The period over which a depreciable asset is expected to be used by the enterprise; or

- The number of production or similar units expected to be obtained from the asset by the enterprise.   *(IAS 16)*

The following factors should be considered when **estimating the useful life** of a depreciable asset.

- Expected **physical wear and tear**
- **Obsolescence**
- Legal or other **limits** on the use of the assets

Once decided, the useful life should be **reviewed at least annually** and depreciation rates adjusted for the current and future periods if expectations vary significantly from the original estimates. The effect of the change should be disclosed in the accounting period in which the change takes place.

The assessment of useful life requires **judgement** based on previous experience with similar assets or classes of asset. When a completely new type of asset is acquired (ie through technological advancement or through use in producing a brand new product or service) it is still necessary to estimate useful life, even though the exercise will be much more difficult.

IAS 16 also points out that the physical life of the asset might be longer than its useful life to the enterprise in question. One of the main factors to be taken into consideration is the **physical wear and tear** the asset is likely to endure. This will depend on various circumstances, including the number of shifts for which the asset will be used and the enterprise's repair and maintenance programme. Other factors to be considered include obsolescence (due to technological advances/improvements in production/reduction in demand for the product/service produced by the asset) and legal restrictions, eg length of a related lease.

4.4 Residual value

The residual value is the net amount which the entity expects to obtain for an asset at the end of its useful life after deducting the expected costs of disposal.

In most cases the residual value of an asset is **likely to be immaterial**. If it is likely to be of any significant value, that value must be estimated at the date of purchase or any subsequent revaluation. The amount of residual value should be estimated based on the current situation with other similar

assets, used in the same way, which are now at the end of their useful lives. Any expected costs of disposal should be offset against the gross residual value. For example:

(a) A non-current asset costing $20,000 which has an expected life of 5 years and an expected residual value of nil should be depreciated by $20,000 in total over the 5 year period.

(b) A non-current asset costing $20,000 which has an expected life of 5 years and an expected residual value of $3,000 should be depreciated by $17,000 in total over the 5 year period.

4.5 Depreciation methods

Depreciation is a means of **spreading the cost** of a non-current asset over its useful life in order to match the cost of the asset with the consumption of the asset's economic benefits.

So for each accounting period, depreciation is charged to the statement of profit or loss and also deducted from the non-current asset balance to give the asset's carrying amount.

The amount of depreciation deducted from the cost of a non-current asset to arrive at its carrying amount will accumulate over time, as more depreciation is charged in each successive accounting period.

For example, if a non-current asset costing $40,000 has an expected life of 4 years and an estimated residual value of nil, it might be depreciated by $10,000 per annum.

	Depreciation charge for the year (statement of profit or loss) (A) $	Accumulated depreciation at end of year (B) $	Cost of the asset (C) $	Carrying amount at end of year (C – B) $
At beginning of its life	–	–	40,000	40,000
Year 1	10,000	10,000	40,000	30,000
Year 2	10,000	20,000	40,000	20,000
Year 3	10,000	30,000	40,000	10,000
Year 4	10,000	40,000	40,000	0
	40,000			

At the end of year 4, the full $40,000 of depreciation charges have been made in the statements of profit or loss of the four years. The carrying amount of the non-current asset is now nil. In theory (although perhaps not in practice) the business will no longer use the non-current asset, which now needs replacing.

There are several different methods of depreciation. For your syllabus, you only need to know about the straight line and the reducing balance methods.

4.6 The straight line method

This is the most commonly used method of all. The total depreciable amount is charged in equal instalments to each accounting period over the expected useful life of the asset. In this way, the carrying amount of the non-current asset declines at a steady rate, or in a 'straight line' over time.

The annual depreciation charge is calculated as: $\dfrac{\text{Cost of asset } - \text{ residual value}}{\text{Expected useful life of the asset}}$

4.7 Example: straight line depreciation

(a) A non-current asset costing $20,000 with an estimated life of 10 years and no residual value would be depreciated at the rate of:

$$\frac{\$20,000}{10 \text{ years}} = \$2,000 \text{ per annum}$$

(b) A non-current asset costing $60,000 has an estimated life of 5 years and a residual value of $7,000. The annual depreciation charge using the straight line method would be:

$$\frac{\$(60,000 - 7,000)}{5 \text{ years}} = \$10,600 \text{ per annum}$$

The carrying amount of the non-current asset would be:

	After 1 year $	After 2 years $	After 3 years $	After 4 years $	After 5 years $
Cost of the asset	60,000	60,000	60,000	60,000	60,000
Accumulated depreciation	10,600	21,200	31,800	42,400	53,000
Carrying amount	49,400	38,800	28,200	17,600	7,000*

* ie its estimated residual value

Since the depreciation charge per annum is the same amount every year with the straight line method, it is often convenient to state that depreciation is charged at the rate of x% per annum on the cost of the asset. So for example, a non-current asset costing $20,000 with an expected residual value of nil and an expected useful life of 10 years would be depreciated on a straight line basis at $20,000/10 = $2,000 per year. This is the same as saying 'the depreciation charge per annum is 10% of cost' (ie 10% of $20,000 = $2,000).

EXAM FOCUS POINT

Examination questions often describe straight line depreciation in this way.

The straight line method of depreciation is a fair allocation of the total depreciable amount between the different accounting periods, **provided that** it is reasonable to assume that the business enjoys equal benefits from the use of the asset in every period throughout its life. An example of this could be shelving (fixtures and fittings) in the accounts department.

4.8 Assets acquired part-way through an accounting period

A business can purchase new non-current assets at any time during the course of an accounting period. It is reasonable to charge an amount for depreciation only from the date that the business has owned the asset, which might be part-way through an accounting period.

4.9 Example: assets acquired part-way through an accounting period

A business which has an accounting year that runs from 1 January to 31 December purchases a new non-current asset on 1 April 20X1, at a cost of $24,000. The expected life of the asset is 4 years, and its residual value is nil. What should the depreciation charge for 20X1 be?

Solution

The annual depreciation charge will be $\dfrac{\$24,000}{4 \text{ years}} = \$6,000$ per annum

However, since the asset was acquired on 1 April 20X1, the business has only benefited from the use of the asset for 9 months instead of a full 12 months. It would therefore seem fair to charge depreciation in 20X1 of only:

$$\frac{9}{12} \times \$6,000 = \$4,500$$

EXAM FOCUS POINT

If an exam question gives you the purchase date of a non-current asset which is part-way through an accounting period, you should generally assume that depreciation should be calculated in this way as a 'part-year' amount, unless the question states otherwise.

In practice, many businesses take a simplified approach where an asset has been purchased part-way through an accounting period. Instead of calculating the depreciation from the date the asset is acquired, the business instead charges a full year's depreciation in the year it is purchased and then no depreciation in the year it is disposed of.

4.10 The reducing balance method

The **reducing balance method** of depreciation calculates the annual depreciation charge as a fixed percentage of the carrying amount of the asset, as at the end of the previous accounting period.

For example, a business purchases a non-current asset at a cost of $10,000. Its estimated residual value is $2,160. The business wishes to use the reducing balance method to depreciate the asset, and calculates that the rate of depreciation should be 40% of the reducing (carrying) amount of the asset. (The method of deciding that 40% is a suitable annual percentage is a problem of mathematics, not financial accounting, and is not described here.)

EXAM FOCUS POINT

If you are expected to use the reducing balance method in the exam, you will be given the percentage rate to apply; you will not have to calculate it.

Under the reducing balance method, unlike the straight line method, we **do not** deduct the residual value from the cost before depreciating. Instead, we depreciate the asset using the percentage given, until we reach the residual value, and then we stop depreciating, as illustrated in the table below.

	$	Accumulated depreciation $	
Asset at cost	10,000		
Depreciation in year 1 (40%)	4,000	4,000	
Carrying amount at end of year 1	6,000		
Depreciation in year 2			
(40% of reducing balance)	2,400	6,400	(4,000 + 2,400)
Carrying amount at end of year 2	3,600		
Depreciation in year 3 (40%)	1,440	7,840	(6,400 + 1,440)
Carrying amount at end of year 3	2,160 =	residual value	

EXAM FOCUS POINT

There are different ways to apply the reducing balance method when the asset has a residual value. The method we have used here is the one preferred by the ACCA examining team.

You should note that with the reducing balance method, the annual charge for depreciation is higher in the earlier years of the asset's life, and lower in the later years. In the example above, the annual charges for years 1, 2 and 3 are $4,000, $2,400 and $1,440 respectively.

The reducing balance method might therefore be used when it is considered fair to allocate a greater proportion of the total depreciable amount to the earlier years and a lower proportion to later years, on the assumption that the benefits obtained by the business from using the asset decline over time. An example of this could be machinery in a factory, where productivity falls as the machine gets older.

It is permissible for a business to depreciate different categories of non-current assets in different ways. For example, if a business owns three cars, then each car would normally be depreciated in the same way (eg by the straight line method); but another category of non-current asset, say, computer equipment, might be depreciated using a different method (eg by the reducing balance method).

QUESTION

Depreciation methods

A lorry bought for a business cost $17,000. It is expected to last for 5 years and then be sold for scrap for $2,000.

Required

Work out the depreciation to be charged each year under:

A   The straight line method   *1,7K − 2K = 15K ∴ 5/15000 = 3K*

B   The reducing balance method (using a rate of 35%)   *17K − 35% = 5950 = 11,050*
11,050 × 35% = 3868 = 7,182

ANSWER
7,182 × 35% = 2514 = 4,668

A   Under the straight line method, depreciation for each of the 5 years is: *4,668 × 35 = 1,634 = 3,034*

$$\text{Annual depreciation} = \frac{\$(17,000 - 2,000)}{5} = \$3,000$$

3,034 − 2000 = 1034

B   Under the reducing balance method, depreciation for each of the 5 years is:

Year	Depreciation	
1	35% × $17,000	= $5,950
2	35% × ($17,000 − $5,950) = 35% × $11,050	= $3,868
3	35% × ($11,050 − $3,868) = 35% × $7,182	= $2,514
4	35% × ($7,182 − $2,514) = 35% × $4,668	= $1,634
5	Balance to bring book value down to $2,000 = $4,668 − $1,634 − $2,000	= $1,034

4.11 Change in method of depreciation

It is up to the business concerned to decide which method of depreciation to apply to its non-current assets. Once that decision has been made, the chosen method of depreciation should be applied **consistently from year to year**. However, IAS 16 requires that the **depreciation method** should be reviewed **periodically**. If there has been a significant change in the expected pattern of economic benefits from those assets, the method should be changed to suit this new pattern. When such a change in depreciation method takes place, the remaining carrying amount is depreciated under the new method, ie only current and future periods are affected; the change is not retrospective.

4.12 Example: change in method of depreciation

Jakob Co purchased an asset for $100,000 on 1.1.X1. It had an estimated useful life of 5 years and it was depreciated using the reducing balance method at a rate of 40%. On 1.1.X3 it was decided to change the method to straight line.

Show the depreciation charge for each year (to 31 December) of the asset's life.

	value	Depn	Prov & Depn	NBV	
Yr 1	100K	40K	40K	60,000	100,000 × 40%
Yr 2	60,000	24K	64K	36,000	60,000 × 40%
Yr 3	36,000	12K	76K	24,000	(100,000 − 64,000)/3 = 12K
Yr 4	24,000	12K	88K	12,000	
Yr 5	12,000	12K	100K	0	

Solution

Year		Depreciation charge $	Aggregate depreciation $
20X1	$100,000 × 40%	40,000	40,000
20X2	$60,000 × 40%	24,000	64,000
20X3	$\dfrac{\$100,000 - \$64,000}{3}$	12,000	76,000
20X4		12,000	88,000
20X5		12,000	100,000

4.13 Change in expected useful life or residual value of an asset

The depreciation charge on a non-current asset depends not only on the cost (or value) of the asset and its estimated residual value but also on its **estimated useful life**.

A business purchased a non-current asset costing $12,000 with an estimated life of four years and no residual value. If it used the straight line method of depreciation, it would make an annual provision of 25% of $12,000 = $3,000.

Now what would happen if the business decided after two years that the useful life of the asset has been underestimated, and it still had five more years in use to come (making its total life seven years)?

For the first two years, the asset would have been depreciated by $3,000 per annum, so that its carrying amount after two years would be $(12,000 – 6,000) = $6,000. If the remaining life of the asset is now revised to five more years, the remaining amount to be depreciated (here $6,000) should be spread over the remaining life, giving an annual depreciation charge for the final five years of:

$$\frac{\text{Carrying amount at time of life readjustment } - \text{ residual value}}{\text{New estimate of remaining useful life}} = \frac{\$6,000}{5 \text{ years}} = \$1,200 \text{ per year}$$

FORMULA TO LEARN

$$\text{New depreciation} = \frac{\text{Carrying amount } - \text{ residual value}}{\text{Revised useful life}}$$

Similar adjustments are made when there is a change in the expected residual value of the asset. For example, assume that the residual value was changed to $500 at the same time as the remaining useful life was revised. The new depreciation would then be (6,000 – 500)/5 = $1,100 per year.

4.14 Depreciation is not a cash expense

Depreciation spreads the cost of a non-current asset (less its estimated residual value) over the asset's life. The cash payment for the non-current asset will be made when, or soon after, the asset is purchased. Annual depreciation of the asset in subsequent years is not a cash expense – rather it allocates costs to those later years for a cash payment that has occurred previously.

For example, a business purchased some shop fittings for $6,000 on 1 July 20X5 and paid for them in cash on that date.

Subsequently, depreciation may be charged at $600 every year for ten years. So each year $600 is deducted from profits and the carrying amount of the fittings goes down, but no actual cash is being paid. The cash was all paid on 1 July 20X5. So annual depreciation is not a cash expense, but rather an allocation of the original cost to later years.

QUESTION

A   What is the purpose of depreciation?

B   In what circumstances is the reducing balance method more appropriate than the straight line method? Give reasons for your answer.

ANSWER

A   The purpose of depreciation is to spread the cost of a non-current asset over its useful life in order to match the cost of the asset over the full period during which the asset consumes economic benefits for the business. Charging depreciation is an application of the accruals concept.

B   The reducing balance method of depreciation is used instead of the straight line method when it is considered fair to allocate a greater proportion of the total depreciable amount to the earlier years and a lower proportion to the later years, on the assumption that the benefits obtained by the business from using the asset decline over time.

   In favour of this method, it may be argued that it links the depreciation charge to the costs of maintaining and running the asset. In the early years these costs are low and the depreciation charge is high, while in later years this is reversed.

4.15 Ledger entries for depreciation

The ledger accounting entries for depreciation are as follows.

(a)   There is an accumulated depreciation account for each separate category of non-current assets; for example, plant and machinery, land and buildings, fixtures and fittings.

(b)   The depreciation charge for an accounting period is a charge against profit. It is accounted for as follows.

   DEBIT   Depreciation expense (statement of profit or loss)
   CREDIT   Accumulated depreciation account (statement of financial position)

   with the depreciation charge for the period.

(c)   The balance on the statement of financial position depreciation account is the total accumulated depreciation. This is always a credit balance brought forward in the ledger account for depreciation.

(d)   The non-current asset accounts are unaffected by depreciation. Non-current assets are recorded in these accounts at cost (or, if they are revalued, at their revalued amount).

(e)   In the statement of financial position of the business, the total balance on the accumulated depreciation account is set against the value of non-current asset accounts (ie non-current assets at cost or revalued amount) to derive the carrying amount of the non-current assets.

This is how the non-current asset accounts might appear in a trial balance.

	Dr	Cr
Freehold building – cost	2,000,000	
Freehold building – accumulated depreciation		500,000
Motor vehicles – cost	70,000	
Motor vehicles – accumulated depreciation		40,000
Office equipment – cost	25,000	
Office equipment – accumulated depreciation		15,000

And this is how they would be shown in the statement of financial position.

Non-current assets	$
Freehold building (2,000,000 – 500,000)	1,500,000
Motor vehicles (70,000 – 40,000)	30,000
Office equipment (25,000 – 15,000)	10,000

4.16 Example: depreciation

Brian Box set up his own computer software business on 1 March 20X6. He purchased a computer system on credit from a manufacturer, at a cost of $16,000. The system has an expected life of 3 years and a residual value of $2,500. Using the straight line method of depreciation, the non-current asset account, accumulated depreciation account and statement of profit or loss (extract) and statement of financial position (extract) would be as follows, for each of the next 3 years, 28 February 20X7, 20X8 and 20X9.

NON-CURRENT ASSET: COMPUTER EQUIPMENT

	Date		$	Date		$
(a)	1.3.X6	Accounts payable	16,000	28.2.X7	Balance c/d	16,000
(b)	1.3.X7	Balance b/d	16,000	28.2.X8	Balance c/d	16,000
(c)	1.3.X8	Balance b/d	16,000	28.2.X9	Balance c/d	16,000
(d)	1.3.X9	Balance b/d	16,000			

In theory, the non-current asset has now lasted out its expected useful life. However, until it is sold off or scrapped, the asset will still appear in the statement of financial position at cost (less accumulated depreciation) and it should remain in the ledger account for computer equipment until it is eventually disposed of.

ACCUMULATED DEPRECIATION

	Date		$	Date		$
(a)	28.2.X7	Balance c/d	4,500	28.2.X7	P/L account	4,500
(b)	28.2.X8	Balance c/d	9,000	1.3.X7	Balance b/d	4,500
				28.2.X8	P/L account	4,500
			9,000			9,000
(c)	28.2.X9	Balance c/d	13,500	1.3.X8	Balance b/d	9,000
				28.2.X9	P/L account	4,500
			13,500			13,500
				1.3.X9	Balance b/d	13,500

The annual depreciation charge is $\dfrac{\$(16{,}000 - 2{,}500)}{3 \text{ years}} = \$4{,}500 \text{ p.a.}$

At the end of the 3 years, the asset is fully depreciated down to its residual value (16,000 – 13,500 = 2,500). If it continues to be used by Brian Box, it will not be depreciated any further (unless its estimated residual value is reduced).

STATEMENT OF PROFIT OR LOSS (EXTRACT)

	Date		$
(a)	28 Feb 20X7	Depreciation	4,500
(b)	28 Feb 20X8	Depreciation	4,500
(c)	28 Feb 20X9	Depreciation	4,500

STATEMENT OF FINANCIAL POSITION (EXTRACT) AS AT 28 FEBRUARY

	20X7	20X8	20X9
	$	$	$
Computer equipment at cost	16,000	16,000	16,000
Less accumulated depreciation	4,500	9,000	13,500
Carrying amount	11,500	7,000	2,500

4.17 Example: depreciation for assets acquired part-way through the year

Brian Box prospers in his computer software business, and before long he purchases a car for himself, and later for his chief assistant Bill Ockhead. Relevant data is as follows.

	Date of purchase	Cost	Estimated life	Estimated residual value
Brian Box car	1 June 20X6	$20,000	3 years	$2,000
Bill Ockhead car	1 June 20X7	$8,000	3 years	$2,000

The straight line method of depreciation is to be used.

Prepare the motor vehicles account and motor vehicle depreciation account for the years to 28 February 20X7 and 20X8. (You should allow for the part-year's use of a car in computing the annual charge for depreciation.)

Calculate the carrying amount of the motor vehicles as at 28 February 20X8.

Solution

(a) (i) Brian Box car Annual depreciation $\dfrac{\$(20,000 - 2,000)}{3 \text{ years}} =$ $6,000 p.a.

Monthly depreciation = $500

Depreciation	1 June 20X6 – 28 February 20X7 (9 months)	$4,500
	1 March 20X7 – 28 February 20X8	$6,000

(ii) Bill Ockhead car Annual depreciation $\dfrac{\$(8,000 - 2,000)}{3 \text{ years}} =$ $2,000 p.a.

Depreciation	1 June 20X7 – 28 February 20X8 (9 months)	$1,500

(b)

MOTOR VEHICLES

Date		$	Date		$
1 Jun 20X6	Payables (or cash) (car purchase)	20,000	28 Feb 20X7	Balance c/d	20,000
1 Mar 20X7	Balance b/d	20,000			
1 Jun 20X7	Payables (or cash) (car purchase)	8,000	28 Feb 20X8	Balance c/d	28,000
		28,000			28,000
1 Mar 20X8	Balance b/d	28,000			

MOTOR VEHICLES – ACCUMULATED DEPRECIATION

Date		$	Date		$
28 Feb 20X7	Balance c/d	4,500	28 Feb 20X7	P/L account	4,500
			1 Mar 20X7	Balance b/d	4,500
28 Feb 20X8	Balance c/d	12,000	28 Feb 20X8	P/L account (6,000+1,500)	7,500
		12,000			12,000
			1 Mar 20X8	Balance b/d	12,000

STATEMENT OF FINANCIAL POSITION (WORKINGS) AS AT 28 FEBRUARY 20X8

	Brian Box car		Bill Ockhead car		Total
	$	$	$	$	$
Asset at cost		20,000		8,000	28,000
Accumulated depreciation					
Year to 28 Feb 20X7	4,500		–		
Year to 28 Feb 20X8	6,000		1,500		
		10,500		1,500	12,000
Carrying amount		9,500		6,500	16,000

5 Revaluation of non-current assets

IAS 16 allows entities to **revalue** non-current assets to fair value.

When a non-current asset is **revalued**, depreciation is charged on the **revalued amount**.

Largely because of inflation, it is now quite common for the market value of certain non-current assets to **go up, in spite of getting older**. The most obvious example of rising market values is land and buildings.

IAS 16 allows entities to choose between keeping an asset recorded at cost or revaluing it to **fair value**. An entity may decide that in order to give a fairer view of the position of the business, some non-current assets should be revalued, otherwise the total value of the assets of the business might seem unrealistically low.

IAS 16 requires that when an item of property, plant and equipment is revalued, **the whole class of assets to which it belongs should be revalued**. A 'class' of assets is simply a group of assets of similar nature and use – eg land and buildings, machinery, motor vehicles, fixtures and fittings. All the items within a class should be revalued at the same time to prevent selective revaluation of certain assets and to avoid disclosing a mixture of costs and values from different dates in the financial statements.

When non-current assets are revalued, depreciation should be charged on the **revalued amount**.

5.1 Example: the revaluation of non-current assets

When Ira Vann commenced trading as a car hire dealer on 1 January 20X1, he purchased business premises at a cost of $50,000.

For the purpose of accounting for depreciation, he decided the following.

(a) The land part of the business premises was worth $20,000; this would not be depreciated.

(b) The building part of the business premises was worth the remaining $30,000. This would be depreciated by the straight line method to a nil residual value over 30 years.

After 5 years of trading, on 1 January 20X6 Ira decides that his business premises are now worth $150,000, divided into:

	$
Land	75,000
Building	75,000
	150,000

He estimates that the building still has a further 25 years' useful life remaining.

Required

(a) Calculate the annual charge for depreciation for the first five years of the building's life and the statement of financial position value of the land and building as at the end of each of the first five years.

(b) Demonstrate the impact the revaluation will have on the depreciation charge and the statement of financial position value of the land and building.

Solution

(a) **Before the revaluation**, the annual depreciation charge is $1,000 per annum on the building. This charge is made in each of the first five years of the asset's life.

The carrying amount of the asset will decline by $1,000 per annum, to:

(i) $49,000 as at 31.12.X1
(ii) $48,000 as at 31.12.X2
(iii) $47,000 as at 31.12.X3
(iv) $46,000 as at 31.12.X4
(v) $45,000 as at 31.12.X5

(b) **When the revaluation takes place**, the amount of the revaluation is:

	$
New asset value (to be shown in statement of financial position)	150,000
Carrying amount as at end of 20X5 ($20,000 + ($30,000 – $5,000))	45,000
Amount of revaluation	105,000

The asset will be revalued by $105,000 to $150,000. If you remember the accounting equation, that the total value of assets must be equalled by the total value of capital and liabilities, you should recognise that if assets go up in value by $105,000, capital or liabilities must also go up by the same amount. Since the increased value benefits the owners of the business, the amount of the revaluation is **added to capital**.

However, the gain on revaluation cannot go to the statement of profit or loss, as it has not been realised. Instead, it is recognised in the **statement of profit or loss and other comprehensive income**, as **other comprehensive income**. From here, the 'gain' is transferred to a **revaluation surplus** (sometimes called a revaluation reserve), part of **capital** in the **statement of financial position**.

This treatment may surprise you at first. However, a profit cannot be anticipated before it is realised. Therefore the 'profit' cannot be dealt with as income in the statement of profit or loss. **If the building were to be subsequently sold for the revalued amount, the profit would be realised and could be taken to the statement of profit or loss**.

After the revaluation, depreciation will be charged on the building at a new rate of:

$$\frac{\text{Revalued amount}}{\text{Remaining useful life}} = \frac{\$75,000}{25 \text{ years}} = \$3,000 \text{ per year}$$

The carrying amount of the property will then be reduced by $3,000 per year over the remaining useful life of 25 years.

One consequence of a revaluation is therefore a higher annual depreciation charge.

5.2 Accounting entries

The accounting treatment for the revaluation above will be:

DEBIT	Building	– cost ($75,000 – $30,000)	$45,000	
	Building	– accumulated depreciation	$5,000	
	Land	– cost ($75,000 – $20,000)	$55,000	
CREDIT	Revaluation surplus			$105,000

The effect of these entries is as follows.

BUILDING – COST OR VALUATION

	$		$
Balance b/d	30,000	Balance c/d	75,000
Revaluation surplus	45,000		
	75,000		75,000

BUILDING – ACCUMULATED DEPRECIATION

	$		$
Revaluation surplus	5,000	Balance b/d	5,000
Balance c/d	–		
	5,000		5,000

LAND – COST

	$		$
Balance b/d	20,000	Balance c/d	75,000
Revaluation surplus	55,000		
	75,000		75,000

REVALUATION SURPLUS

	$		$
Balance c/d	105,000	Building – cost	45,000
		Building – acc depreciation	5,000
		Land – cost	55,000
	105,000		105,000

5.3 Excess depreciation

As we saw above, the consequence of the revaluation is a higher annual depreciation charge. The difference between the new depreciation charge based on the revalued carrying amount and the old depreciation charge based on the original cost of the asset is known as the '**excess depreciation**'. IAS 16 allows entities to transfer an amount equal to the excess depreciation from the revaluation surplus to retained earnings in the equity section of the statement of financial position, **if they wish to do so**.

Applying this to the example above gives the following.

$$\text{Old depreciation} = \frac{\$30,000}{30 \text{ years}} = \$1,000 \text{ per year}$$

$$\text{New depreciation} = \frac{\$75,000}{25 \text{ years}} = \$3,000 \text{ per year}$$

Excess depreciation = $3,000 – $1,000 = $2,000

An amount of $2,000, representing the excess depreciation, can be transferred each year from the revaluation surplus to retained earnings.

The accounting entries to record the depreciation charge each year would therefore be as follows.

DEBIT	Depreciation expense (statement of profit or loss)	$3,000	
CREDIT	Accumulated depreciation account (statement of financial position)		$3,000
	To record the new annual depreciation charge		

DEBIT	Revaluation surplus (statement of financial position)	$2,000	
CREDIT	Retained earnings (statement of financial position)		$2,000
	To record the transfer of the excess depreciation		

This transfer between the revaluation surplus to retained earnings is shown in the financial statements in the **statement of changes in equity**. The statement of changes in equity is covered in Chapter 20 where we take a look at financial statements for companies.

5.4 Revaluation downwards

After some years, it may become apparent that the building is overvalued and needs to be revalued downwards.

Carrying on the example from above, the carrying amount of the building five years after the revaluation to $75,000 is $75,000 – ($3,000 × 5) = $60,000. However, the market value of building has fallen to $40,000. (In order to make the double entry clear in this example, we will assume that the entity **does not** transfer the excess depreciation from the revaluation surplus to retained earnings.)

The accounting treatment for the downward revaluation is:

DEBIT	Revaluation surplus	$20,000
	Buildings – accumulated depreciation	$15,000
CREDIT	Buildings – cost ($75,000 – $40,000)	$35,000

The effect of these entries is as follows.

BUILDING – COST OR VALUATION

	$		$
Balance b/d	75,000	Revaluation surplus	35,000
		Balance c/d	40,000
	75,000		75,000

BUILDING – ACCUMULATED DEPRECIATION

	$		$
Revaluation surplus	15,000	Balance b/d (5 × $3,000)	15,000

LAND – COST OR VALUATION

	$		$
Balance b/d	75,000	Balance c/d	75,000

REVALUATION SURPLUS

	$		$
Cost	35,000	Balance b/d	105,000
Balance c/d	85,000	Accumulated depreciation	15,000
	120,000		120,000

6 Non-current asset disposals

> When a non-current asset is **sold**, there is likely to be a **profit or loss on disposal**. This is the difference between the net sale price of the asset and its carrying amount at the time of disposal.

6.1 The disposal of non-current assets

Non-current assets are not purchased by a business with the intention of reselling them in the normal course of trade. However, they might be sold off at some stage during their life, either when their useful life is over or before then. A business might decide to sell off a non-current asset long before its useful life has ended.

Whenever a business sells something, it will make a profit or a loss. When non-current assets are disposed of, there will be a profit or loss on disposal. As it is a capital item being sold, the profit or loss will be a capital gain or a capital loss. These gains or losses are reported in the income and expenses part of the statement of profit or loss of the business, after gross profit. They are commonly referred to as '**profit on disposal of non-current assets**' or '**loss on disposal**'.

Examination questions on the disposal of non-current assets are likely to ask for ledger accounts to be prepared, showing the entries in the accounts to record the disposal. But before we look at the ledger accounting for disposing of assets, we had better look at the principles behind calculating the profit (or loss) on disposing of assets.

6.2 The principles behind calculating the profit or loss on disposal

The profit or loss on the disposal of a non-current asset is the difference between (a) and (b) below.

(a)   The carrying amount of the asset at the time of its sale
(b)   Its net sale price, which is the price minus any costs of making the sale

A profit is made when the sale price exceeds the carrying amount, and a loss is made when the sale price is less than the carrying amount.

6.3 Example: disposal of a non-current asset

A business purchased a non-current asset on 1 January 20X1 for $25,000. It had an estimated life of 6 years and an estimated residual value of $7,000. The asset was eventually sold after 3 years on 1 January 20X4 to another trader who paid $17,500 for it.

What was the profit or loss on disposal, assuming that the business uses the straight line method for depreciation?

Solution

$$\text{Annual depreciation} = \frac{\$(25,000 - 7,000)}{6 \text{ years}} = \$3,000 \text{ per annum}$$

	$
Cost of asset	25,000
Less accumulated depreciation (three years)	9,000
Carrying amount at date of disposal	16,000
Sale price	17,500
Profit on disposal	1,500

This profit will be shown in the statement of profit or loss of the business where it will be an item of other income, below gross profit.

6.4 Example 2: disposal of a non-current asset

A business purchased a machine on 1 July 20X1 at a cost of $35,000. The machine had an estimated residual value of $3,000 and a life of 8 years. The machine was sold for $18,600 on 31 December 20X4, the last day of the accounting year of the business. To make the sale, the business had to incur dismantling costs and costs of transporting the machine to the buyer's premises. These amounted to $1,200.

The business uses the straight line method of depreciation. What was the profit or loss on disposal of the machine?

Solution

Annual depreciation $\dfrac{\$(35,000 - 3,000)}{8 \text{ years}}$ = $4,000 per annum

It is assumed that in 20X1 only six months' depreciation was charged, because the asset was purchased six months into the year.

	$	$
Non-current asset at cost		35,000
Depreciation in 20X1 (½ year)	2,000	
20X2, 20X3 and 20X4	12,000	
Accumulated depreciation		14,000
Carrying amount at date of disposal		21,000
Sale price	18,600	
Costs incurred in making the sale	(1,200)	
Net sale price		17,400
Loss on disposal		(3,600)

This loss will be shown as an expense in the statement of profit or loss of the business, below gross profit.

6.5 The disposal of non-current assets: ledger accounting entries

We have already seen how the profit or loss on disposal of a non-current asset should be computed. A profit on disposal is an item of 'other income' in the statement of profit or loss, and a loss on disposal is an item of expense in the statement of profit or loss.

It is customary in ledger accounting to record the disposal of non-current assets in a **disposal of non-current assets account**.

(a) The profit or loss on disposal is the difference between:

   (i)   The sale price of the asset (if any); and
   (ii) The carrying amount of the asset at the time of sale.

(b) The following items must appear in the disposal of non-current assets account.

   (i)   The value of the asset (at cost, or revalued amount*)
   (ii)   The accumulated depreciation up to the date of sale
   (iii) The sale price of the asset

   * To simplify the explanation of the rules, we will assume now that the non-current assets disposed of are valued at cost.

(c) The ledger accounting entries are as follows.

   (i)   DEBIT   Disposal of non-current asset account
          CREDIT   Non-current asset account

   with the cost of the asset disposed of.

   (ii)   DEBIT   Accumulated depreciation account
          CREDIT   Disposal of non-current asset account

   with the accumulated depreciation on the asset as at the date of sale.

   (iii) DEBIT   Receivable account or cash book
          CREDIT   Disposal of non-current asset account

   with the sale price of the asset. The sale is therefore not recorded in a sales account, but in the disposal of non-current asset account itself. You will notice that the effect of these entries is to remove the asset, and its accumulated depreciation, from the statement of financial position.

   The balance on the disposal account is the profit or loss on disposal and the corresponding double entry is recorded in the profit or loss account.

6.6 Example: disposal of assets: ledger accounting entries

A business includes $110,000 worth of machinery at cost in its accounts. Its policy is to make a provision for depreciation at 20% per annum straight line. The total provision now stands at $70,000. The business sells for $19,000 a machine which it purchased exactly 2 years ago for $30,000.

Show the relevant ledger entries.

Solution

PLANT AND MACHINERY ACCOUNT

	$		$
Balance b/d	110,000	Plant and machinery disposals a/c	30,000
		Balance c/d	80,000
	110,000		110,000
Balance b/d	80,000		

PLANT AND MACHINERY ACCUMULATED DEPRECIATION

	$		$
Plant and machinery disposals (20% of $30,000 for 2 years)	12,000	Balance b/d	70,000
Balance c/d	58,000		
	70,000		70,000
		Balance b/d	58,000

PLANT AND MACHINERY DISPOSALS

	$		$
Plant and machinery account	30,000	Accumulated depreciation	12,000
P/L a/c (profit on sale)	1,000	Cash	19,000
	31,000		31,000

Check

	$
Asset at cost	30,000
Accumulated depreciation at time of sale	12,000
Carrying amount at time of sale	18,000
Sale price	19,000
Profit on sale	1,000

6.7 Example continued: part exchange

Exchange or part exchange of assets occurs frequently for items of property, plant and equipment. IAS 16 states that the cost of an item obtained through (part) exchange is the **fair value of the asset received (unless this cannot be measured reliably).**

Taking the example above assume that, instead of the machine being sold for $19,000, it was exchanged for a new machine costing $60,000, a credit of $19,000 being received upon exchange. In other words, $19,000 is the trade-in price of the old machine. Now what are the relevant ledger account entries?

Solution

PLANT AND MACHINERY ACCOUNT

	$		$
Balance b/d	110,000	Plant disposal	30,000
Cash $(60,000 − 19,000)	41,000	Balance c/d	140,000
Plant disposals	19,000		
	170,000		170,000
Balance b/d	140,000		

The new asset is recorded in the non-current asset account at cost $(41,000 + 19,000) = $60,000.

PLANT AND MACHINERY ACCUMULATED DEPRECIATION

	$		$
Plant disposals (20% of $30,000 for 2 years)	12,000	Balance b/d	70,000
Balance c/d	58,000		
	70,000		70,000
		Balance b/d	58,000

PLANT AND MACHINERY DISPOSALS

	$		$
Plant and machinery	30,000	Accumulated depreciation	12,000
P/L a/c (profit on disposal)	1,000	Plant and machinery part exchange	19,000
	31,000		31,000

QUESTION
Non-current asset ledger accounts

A business purchased two rivet-making machines on 1 January 20X5 at a cost of $15,000 each. Each had an estimated life of five years and a nil residual value. The straight line method of depreciation is used.

Owing to an unforeseen slump in market demand for rivets, the business decided to reduce its output of rivets, and switch to making other products instead. On 31 March 20X7, one rivet-making machine was sold (on credit) to a buyer for $8,000.

Later in the year, however, it was decided to abandon production of rivets altogether, and the second machine was sold on 1 December 20X7 for $2,500 cash.

Prepare the machinery account, depreciation of machinery account and disposal of machinery account for the accounting year to 31 December 20X7.

ANSWER

MACHINERY ACCOUNT

20X7		$	20X7		$
1 Jan	Balance b/d	30,000	31 Mar	Disposal of machinery account	15,000
			1 Dec	Disposal of machinery account	15,000
		30,000			30,000

MACHINERY – ACCUMULATED DEPRECIATION

20X7		$	20X7		$
31 Mar	Disposal of machinery account*	6,750	1 Jan	Balance b/d	12,000
1 Dec	Disposal of machinery account**	8,750	31 Dec	P/L account***	3,500
		15,500			15,500

* Depreciation at date of disposal = $6,000 + $750
** Depreciation at date of disposal = $6,000 + $2,750
*** Depreciation charge for the year = $750 + $2,750

DISPOSAL OF MACHINERY

20X7		$	20X7			$
31 Mar	Machinery account	15,000	31 Mar	Account receivable (sale price)		8,000
			31 Mar	Accumulated depreciation		6,750
1 Dec	Machinery	15,000	1 Dec	Cash (sale price)		2,500
			1 Dec	Accumulated depreciation		8,750
			31 Dec	P/L a/c (loss on disposal)		4,000
		30,000				30,000

You should be able to calculate that there was a loss on the first disposal of $250, and on the second disposal of $3,750, giving a total loss of $4,000.

Workings

1   At 1 January 20X7, accumulated depreciation on the machines will be:

$$2 \text{ machines} \times 2 \text{ years} \times \frac{\$15,000}{5} \text{ per machine p.a.} = \$12,000, \text{ or } \$6,000 \text{ per machine}$$

2   Monthly depreciation is $\dfrac{\$3,000}{12}$ = $250 per machine per month

3   The machines are disposed of in 20X7

    (a)   On 31 March – after 3 months of the year
            Depreciation for the year on the machine = 3 months × $250 = $750

    (b)   On 1 December – after 11 months of the year
            Depreciation for the year on the machine = 11 months × $250 = $2,750

6.8 Example: disposal of a revalued asset

Returning to the case of the revalued asset in Section 5, suppose that two years after the revaluation to $150,000 the land and building are sold for $200,000. (Assume that the entity **does not** transfer the excess depreciation from the revaluation surplus to retained earnings.) What is the profit on disposal?

BUILDING – COST

	$		$
Balance b/d	75,000	Disposal account	75,000

BUILDING – ACCUMULATED DEPRECIATION

	$		$
Disposal account	6,000	Balance b/d ($3,000 × 2)	6,000

LAND – COST

	$		$
Balance b/d	75,000	Disposal account	75,000

REVALUATION SURPLUS

	$		$
Disposal account	105,000	Balance b/d	105,000

DISPOSAL ACCOUNT

	$		$
Building – cost	75,000	Cash	200,000
Land – cost	75,000	Building – acc dep'n	6,000
a/c (profit on disposal)	161,000	Revaluation surplus	105,000
	311,000		311,000

Ignoring the revaluation:

	$
Original cost of building	30,000
Original cost of land	20,000
	50,000
Depreciation ($5,000 + $6,000)	(11,000)
Carrying amount	39,000
Sale proceeds	200,000
Profit on sale	161,000

7 Disclosure in financial statements

IAS 16 requires a reconciliation of the opening and closing carrying amounts of non-current assets to be given in the financial statements.

The disclosure requirements in IAS 16 are extensive and include both numerical and narrative disclosures.

The financial statements should show a reconciliation of the carrying amount of non-current assets at the beginning and end of the period. The reconciliation should show the movement on the non-current asset balance and include the following.

- Additions
- Disposals
- Increases/decreases from revaluations
- Reductions in carrying amount
- Depreciation
- Any other movements

The following format is commonly used.

PROPERTY, PLANT AND EQUIPMENT NOTE

	Total $	Land and buildings $	Plant and equipment $
Cost or valuation			
At 1 January 20X4	50,000	40,000	10,000
Revaluation surplus	12,000	12,000	–
Additions in year	4,000	–	4,000
Disposals in year	(1,000)	–	(1,000)
At 31 December 20X4	65,000	52,000	13,000
Depreciation			
At 1 January 20X4	16,000	10,000	6,000
Charge for year	4,000	1,000	3,000
Eliminated on disposals	(500)	–	(500)
At 31 December 20X4	19,500	11,000	8,500
Carrying amount			
At 31 December 20X4	45,500	41,000	4,500
At 1 January 20X4	34,000	30,000	4,000

As well as the reconciliation above, the financial statements should disclose the following.

(a) An accounting policy note should disclose the **measurement bases** used for determining the amounts at which depreciable assets are stated, along with the other accounting policies.

(b) For each class of **property, plant and equipment**:

- Depreciation methods used
- Useful lives or the depreciation rates used

- Total depreciation allocated for the period

- Gross amount of depreciable assets and the related accumulated depreciation at the beginning and end of the period

(c) For **revalued** assets:

- **Basis** used to revalue the assets

- **Effective date** of the revaluation

- Whether an **independent valuer** was involved

- **Carrying amount** of each class of property, plant and equipment that would have been included in the financial statements had the assets been carried at cost less depreciation

- **Revaluation surplus**, indicating the movement for the period and any restrictions on the distribution of the balance to shareholders.

EXAM FOCUS POINT

Disclosure notes can and will be tested. You need to learn the disclosures required here.

QUESTION

Carrying amount

A In a statement of financial position prepared in accordance with IAS 16, what does the carrying amount represent?

B In a set of financial statements prepared in accordance with IAS 16, is it correct to say that the carrying amount figure in a statement of financial position cannot be greater than the market (net realisable) value of the partially used asset as at the reporting date? Explain your reasons for your answer.

ANSWER

A In simple terms, the carrying amount of an asset is the cost of an asset less the 'accumulated depreciation'; that is, all depreciation charged so far. It should be emphasised that the main purpose of charging depreciation is to ensure that profits are fairly reported. Thus depreciation is concerned with the statement of profit or loss rather than the statement of financial position. In consequence, the carrying amount figure in the statement of financial position can be quite arbitrary. In particular, it does not necessarily bear any relation to the market value of an asset and is of little use for planning and decision making.

An obvious example of the disparity between carrying amount and market value is found in the case of buildings, which may be worth more than ten times as much as their carrying amount.

B Carrying amount can in some circumstances be higher than market value (net realisable value). IAS 16 *Property, plant and equipment* states that the value of an asset cannot be greater than its 'recoverable amount'. However, 'recoverable amount' as defined in IAS 16 is the amount recoverable from further use. This may be higher than the market value.

This makes sense if you think of a specialised machine which could not fetch much on the secondhand market but which will produce goods which can be sold at a profit for many years.

8 The asset register

> An **asset register** is used to record all non-current assets and is an **internal check** on the accuracy of the nominal ledger.

The asset register lists out all the details of each non-current asset that is owned by the business. Most businesses will keep an asset register.

8.1 Data kept in an asset register

Data kept in an asset register about each non-current asset usually include the following.

- The internal reference number (for physical identification purposes)
- Manufacturer's serial number (for maintenance purposes)
- Description of asset
- Location of asset
- Department which 'owns' asset
- Purchase date (for calculation of depreciation)
- Cost
- Depreciation method and estimated useful life (for calculation of depreciation)
- Carrying amount

8.2 Purpose and function of an asset register

The asset register is separate from the nominal ledger and contains much more detail about the assets owned by the business. Its main use is as an internal control, to make sure that the information about non-current assets reported in the nominal ledger (and therefore the financial statements) is accurate and correct.

The asset register can be used as an internal control by regularly reconciling the net carrying amounts of all the assets on the asset register with the net carrying amount of non-current assets recorded in the nominal ledger. This can be done as follows.

	$
Assets at cost (from the non-current asset cost ledger account)	X
Accumulated depreciation (from the ledger account)	(X)
Total of carrying amounts listed in the asset register	X

Any difference should be investigated and corrected. Differences usually arise from computational errors or from items being taken out of the asset register with no equivalent change being made in the ledger accounts, or vice versa, for instance because:

- Assets have been stolen, damaged or scrapped (for nil proceeds)
- Assets are obsolete
- There are new assets, not yet recorded in the register
- There have been enhancements not yet recorded in the register
- There are errors in the register

Periodically, all physical non-current assets should be checked to the current register. This helps to deter theft and ensures that all items are accounted for.

9 Worked example

You have already had practice at preparing a statement of profit or loss and statement of financial position from a simple trial balance. Now see if you can do the same thing but at a more advanced level, taking account of adjustments for depreciation and inventory. Have a go at the following question.

QUESTION

The following list of account balances was extracted from the ledger of Roger Jones, a sole trader, as at 31 May 20X1, the end of his financial year.

ROGER JONES
TRIAL BALANCE AS AT 31 MAY 20X1

	Dr	Cr
	$	$
Property, at cost	120,000	
Equipment, at cost	80,000	
Accumulated depreciation (as at 1 June 20X0)		
on property		20,000
on equipment		38,000
Purchases	250,000	
Sales		402,200
Inventory, as at 1 June 20X0	50,000	
Returns out (purchase returns)		15,000
Wages and salaries	58,800	
Selling expenses	22,600	
Loan interest	5,100	
Other operating expenses	17,700	
Trade accounts payable		36,000
Trade accounts receivable	38,000	
Cash in hand	300	
Bank	1,300	
Drawings	24,000	
17% long-term loan		30,000
Capital, as at 1 June 20X0		126,600
	667,800	667,800

The following additional information as at 31 May 20X1 is available.

(a)   Inventory as at the close of business has been valued at cost at $42,000.

(b)   Depreciation for the year ended 31 May 20X1 has still to be charged as follows.

Property: 1.5% per annum using the straight line method

Equipment: 25% per annum using the reducing balance method

Required

Prepare Roger Jones's statement of profit or loss for the year ended 31 May 20X1 and his statement of financial position as at that date.

ANSWER

ROGER JONES
STATEMENT OF PROFIT OR LOSS FOR THE YEAR ENDED 31 MAY 20X1

	$	$
Revenue		402,200
Cost of sales		
Opening inventory	50,000	
Purchases	250,000	
Purchases returns	(15,000)	
	285,000	
Closing inventory	42,000	
		243,000
Gross profit		159,200

	$	$
Expenses		
Wages and salaries	58,800	
Selling expenses	22,600	
Loan interest	5,100	
Depreciation (W1)	12,300	
Other operating expenses	17,700	
		116,500
Profit for the year		42,700

ROGER JONES
STATEMENT OF FINANCIAL POSITION AS AT 31 MAY 20X1

	$	$
Assets		
Non-current assets		
Property: cost	120,000	
accumulated depreciation (W1)	21,800	
		98,200
Equipment: cost	80,000	
accumulated depreciation (W1)	48,500	
		31,500
Current assets		
Inventory	42,000	
Trade accounts receivable	38,000	
Bank	1,300	
Cash in hand	300	
		81,600
Total assets		211,300
Capital and liabilities		
Capital		
Balance at 1 June 20X0	126,600	
Profit for the year	42,700	
Drawings	(24,000)	
Balance at 31 May 20X1		145,300
Non-current liabilities		
17% loan		30,000
Current liabilities		
Trade accounts payable		36,000
Total capital and liabilities		211,300

Working

1	Depreciation	
	Property	$
	Opening balance	20,000
	Charge for the year (1.5% × 120,000)	1,800
	Closing balance	21,800
	Equipment	
	Opening balance	38,000
	Charge for the year (25% × (80,000 – 38,000))	10,500
	Closing balance	48,500
	Depreciation charge in statement of profit or loss (1,800 + 10,500)	12,300

EXAM FOCUS POINT

There are a number of articles on property, plant and equipment in the Paper F7 exam resources section of the ACCA website. Although these articles were written for Paper F7, they are relevant to

CHAPTER ROUNDUP

⤷ **Non-current assets** are assets which are bought by the business for **continuing use**. **Tangible non-current assets** are those with **physical form**.

⤷ **Capital expenditure** is expenditure which forms part of the cost **of non-current assets**. **Revenue expenditure** is expenditure incurred for the **purpose of the trade** or to **maintain non current assets**.

⤷ The accounting treatment of tangible non-current assets is covered by IAS 16 *Property, plant and equipment*.

⤷ The **cost** of a non-current asset, less its **estimated residual value**, is allocated fairly between accounting periods by means of **depreciation**. Depreciation is both of the following.

–   Charged against profit
–   Deducted from the value of the non-current asset in the statement of financial position

⤷ Two methods of depreciation are specified in your syllabus.

–   The straight line method
–   The reducing balance method

⤷ IAS 16 allows entities to **revalue** non-current assets to fair value.

⤷ When a non-current asset is **revalued**, depreciation is charged on the **revalued amount**.

⤷ When a non-current asset is **sold**, there is likely to be a **profit or loss on disposal**. This is the difference between the net sale price of the asset and its carrying amount at the time of disposal.

⤷ IAS 16 requires a reconciliation of the opening and closing carrying amounts of non-current assets to be given in the financial statements.

⤷ An **asset register** is used to record all non-current assets and is an **internal check** on the accuracy of the nominal ledger.

1   Which of the following statements regarding non-current asset accounting is correct?

    A   All non-current assets should be revalued each year.

    B   Non-current assets may be revalued at the discretion of management. Once revaluation has occurred it must be repeated regularly for all non-current assets in a class.

    C   Management can choose which non-current assets in a class of non-current assets should be revalued.

    D   Non-current assets should only be revalued to reflect rising prices.

2   Which of the following statements regarding depreciation is correct?

    A   All non-current assets must be depreciated.

    B   Straight line depreciation is usually the most appropriate method of depreciation.

    C   A change in the chosen depreciation method is accounted for retrospectively, with all previous depreciation charges reversed and recalculated.

    D   Depreciation charges must be based on the carrying amount of an asset (less residual value if appropriate).

3   What is an asset's carrying amount?

    A   Its cost less annual depreciation
    B   Its cost less accumulated depreciation
    C   Its net realisable value
    D   Its replacement value

4   Give two common depreciation methods.

5   A non-current asset (cost $10,000, depreciation $7,500) is given in part exchange for a new asset costing $20,500. The agreed trade-in value was $3,500. Which of the following will the statement of profit or loss include?

    A   A loss on disposal $1,000
    B   A profit on disposal $1,000
    C   A loss on purchase of a new asset $3,500
    D   A profit on disposal $3,500

6   What details about a non-current asset might be included in an asset register?

7   Why might the asset register not reconcile with the non-current assets?

    A   Asset stolen or damaged
    B   New asset, not yet recorded in the register
    C   Errors in the register
    D   All of the above

ANSWERS TO QUICK QUIZ

1	B	Correct
	A	Non-current assets may be revalued, there is no requirement to do so in IAS 16
	C	Incorrect, all non-current assets in a class must be revalued
	D	Incorrect, non-current assets may be reduced in value as well as being increased
2	D	Correct
	A	Incorrect, some non-current assets are not depreciated eg land
	B	Incorrect, management should choose the most appropriate method
	C	Incorrect, a method change should be accounted for prospectively, not retrospectively, previous depreciation charges are not recalculated
3	B	Its cost less accumulated depreciation
4		Straight line and reducing balance

5   B

	$
Carrying amount at disposal (10,000 – 7,500)	2,500
Trade-in allowance	3,500
Profit	1,000

6
- Date of purchase
- Description
- Original cost
- Depreciation rate and method
- Accumulated depreciation to date
- Date and amount of any revaluation

7   D   Other reasons include an asset that is obsolete and so scrapped or improvements not yet recorded in the register.

Now try ...

Attempt the questions below from the **Practice Question Bank**

Number

Qs 34 - 39

CHAPTER

09

Intangible non-current assets

Intangible non-current assets are long-term assets that have a value to the business because they have been paid for, but which do not have any physical substance. The most significant of such intangible assets are research and deferred development costs.

In many companies, especially those which produce food or 'scientific' products, such as medicines and 'high technology' products, the expenditure on **research and development (R&D)** is considerable. When R&D is a large item of cost its accounting treatment may have a significant influence on the profits of a business and its statement of financial position valuation. Because of this, attempts have been made to standardise the treatment, and these are discussed in this chapter.

TOPIC LIST	SYLLABUS REFERENCE
1 Intangible assets	D6(a),(b)
2 Research and development costs	D6(c)–(f)
3 Disclosure in financial statements	F3(b)

Study Guide	Intellectual level
D **Recording transactions and events**	
6 **Intangible non-current assets and amortisation**	
(a) Recognise the difference between tangible and intangible non-current assets.	K
(b) Identify types of intangible assets.	K
(c) Identify the definition and treatment of 'research costs' and 'development costs' in accordance with IFRSs.	K
(d) Calculate amounts to be capitalised as development expenditure or to be expensed from given information.	S
(e) Explain the purpose of amortisation.	K
(f) Calculate and account for the charge for amortisation.	S
F **Preparing basic financial statements**	
3 **Disclosure notes**	
(b) Draft the following disclosure notes.	S
(i) Non-current assets including tangible and intangible assets	

EXAM FOCUS POINT

The ACCA examining team has highlighted intangible non-current assets as one of the areas that consistently causes problems for students.

1 Intangible assets

Intangible assets are non-current assets with no **physical substance**.

1.1 Intangible assets

'Intangible assets' means assets that literally cannot be touched, as opposed to tangible assets (such as plant and machinery) which have a physical existence. Intangible assets include goodwill (which we will meet in Chapter 24 on consolidated financial statements), intellectual rights (eg patents, performing rights and authorship rights), and research and development costs.

1.2 Accounting treatment

In accordance with IAS 38, intangible assets are capitalised in the accounts and amortised (another word for depreciation but referring specifically to intangible assets). Amortisation is intended to write off the asset over its useful life (under the accruals concept).

1.3 Example: patent

A business buys a patent for $50,000. It expects to use the patent for the next ten years, after which it will be valueless. Amortisation is calculated in the same way as for tangible assets:

$$\frac{\text{Cost} - \text{residual value}}{\text{Estimated useful life}}$$

In this case, amortisation will be $5,000 per annum (50,000/10).

The double entry treatment is similar to that for depreciation. The entries for the amortisation calculated above will be:

DEBIT   Amortisation account (statement of profit or loss) $5,000
CREDIT   Accumulated amortisation account (statement of financial position) $5,000

2 Research and development costs

Expenditure on **research** must always be written off in the period in which it is incurred.

If the criteria laid down by IAS 38 are satisfied, development expenditure must be capitalised as an **intangible asset**. If it has a **finite useful life**, it should then be amortised over that life. If the criteria in IAS 38 are not satisfied, development expenditure must be written off in the period in which it is incurred.

2.1 Introduction to research and development (R&D)

Large companies may spend significant amounts of money on research and development (R&D) activities. Obviously, any amounts so expended must be credited to cash and debited to an account for research and development expenditure. The accounting problem is **how to treat the debit balance on the R&D account** at the reporting date.

There are two possibilities.

(a)   The debit balance may be classified as an **expense** and transferred to the statement of profit or loss. This is referred to as 'writing off' the expenditure. The argument here is that it is an expense just like rent or wages and its accounting treatment should be the same.

(b)   The debit balance may be classified as an **asset** and included in the statement of financial position. This is referred to as 'capitalising' or 'carrying forward' or 'deferring' the expenditure. This argument is based on the accrual assumption. The costs should be carried forward and written off to reflect the pattern of economic benefits consumed by the asset.

So the main question surrounding research and development (R&D) costs is whether they should be treated as an expense or capitalised as an asset. This question is dealt with in IAS 38 *Intangible assets*.

2.2 Definitions

The following definitions are given by IAS 38.

- An intangible asset is an identifiable non-monetary asset without physical substance. The asset must be:

    - Controlled by the entity as a result of events in the past
    - Something from which the entity expects future economic benefits to flow

- Research is original and planned investigation undertaken with the prospect of gaining new scientific or technical knowledge and understanding.

- Development is the application of research findings or other knowledge to a plan or design for the production of new or substantially improved materials, devices, products, processes, systems or services prior to the commencement of commercial production or use.

- **Amortisation** is the systematic allocation of the depreciable amount of an intangible asset over its useful life. Amortisation period and amortisation method should be reviewed at each financial year end.

- **Depreciable amount** is the cost of an asset, or other amount substituted for cost, less its residual value.

- **Useful life** is:

  (a) The period over which an asset is expected to be available for use by an entity; or

  (b) The number of production or similar units expected to be obtained from the asset by an entity.
  (IAS 38)

Although these definitions are usually well understood, **in practice** it may not be so easy to identify the activities encompassed by R&D and the dividing line between the categories may be indistinct. Identification often depends on the type of business involved, the projects it undertakes and how it is organised.

The standard gives examples of activities which might be included in either research or development, or which are neither but may be closely associated with both.

- **Research**

  - Activities aimed at obtaining new knowledge
  - The search for applications of research findings or other knowledge
  - The search for product or process alternatives
  - The formulation and design of possible new or improved product or process alternatives

- **Development**

  - The design, construction and testing of pre-production prototypes and models

  - The design of tools, jigs, moulds and dies involving new technology

  - The design, construction and operation of a pilot plant that is not of a scale economically feasible for commercial production

  - The design, construction and testing of a chosen alternative for new/improved materials

2.3 Components of R&D costs

R&D costs will include all costs that are **directly attributable** to R&D activities, or that can be **allocated on a reasonable basis**.

The standard lists the costs which may be included in R&D, where applicable (note that **selling costs are excluded**).

- **Salaries, wages** and other employment-related costs of personnel engaged in R&D activities

- Costs of **materials and services** consumed in R&D activities

- **Depreciation** of property, plant and equipment to the extent that these assets are used for R&D activities

- **Overhead costs**, other than general administrative costs, related to R&D activities; these costs are allocated on bases similar to those used in allocating overhead costs to inventories (see IAS 2 *Inventories*)

- **Other costs**, such as the amortisation of patents and licences, to the extent that these assets are used for R&D activities

2.4 Recognition of R&D costs

The relationship between the R&D costs and the **economic benefit** expected to derive from them will determine the allocation of those costs to different periods. Recognition of the costs as an asset will only occur where it is probable that the cost will produce future economic benefits for the entity and where the costs can be measured reliably.

(a)   In the case of **research costs**, this will not be the case due to uncertainty about the resulting benefit from them. So they should be expensed in the period in which they arose.

(b)   **Development activities** tend to be much further advanced than the research stage and so it may be possible to determine the likelihood of future economic benefit. Where this can be determined, the development costs should be carried forward as an asset.

2.4.1 Research costs

Research costs should be recognised as an **expense in the period in which they are incurred**. They should not be recognised as an asset in a later period.

2.4.2 Development costs

Development expenditure must be recognised as an intangible asset (sometimes called 'deferred development expenditure') if, and only if, the business can demonstrate that **all** of the criteria in IAS 38 have been met.

EXAM FOCUS POINT

The recognition criteria can be summarised by the mnemonic **PIRATE** which makes it easier to learn for your exam.

The recognition criteria are as follows.

The entity must demonstrate:

- **P** – how the intangible asset will generate **Probable** future economic benefits. (This is demonstrated by the existence of an external market or by how the asset will be useful to the business if it is to be used internally.)

- **I** – its **Intention** to complete the intangible asset and use or sell it

- **R** – the availability of adequate technical, financial and other **Resources** to complete the development and to use or sell the intangible asset

- **A** – its **Ability** to use or sell the intangible asset

- **T** – the **Technical** feasibility of completing the intangible asset so that it will be available for use or sale

- **E** – its ability to measure reliably the **Expenditure** attributable to the intangible asset during its development

There is also an important point about the carrying amount of the asset and recoverability. The development costs of a project recognised as an asset should not exceed the amount that it is probable will be **recovered from related future economic benefits**, after deducting further development costs, related production costs, and selling and administrative costs directly incurred in marketing the product.

2.5 Amortisation of development costs

Once capitalised as an asset, development costs must be **amortised** and recognised as an expense to match the costs with the related revenue or cost savings. The amortisation will begin when the **asset is available for use**.

Amortisation must be done on a systematic basis to reflect the pattern in which the related economic benefits are recognised.

It is unlikely to be possible to **match exactly** the economic benefits obtained with the costs which are held as an asset simply because of the nature of development activities. The entity should consider the period of time over which the product/process is expected to be sold/used.

If the pattern cannot be determined reliably, the straight-line method should be used. For example, development costs totalling $150,000 have been capitalised as an asset. The asset is now available for use and economic benefits are expected to arise over the next five years. The amortisation will be 150,000/5 = $30,000 for each year.

If the intangible asset is considered to have an **indefinite** useful life, it should not be amortised but should be subjected to an annual impairment review.

It should be noted that from 1 January 2016, amortisation based on revenue generated from the intangible asset is inappropriate. There are limited exceptions to this:

*   Where the intangible asset is expressed as a measure of revenue: and

*   Where it can be demonstrated that revenue and the consumption of economic benefits of the intangible asset are highly correlated. *(IAS 38)*

2.6 Impairment of development costs

As with all assets, impairment (fall in value of an asset) is a possibility, but is perhaps more likely with development costs, when the asset is linked with success of the development. The development costs should be **written down** to the extent that the unamortised balance (taken together with further development costs, related production costs, and selling and administrative costs directly incurred in marketing the product) is no longer likely to be recovered from the expected future economic benefit.

QUESTION

Research and development

Y Co is a company which specialises in developing new materials and manufacturing processes for the furniture industry. The company receives payments from a variety of manufacturers, which pay for the right to use the company's patented fabrics and processes.

R&D costs for the year ended 30 September 20X5 can be analysed as follows.

	$
Current projects:	

Project A   280,000
New flame-proof padding. Expected to cost a total of $400,000 to complete development. Expected total revenue $2,000,000 once work completed – probably late 20X6. Customers already placed advance orders for the material after seeing demonstrations of its capabilities earlier in the year.

$

Project B   150,000
New colour-fast dye. Expected to cost a total of $3,000,000 to complete. The dye is being developed as a cheaper replacement for a dye already used in Y Co's most successful product; cost savings of over $10,000,000 are expected from its use. Although Y has demonstrated that the dye is a viable product, and has the intention to finish developing it, the completion date is currently uncertain because external funding will have to be obtained before the development work can be completed.

$

Project C   110,000
Investigation of new adhesive recently developed in aerospace industry. If this proves effective then Y Co may well generate significant income because it will be used in place of existing adhesives.

-

Explain how the three research projects A, B and C will be dealt with in Y Co's statement of profit or loss and statement of financial position.

In each case, explain your proposed treatment in terms of IAS 38 *Intangible assets*.

ANSWER

Project A

This project meets the criteria in IAS 38 for development expenditure to be recognised as an asset. These are as follows.

- **P** – how the intangible asset will generate **Probable** future economic benefits: customers have already placed advanced orders for the final product after development
- **I** – its **Intention** to complete the intangible asset and use or sell it: Y Co intends to finish development of the product by late 20X6 and then sell the right to use it to customers
- **R** – the availability of adequate technical, financial and other **Resources** to complete the development and to use or sell the intangible asset: adequate resources do exist, the project seems to be in the late stages of development
- **A** – its **Ability** to use or sell the intangible asset: customers have already placed advanced orders for the final product, so Y Co's ability to use the asset is clear
- **T** – the **Technical** feasibility of completing the intangible asset so that it will be available for use or sale: the capabilities of the product were demonstrated to customers, so the technical feasibility is assured
- **E** – its ability to measure reliably the **Expenditure** attributable to the intangible asset during its development: Y Co has a reliable estimation of costs to date and to complete

Hence the costs of $280,000 incurred to date should be capitalised as an intangible asset in the statement of financial position. Once the material is ready for use, the intangible asset should be amortised over its useful life.

Project B

This project meets most of the criteria discussed above which would enable the costs to be carried forward; however, it fails on the availability of adequate resources to complete the project. As such, the costs cannot be capitalised and should be expensed to the statement of profit or loss.

Once funding is obtained the situation can then be reassessed and future costs may be capitalised.

Project C

This is a research project according to IAS 38, ie original and planned investigation undertaken with the prospect of gaining new scientific or technical knowledge or understanding.

There is no certainty as to its ultimate success or commercial viability and therefore it cannot be considered to be a development project. IAS 38 therefore requires that costs be written off as incurred.

3 Disclosure in financial statements

IAS 38 requires both numerical and narrative disclosures for intangible assets.

The disclosure requirements in IAS 38 are extensive and include both numerical and narrative disclosures.

The financial statements should show a **reconciliation of the carrying amount** of intangible assets at the beginning and at the end of the period. The reconciliation should show the movement on intangible assets, including:

- Additions
- Disposals
- Reductions in carrying amount
- Amortisation
- Any other movements

The following format is commonly used.

INTANGIBLE ASSETS NOTE

	Total $	Development costs $	Patents $
Cost			
At 1 January 20X4	40,000	30,000	10,000
Additions in year	19,000	15,000	4,000
Disposals in year	(1,000)	–	(1,000)
At 31 December 20X4	58,000	45,000	13,000
Amortisation			
At 1 January 20X4	11,000	5,000	6,000
Charge for year	4,000	1,000	3,000
Eliminated on disposals	(500)	–	(500)
At 31 December 20X4	14,500	6,000	8,500
Carrying amount			
At 31 December 20X4	43,500	39,000	4,500
At 1 January 20X4	29,000	25,000	4,000

As well as the reconciliation above, the financial statements should also disclose the following.

(a) The financial statements should disclose the **accounting policies** for intangible assets that have been adopted

(b) For **each class of intangible assets** (including development costs), disclosure is required of the following:

- The method of amortisation used

- The useful life of the assets or the amortisation rate used

- The gross carrying amount, the accumulated amortisation and the accumulated impairment losses as at the beginning and the end of the period

- The carrying amount of internally generated intangible assets

- The line item(s) of the statement of profit or loss in which any amortisation of intangible assets is included

EXAM FOCUS POINT

Disclosure notes can and will be tested. You need to learn the disclosures required here.

QUESTION

Research and development (2)

Y Co had the following balances relating to deferred development expenditure at 30 September 20X4.

	$
Deferred development expenditure (cost)	1,250,000
Amortisation	(125,000)
Carrying value at 30 September 20X4	1,125,000

The existing deferred development expenditure is being amortised over ten years on a straight line basis.

Show how these balances and the R&D costs in the previous question will be disclosed in the accounts of Y Co at 30 September 20X5. Show extracts from the:

A   Statement of profit or loss
B   Statement of financial position
C   Notes to the accounts

ANSWER

A   STATEMENT OF PROFIT OR LOSS (EXTRACT)

	$
Research expenditure (Project C)	110,000
Development costs (Project B)	150,000
Amortisation of capitalised development costs	125,000

B   STATEMENT OF FINANCIAL POSITION (EXTRACT)

	$
Non-current assets	
Intangible assets – deferred development expenditure (1,125 – 125 + 280)	1,280,000

C   NOTES TO THE FINANCIAL STATEMENTS

Note X – *Deferred development costs*

	$
Cost	
Balance b/f	1,250,000
Additions during year (Project A)	280,000
Balance c/f	1,530,000
Amortisation	
Balance b/f	125,000
Charge during year	125,000
Balance c/f	250,000
Carrying value at 30 September 20X5	1,280,000
Carrying value at 30 September 20X4	1,125,000

EXAM FOCUS POINT

There is an article on research and development in the Paper F7 exam resources section of the ACCA website. Although this article was written for Paper F7, it is relevant to F3/FFA and you should take a

CHAPTER ROUNDUP

↳ Intangible assets are non-current assets with no **physical substance**.

↳ Expenditure on **research** must always be written off in the period in which it is incurred.

↳ If the criteria laid down by IAS 38 are satisfied, development expenditure must be capitalised as an **intangible asset**. If it has a **finite useful life**, it should then be amortised over that life. If the criteria in IAS 38 are not satisfied, development expenditure must be written off in the period in which it is incurred.

↳ IAS 38 requires both numerical and narrative disclosures for intangible assets.

QUICK QUIZ

1 The required accounting treatment for expenditure on research is to capitalise it and carry it forward as an asset. True or false?

2 Which of the following items is an intangible asset?

    A   Land
    B   Patents
    C   Buildings
    D   Van

3 Fill in the blank.

.... expenditure is incurred in the application of knowledge for the production of new products.

The following information is relevant for questions 4 and 5.

XY Co has development expenditure of $500,000. Its policy is to amortise development expenditure at 2% per annum. Accumulated amortisation brought forward is $20,000.

4 What is the charge in the statement of profit or loss for the year's amortisation?

    A $10,000
    B $400
    C $20,000
    D $9,600

5 What is the amount shown in the statement of financial position for development expenditure?

    A $500,000
    B $480,000
    C $470,000
    D $490,000

ANSWERS TO QUICK QUIZ

1   False. Research expenditure is always written off as it is incurred.

2   B   All the others are tangible assets.

3   **Development** expenditure is incurred in the application of knowledge for the production of new products.

4   A   2% × $500,000 = $10,000.

5   C   Deferred development expenditure b/f is $480,000 (cost $500,000 – accumulated depreciation $20,000), then deduct annual depreciation of $10,000 to give figure c/f of $470,000.

Now try ...

Attempt the questions below from the **Practice Question Bank**

Number

Qs 40 – 42

CHAPTER

10

Accruals and prepayments

This chapter deals with the adjustments which may need to be made to the **expenses** in the statement of profit or loss.

1 Accruals and prepayments

SYLLABUS REFERENCE

D7(a)–(e)

              Intellectual level

D   **Recording transactions and events**

7   **Accruals and prepayments**

(a)	Understand how the matching concept applies to accruals and prepayments.	K
(b)	Identify and calculate the adjustments needed for accruals and prepayments in preparing financial statements.	S
(c)	Illustrate the process of adjusting for accruals and prepayments in preparing financial statements.	S
(d)	Prepare the journal entries and ledger entries for the creation of an accrual or prepayment.	S
(e)	Understand and identify the impact on profit and net assets of accruals and prepayments.	S

1   Accruals and prepayments

> **Accrued expenses (accruals)** are expenses which relate to an accounting period but have not been paid for. They are shown in the statement of financial position as a **liability**.
>
> **Prepaid expenses (prepayments)** are expenses which have already been paid but relate to a future accounting period. They are shown in the statement of financial position as an **asset**.

1.1 Introduction

We have already seen that the gross profit for a period should be calculated by **matching** sales and the cost of goods sold. In the same way, the profit for the year for a period should be calculated by charging the expenses which relate to that period. For example, in preparing the statement of profit or loss of a business for a period of, say, six months, it would be appropriate to charge six months' expenses for rent and local taxes, insurance costs and telephone costs, etc.

Expenses might not be paid for during the period to which they relate. For example, a business rents a shop for $20,000 per annum and pays the full annual rent on 1 April each year. If we calculate the profit of the business for the first six months of the year 20X7, the correct charge for rent in the statement of profit or loss is $10,000, even though the rent paid is $20,000 in that period. Similarly, the rent charge in the statement of profit or loss for the second six months of the year is $10,000, even though no rent was actually paid in that period.

Accruals or accrued expenses are expenses which are charged against the profit for a particular period, even though they have not yet been paid for. They are shown in the statement of financial position as a **liability**.

Prepayments are payments which have been made in one accounting period, but should not be charged against profit until a later period, because they relate to that later period. They are shown in the statement of financial position as an **asset**.

1.1.1 Difference between accruals and trade accounts payables

You will notice that accruals and trade accounts payables are separate balances within **liabilities** on a statement of financial position.

Accruals generally represent liabilities to pay for goods or services received in a period, that have **not yet been invoiced for by the suppliers**. (Although most accrued expenses are for purchases of goods or services from suppliers, accruals can cover all types of expense, eg bonuses for the year ended 20X4 paid to staff in 20X5, should be accrued for in 20X4.) **Trade accounts payables** are liabilities to pay for goods or services received in a period that **have been invoiced for by the suppliers**.

Accruals are necessary, since the expense and liability must be accounted for in the period they are incurred, even if the invoice has not been received. This is the accruals basis of accounting, which we looked at earlier in Chapter 3.

An accrual can be an **estimated amount**, since the actual cost may not be known until the invoice is received. This is often based on a quote or previous costs. Some companies use **goods received notes (GRNs)** to calculate their accrued purchases (see Section 1.4 in Chapter 4).

When the invoice is received, the expense and liability for the **invoiced amount** is then recorded. However, this effectively accounts for the expense and liability twice.

To counteract this, the accrual must be **reversed** to avoid recording twice (see Section 1.5.1 below).

1.1.2 Example

A business calls in a plumber to fix a leak. The job is done in December 20X4 and the plumber has quoted approximately $500.00. The invoice is received from the plumber in January 20X5 for $525.00.

The double entry for the accrual will be:

December 20X4

DEBIT	Repairs and maintenance costs	$500.00	
CREDIT	Accruals (liability)		$500.00

The double entry for the invoice (ignoring sales tax) will be:

January 20X5

DEBIT	Repairs and maintenance costs	$525.00	
CREDIT	Accounts payable (liability)		$525.00

The double entry for the accrual reversal will be:

January 20X5

DEBIT	Accruals (liability)	$500.00	
CREDIT	Repairs and maintenance costs		$500.00

This results in an estimated cost of $500.00 for the expense being accounted for in 20X4, and the additional $25 accounted for in 20X5.

Accruals and prepayments might seem difficult at first, but the following examples should help to clarify the principle involved, that expenses should be matched against the period to which they relate. We can regard accruals and prepayments as the means by which we move charges into the correct accounting period. If we pay in this period for something which relates to the next accounting period, we use a prepayment to transfer that charge forward to the next period. If we have incurred an expense in this period which will not be paid for until next period, we use an accrual to bring the charge back into this period.

1.2 Example 1: accruals

Horace Goodrunning, trading as Goodrunning Motor Spares, ends his financial year on 28 February each year. His telephone was installed on 1 April 20X6 and he receives his telephone account quarterly at the end of each quarter. On the basis of the following data, you are required to calculate the telephone expense to be charged to the statement of profit or loss for the year ended 28 February 20X7.

Goodrunning Motor Spares – telephone expense for the three months ended:

	$
30.6.20X6	23.50
30.9.20X6	27.20
31.12.20X6	33.40
31.3.20X7	36.00

Solution

The telephone expenses for the year ended 28 February 20X7 are:

	$
1 March – 31 March 20X6 (no telephone)	0.00
1 April – 30 June 20X6	23.50
1 July – 30 September 20X6	27.20
1 October – 31 December 20X6	33.40
1 January – 28 February 20X7 (two months) (2/3 × 36)	24.00
	108.10

The charge for the period 1 January – 28 February 20X7 is two-thirds of the quarterly bill received on 31 March. As at 28 February 20X7, no telephone bill has been received because it is not due for another month. However, it is inappropriate to ignore the telephone expenses for January and February, and so an accrued charge of $24 is made, being two-thirds of the quarter's bill of $36.

The accrued charge will also appear in the statement of financial position of the business as at 28 February 20X7, as a current liability.

1.3 Example 2: accruals

Cleverley started in business as a paper plate and cup manufacturer on 1 January 20X2, making up accounts to 31 December 20X2. Electricity bills received were as follows.

	20X2	20X3	20X4
	$	$	$
31 January	–	6,491.52	6,753.24
30 April	5,279.47	5,400.93	6,192.82
31 July	4,663.80	4,700.94	5,007.62
31 October	4,117.28	4,620.00	5,156.40

What should the electricity charge be for the year ended 31 December 20X2?

Solution

The three invoices received during 20X2 totalled $14,060.55, but this is not the full charge for the year: the November and December electricity charge was not invoiced until the end of January. To show the correct charge for the year, it is necessary to **accrue** the charge for November and December based on January's bill. The charge for 20X2 is:

	$
Paid in year	14,060.55
Accrual (2/3 × $6,491.52)	4,327.68
	18,388.23

The double entry for the accrual (using the **journal**) will be:

DEBIT	Electricity account	$4,327.68	
CREDIT	Accruals (liability)		$4,327.68

1.4 Example 3: prepayments

A business opens on 1 January 20X4 in a shop which is on a 20 year lease. The rent is $20,000 per year and is payable quarterly in advance. Payments were made on what are known as the 'quarter-days' (except the first payment) as follows.

	$
1 January 20X4	5,000.00
25 March 20X4	5,000.00
24 June 20X4	5,000.00
29 September 20X4	5,000.00
25 December 20X4	5,000.00

What will the rental charge be for the year ended 31 December 20X4?

Solution

The total amount paid in the year is $25,000. The yearly rental, however, is only $20,000. The last payment was almost entirely a prepayment (give or take a few days), as it is payment in advance for the first three months of 20X5. The charge for 20X4 is therefore:

	$
Paid in year	25,000.00
Prepayment	(5,000.00)
	20,000.00

The double entry for this prepayment is:

DEBIT	Prepayments (asset)	$5,000.00	
CREDIT	Rent account		$5,000.00

1.5 Double entry for accruals and prepayments

You can see from the double entry shown for both these examples that the other side of the entry is taken to an asset or a liability account.

- **Prepayments** are included in **receivables** in current assets in the statement of financial position. They are **assets**, as they represent money that has been paid out in advance of the expense being incurred.
- **Accruals** are included in **payables** in **current liabilities**, as they represent liabilities which have been incurred but for which no invoice has yet been received.

Transaction	DR	CR	Description
Accrual	Expense	Liability	Expense incurred in period, not recorded
Prepayment	Asset	(Reduction in) expense	Expense recorded in period, not incurred until next period

1.5.1 Reversing accruals and prepayments in subsequent periods

In each of the above examples, as with all prepayments and accruals, the double entry will be **reversed** in the following period, otherwise the organisation will charge itself twice for the same expense (accruals) **or** will never charge itself (prepayments). It may help to see the accounts in question.

Consider Example 2:

ELECTRICITY ACCOUNT

20X2		$	20X2		$
30.4	Cash	5,279.47	31.12	Statement of profit or loss	18,388.23
31.7	Cash	4,663.80			
31.10	Cash	4,117.28			
31.12	Balance c/d (accrual)	4,327.68			
		18,388.23			18,388.23

20X3		$	20X3		$
31.1	Cash	6,491.52	1.1	Balance b/d	
30.4	Cash	5,400.93		(accrual reversed)	4,327.68
31.7	Cash	4,700.94	31.12	Statement of profit or loss	21,387.87
31.10	Cash	4,620.00			
31.12	Balance c/d (accrual)	4,502.16			
		25,715.55			25,715.55

The statement of profit or loss charge and accrual for 20X3 can be checked as follows.

Invoice paid		Proportion charged in 20X3	$
31.1.X3	6,491.52	1/3	2,163.84
30.4.X3	5,400.93	all	5,400.93
31.7.X3	4,700.94	all	4,700.94
31.10.X3	4,620.00	all	4,620.00
31.1.X4	6,753.24	2/3	4,502.16
Charge to statement of profit or loss in 20X3			21,387.87

QUESTION

Accruals

Ratsnuffer is a business dealing in pest control. Its owner, Roy Dent, employs a team of 8 who were paid $12,000 per annum each in the year to 31 December 20X5. At the start of 20X6 he raised salaries by 10% to $13,200 per annum each.

On 1 July 20X6, he hired a trainee at a salary of $8,400 per annum.

He pays his workforce on the first working day of every month, one month in arrears, so that his employees receive their salary for January on the first working day in February, etc.

Required

(a) Calculate the cost of salaries which would be charged in the statement of profit or loss of Ratsnuffer for the year ended 31 December 20X6.

(b) Calculate the amount actually paid in salaries during the year (ie the amount of cash received by the workforce).

(c) State the amount of accrued charges for salaries which would appear in the statement of financial position of Ratsnuffer as at 31 December 20X6.

ANSWER

(a) *Salaries cost in the statement of profit or loss*

	$
Cost of 8 employees for a full year at $13,200 each	105,600
Cost of trainee for a half year	4,200
	109,800

(b) *Salaries actually paid in 20X6*

	$
December 20X5 salaries paid in January (8 employees × $1,000 per month)	8,000
Salaries of 8 employees for January – November 20X6 paid in February – December (8 employees × $1,100 per month × 11 months)	96,800
Salaries of trainee (for July – November paid in August – December 20X6: 5 months × $700 per month)	3,500
Salaries actually paid	108,300

(c) *Accrued salaries costs as at 31 December 20X6*
(ie costs charged in the statement of profit or loss, but not yet paid)

	$
8 employees × 1 month × $1,100 per month	8,800
1 trainee × 1 month × $700 per month	700
	9,500

(d)   *Summary*

	$
Accrued wages costs as at 31 December 20X5	8,000
Add salaries cost for 20X6 (statement of profit or loss)	109,800
	117,800
Less salaries paid	108,300
Equals accrued wages costs as at 31 December 20X6 (liability)	9,500

1.6 Example 4: prepayments

The Square Wheels Garage pays fire insurance annually in advance on 1 June each year. The firm's financial year end is 28 February. From the following record of insurance payments you are required to calculate the charge to statement of profit or loss for the financial year to 28 February 20X8.

Insurance paid

	$
1.6.20X6	600
1.6.20X7	700

Insurance cost for:

		$
(a)	Three months, 1 March – 31 May 20X7 (3/12 × $600)	150
(b)	Nine months, 1 June 20X7 – 28 February 20X8 (9/12 × $700)	525
Insurance cost for the year, charged to the statement of profit or loss		675

At 28 February 20X8 there is a prepayment for fire insurance, covering the period 1 March – 31 May 20X8. This insurance premium was paid on 1 June 20X7, but only 9 months' worth of the full annual cost is chargeable to the accounting period ended 28 February 20X8. The prepayment of (3/12 × $700) $175 as at 28 February 20X8 will appear as a current asset in the statement of financial position of the Square Wheels Garage as at that date.

In the same way, there was a prepayment of (3/12 × $600) $150 in the statement of financial position one year earlier as at 28 February 20X7.

Summary

	$
Prepaid insurance premiums as at 28 February 20X7	150
Add insurance premiums paid 1 June 20X7	700
	850
Less insurance costs charged to the statement of profit or loss for the year ended 28 February 20X8	675
Equals prepaid insurance premiums as at 28 February 20X8 (asset)	175

QUESTION   Accruals and prepayments

The Batley Print Shop rents a photocopying machine from a supplier for which it makes a quarterly payment as follows.

(a)   Three months' rental in advance

(b)   A further charge of 2p per copy made during the quarter just ended

The rental agreement began on 1 August 20X4 and the first 6 quarterly bills were as follows.

Bills dated and received	Rental	Costs of copies taken	Total
	$	$	$
1 August 20X4	2,100	0	2,100
1 November 20X4	2,100	1,500	3,600
1 February 20X5	2,100	1,400	3,500
1 May 20X5	2,100	1,800	3,900
1 August 20X5	2,700	1,650	4,350
1 November 20X5	2,700	1,950	4,650

The bills are paid promptly, as soon as they are received.

(a) Calculate the charge for photocopying expenses for the year to 31 August 20X4 and the amount of prepayments and/or accrued charges as at that date

(b) Calculate the charge for photocopying expenses for the following year to 31 August 20X5, and the amount of prepayments and/or accrued charges as at that date

ANSWER

(a) *Year to 31 August 20X4*

	$
One month's rental (1/3 × $2,100) *	700
Accrued copying charges (1/3 × $1,500) **	500
Photocopying expense (statement of profit or loss)	1,200

* From the quarterly bill dated 1 August 20X4
** From the quarterly bill dated 1 November 20X4

There is a prepayment for 2 months' rental ($1,400) as at 31 August 20X4.

(b) *Year to 31 August 20X5*

	$	$
Rental from 1 September 20X4 – 31 July 20X5 (11 months at $2,100 per quarter or $700 per month)		7,700
Rental from 1 August – 31 August 20X5 (1/3 × $2,700)		900
Rental charge for the year		8,600
Copying charges:		
1 September – 31 October 20X4 (2/3 × $1,500)	1,000	
1 November 20X4 – 31 January 20X5	1,400	
1 February – 30 April 20X5	1,800	
1 May – 31 July 20X5	1,650	
Accrued charges for August 20X5 (1/3 × $1,950)	650	
		6,500
Total photocopying expenses (statement of profit or loss)		15,100

There is a prepayment for two months' rental ($1,800) as at 31 August 20X5.

Summary of year 1 September 20X4 – 31 August 20X5

	Rental charges $	Copying costs $
Prepayments as at 31.8.20X4	1,400	
Accrued charges as at 31.8.20X4		(500)
Bills received during the year		
1 November 20X4	2,100	1,500
1 February 20X5	2,100	1,400
1 May 20X5	2,100	1,800
1 August 20X5	2,700	1,650
Prepayment as at 31.8.20X5	(1,800)	
Accrued charges as at 31.8.20X5		650
Charge to the statement of profit or loss for the year	8,600	6,500
Statement of financial position items as at 31 August 20X5		
Prepaid rental (current asset)	1,800	
Accrued copying charges (current liability)		650

1.7 Example 5: accruals

Willie Woggle opens a shop on 1 May 20X6 to sell hiking and camping equipment. The rent of the shop is $12,000 per annum, payable quarterly in arrears (with the first payment on 31 July 20X6). Willie decides that his accounting period should end on 31 December each year.

The rent account as at 31 December 20X6 will record only two rental payments (on 31 July and 31 October). There will be two months' accrued rental expenses for November and December 20X6 ($2,000), since the next rental payment is not due until 31 January 20X7.

The charge to the statement of profit or loss for the period to 31 December 20X6 will be for eight months' rent (May-December inclusive) and so it follows that the total rental cost should be $8,000.

So far, the rent account appears as follows.

RENT ACCOUNT

20X6		$	20X6		$
31 Jul	Cash	3,000			
31 Oct	Cash	3,000	31 Dec	Statement of profit or loss	8,000

To complete the picture, the accrual of $2,000 has to be put in, to bring the balance on the account up to the full charge for the year. At the beginning of the next year the accrual is reversed.

RENT ACCOUNT

20X6		$	20X6		$
31 Jul	Cash *	3,000			
31 Oct	Cash *	3,000			
31 Dec	Balance c/d (accruals)	2,000	31 Dec	Statement of profit or loss	8,000
		8,000			8,000
			20X7		
			1 Jan	Balance b/d (accrual reversed)	2,000

* The corresponding credit entry would be cash if rent is paid without the need for an invoice – eg with payment by standing order or direct debit at the bank. If there is always an invoice where rent becomes payable, the double entry would be:

DEBIT	Rent account	$2,000	
CREDIT	Payables		$2,000

Then when the rent is paid, the ledger entries would be:

DEBIT	Payables	$2,000	
CREDIT	Bank		$2,000

The rent account for the **next** year to 31 December 20X7, assuming no increase in rent in that year, would be as follows.

RENT ACCOUNT

20X7		$	20X7		$
31 Jan	Cash	3,000	1 Jan	Balance b/d	
30 Apr	Cash	3,000		(accrual reversed)	2,000
31 Jul	Cash	3,000			
31 Oct	Cash	3,000			
31 Dec	Balance c/d (accruals)	2,000	31 Dec	Statement of profit or loss	12,000
		14,000			14,000
			20X8		
			1 Jan	Balance b/d (accrual reversed)	2,000

A full 12 months' rental charges are taken as an expense to the statement of profit or loss.

1.8 Further example: prepayments of income (also referred to as deferred or unearned income)

Income can be prepaid, for example rent paid in advance and subscriptions to a trade association as in the following example). This is income the recipient has not yet earned and could be repayable. Therefore the treatment is to exclude the prepaid income from the statement of profit or loss.

Terry Trunk commences business as a landscape gardener on 1 September 20X5. He immediately decides to join his local trade association, the Confederation of Luton Gardeners, for which the annual membership subscription is $180, payable annually in advance. He paid this amount on 1 September. The Confederation makes up its accounts to 30 June each year.

In the first period to 30 June 20X6, Terry has paid a full year's membership, but only ten-twelfths of the subscription should be charged to the period (ie $10/12 \times \$180 = \$150$). There is a prepayment of two months' membership subscription (ie $2/12 \times \$180 = \$30$).

The prepayment is recognised in the Confederation's ledger account for subscriptions. For simplicity, only Terry's subscription is shown. This is done in much the same way as accounting for accruals, by using the balance carried down / brought down technique.

DEBIT	Subscriptions account with prepayment as a balance c/d	$30
CREDIT	Subscriptions account with the same balance b/d	$30

Remember that the prepaid subscription is a liability because, theoretically, this amount could be repaid to Terry.

The remaining expenses in the subscriptions account should then be taken to the statement of profit or loss. The balance on the account will appear as a current liability (prepaid subscriptions) in the statement of financial position as at 30 June 20X6.

SUBSCRIPTIONS ACCOUNT

20X6		$	20X5		$
30 Jun	Statement of profit or loss	150	1 Sep	Cash	180
30 Jun	Balance c/d (prepayment)	30			
		180			180
			20X6		
			1 Jul	Balance b/d (prepayment reversed)	30

The subscription account for the next year, assuming no increase in the annual charge, will be:

SUBSCRIPTIONS ACCOUNT

20X7		$	20X6		$
30 Jun	Statement of profit or loss	180	1 Jul	Balance b/d	30
30 Jun	Balance c/d (prepayment)	30	1 Sep	Cash	180
		210			210
			20X7		
			1 Jul	Balance b/d (prepayment reversed)	30

Again, the charge to the statement of profit or loss is for a full year's subscription. Remember that the prepaid subscription b/d is, theoretically, repayable if Terry ceases to be a member. Therefore it is a liability.

EXAM FOCUS POINT

You will almost certainly have to deal with accruals and/or prepayments in the exam. Make sure you understand the logic, then you will be able to do whatever question comes up.

1.9 Effect on profit and net assets

You may find the following table a useful summary of the effects of accruals and prepayments.

	Effect on income/expenses	Effect on profit	Effect on assets/liabilities
Accruals	Increases expenses	Reduces profit	Increases liabilities
Prepayments	Reduces expenses	Increases profit	Increases assets
Prepayments of income	Reduces income	Reduces profit	Increases liabilities

QUESTION

Statement of profit or loss and statement of financial position

The Umbrella Shop has the following trial balance as at 30 September 20X8.

	$	$
Sales		156,000
Purchases	65,000	
Land and buildings – carrying value at 30.9.X8	125,000	
Plant and machinery – carrying value at 30.9.X8	75,000	
Inventory at 1.10.X7	10,000	
Cash at bank	12,000	
Trade accounts receivable	54,000	
Trade accounts payable		40,000
Selling expenses	10,000	
Cash in hand	2,000	
Administration expenses	15,000	
Finance expenses	5,000	
Carriage inwards	1,000	
Carriage outwards	2,000	
Capital account at 1.10.X7		180,000
	376,000	376,000

The following information is available.

(a)   Closing inventory at 30.9.X8 is $13,000, after writing off damaged goods of $2,000.

(b)   Included in administration expenses is machinery rental of $6,000 covering the year to 31 December 20X8.

(c)   A late invoice for $12,000 covering rent for the year ended 30 June 20X9 has not been included in the trial balance.

Prepare a statement of profit or loss and statement of financial position for the year ended 30 September 20X8.

ANSWER

THE UMBRELLA SHOP
STATEMENT OF PROFIT OR LOSS FOR THE YEAR ENDED 30 SEPTEMBER 20X8

	$	$
Revenue		156,000
Opening inventory	10,000	
Purchases	65,000	
Carriage inwards	1,000	
	76,000	
Closing inventory (W1)	13,000	
Cost of goods sold		63,000
Gross profit		93,000

	$	$
Selling expenses	10,000	
Carriage outwards	2,000	
Administration expenses (W2)	16,500	
Finance expenses	5,000	
		33,500
Profit for the year		59,500

THE UMBRELLA SHOP
STATEMENT OF FINANCIAL POSITION AS AT 30 SEPTEMBER 20X8

	$	$
Assets		
Non-current assets		
Land and buildings		125,000
Plant and machinery		75,000
		200,000
Current assets		
Inventory (W1)	13,000	
Trade accounts receivable	54,000	
Prepayments (W4)	1,500	
Cash at bank and in hand	14,000	
		82,500
		282,500
Capital and liabilities		
Proprietor's capital		
Balance brought forward	180,000	
Profit for the year	59,500	
		239,500
Current liabilities		
Trade account payable	40,000	
Accruals (W3)	3,000	
		43,000
		282,500

Workings

1   *Closing inventory*

As the figure of $13,000 is **after** writing off damaged goods, no further adjustments are necessary. Remember that you are effectively crediting closing inventory to the statement of profit or loss and the corresponding debit is to the statement of financial position.

2   *Administration expenses*

	$
Per trial balance	15,000
Add accrual (W3)	3,000
	18,000
Less prepayment (W4)	(1,500)
	16,500

3   *Accrual*

	$
Rent for year to 30 June 20X9	12,000
Accrual for period to 30 September 20X8 ($^3/_{12} \times \$12,000$)	3,000

4   *Prepayment*

	$
Machinery rental for the year to 31 December 20X8	6,000
Prepayment for period 1 October to 31 December 20X8 ($^3/_{12} \times \$6,000$)	1,500

CHAPTER ROUNDUP

↳ **Accrued expenses (accruals)** are expenses which relate to an accounting period but have not yet been paid for. They are shown in the statement of financial position as a **liability**.

↳ **Prepaid expenses (prepayments)** are expenses which have already been paid but relate to a future accounting period. They are shown in the statement of financial position as an **asset**.

QUICK QUIZ

1 How is the cost of goods sold calculated?

2 Electricity paid during the year is $14,000. There was an opening accrual b/f of $500. A bill for the quarter ended 31 January 20X7 was $900. What is the electricity charge in the statement of profit or loss for the year ended 31 December 20X6?

    A $14,000
    B $14,100
    C $13,900
    D $14,400

3 If a business has paid rent of $1,000 for the year to 31 March 20X9, what is the prepayment in the accounts for the year to 31 December 20X8?

4 What is the correct journal for an electricity prepayment of $500?

	Debit	*Credit*
Prepayment		
Expense		

5 An accrual is an expense charged against profit for a period, even though it has not yet been paid or invoiced. True or false?

1   Opening inventory + purchases – closing inventory

2   B

	ELECTRICITY		
	$		$
Cash	14,000	Accrual b/f	500
Accrual c/f (2/3 × 900)	600	Statement of profit or loss	14,100
	14,600		14,600

3   $^{3}/_{12} \times \$1,000 = \$250$

4

	Debit	Credit
Prepayment	$500	
Expense		$500

5   True

Now try ...

Attempt the questions below from the **Practice Question Bank**

Number

Qs 43 – 46

Provisions and contingencies

This chapter considers provisions and contingencies which are the subject of an IFRS – IAS 37 *Provisions, contingent liabilities and contingent assets*. Provisions are concerned with anticipating losses.

IAS 37 is an important standard and will be examined. You need to understand the basic definitions given in IAS 37 and be able to work out whether an item needs to be recognised or disclosed in the financial statements.

TOPIC LIST	SYLLABUS REFERENCE
1 Provisions	D9(a)–(f)
2 Contingent liabilities and contingent assets	D9(a)–(c)
3 Disclosure in financial statements	F3(b)

1   Provisions

A **provision** should be recognised:

- When an entity has incurred a **present obligation**
- When it is **probable** that a **transfer of economic benefits** will be required to settle it
- When a **reliable estimate** can be made of the amount involved

1.1 Provisions

EXAM FOCUS POINT

This subject area was highlighted by the ACCA examining team at the 2013 ACCA Learning Providers Conference as being one of the least well answered in the exam. The examining team commented that students were not learning key definitions and displayed an inability to apply the theory to practical situations. Make sure you read this material thoroughly and work through the examples and questions to cement your understanding.

IAS 37 *Provisions, contingent liabilities and contingent assets* views a provision as a **liability**.

A provision is a liability of uncertain timing or amount.

A liability is an obligation of an entity to transfer economic benefits as a result of past transactions or events. *(IAS 37)*

IAS 37 distinguishes provisions from other liabilities, such as trade payables and accruals. This is on the basis that for a provision there is **uncertainty** about the timing or amount of the future expenditure.

While uncertainty is clearly present in the case of certain accruals, the uncertainty is generally much less than for provisions.

IAS 37 states that a provision should be **recognised** (which simply means 'included') as a liability in the financial statements when **all three** of the following conditions are met.

- An entity has a **present obligation** (legal or constructive) as a result of a past event.

- It is **probable** (ie more than 50% likely) that a **transfer of economic benefits** will be required to settle the obligation.

- A **reliable estimate** can be made of the obligation.

What do we mean by a legal or constructive obligation? An **obligation** means in simple terms that the business owes something to someone else. A **legal** obligation usually arises from a contract and might, for example, include warranties sold with products to make good any repairs required within a certain time frame. A **constructive** obligation arises through past behaviour and actions where the entity has raised a valid expectation that it will carry out a particular action. For example, a constructive obligation would arise if a business which doesn't offer warranties on its products has a history of usually carrying out free small repairs on its products, so that customers have come to expect this benefit when they make a purchase.

1.2 Provisions: ledger accounting entries

When a business first sets up a provision, the full amount of the provision should be debited to the statement of profit or loss and credited to the statement of financial position as follows.

DEBIT   Expenses (statement of profit or loss)
CREDIT   Provisions (statement of financial position)

In subsequent years, adjustments may be needed to the amount of the provision. The procedure to be followed then is as follows.

(a)   Calculate the new provision required.

(b)   Compare it with the existing balance on the provision account (ie the balance b/f from the previous accounting period).

(c)   Calculate increase or decrease required.

    (i)   If a higher provision is required now:

        DEBIT   Expenses (statement of profit or loss)
        CREDIT   Provisions (statement of financial position)

        with the amount of the increase.

    (ii)   If a lower provision is needed now than before:

        DEBIT   Provisions (statement of financial position)
        CREDIT   Expenses (statement of profit or loss)

        with the amount of the decrease.

1.3 Example: provisions

A business has been told by its lawyers that it is likely to have to pay $10,000 damages for a product that failed. The business duly set up a provision at 31 December 20X7. However, the following year, the lawyers found that damages were more likely to be $50,000.

Required

How is the provision treated in the accounts at:

(a)   31 December 20X7?
(b)   31 December 20X8?

Solution

(a)   The business needs to set up a provision as follows.

| DEBIT | Damages (SPL) | $10,000 | |
| CREDIT | Provision (SOFP) | | $10,000 |

EXTRACT FROM STATEMENT OF PROFIT OR LOSS

	$
Expenses	
Provision for damages	10,000

EXTRACT FROM STATEMENT OF FINANCIAL POSITION

	$
*Non-current liabilities**	
Provision for damages	10,000

* Because it is uncertain when the amount relating to the provision will be paid, or indeed if it **definitely will** be paid, it is classified as a non-current liability.

(b)   The business needs to increase the provision.

| DEBIT | Damages (SPL) | $40,000 | |
| CREDIT | Provision (SOFP) | | $40,000 |

Do not forget that the provision account already has a balance brought forward of $10,000, so we only need to account for the **increase** in the provision.

EXTRACT FROM STATEMENT OF PROFIT OR LOSS

	$
Expenses	
Provision for damages	40,000

EXTRACT FROM STATEMENT OF FINANCIAL POSITION

	$
Non-current liabilities	
Provision for damages (10,000 + 40,000)	50,000

1.4 Measurement of provisions

The amount recognised as a provision should be the **best estimate** of the expenditure required to settle the present obligation at the end of the reporting period. The estimates will be determined by the **judgement** of the entity's management supplemented by the experience of similar transactions. If the provision relates to just one item, the best estimate of the expenditure will be the most likely outcome.

When a provision is needed that involves a lot of items (for example, a warranty provision, where each item sold has a warranty attached to it), then the provision is calculated using the **expected value approach**. The expected value approach takes each possible outcome (ie the amount of money that will need to be paid under each circumstance) and weights it according to the probability of that outcome happening. This is illustrated in the following example.

1.5 Difference between provision and accruals

Whilst accruals and provisions are both liabilities, a **provision** is a **liability** of uncertain timing or amount, however for an accrual, the timing and amount to be paid is almost certain. An estimate is still required for an accrual but it is more reliable than provision.

1.6 Example: warranty provision

Parker Co sells goods with a warranty under which customers are covered for the cost of repairs of any manufacturing defect that becomes apparent within the first six months of purchase. The company's past experience and future expectations indicate the following pattern of likely repairs.

% of goods sold	Defects	Cost of repairs $m
75	None	–
20	Minor	1.0
5	Major	4.0

What should the warranty provision in Parker Co's financial statements be?

Solution

Parker Co should provide on the basis of the **expected cost** of the repairs under warranty.

The expected cost is calculated as (75% × $nil) + (20% × $1.0m) + (5% × $4.0m) = $400,000.

Parker Co should include a provision of $400,000 in the financial statements.

2 Contingent liabilities and contingent assets

A **contingent liability must not be recognised** as a liability in the financial statements. Instead it should be **disclosed** in the notes to the accounts, unless the possibility of an outflow of economic benefits is **remote**.

A **contingent asset must not be recognised** as an asset in the financial statements. Instead it should be **disclosed** in the notes to the accounts if it is **probable** that the economic benefits associated with the asset will flow to the entity.

2.1 Contingent liabilities

Contingent liabilities are defined as follows.

IAS 37 defines a contingent liability as:

- A possible obligation that arises from past events and whose existence will be confirmed only by the occurrence or non-occurrence of one or more uncertain future events not wholly within the entity's control; or

- A present obligation that arises from past events but is not recognised because:

    - It is not probable that a transfer of economic benefits will be required to settle the obligation; or

    - The amount of the obligation cannot be measured with sufficient reliability.

As a general rule, probable means more than 50% likely. **If an obligation is probable, it is not a contingent liability** – instead, a **provision is needed**. If the obligation is **remote**, it does not need to be disclosed in the accounts.

Contingent liabilities **should not be recognised in financial statements** but they **should be disclosed in the notes**. The required disclosures are:

- A brief description of the nature of the contingent liability
- An estimate of its financial effect
- An indication of the uncertainties that exist
- The possibility of any reimbursement

2.2 Contingent assets

IAS 37 defines a contingent asset as:

A possible asset that arises from past events and whose existence will be confirmed by the occurrence of one or more uncertain future events not wholly within the enterprise's control.

A contingent asset **must not be recognised** in the accounts, but should be **disclosed** if it is **probable** that the economic benefits associated with the asset will flow to the entity.

A brief description of the contingent asset should be provided, along with an estimate of its likely financial effect.

If the flow of economic benefits associated with the contingent asset becomes **virtually certain**, it should then be **recognised as an asset** in the statement of financial position, as it is no longer a contingent asset.

For example, a company expects to receive damages of $100,000 and this is virtually certain. **An asset is recognised**. If, however, the company expects to probably receive damages of $100,000, **a contingent asset is disclosed**.

2.3 IAS 37 flow chart

You must practise the questions below to get the hang of the IAS 37 rules on contingencies. But first, study the flow chart, taken from IAS 37, which is a good summary of its requirements.

EXAM FOCUS POINT

If you learn this flow chart you should be able to deal with most questions you are likely to meet in the exam.

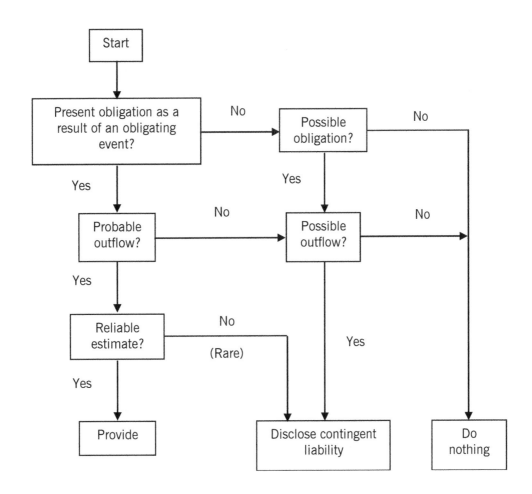

QUESTION

During 20X9 Smack Co gives a guarantee of certain borrowings of Pony Co, whose financial condition at that time is sound. During 20Y0, the financial condition of Pony Co deteriorates and at 30 June 20Y0 Pony Co files for protection from its creditors.

What accounting treatment is required:

(a)   At 31 December 20X9?
(b)   At 31 December 20Y0?

ANSWER

(a)   At 31 December 20X9

There is a present obligation as a result of a past obligating event. The obligating event is the giving of the guarantee, which gives rise to a legal obligation. However, at 31 December 20X9 no transfer of economic benefits is probable in settlement of the obligation.

No provision is recognised. The guarantee is disclosed as a contingent liability unless the probability of any transfer is regarded as remote.

An appropriate note to the accounts would be as follows.

Contingent liability

The company has given a guarantee in respect of the bank borrowings (currently $500,000) of Pony Co. At the reporting date, Pony Co was sound and it is unlikely that the company will be required to fulfil its guarantee.

(b)   At 31 December 20Y0

As above, there is a present obligation as a result of a past obligating event, namely the giving of the guarantee.

At 31 December 20Y0 it is probable that a transfer of economic benefits will be required to settle the obligation. A provision is therefore recognised for the best estimate of the obligation.

QUESTION   Provisions and contingencies II

After a wedding in 20X0 ten people became seriously ill, possibly as a result of food poisoning from products sold by Callow Co. Legal proceedings are started seeking damages from Callow but it disputes liability. Up to the date of approval of the financial statements for the year to 31 December 20X0, Callow's lawyers advise that it is probable that it will not be found liable. However, when Callow prepares the financial statements for the year to 31 December 20X1 its lawyers advise that, owing to developments in the case, it is probable that it will be found liable.

What is the required accounting treatment:

(a)   At 31 December 20X0?
(b)   At 31 December 20X1?

ANSWER

(a)   On the basis of the evidence available when the financial statements were approved, there is no obligation as a result of past events. No provision is recognised. The matter is disclosed as a contingent liability unless the probability of any transfer is regarded as remote.

(b)   On the basis of the evidence available, there is a present obligation. A transfer of economic benefits in settlement is probable.

A provision is recognised for the best estimate of the amount needed to settle the present obligation.

QUESTION   Provisions and contingencies III

An oil company causes environmental contamination in the course of its operations, but cleans up only when required to do so under the laws of the country in which it is operating. One country in which it has been operating for several years has up to now had no legislation requiring cleaning up. However, there is now an environmental lobby in this country. At the date of the company's year end, it is virtually certain that a draft law requiring clean-up of contaminated land will be enacted very shortly. The oil company will then be obliged to deal with the contamination it has caused over the past several years.

What accounting treatment is required at the year end?

ANSWER

At the year end there is a **present obligation** as a result of a **past obligating event**. Because it is 'virtually certain' that the law will be enacted, the past contamination becomes an obligating event. It is highly probable that an **outflow of economic resources** will be required to settle this. A provision should therefore be made of the best estimate of the costs involved.

3 Disclosure in financial statements

> IAS 37 requires certain items for provisions and contingent assets and liabilities to be disclosed in the financial statements.

3.1 Disclosures for provisions

Disclosures required in the financial statements for provisions fall into two parts.

(a)   Disclosure of details of the change in carrying amount of a provision from the beginning to the end of the year, including additional provisions made, amounts used and other movements.

(b)   For each class of provision, disclosure of the background to the making of the provision and the uncertainties affecting its outcome, including:

    (i)   A brief description of the nature of the provision and the expected timing of any resulting outflows relating to the provision

    (ii)   An indication of the uncertainties about the amount or timing of those outflows and, where necessary to provide adequate information, the major assumptions made concerning future events

    (iii)   The amount of any expected reimbursement relating to the provision and whether any asset that has been recognised for that expected reimbursement

Example: disclosure in the financial statements of a warranty provision

Warren Tees Ltd. is a manufacturer of golf tees. Tees purchased are covered by a three year warranty, whereby the company will replace any defective tees.

At the end of last year on 31 March 20X6, a provision of $150,000 was made. During this year, $75,000 was paid for the cost of replacing tees under warranty. At the end of this year, the company estimated that a provision of $135,000 was needed.

ACCOUNTING ENTRIES

The cost of replacing tees under warranty is a utilisation of the provision:

DEBIT	Provision (SOFP)	$75,000	
CREDIT	Bank (SOFP)		$75,000

The increase in the provision during the year of $60,000 is the charge to the statement of profit or loss for the year:

DEBIT	Warranty costs (SPL)	$60,000	
CREDIT	Provision (SOFP)		$60,000

DISCLOSURE

Below is an example of how the warranty provision might be disclosed in the notes to the financial statements.

Note X: Provisions

	Warranty provision $'000
At 1 April 20X6	150
Increase in the provision during the year	60
Amounts used during year	(75)
At 31 March 20X7	135

The warranty provision relates to estimated claims on those products sold in the year ended 31 March 20X7 which come with a three year warranty. The expected value method is used to provide a best estimate. It is expected that the expenditure will be incurred in the next three years.

The table above is essentially a T-account, as set out below.

WARRANTY PROVISION

	$'000		$'000
Utilised	75	Balance b/f 1 April 20X6	150
Balance c/f 31 March 20X7	135	Increase during the year	60
	210		210

3.2 Disclosures for contingent liabilities

Unless remote, disclose for each contingent liability:

- A brief description of its nature, and where practicable
- An estimate of the financial effect
- An indication of the uncertainties relating to the amount or timing of any outflow
- The possibility of any reimbursement

3.3 Disclosures for contingent assets

Where an inflow of economic benefits is **probable**, an entity should disclose:

- A brief description of its nature, and where practicable
- An estimate of the financial effect

CHAPTER ROUNDUP

↳ A **provision** should be recognised:

- When an entity has a **present obligation**
- When it is **probable** that a **transfer of economic benefits** will be required to settle it
- When a **reliable estimate** can be made of its amount

↳ A **contingent liability must not be recognised** as a liability in the financial statements. Instead it should be **disclosed** in the notes to the accounts, unless the possibility of an outflow of economic benefits is **remote**.

↳ A **contingent asset must not be recognised** as an asset in the financial statements. Instead it should be **disclosed** in the notes to the accounts if it is **probable** that the economic benefits associated with the asset will flow to the entity.

↳ IAS 37 requires certain items for provisions and contingent assets and liabilities to be disclosed in the financial statements.

QUICK QUIZ

1 A company is being sued for $10,000 by a customer. The company's lawyers reckon that it is likely that the claim will be upheld. Legal fees are currently $5,000.

How should the company account for this?

2 Given the facts in 1 above, how much of a provision should be made if further legal fees of $2,000 are likely to be incurred?

A $10,000
B $5,000
C $15,000
D $12,000

3 A company has a provision for warranty claims b/f of $50,000. It does a review and decides that the provision needed in future should be $45,000. What is the effect on the financial statements?

	Statement of profit or loss	Statement of financial position
A	Increase expenses by $5,000	Provision $50,000
B	Increase expenses by $5,000	Provision $45,000
C	Decrease expenses by $5,000	Provision $50,000
D	Decrease expenses by $5,000	Provision $45,000

4 A contingent liability is always disclosed on the face of the statement of financial position.
True or false?

5 How does a company account for a contingent asset that is not probable?

A By way of note
B As an asset in the statement of financial position
C It does nothing
D Offset against any associated liability

1   A provision in the statement of financial position

2   D   The legal fees currently incurred of $5,000 are current liabilities and should already be included in the accounts. The provision is for the claim of $10,000 plus the additional legal fees of $2,000.

3   D

PROVISION ACCOUNT

	$		$
P/L account	5,000	Bal b/f	50,000
Bal c/f	45,000		
	50,000		50,000

Note. We are debiting provision account $5,000 and so crediting statement of profit or loss $5,000. Therefore, we are **decreasing** expenses.

4   False. A contingent liability is disclosed by way of notes to the financial statements.

5   C   It does nothing.

Now try ...

Attempt the questions below from the **Practice Question Bank**

Number

Qs 51 – 54

CHAPTER

12

Irrecoverable debts and allowances

In this chapter we look at two types of adjustment which need to be made in respect of credit sales.

- Irrecoverable debts
- Allowance for receivables

TOPIC LIST	SYLLABUS REFERENCE
1 Irrecoverable debts	D8(b)–(g)
2 Allowances for receivables	D8(h)–(i)

D   Recording transactions and events

8   Receivables and payables

(b)	Identify the benefits and costs of offering credit facilities to customers.	K
(c)	Understand the purpose of an aged receivables analysis.	K
(d)	Understand the purpose of credit limits.	K
(e)	Prepare the bookkeeping entries to write off an irrecoverable debt.	S
(f)	Record an irrecoverable debt recovered.	S
(g)	Identify the impact of irrecoverable debts on the statement of profit or loss and statement of financial position.	S
(h)	Prepare the bookkeeping entries to create and adjust an allowance for receivables.	S
(i)	Illustrate how to include movements in the allowance for receivables in the statement of profit or loss and how the closing balance of the allowance should appear in the statement of financial position.	S

1   Irrecoverable debts

> **Irrecoverable debts** are specific debts owed to a business which it decides are never going to be paid. They are written off as an expense in the statement of profit or loss.

1.1 Introduction

Very few businesses expect to be paid immediately in cash, unless they are retail businesses on the high street. Most businesses buy and sell to one another on credit terms. This has the **benefit** of allowing businesses to keep trading without having to provide cash 'up front'. So a business will allow credit terms to customers and receive credit terms from its suppliers. Ideally a business wants to receive money from its customers as quickly as possible, but delay paying its suppliers for as long as possible. This can lead to problems.

Most businesses aim to control such problems by means of **credit control**. A customer will be given a **credit limit**, which cannot be exceeded (compare an overdraft limit or a credit card limit). If an order would take the customer's account over its credit limit, it will not be actioned until a payment is received to reduce the customer's outstanding balance.

Another tool in **credit control** is the **aged receivables analysis**. An aged receivables analysis is a report of all receivables analysed by customer and by age of the receivable, eg balances outstanding for 30 days, 60 days and 90+ days. If a balance has been outstanding for a long period of time, it may indicate that a customer is unable to pay. Most credit controllers will have a system of chasing up payment for long outstanding invoices.

Customers might fail to pay, perhaps out of dishonesty or because they have gone bankrupt and cannot pay. Customers in another country might be prevented from paying by the unexpected introduction of foreign exchange control restrictions by their country's government during the credit period. Therefore, the **costs** of offering credit facilities to customers can include:

* Interest costs of an overdraft, if customers do not pay promptly
* Costs of trying to obtain payment
* Court costs

For one reason or another, a business might decide to give up expecting payment and to write the debt off.

An irrecoverable (or 'bad') debt is a debt which is definitely not expected to be paid. An irrecoverable debt could occur when, for example, a customer has gone bankrupt.

1.2 Writing off irrecoverable debts

To begin with, let's recap the ledger entries when a sale on credit is made to a customer.

DEBIT Trade receivables
CREDIT Sales

All being well, a few weeks later the customer will pay the debt and cash will be received, at which point the double entry is:

DEBIT Cash account
CREDIT Trade receivables

But what happens if, instead, the customer goes bankrupt and then can't pay? Remember that according to the *Conceptual Framework* an asset is a resource controlled by an entity from which **future economic benefits are expected to flow**. If the customer can't pay, then no economic benefits are expected to flow from the trade receivable. So the trade receivable no longer meets the definition of an asset and it must be removed from the statement of financial position and is charged as an expense in the statement of profit or loss. The ledger entries to write off an irrecoverable debt are:

DEBIT Irrecoverable debts expense (statement of profit or loss)
CREDIT Trade receivables (statement of financial position)

QUESTION
Irrecoverable debts I

Design Co has a total balance for trade receivables of $25,000 at the year end. A review of the receivables balances highlights that one of its customers, Mann Co, has gone bankrupt. Design Co is owed $4,000 by Mann Co for design work done during the year. This debt is now considered irrecoverable.

Required

(a) What is the balance for trade receivables to be shown in the statement of financial position at the year end?

(b) What is the irrecoverable debts expense to be shown in the statement of profit or loss at the year end?

ANSWER

TRADE RECEIVABLES (SOFP)

	$		$
Balance b/d	25,000	Irrecoverable debts expense	4,000
	–	Balance c/d	21,000
	25,000		25,000
Balance b/d	21,000		

Trade receivables will be shown at **$21,000** in the statement of financial position.

IRRECOVERABLE DEBTS EXPENSE (SPL)

	$		$
Trade receivables	4,000	P/L account	4,000

The irrecoverable debt expense in the statement of profit or loss is **$4,000**.

QUESTION

At 1 October 20X5 a business had total outstanding debts of $8,600. During the year to 30 September 20X6 the following transaction took place.

(a) Credit sales amounted to $44,000.

(b) Payments from various customers (accounts receivable) amounted to $49,000.

(c) Two debts, for $180 and $420, were declared irrecoverable and the customers are no longer purchasing goods from the company. These are to be written off.

Required

Prepare the trade receivables ledger account and the irrecoverable debts expense account for the year.

ANSWER

TRADE RECEIVABLES (SOFP)

	$		$
Opening balance b/f	8,600	Cash	49,000
Sales	44,000	Irrecoverable debts	180
		Irrecoverable debts	420
		Closing balance c/d	3,000
	52,600		52,600
Opening balance b/d	3,000		

IRRECOVERABLE DEBTS EXPENSE (SPL)

	$		$
Receivables	180	P/L a/c	600
Receivables	420		
	600		600

In the receivables ledger, personal accounts of the customers whose debts are irrecoverable will be taken off the ledger.

1.3 Irrecoverable debts written off and subsequently paid

An irrecoverable debt which has been written off might occasionally be unexpectedly paid. Because the debt has already been written off, it no longer exists in the statement of financial position and so the cash received cannot be offset against it in the usual way. Instead, the cash received is offset against the irrecoverable debts expense. Regardless of when the payment is received, the ledger entries are as follows.

DEBIT   Cash account

CREDIT   Irrecoverable debts expense

For example, a statement of profit or loss for the Blacksmith's Forge for the year to 31 December 20X5 could be prepared as shown below from the following information.

	$
Inventory, 1 January 20X5	6,000
Purchases of goods	122,000
Inventory, 31 December 20X5	8,000
Cash sales	100,000
Credit sales	70,000
Irrecoverable debts written off	9,000
Debts paid in 20X5 which were previously written off as irrecoverable in 20X4	2,000
Other expenses	31,800
Trade receivables	24,000

BLACKSMITH'S FORGE
STATEMENT OF PROFIT OR LOSS FOR THE YEAR ENDED 31.12.20X5

	$	$
Revenue		170,000
Opening inventory	6,000	
Purchases	122,000	
	128,000	
Less closing inventory	8,000	
Cost of goods sold		120,000
Gross profit		50,000
Expenses		
Irrecoverable debts expense (9,000 – 2,000)	7,000	
Other expenses	31,800	
		38,800
Profit for the year		11,200
STATEMENT OF FINANCIAL POSITION (EXTRACT)		
Trade receivables (24,000 – 9,000)		15,000

2 Allowances for receivables

In addition to irrecoverable debts, a business may make an **allowance for receivables** as a prudent precaution to account for the fact that some receivables balances might not be collectable.

An increase in the allowance for receivables is shown as an expense in the statement of profit or loss.

Trade receivables in the statement of financial position are shown **net** of any receivables allowance.

2.1 Doubtful debts

Irrecoverable debts are specific debts which are **definitely not** expected to be paid. However, there may be some debts which the business thinks **might not** be paid; these are known as **doubtful debts**.

A doubtful debt is a debt which is **possibly** irrecoverable.

Doubtful debts may occur, for example, when an invoice is in dispute, or when a customer is in financial difficulty.

In this situation, the debt is not written off, as it is not certain that the debt is irrecoverable. But because there is doubt over whether the debt will be paid, an **allowance for receivables** is made against the doubtful debt.

Allowance for receivables. An **impairment** amount in relation to receivables that reduces the receivables asset to its **recoverable amount** in the statement of financial position. It is offset against trade receivables, which are shown at the net amount.

An allowance for receivables accounts for potential irrecoverable debts, as a **prudent precaution** by the business. The business will therefore be more likely to avoid claiming profits which subsequently fail to materialise because some specific debts turn out to be irrecoverable.

You may sometimes see an allowance for receivables referred to as a **bad debt provision**. This term is not correct, since it is not a provision. A provision must be a liability (see Chapter 11) which is not the case here.

2.2 Determining the allowance for receivables

The methods of determining the allowance for trade receivables fall under IAS 39/IFRS 9 as part of an impairment review of trade receivables, and can be quite complex. Fortunately, these are beyond the scope of this syllabus. In this paper, the allowance for receivables is likely to be expressed simply as a percentage of trade receivables, eg 'an allowance equivalent to 2% of trade receivables'.

The allowance against the trade receivables balance is made **after** writing off any irrecoverable debts.

2.3 Accounting treatment in the financial statements

The accounting treatment for an allowance for receivables is as follows.

(a)   When an allowance is first made, the amount of this initial allowance is charged as an expense in the statement of profit or loss for the period in which the allowance is created.

(b)   When an allowance already exists, but is subsequently increased in size, the amount of the **increase** in allowance is charged as an **expense** in the statement of profit or loss for the period in which the increased allowance is made.

(c)   When an allowance already exists, but is subsequently reduced in size, the amount of the **decrease** in allowance is credited back to the statement of profit or loss for the period in which the reduction in allowance is made.

EXAM FOCUS POINT

In the exam it is highly likely that you will have to calculate the increase or decrease in the allowance for receivables and show the effect of this on the statement of profit or loss.

The statement of financial position, as well as the statement of profit or loss of a business, must be adjusted to show the allowance.

IMPORTANT

The value of trade receivables in the statement of financial position must be shown after deducting the allowance for receivables.

This is because the net realisable value of all the receivables of the business is estimated to be less than their 'sales value'. After all, this is the reason for making the allowance in the first place. The net realisable value of trade accounts receivable is the total value of receivables minus receivables allowance.

For example, a company has a trade receivables balance of $50,000 but requires an allowance for receivables equivalent to 5% of the balance. Therefore the allowance for receivables will be 5% of $50,000 = $2,500. This means that although total trade receivables are $50,000, eventual payment of only $47,500 is expected.

(a)   In the statement of profit or loss, the newly created allowance of $2,500 will be shown as an expense.

(b)   In the statement of financial position, trade receivables will be shown as:

	$
Trade receivables (50,000 – 2,500)	47,500

2.4 Allowance for receivables: ledger accounting entries

When an allowance for receivables is first set up, the whole amount is debited to the statement of profit or loss.

In subsequent years, only the **movement** on the receivables allowance is debited or credited to irrecoverable debts expense in the statement of profit or loss.

When a business first sets up an allowance for receivables, the full amount of the allowance should be debited to irrecoverable debts expense as follows.

DEBIT   Irrecoverable debts expense (statement of profit or loss)
CREDIT   Allowance for receivables (statement of financial position)

In subsequent years, adjustments may be needed to the amount of the allowance. The procedure to be followed then is as follows.

(a)   Calculate the new allowance required

(b)   Compare it with the existing balance on the allowance account (ie the balance b/f from the previous accounting period)

(c)   Calculate increase or decrease required

      (i)   If a higher allowance is required now:

            DEBIT   Irrecoverable debts expense (statement of profit or loss)
            CREDIT   Allowance for receivables (statement of financial position)

            with the amount of the increase

      (ii)   If a lower allowance is needed now than before:

            DEBIT   Allowance for receivables (statement of financial position)
            CREDIT   Irrecoverable debts expense (statement of profit or loss)

            with the amount of the decrease

2.5 Example: accounting entries for allowance for receivables

Alex Gullible has total receivables outstanding at 31 December 20X2 of $28,000. He has calculated that the equivalent of 1% of the these balances might not be collected and wishes to make an appropriate allowance. Before now, he has not made any allowance for receivables at all.

On 31 December 20X3 his trade accounts receivable amounted to $40,000. Upon reviewing the balances, he calculated that an allowance should be made equivalent to 5% of the total balance.

What accounting entries should Alex make on 31 December 20X2 and 31 December 20X3, and what figures for trade receivables will appear in his statements of financial position as at those dates?

Solution

At 31 December 20X2

Allowance required = 1% × $28,000
                = $280

Alex will make the following entries.

DEBIT   Irrecoverable debts expense (statement of profit or loss) $280
CREDIT   Allowance for receivables (statement of financial position) $280

Receivables will appear as follows under current assets.

	$
Receivables ledger balances	28,000
Less allowance for receivables	(280)
	27,720

At 31 December 20X3

Following the procedure described above, Alex will calculate as follows.

	$
Allowance required now (5% × $40,000)	2,000
Existing allowance	(280)
∴ Additional allowance required	1,720

He will make the following entries.

DEBIT	Irrecoverable debts expense	$1,720	
CREDIT	Allowance for receivables		$1,720

The allowance account will now appear as follows.

ALLOWANCE FOR RECEIVABLES (SOFP)

20X2			$	20X2			$
31 Dec	Balance c/d		280	31 Dec	P/L account		280
20X3				20X3			
31 Dec	Balance c/d		2,000	1 Jan	Balance b/d		280
				31 Dec	P/L account		1,720
			2,000				2,000
				20X4			
				1 Jan	Balance b/d		2,000

Trade receivables will be valued as follows.

	$
Receivables ledger balances	40,000
Less allowance for receivables	2,000
	38,000

In practice, it is unnecessary to show the total receivables balances and the allowance as separate items in the statement of financial position. Normally it shows only the net figure ($27,720 in 20X2, $38,000 in 20X3).

Now try the following questions on allowance for receivables for yourself.

QUESTION

Receivables allowance I

Corin Flake owns and runs the Aerobic Health Foods Shop in Dundee. He commenced trading on 1 January 20X1, selling health foods to customers, most of whom make use of a credit facility that Corin offers. (Customers are allowed to purchase up to $200 of goods on credit but must repay a certain proportion of their outstanding debt every month.)

This credit system gives rise to a large number of irrecoverable debts, and Corin Flake's results for his first three years of operations are as follows.

Year to 31 December 20X1

Gross profit	$27,000
Irrecoverable debts written off	$8,000
Debts owed by customers as at 31 December 20X1	$40,000
Allowance for receivables	2½% of outstanding receivables
Other expenses	$20,000

Year to 31 December 20X2

Gross profit	$45,000
Irrecoverable debts written off	$10,000
Debts owed by customers as at 31 December 20X2	$50,000
Allowance for receivables	2½% of outstanding receivables
Other expenses	$28,750

Year to 31 December 20X3

Gross profit	$60,000
Irrecoverable debts written off	$11,000
Debts owed by customers as at 31 December 20X3	$30,000
Allowance for receivables	3% of outstanding receivables
Other expenses	$32,850

Required

For each of these three years, prepare the statement of profit or loss of the business, and state the value of trade receivables appearing in the statement of financial position as at 31 December.

ANSWER

AEROBIC HEALTH FOODS SHOP
STATEMENTS OF PROFIT OR LOSS FOR THE YEARS ENDED 31 DECEMBER

	20X1		20X2		20X3	
	$	$	$	$	$	$
Gross profit		27,000		45,000		60,000
Expenses:						
Irrecoverable debts written off	8,000		10,000		11,000	
Increase/decrease in						
allowance for receivables*	1,000		250		(350)	
Other expenses	20,000		28,750		32,850	
		29,000		39,000		43,500
Profit/(loss) for the year		(2,000)		6,000		16,500

* At 1 January 20X1 when Corin began trading, the allowance for receivables was nil. At 31 December 20X1 the allowance required was 2½% of $40,000 = $1,000. The increase in the allowance is therefore $1,000. At 31 December 20X2 the allowance required was equivalent to 2½% of $50,000 = $1,250. The 20X1 allowance must therefore be increased by $250. At 31 December 20X3 the allowance required is equivalent to 3% × $30,000 = $900. The 20X2 allowance is therefore reduced by $350.

VALUE OF TRADE RECEIVABLES IN THE STATEMENT OF FINANCIAL POSITION

	As at 31.12.20X1	As at 31.12.20X2	As at 31.12.20X3
	$	$	$
Total value of receivables	40,000	50,000	30,000
Less allowance for receivables	1,000	1,250	900
Statement of financial position value	39,000	48,750	29,100

QUESTION

Receivables allowance II

Horace Goodrunning fears that his business will suffer an increase in defaulting receivables in the future and so he needs to make an allowance for receivables equivalent to 2% of outstanding trade receivables at the reporting date from 28 February 20X6. On 28 February 20X8, Horace determines that the allowance has been overestimated and he recalculates it to be the equivalent of 1% of outstanding trade receivables. Outstanding receivables balances at the various reporting dates are as follows.

	$
28.2.20X6	15,200
28.2.20X7	17,100
28.2.20X8	21,400

Required

Show extracts from the following ledger accounts for each of the three years above.

(a) Trade receivables
(b) Allowance for receivables
(c) Profit or loss account

Show how receivables would appear in the statement of financial position at the end of each year.

ANSWER

The entries for the three years are denoted by (a), (b) and (c) in each account.

TRADE RECEIVABLES (EXTRACT)

			$
(a)	28.2.20X6	Balance	15,200
(b)	28.2.20X7	Balance	17,100
(c)	28.2.20X8	Balance	21,400

ALLOWANCE FOR RECEIVABLES

			$			$
(a)	28.2.20X6	Balance c/d (2% of 15,200)	304	28.2.20X6	P/L account	304
			304			304
(b)	28.2.20X7	Balance c/d (2% of 17,100)	342	1.3.20X6	Balance b/d	304
				28.2.20X7	P/L account (note (1))	38
			342			342
(c)	28.2.20X8	P/L account (note (2))	128	1.3.20X7	Balance b/d	342
	28.2.20X8	Balance c/d (1% of 21,400)	214			
			342			342
				1.3.20X8	Balance b/d	214

PROFIT OR LOSS (EXTRACT)

		$			$
28.2.20X6	Allowance for receivables	304			
28.2.20X7	Allowance for receivables	38			
			28.2.20X8	Allowance for receivables	128

Notes

1. The increase in the allowance is $(342 − 304) = $38

2. The decrease in the allowance is $(342 − 214) = $128

3. We calculate the net receivables figure for inclusion in the statement of financial position as follows:

	20X6 $	20X7 $	20X8 $
Current assets			
Trade accounts receivable	15,200	17,100	21,400
Less allowance for receivables	304	342	214
	14,896	16,758	21,186

2.6 Example: irrecoverable debts and allowance for receivables combined

Consider the following example.

Fatima's receivables at 31 May 20X7 were $723,800. The balance on the allowance for receivables account at 1 June 20X6 was $15,250. Fatima needs to adjust the allowance for receivables to be the equivalent of 1.5% of receivables at 31 May 20X7.

On 14 May 20X7 Fatima received $540 in final settlement of an amount written off during the year ended 31 May 20X6.

Required

What total amount should be recognised for receivables in the statement of profit or loss for the year ended 31 May 20X7?

Solution

First, note the requirement's wording 'recognised for receivables in the statement of profit or loss'. This means the total charge (or recovery) for irrecoverable debts **and** the allowance for receivables in the statement of profit or loss.

Secondly, consider the allowance for receivables.

	$
Closing allowance required (723,800 × 1.5%)	10,857
Opening allowance	(15,250)
Reduction needed in allowance	(4,393)

Remember that a reduction to the allowance for receivables is a **credit** to the statement of profit or loss.

Thirdly, the amount received of $540 had already been written off the previous year and now needs to be **credited** to irrecoverable debts.

Therefore the total credit to the statement of profit or loss = 540 + 4,393 = $4,933

EXAM FOCUS POINT

It is highly likely that you will get a question like this in the exam. Make sure you understand the solution.

2.7 Question to test your learning

You should now try to use what you have learned to attempt a solution to the following exercise, which involves preparing a statement of profit or loss and statement of financial position.

QUESTION

Newbegin tools

The financial affairs of Newbegin Tools prior to the commencement of trading were as follows.

NEWBEGIN TOOLS
STATEMENT OF FINANCIAL POSITION AS AT 1 AUGUST 20X5

	$	$
Assets		
Non-current assets		
Motor vehicle	2,000	
Shop fittings	3,000	
		5,000
Current assets		
Inventories	12,000	
Cash	1,000	
		13,000
		18,000
Equity and liabilities		
Equity		12,000
Current liabilities		
Bank overdraft	2,000	
Trade payables	4,000	
		6,000
Total equity and liabilities		18,000

At the end of six months the business had made the following transactions.

(a)   Goods were purchased on credit for $10,000.

(b)   Closing inventories were valued at $5,450.

(c)   Cash sales and credit sales together totalled $27,250.

(d)   Outstanding trade accounts receivable balances at 31 January 20X6 amounted to $3,250, of which $250 were to be written off.

(e)   An allowance for receivables is to be made equivalent to 2% of the remaining outstanding receivables.

(f)   Cash payments were made in respect of the following expenses.

			$
(i)	Stationery, postage and wrapping		500
(ii)	Telephone charges		200
(iii)	Electricity		600
(iv)	Cleaning and refreshments		150
(v)	Suppliers		8,000

(g)   Cash drawings by the proprietor, Alf Newbegin, amounted to $6,000.

(h)   The outstanding overdraft balance as at 1 August 20X5 was paid off. Interest charges and bank charges on the overdraft amounted to $40.

Alf Newbegin knew the balance of cash in hand at 31 January 20X6 but he wanted to know if the business had made a profit for the six months that it had been trading, and so he asked his friend, Harry Oldhand, if he could tell him.

Required

Prepare the statement of profit or loss of Newbegin Tools for the six months to 31 January 20X6 and a statement of financial position as at that date.

ANSWER

NEWBEGIN TOOLS
STATEMENT OF PROFIT OR LOSS FOR THE SIX MONTHS ENDED
31 JANUARY 20X6

	$	$
Revenue		27,250
Opening inventories	12,000	
Purchases	10,000	
	22,000	
Less closing inventories	5,450	
Cost of goods sold		16,550
Gross profit		10,700
Electricity	600	
Stationery, postage and wrapping	500	
Irrecoverable debts written off	250	
Allowance for receivables*	60	
Telephone charges	200	
Cleaning and refreshments	150	
Interest and bank charges	40	
		1,800
Profit for the period		8,900

* 2% of $3,000 = $60.

The preparation of a statement of financial position is more complex, because we must calculate the value of trade payables and cash in hand.

(a)   **Trade payables as at 31 January 20X6**

The amount owing on trade accounts is the sum of the amount owing at the beginning of the period, plus the cost of purchases during the period, less the payments already made for purchases. If you think carefully about this, you might see that this calculation is logical. What is still owed is the total amount of costs incurred less payments already made.

	$
Accounts payable as at 1 August 20X5	4,000
Add purchases during the period	10,000
	14,000
Less payments to suppliers' accounts during the period	(8,000)
	6,000

(b) **Cash at bank and in hand as at 31 January 20X6**

You need to identify cash payments received and cash payments made.

(i) Cash received from sales

	$
Total sales in the period	27,250
Add trade accounts receivable as at 1 August 20X5	0
	27,250
Less unpaid debts as at 31 January 20X6	3,250
Cash received	24,000

(ii) *Cash paid*

	$
Trade accounts payable	8,000
Stationery, postage and wrapping	500
Telephone charges	200
Electricity	600
Cleaning and refreshments	150
Bank charges and interest	40
Bank overdraft repaid	2,000
Drawings by proprietor	6,000
	17,490

Note. It is easy to forget some of these payments, especially drawings.

		$
(iii)	Cash in hand as at 1 August 20X5	1,000
	Cash received in the period	24,000
		25,000
	Cash paid in the period	(17,490)
	Cash at bank and in hand as at 31 January 20X6	7,510

(c) When irrecoverable debts are written off, the value of outstanding receivables must be reduced by the amount written off. This is because the customers are no longer expected to pay, and it would be misleading to show them in the statement of financial position as current assets of the business for which cash payment is expected within one year. Receivables will be valued at $3,250 less the irrecoverable debt of $250 less the allowance for receivables of $60 – ie at $2,940.

NEWBEGIN TOOLS
STATEMENT OF FINANCIAL POSITION AS AT 31 JANUARY 20X6

	$	$
Assets		
Non-current assets		
Motor vehicles	2,000	
Shop fittings	3,000	
		5,000
Current assets		
Inventory	5,450	
Trade accounts receivable	2,940	
Cash	7,510	
		15,900
		20,900

Equity and liabilities
Equity
Capital as at 1 August 20X5	12,000	
Profit for the period	8,900	
Less drawings	(6,000)	
Capital as at 31 January 20X6		14,900
Current liabilities		
Trade accounts payable		6,000
Total equity and liabilities		20,900

The bank overdraft has now been repaid and is therefore not shown.

CHAPTER ROUNDUP

⤷ **Irrecoverable debts** are specific debts owed to a business which it decides are never going to be paid. They are written off as an expense in the statement of profit or loss.

⤷ In addition to irrecoverable debts, a business may make an **allowance for receivables** as a prudent precaution to account for the fact that some receivables balances might not be collectable.

⤷ An increase in the allowance for receivables is shown as an expense in the statement of profit or loss and other comprehensive income.

⤷ Trade receivables in the statement of financial position are shown **net** of any receivables allowance.

⤷ When an allowance for receivables is first set up, the whole amount is debited to the statement of profit or loss.

⤷ In subsequent years, only the **movement** on the receivables allowance is debited or credited to irrecoverable debts in the statement of profit or loss.

QUICK QUIZ

1   An irrecoverable debt arises in which of the following situations?

    A   A customer pays part of the account.
    B   An invoice is in dispute.
    C   The customer goes bankrupt.
    D   The invoice is not yet due for payment.

2   Irrecoverable debts are $5,000. Trade receivables at the year end are $120,000. If an allowance for receivables equivalent to 5% of trade receivables is required, what is the entry for irrecoverable debts and allowance for receivables in the statement of profit or loss?

    A $5,000
    B $11,000
    C $6,000
    D $10,750

3   An allowance for receivables equivalent to 2% of trade receivables is required. Trade receivables at the period end are $200,000 and the allowable for receivables brought forward from the previous period is $2,000. What movement is required this year?

4   Fill in the blank.
     If a receivables allowance is increased, expenses in the statement of profit or loss are ....

5   What is the double entry to record an irrecoverable debt written off?

     Mark the correct boxes below.

	Debit	Credit
Irrecoverable debts expense		
Trade receivables		
Allowance for receivables		

ANSWERS TO QUICK QUIZ

1   C   The customer goes bankrupt

2   B $5,000 + (5% × 120,000) = $11,000

3   2% of $200,000 = $4,000. Therefore the allowable needs to be increased by $2,000.

4   If a receivables allowance is increased, expenses in the statement of profit or loss are **increased**.

5

	Debit	Credit
Irrecoverable debts expense	X	
Trade receivables		X
Allowance for receivables		

The allowance for receivables balance is not affected.

Now try ...

Attempt the questions below from the **Practice Question Bank**

Number

Qs 47 – 50

Sales tax

Many business transactions involve sales tax (eg VAT in the UK). Invoices and bills show any sales tax charged separately.

Sales tax is charged on the supply of goods and services. It is an **indirect tax**.

Section 1 explains how sales tax works.

Section 2 deals with the accounting treatment of sales tax. If you understand the principle behind the tax and how it is collected, you will understand the accounting treatment.

TOPIC LIST	SYLLABUS REFERENCE
1 The nature of sales tax and how it is collected	D1(c),(d)
2 Accounting for sales tax	D1(d)

D   Recording transactions and events

1   Sales and purchases

(c)   Understand the general principles of the operation of a sales tax.   K

(d)   Calculate sales tax on transactions and record the consequent accounting entries.   S

1   The nature of sales tax and how it is collected

Sales tax is an indirect tax levied on the sale of goods and services. It is usually administered by the local tax authorities.

1.1 How is sales tax collected?

Sales tax is a cumulative tax, collected at various stages during the life of goods or services. In the illustrative example below, a manufacturer of a television buys materials and components and then sells the television to a wholesaler, who in turn sells it to a retailer, who then sells it to a customer. It is assumed that the rate for sales tax is 15% on all items. All the other figures are for illustration only.

1.2 Example

			Price net of sales tax $	Sales tax 15% $	Total price $
(a)	(i)	Manufacturer purchases raw materials and components	40	6	46
	(ii)	Manufacturer sells the completed television to a wholesaler	200	30	230
		The manufacturer hands over to tax authorities		24	
(b)	(i)	Wholesaler purchases television	200	30	230
	(ii)	Wholesaler sells television to a retailer	320	48	368
		Wholesaler hands over to tax authorities		18	
(c)	(i)	Retailer purchases television	320	48	368
	(ii)	Retailer sells television	480	72	552
		Retailer hands over to tax authorities		24	
(d)		Customer purchases television	480	72	552

The total tax of $72 is borne by the ultimate consumer but is collected on behalf of the tax authorities at the different stages in the product's life. If we assume that the sales tax of $6 on the initial supplies to the manufacturer is paid by the supplier, the tax authorities would collect the sales tax as follows.

	$
Supplier of materials and components	6
Manufacturer	24
Wholesaler	18
Retailer	24
Total sales tax paid	72

So sales tax does not affect the statement of profit or loss, unless it is irrecoverable (see below), but is simply being collected on behalf of the tax authorities to whom a payment is made.

1.3 Input and output sales tax

Registered businesses charge **output sales tax** on sales and suffer **input sales tax** on purchases. If output sales tax exceeds input sales tax, the business pays the difference in tax to the authorities. If output sales tax is less than input sales tax in a period, the tax authorities will refund the difference to the business.

Sales tax charged (or 'collected') on goods and services sold by a business is referred to as output sales tax. Sales tax paid (or 'suffered') on goods and services bought by a business is referred to as input sales tax.

(It may be easier to think of output sales tax as sales tax paid by others on goods and services going 'out' of a business and input sales tax as sales tax paid on goods and services going 'in' to a business.)

The example above assumes that the supplier, manufacturer, wholesaler and retailer are all sales tax registered traders. In order to charge sales tax, a business must be **registered for sales tax**.

A sales tax registered trader must carry out the following tasks.

(a)   Charge sales tax on the goods and services sold at the rate prescribed by the Government. This is output sales tax.

(b)   Pay sales tax on goods and services purchased from other businesses. This is input sales tax.

(c)   Pay to the tax authorities the difference between the sales tax collected on sales and the sales tax paid to suppliers for purchases. Payments are made at prescribed intervals.

1.4 Irrecoverable sales tax

Some sales tax is **irrecoverable**. Where sales tax is irrecoverable it must be regarded as part of the cost of the items purchased and included in the statement of profit or loss charge or in the statement of financial position as appropriate.

There are some circumstances in which sales tax paid on inputs cannot be reclaimed (eg where a trader is not registered for sales tax or where inputs are not related to taxable business activities). This is referred to as **irrecoverable sales tax**. In these cases the trader must bear the cost of the sales tax and account for it accordingly.

For example, if a business pays $500 for entertaining expenses and suffers irrecoverable input sales tax of $75 on this amount, the total of $575 paid should be charged to the statement of profit or loss as an expense. Similarly, if a business pays $5,000 for a motor vehicle and suffers irrecoverable input sales tax of $400, the business should capitalise the full amount of $5,400 as a non-current asset in the statement of financial position.

1.5 Amounts inclusive and exclusive of tax

In business, you are likely to come across sales and purchases figures quoted as gross or net of sales tax.

The **gross amount** of a sale or purchase is the amount **inclusive of sales tax**.

The **net amount** of a sale or purchase is the amount **exclusive of sales tax**.

For example, if the net amount of a purchase is $100, and the rate of sales tax is 15%, the amounts are as follows.

Net amt exclusive of sales tax:		= $100
Sales tax:	= $100 × 15%	= $15
Gross amt inclusive of sales tax:	= $100 + $15	= $115

It is a bit more difficult to calculate the net amount, or sales tax, from the gross amount and the rate of tax. The **net amount** is equal to the **gross amount / (1 + tax rate)**.

For example, if the gross amount of a purchase is $80, and the rate of sales tax is 15%, the sales tax and net amounts are as follows.

Gross amt		= $80
Net amt	= $80 / (1 + 0.15)	= $69.57
Sales tax	= $80 – $69.57	= $10.43

2 Accounting for sales tax

2.1 Statement of profit or loss

Sales tax charged on sales is collected by the business on behalf of the tax authorities. It does not form part of the revenue of the business. For example, if a business sells goods for $600 + sales tax $90, ie for $690 total price, the sales account should only record the $600 excluding sales tax. The accounting entries to record the sale would be as follows.

DEBIT	Cash or trade receivables	$690	
CREDIT	Sales		$600
CREDIT	Sales tax control account (output sales tax)		$90

If input sales tax is **recoverable**, the cost of purchases should exclude the sales tax and be recorded net of tax. For example, if a business purchases goods on credit for $400 + sales tax $60, the transaction would be recorded as follows.

DEBIT	Purchases	$400	
DEBIT	Sales tax control account (input sales tax recoverable)	$60	
CREDIT	Trade payables		$460

If the input sales tax is not recoverable (irrecoverable), the cost of purchases must **include** the tax, ie purchases would be $460 in the example above, because it is the business itself which must bear the cost of the tax.

EXAM FOCUS POINT		
	Purchases	*Sales*
Statement of profit or loss	Irrecoverable input sales tax: include	Exclude sales tax
	Recoverable input sales tax: exclude	

2.2 Sales tax in the cash book, sales day book and purchase day book

When a business makes a credit sale the total amount invoiced, including sales tax, will be recorded in the sales day book. The analysis columns will then separate the sales tax from the sales income of the business as follows.

SALES DAY BOOK

Date	Invoice	Customer	Total $	Sales income $	Sales tax $
10 Jan 20X1	247	A Detter and Sons	230	200	30

When a business is invoiced by a supplier the total amount payable, including sales tax, will be recorded in the purchase day book. The analysis columns will then separate the recoverable input sales tax from the net purchase cost to the business as follows.

PURCHASES DAY BOOK

Date	Customer	Total	Purchase	Sales tax
		$	$	$
15 Mar 20X1	A Splier (Merchants)	184	160	24

When receivables pay what they owe, or payables are paid, there is **no need to show** the sales tax in an analysis column of the cash book, because input and output sales tax arise when the sale is made, not when the debt is settled.

However, sales tax charged on **cash sales** or sales tax paid on **cash purchases** will be analysed in a separate column of the cash book. This is because output sales tax has just arisen from the cash sale and must be credited to the sales tax payables in the ledger accounts. Similarly, input sales tax paid on cash purchases, having just arisen, must be debited to the sales tax payable.

For example, the receipts side of a cash book might be written up as follows.

CASH BOOK (RECEIPTS)

				Analysis columns	
			Sales	Cash	Output sales tax on cash
Date	Narrative	Total	ledger	sales	sales
20X1		$	$	$	$
10 Feb	A Detter & Sons	230	230		
10 Feb	Owen	660	660		
12 Feb	Cash sales	322		280	42
15 Feb	Newgate Merchants	184	184		
20 Feb	Cash sales	92		80	12
		1,488	1,074	360	54

The payments side of a cash book might be written up as follows.

CASH BOOK (PAYMENTS)

				Analysis columns	
				Cash purchases	
			Purchase	and sun-	Input sales tax on cash
Date	Narrative	Total	ledger	dry items	purchases
20X1		$	$	$	$
10 Apr	A Splier (Merchants)	184	184		
20 Apr	Telephone bill paid	138		120	18
25 Apr	Cash purchase of stationery	46		40	6
26 Apr	Sales tax paid to tax authorities	1,400		1,400	
		1,768	184	1,560	24

QUESTION

Statement of profit or loss

Are trade receivables and trade payables shown in the accounts inclusive of sales tax or exclusive of sales tax?

ANSWER

They are shown inclusive of sales tax, as the statement of financial position must reflect the total amount due from receivables and due to payables.

EXAM FOCUS POINT

A small element of sales tax is quite likely in questions. It is worth spending a bit of time ensuring that you understand the logic behind the way sales tax is accounted for, rather than trying to learn the rules by rote. This will ensure that even if you forget the rules, you will be able to work out what should be done.

2.3 Payable for sales tax

An outstanding payable for sales tax will appear as a current liability in the statement of financial position.

The sales tax paid to the authorities each quarter is the difference between recoverable input sales tax on purchases and output sales tax on sales. For example, if a business is invoiced for input sales tax of $8,000 and charges sales tax of $15,000 on its credit sales and sales tax of $2,000 on its cash sales, the sales tax control account would be as follows.

SALES TAX CONTROL ACCOUNT

	$		$
Payables (input sales tax)	8,000	Receivables (output sales	
Cash (payment to authorities)	9,000	tax invoiced)	15,000
		Cash (output sales tax on cash sales)	2,000
	17,000		17,000

Payments to the authorities will not generally coincide with the end of the accounting period of a business, and so at the reporting date there will be a balance on the sales tax control account. If this balance is for an amount payable to the authorities, the outstanding payable for sales tax will appear as a current liability in the statement of financial position.

Occasionally, a business will be owed money by the authorities. In such a situation, the sales tax refund owed by the authorities would be a current asset in the statement of financial position.

QUESTION

Sales tax payable

A business in its first period of trading charges $4,000 of sales tax on its sales and suffers $3,500 of sales tax on its purchases which includes $250 irrecoverable sales tax on business entertaining. Prepare the sales tax control account.

ANSWER

SALES TAX CONTROL ACCOUNT

	$		$
Payables	3,250	Receivables	4,000
Balance c/d (owed to tax authorities)	750		
	4,000		4,000
		Balance b/d	750

EXAM FOCUS POINT

The ACCA examining team commented that in the December 2013 exam, a question on calculating and accounting for sales tax had one of the lowest pass rates.

Specifically, some students accounted for sales tax on **payments** to **credit suppliers**.

This is incorrect, as the sales tax will have already been accounted for when the **credit purchase** was recorded.

Sales tax – the main points

(a) **Credit sales**

    (i)   Include sales tax in sales day book; show it separately

    (ii)   Include gross receipts from receivables in cash book; no need to show sales tax separately

    (iii)   Exclude sales tax element from statement of profit or loss

    (iv)   Credit sales tax control account with output sales tax element of receivables invoiced

(b) **Credit purchases**

    (i)   Include sales tax in purchases day book; show it separately

    (ii)   Include gross payments in cashbook; no need to show sales tax separately

    (iii)   Exclude recoverable sales tax from statement of profit or loss

    (iv)   Include irrecoverable sales tax in statement of profit or loss

    (v)   Debit sales tax control account with recoverable input sales tax element of credit purchases

(c) **Cash sales**

    (i)   Include gross receipts in cash book; show sales tax separately

    (ii)   Exclude sales tax element from statement of profit or loss

    (iii)   Credit sales tax control account with output sales tax element of cash sales

(d) **Cash purchases**

    (i)   Include gross payments in cash book: show sales tax separately

    (ii)   Exclude recoverable sales tax from statement of profit or loss

    (iii)   Include irrecoverable sales tax in statement of profit or loss

    (iv)   Debit sales tax control account with recoverable input sales tax element of cash purchases

EXAM FOCUS POINT

In sales tax questions, remember to check the tax rate used. If you are required to calculate sales tax, the rate will always be given.

CHAPTER ROUNDUP

↳ **Sales tax** is an indirect tax levied on the sale of goods and services. It is usually administered by the local tax authorities.

↳ **Registered** businesses charge **output sales tax** on sales and suffer **input sales tax** on purchases. If output sales tax exceeds input sales tax, the business pays the difference in tax to the authorities. If output sales tax is less than input sales tax in a period, the tax authorities will refund the difference to the business.

↳ Some sales tax is **irrecoverable**. Where sales tax is irrecoverable it must be regarded as part of the cost of the items purchased and included in the statement of profit or loss charge or in the statement of financial position as appropriate.

↳ An outstanding payable for sales tax will appear as a current liability in the statement of financial position.

QUICK QUIZ

1   Which **one** of the following statements about sales tax is correct?

A   Sales tax is a direct tax levied on sales of goods and services.
B   Sales tax is an indirect tax levied on the sales of goods and services.
C   Traders can always reclaim all sales tax paid on their inputs.
D   Sales tax is charged by all businesses on taxable supplies.

2   When sales tax is not recoverable on the cost of a motor vehicle, it should be treated in which of the following ways?

A   Deducted from the cost of the asset capitalised
B   Included in the cost of the asset capitalised
C   Deducted from output tax for the period
D   Written off to the statement of profit or loss as an expense

3   Purchases of goods costing $500 subject to sales tax at 15% occur. Which of the following correctly records the **credit purchase**?

A	DEBIT	Purchases	$500.00	
	DEBIT	Sales tax	$75.00	
	CREDIT	Payables		$575.00
B	DEBIT	Purchases	$575.00	
	CREDIT	Payables		$575.00
C	DEBIT	Purchases	$434.78	
	DEBIT	Sales tax	$65.22	
	CREDIT	Payables		$500.00
D	DEBIT	Purchases	$500.00	
	CREDIT	Sales tax		$65.22
	CREDIT	Payables		$434.78

4   A business purchases goods valued at $400. Sales tax is charged at 15%. What is the double entry to record the purchase?

DEBIT   .... $...............
DEBIT   .... $...............
CREDIT   .... $...............

5   Fill in the blanks.
Input sales tax is the sales tax .... on goods and services .... by the business; output sales tax is the sales tax .... on goods and services .... by the business.

6   When a cash sale is made for $316.25 (including sales tax at 15%) the entries made are:

DEBIT   .... account $...............
CREDIT   .... account $...............
CREDIT   .... account $...............

7   When a cash purchase of $172.50 is made (including sales tax at 15%), what are the double entries required?

A	DEBIT	Purchases	172.50	
	CREDIT	Cash		172.50
B	DEBIT	Purchases	150.00	
	DEBIT	Sales tax	22.50	
	CREDIT	Cash		172.50
C	DEBIT	Cash	150.00	
	DEBIT	Sales tax	22.50	
	CREDIT	Purchases		172.50
D	DEBIT	Cash	172.50	
	CREDIT	Purchases		172.50

8   Fill in the blanks.

The sales tax paid to the tax authorities is the difference between ....
.... and ....

9   A trader is registered for sales tax. During a period, they have sales of $5,750 including sales tax at 15% and purchases of $2,500 excluding sales tax. What amount is owed to or due from the tax authorities at the end of the period?

A $487.50 owed to
B $487.50 due from
C $375.00 owed to
D $375.00 due from

ANSWERS TO QUICK QUIZ

1   B   Sales tax is an indirect tax. Some sales tax paid on inputs is irrecoverable and cannot be reclaimed. Only sales tax registered traders can charge sales tax.

2   B   The irrecoverable sales tax should be included in the cost of the asset capitalised. The statement of financial position value will therefore include sales tax and the depreciation charge will rise accordingly.

3   A   Correct, recoverable input tax is debited to the sales tax a/c and the purchases account is debited net of sales tax.
    B   Incorrect, the sales tax has not been reclaimed.
    C   Incorrect, the $500 is subject to sales tax.
    D   Incorrect, reversal of the sales tax transaction has occurred.

4   DEBIT   **Purchases**   **$400**
    DEBIT   **Sales tax**   **$60**
    CREDIT   **Cash or payables**   **$460**

5   Input sales tax is the sales tax **suffered** on goods and services **bought** by the business; output sales tax is the sales tax **collected** on goods and services **sold** by the business.

6   $316.25 is the gross amount including VAT. The net amount is equal to the gross amount ÷ (1 + tax rate), ie $316.25 ÷ 1.15 = $275. The VAT is therefore the difference between the gross and net amounts ie. $316.25 − $275 = $41.25

    DEBIT   **Cash** account   **$316.25**
    CREDIT   **Sales** account   **$275.00**
    CREDIT   **Sales tax** account   **$41.25**

7
    B   DEBIT   Purchases $150.00
        DEBIT   Sales tax $22.50
        CREDIT Cash $172.50

8   The sales tax paid to the tax authorities is the difference between **output sales tax collected on sales** and **input sales tax suffered on purchases and expenses**.

9   C $375.00 owed to the tax authorities. Output tax on sales $750.00 (5,750/1.15 × 0.15) less input tax on purchases $375.00 (2,500 × 0.15), leaves a net amount of $375.00 due to the tax authorities.

Now try ...

Attempt the questions below from the **Practice Question Bank**

Number

Qs 25 – 28

E

Preparing a trial balance

Control accounts

So far in this Text we have assumed that the bookkeeping and double entry (and subsequent preparation of financial accounts) has been carried out by a business without any mistakes. This is not likely to be the case in real life: even the bookkeeper of a very small business with hardly any accounting entries to make will be prone to human error. If a debit is written as $123 and the corresponding credit as $321, then the books of the business are immediately out of balance by $198.

Once an error has been detected, it has to be corrected.

In this chapter and in the following two chapters we explain how errors can be **detected**, what kinds of error might **exist**, and how to post **corrections** and adjustments to produce final accounts.

TOPIC LIST	SYLLABUS REFERENCE
1 What are control accounts?	E3(b)
2 Discounts	D1(e), D8(k)
3 The operation of control accounts	D8(j), E3(c)
4 The purpose of control accounts	E3(a), (d)–(f)

1   What are control accounts?

A **control account** keeps a total record of a number of individual items. It is an **impersonal** account which is part of the double entry system.

A control account is an account in the nominal ledger in which a record is kept of the total value of a number of similar but individual items. Control accounts are used chiefly for trade receivables and payables.

(a)   A receivables control account is an account in which records are kept of transactions involving all receivables in total. The balance on the receivables control account at any time will be the total amount due to the business at that time from its receivables.

(b)   A payables control account is an account in which records are kept of transactions involving all payables in total. The balance on this account at any time will be the total amount owed by the business at that time to its payables.

Although control accounts are used mainly in accounting for receivables and payables, they can also be kept for other items, such as inventories, wages and salaries, and cash. The first important idea to remember, however, is that a control account is an account which keeps a total record for a collective item (eg receivables), which in reality consists of many individual items (eg individual trade receivables).

A control account is an (impersonal) ledger account which will appear in the nominal ledger.

1.1 Control accounts and personal accounts

The personal accounts of individual customers of the business are kept in the receivables ledger, and the amount owed by each receivable will be a balance on the receivable's personal account. The amount owed by all the receivables together (ie all the trade receivables) will be a balance on the receivables control account.

At any time the balance on the receivables control account should be equal to the sum of the individual balances on the personal accounts in the receivables ledger.

For example, a business has three trade accounts receivable: A Arnold owes $80, B Bagshaw owes $310 and C Cloning owes $200. The debit balances on the various accounts would be:

Receivables ledger (personal accounts)

	$
A Arnold	80
B Bagshaw	310
C Cloning	200
	590

Nominal ledger: receivables control account	590

What has happened here is that the three entries of $80, $310 and $200 were first entered into the sales day book. They were also recorded in the three personal accounts of Arnold, Bagshaw and Cloning in the receivables ledger – but remember that this is not part of the double entry system.

Later, the **total** of $590 is posted from the sales day book by a debit into the receivables (control) account and a credit to sales. If you add up all the debit figures on the personal accounts, they also total $590, as shown above.

2 Discounts

Discounts can be defined as follows.

- A **trade discount** is a reduction in the list price of an article, given by a wholesaler or manufacturer to a retailer. It is often given in return for bulk purchase orders.

- A **cash (or settlement) discount** is a reduction in the amount payable in return for payment in cash, or within an agreed period.

Before looking at control accounts for accounts receivable and payable, we need to consider the accounting treatment for discounts.

2.1 Types of discount

A discount is a reduction in the price of goods below the amount at which those goods would normally be sold to other customers. There are two types of discount.

- **Trade** discount
- **Cash or settlement** discount

A trade discount is a reduction in the cost of goods owing to the nature of the trading transaction. It usually results from buying goods in bulk.

2.1.1 Examples of trade discount

(a)   A customer is quoted a price of $1 per unit for a particular item, but a lower price of 95 cents per unit if the item is bought in quantities of 100 units or more at a time.

(b)   An important customer or a regular customer is offered a discount on all the goods the customer buys, regardless of the size of each individual order, because the total volume of the customer's purchases over time is so large.

A cash discount (or settlement discount) is a reduction in the amount payable to the supplier, in return for immediate payment in cash, by credit card or by other electronic payment, rather than purchase on credit, or for payment within an agreed period.

For example, a supplier charges $1,000 for goods, but offers a discount of 5% if the goods are paid for immediately in cash. Alternatively, a supplier charges $2,000 to a credit customer for goods purchased, but offers a discount of 10% for payment within so many days of the invoice date.

2.2 Accounting for discounts

Trade discounts received are deducted from the cost of purchases. Cash discounts received are included as 'other income' of the period. Trade discounts allowed are deducted from sales and cash discounts allowed are shown as expenses of the period.

2.2.1 Trade discounts

A trade discount is a reduction in the amount of money demanded from a customer.

(a)   If a trade discount is received by a business for goods purchased from a supplier, the amount of money demanded from the business by the supplier will be net of discount (ie it will be the normal sales value less the discount).

(b)   Similarly, if a trade discount is given by a business for goods sold to a customer, the amount of money demanded by the business will be after deduction of the discount.

Trade discounts should therefore be accounted for as follows.

(a)   **Trade discounts received** should be deducted from the gross cost of purchases. In other words, the cost of purchases in the trading account will be stated at gross cost minus discount (ie it will be stated at the invoiced amount).

For example, Company A purchases inventory on credit from Supplier B at a gross cost of $100, and receives a trade discount of 5% from the supplier. The double entry for the purchase is as follows:

DEBIT	Inventory	$95
CREDIT	Trade payables	$95

(b)   **Trade discounts allowed** should be deducted from the gross sales price, so that sales for the period will be reported in the trading account at their invoice value.

For example, Company B sells inventory on credit to Customer A at a gross sale price of $100 and offers a trade discount of 10% to the customer. The double entry for the sale is as follows:

DEBIT	Income	$90
CREDIT	Trade receivables	$90

2.2.2 Cash discounts received

When a business is given the opportunity to take advantage of a cash discount or a settlement discount for prompt payment, the decision whether or not to take the discount is a matter of financing policy, not of trading policy.

For example, A buys goods from B, on the understanding that A will be allowed a period of credit before having to pay for the goods. The terms of the transaction are as follows.

(a)   Date of sale: 1 July 20X6
(b)   Credit period allowed: 30 days
(c)   Invoice price of the goods: $2,000
(d)   Cash discount offered: 4% discount for prompt payment

A has the following choices.

(a)   Holding on to its money for 30 days and then paying the full $2,000
(b)   Paying $2,000 less 4% – ie $1,920 now

This is a financing decision about whether it is worthwhile for A to save $80 by paying its debts sooner, or whether it can employ its cash more usefully for 30 days, and pay the debt at the latest acceptable moment.

If A decides to take the cash discount, it will pay $1,920, instead of the invoiced amount of $2,000. The cash discount received ($80) will be accounted for in the books of A as follows.

(a)   In the purchases account, the cost of purchases will be at the invoiced price (or 'full trade' price) of $2,000. When the invoice for $2,000 is received by A, it will be recorded in A's books of account at that price, and the subsequent financing decision about accepting the cash discount is ignored.

(b)   In the statement of profit or loss, the cash discount received is shown as income received. There is no expense in the statement of profit or loss from which the cash discount can be deducted, and so there is no alternative other than to show the discount received as 'other income'.

IMPORTANT

Cash (or settlement) discounts received are included as other income in the statement of profit or loss.

QUESTION   Discounts

Soft Supplies Co recently purchased from Hard Imports Co 10 printers originally priced at $200 each. A 10% trade discount was negotiated together with a 5% cash discount if payment was made within 14 days. Calculate the following.

A   The total of the trade discount
B   The total of the cash discount

ANSWER

A $200 ($200 × 10 × 10%)
B $90 ($200 × 10 × 90% × 5%)

2.2.3 Cash discounts allowed

The same principle is applied in accounting for cash discounts or settlement discounts allowed to customers. Goods are sold at a trade price, and the offer of a discount on that price is a matter of financing policy for the business and not a matter of trading policy.

For example, X sells goods to Y at a price of $5,000. Y is allowed 60 days' credit before payment, but is also offered a discount of 2% for payment within 10 days of the invoice date.

X will issue an invoice to Y for $5,000 when the goods are sold. X has no idea whether or not Y will take advantage of the discount. In trading terms, and in terms of the amount charged in the invoice to Y, Y is a debtor for $5,000.

If Y subsequently decides to take the discount, Y will pay $5,000 less 2% – ie $4,900 – 10 days later. The discount allowed ($100) will be accounted for by X as follows.

(a)   Sales will be valued at their full invoice price, $5,000.
(b)   The discount allowed will be shown as an expense.

IMPORTANT

Cash (or settlement) discounts allowed are included as expenses in the statement of profit or loss.

QUESTION

Discounts

You are required to prepare the statement of profit or loss of Seesaw Timber Merchants for the year ended 31 March 20X6, given the following information.

	$
Purchases at gross cost	120,000
Trade discounts received	4,000
Settlement discounts received	1,500
Cash sales	34,000
Credit sales at invoice price	150,000
Cash discounts allowed	8,000
Selling expenses	32,000
Administrative expenses	40,000
Drawings by proprietor, Tim Burr	22,000

ANSWER

SEESAW TIMBER MERCHANTS
STATEMENT OF PROFIT OR LOSS FOR THE YEAR ENDED 31 MARCH 20X6

	$	$
Revenue (Note 1)		184,000
Purchases (Note 2)		116,000
Gross profit		68,000
Discounts received		1,500
		69,500
Expenses		
Selling expenses	32,000	
Administrative expenses	40,000	
Discounts allowed	8,000	
		80,000
Loss for the year (transferred to statement of financial position)		(10,500)

Notes

1   $(34,000 + 150,000)
2   $(120,000 – 4,000)
3   Drawings are not an expense, but an appropriation of profit

2.3 Supplier statements

A supplier will usually send a monthly statement showing invoices issued, credit notes, payments received and discounts given. It is **vitally important** that these statements are compared to the supplier's personal account in the payables ledger. Any discrepancies need to be identified and any errors corrected.

A statement of account is reproduced below.

STATEMENT OF ACCOUNT

Pickett (Handling Equipment) Co
Unit 7, Western Industrial Estate
Dunford DN2 7RJ

Tel: (01990) 72101   Fax: (01990) 72980   VAT Reg No 982 7213 49

Accounts Department
Finstar Co
67 Laker Avenue
Dunford DN4 5PS

RECEIVED 1 JUN X1

Date: 31 May 20X1

A/c No: F023

Date	Details	Debit $ c	Credit $ c	Balance $ c
30/4/X1	Balance brought forward from previous statement			492 22
3/5/X1	Invoice no. 34207	129 40√		621 62
4/5/X1	Invoice no. 34242	22 72√		644 34
5/5/X1	Payment received - thank you		412 17√	232 17
17/5/X1	Invoice no. 34327	394 95√		627 12
18/5/X1	Credit note no. 00192		64 40√	562 72
21/5/X1	Invoice no. 34392	392 78		955 50
28/5/X1	Credit note no. 00199		107 64√	847 86

Amount now due	$	847 86

Terms: 30 days net, 1% discount for payment in 7 days. E & OE

Registered office: 4 Arkwright Road, London E16 4PQ Registered in England No 2182417

The statement is received on 1 June 20X1 and is passed to Linda Kelly who is the payables ledger clerk at Finstar Co. Linda obtains a printout of the transactions with Pickett (Handling Equipment) Co from Finstar's payables ledger system. (The reason why Linda has made ticks on the statement and on the printout which follows will be explained below.)

FINSTAR CO		PAYABLES LEDGER
ACCOUNT NAME:	PICKETT (HANDLING EQUIPMENT) CO	
ACCOUNT REF:	PO42	
DATE OF REPORT:	1 JUNE 20X1	

Date	Transaction	(Debit)/Credit $
16.3.X1	Invoice 33004	350.70
20.3.X1	Invoice 33060	61.47
6.4.X1	Invoice 34114	80.05
3.5.X1	Invoice 34207	129.40 ✓
4.5.X1	Payment	(412.17) ✓
6.5.X1	Invoice 34242	22.72 ✓
19.5.X1	Invoice 34327	394.95 ✓
19.5.X1	Credit note 00192	(64.40) ✓
28.5.X1	Payment	(117.77)
30.5.X1	Credit note 00199	(107.64) ✓
	Balance	337.31

The payables ledger of Finstar shows a balance due to Pickett of $337.31, while Pickett's statement shows a balance due of $847.86.

2.3.1 Supplier statement reconciliations

Linda wants to be sure that her payables ledger record for Pickett is correct and so she prepares a **supplier statement reconciliation**.

These are the steps to follow.

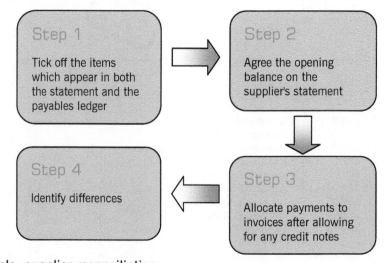

Step 1
Tick off the items which appear in both the statement and the payables ledger

Step 2
Agree the opening balance on the supplier's statement

Step 4
Identify differences

Step 3
Allocate payments to invoices after allowing for any credit notes

2.3.2 Example: supplier reconciliation

Linda applies the above steps to Pickett's statement.

Step 1	The common items have been ticked off on the statement and payables ledger above.

Step 2   The balance brought forward at 30.4.X1 consists of three invoices.

	$
33004	350.70
33060	61.47
34114	80.05
	492.22

Step 3	Invoices 33004 and 33060 were paid on 4 May and 34114 was part of the payment on 28 May.

Step 4	Pickett's statement does not show the payment of $117.77 made on 28 May. However, this is reasonable, as the cheque was probably still in the post. The statement also shows an invoice 34392 dated 21 May, which is not in the payables ledger. This is surprising. Finstar needs to check if the invoice has been received (using the purchase day book) and, if so, has it been posted to the wrong account? If it has not been received, Linda will need to contact Pickett and ask for a duplicate.

SUPPLIER STATEMENT RECONCILIATION
ACCOUNT: PICKETT (HANDLING EQUIPMENT) CO (PO42)

	$
Balance per supplier's statement	847.86
Less payment (28 May) not on statement	(117.77)
invoice (supplier no 34392) on statement,	
not on payables ledger	(392.78)
Balance per payables ledger	337.31

2.3.3 The reasons for reconciling items

Reconciling items may occur as a result of the following items.

Reconciling item	Effect	Status
Payments in transit	A payment will go in the payables ledger when the cheque is issued or when a bank transfer instruction is made. There will be delay (postal, processing) before this payment is entered in the records of the supplier. Any statement of account received by post will also be out of date by the length of time taken to deliver it.	Timing difference
Omitted invoices and credit notes	Invoices or credit notes may appear in the ledger of one business but not in that of the other due to error or omission. However, the most common reason will be a timing difference in recording the items in the different ledgers.	Error or omission or timing difference
Other errors	Addition errors can occur, particularly if a statement of account is prepared manually. Invoice, credit note or payment amounts can be misposted. Regular reconciliation of supplier statements will minimise the possibility of missing such errors.	Error

3 The operation of control accounts

The two most important **control accounts** are those for **receivables** and **payables**. They are part of the double entry system.

3.1 Example: accounting for receivables

You might still be uncertain why we need to have control accounts at all. Before turning our attention to this question, it will be useful first of all to see how transactions involving receivables are accounted for

by means of an illustrative example. Reference numbers are shown in the accounts to illustrate the cross referencing that is needed, and in the example:

(a)   Reference numbers beginning SDB refer to a page in the sales day book
(b)   Reference numbers beginning RL refer to a particular account in the receivables ledger
(c)   Reference numbers beginning NL refer to a particular account in the nominal ledger
(d)   Reference numbers beginning CB refer to a page in the cash book

At 1 July 20X2, the Outer Business Company had no trade accounts receivable. During July, the following transactions affecting credit sales and customers occurred.

(a)   3 July: invoiced A Arnold for the sale on credit of hardware goods: $100

(b)   11 July: invoiced B Bagshaw for the sale on credit of electrical goods: $150

(c)   15 July: invoiced C Cloning for the sale on credit of hardware goods: $250

(d)   10 July: received payment from A Arnold of $90, in settlement of their debt in full, having taken a permitted discount of $10 for payment within seven days

(e)   18 July: received a payment of $72 from B Bagshaw in part settlement of $80 of their debt; a discount of $8 was allowed for payment within seven days of invoice

(f)   28 July: received a payment of $120 from C Cloning, who was unable to claim any discount

Account numbers are as follows.

RL 4   Personal account: A Arnold
RL 9   Personal account: B Bagshaw
RL 13   Personal account: C Cloning
NL 6   Receivables control account
NL 7   Discounts allowed
NL 21   Sales: hardware
NL 22   Sales: electrical
NL 1   Cash at bank

The accounting entries would be as follows.

SALES DAY BOOK   SDB 35

Date 20X2	Name	Ref.	Total $	Hardware $	Electrical $
3 July	A Arnold	RL 4 Dr	100.00	100.00	
11 July	B Bagshaw	RL 9 Dr	150.00		150.00
15 July	C Cloning	RL 13 Dr	250.00	250.00	
			500.00	350.00	150.00
			NL 6 Dr	NL 21 Cr	NL 22 Cr

Note. The personal accounts in the receivables ledger are debited on the day the invoices are sent out. The double entry in the ledger accounts might be made at the end of each day, week or month; here it is made at the end of the month, by posting from the sales day book as follows.

			$	$
DEBIT	NL 6	Receivables control account	500	
CREDIT	NL 21	Sales: hardware		350
	NL 22	Sales: electrical		150

CASH BOOK EXTRACT
RECEIPTS – JULY 20X2   CB 23

Date 20X2	Narrative	Ref.	Total $	Discount allowed $	Accounts receivable $
10 July	A Arnold	RL 4 Cr	90.00	10.00	100.00
18 July	B Bagshaw	RL 9 Cr	72.00	8.00	80.00
28 July	C Cloning	RL 13 Cr	120.00	–	120.00
			282.00	18.00	300.00
			NL 1 Dr	NL 7 Dr	NL 6 Cr

At the end of July, the cash book is posted to the nominal ledger.

		$	$
DEBIT	Cash at bank	282.00	
	Discount allowed	18.00	
CREDIT	Receivables control account		300.00

The personal accounts in the receivables ledger are memorandum accounts, because they are not a part of the double entry system.

MEMORANDUM RECEIVABLES LEDGER
ARNOLD
A/c no: RL 4

Date 20X2	Narrative	Ref.	$	Date 20X2	Narrative	Ref.	$
3 July	Sales	SDB 35	100.00	10 Jul	Cash	CB 23	90.00
					Discount	CB 23	10.00
			100.00				100.00

B BAGSHAW
A/c no: RL 9

Date 20X2	Narrative	Ref.	$	Date 20X2	Narrative	Ref.	$
11 July	Sales	SDB 35	150.00	18 Jul	Cash	CB 23	72.00
					Discount	CB 23	8.00
				31 Jul	Balance	c/d	70.00
			150.00				150.00
1 August	Balance	b/d	70.00				

C CLONING
A/c no: RL 13

Date 20X2	Narrative	Ref.	$	Date 20X2	Narrative	Ref.	$
15 July	Sales	SDB 35	250.00	28 Jul	Cash	CB 23	120.00
				31 Jul	Balance	c/d	130.00
			250.00				250.00
1 August	Balance	b/d	130.00				

In the nominal ledger, the accounting entries are made from the books of prime entry to the ledger accounts, in this example at the end of the month.

NOMINAL LEDGER (EXTRACT)
RECEIVABLES LEDGER CONTROL ACCOUNT
A/c no: NL 6

Date 20X2	Narrative	Ref.	$	Date 20X2	Narrative	Ref.	$
31 July	Sales	SDB 35	500.00	31 Jul	Cash and discount	CB 23	300.00
				31 Jul	Balance	c/d	200.00
			500.00				500.00
1 August	Balance	b/d	200.00				

Note. At 31 July the closing balance on the receivables control account ($200) is the same as the total of the individual balances on the personal accounts in the receivables ledger ($0 + $70 + $130).

DISCOUNT ALLOWED
A/c no: NL 7

Date 20X2	Narrative	Ref.	$	Date	Narrative	Ref.	$
31 July	Receivables	CB 23	18.00				

CASH CONTROL ACCOUNT
A/c no: NL 1

Date 20X2	Narrative	Ref.	$	Date	Narrative	Ref.	$
31 July	Cash received	CB 23	282.00				

SALES: HARDWARE   A/c no: NL 21

Date	Narrative	Ref.	$	Date	Narrative	Ref.	$
				20X2			
				31 Jul	Receivables	SDB 35	350.00

SALES: ELECTRICAL   A/c no: NL 22

Date	Narrative	Ref.	$	Date	Narrative	Ref.	$
				20X2			
				31 Jul	Receivables	SDB 35	150.00

If we take the balance on the accounts shown in this example as at 31 July 20X2, the trial balance is as follows.

TRIAL BALANCE

	Debit	Credit
	$	$
Cash (all receipts)	282	
Receivables	200	
Discount allowed	18	
Sales: hardware		350
Sales: electrical		150
	500	500

The trial balance is shown here to emphasise the point that a trial balance includes the balances on control accounts, but excludes the balances on the personal accounts in the receivables ledger and payables ledger.

3.2 Accounting for payables

If you are able to follow the example above dealing with the receivables control account, you should have no difficulty in dealing with similar examples relating to purchases/payables. If necessary refer back to revise the entries made in the purchase day book and payables ledger personal accounts.

3.3 Entries in control accounts

Typical entries in the control accounts are listed below. Reference 'Jnl' indicates that the transaction is first lodged in the journal before posting to the control account and other accounts indicated. References SRDB and PRDB are to sales returns and purchase returns day books respectively.

RECEIVABLES CONTROL ACCOUNT

	Ref.	$		Ref.	$
Opening debit balances	b/d	7,000	Opening credit balances		
Sales	SDB	52,390	(if any)	b/d	200
Dishonoured bills or	Jnl	1,000	Cash received	CB	52,250
cheques			Discounts allowed	CB	1,250
Cash paid to clear credit			Returns inwards from		
balances	CB	110	customers	SRDB	800
Interest changed on late			Irrecoverable debts	Jnl	300
paid accounts	Jnl	30			
Closing credit balances	c/d	90	Closing debit balances	C/d	5,820
		60,620			60,620
Debit balances b/d		5,820	Credit balances b/d		90

Note. Opening credit balances are unusual in the receivables control account. They represent customers to whom the business owes money, probably as a result of the overpayment of debts or for advance payments of debts for which no invoices have yet been sent.

PAYABLES CONTROL ACCOUNT

	Ref.	$		Ref.	$
Opening debit balances (if any)	b/d	70	Opening credit balances	b/d	8,300
			Purchases	PDB	31,000
Cash paid	CB	29,840	Interest paid on overdue accounts	CB	35
Discounts received	CB	35	Cash received clearing debit balances	CB	25
Returns outwards to suppliers	PRDB	60	Closing debit balances (if any)	c/d	45
Closing credit balances	c/d	9,400			
		39,405			39,405
Debit balances	b/d	45	Credit balances	b/d	9,400

Note. Opening debit balances in the payables control account would represent suppliers who owe the business money, perhaps because the business has overpaid or because a credit note is awaited for returned goods.

Posting from the journal to the memorandum receivables or payables ledgers and to the nominal ledger may be effected at the same time; as in the following example, where C Cloning has returned goods with a sales value of $50.

Journal entry	Ref.	Dr $	Cr $
Sales	NL 21	50	
To receivables control	NL 6		50
To C Cloning (memorandum)	RL 13	–	50
Return of electrical goods inwards			

3.4 Contra entries

Sometimes the same business may be both a receivable and a payable. For example, C Cloning buys hardware from you and you buy stationery from C Cloning. In the receivables ledger, C Cloning owes you $130. However, you owe C Cloning $250. You may reach an agreement to offset the balances receivable and payable. This is known as a 'contra'. The double entry is as follows.

DEBIT	Payables control	$130
CREDIT	Receivables control	$130

You will also need to make the appropriate entries in the memorandum receivables and payables ledger. After this, C Cloning will owe you nothing and you will owe C Cloning $120 ($250 – $130).

QUESTION

Payables control account

A payables control account contains the following entries.

	$
Bank	79,500
Credit purchases	83,200
Discounts received	3,750
Contra with receivables control account	4,000
Balance c/f at 31 December 20X8	12,920

There are no other entries in the account. What was the opening balance brought forward at 1 January 20X8?

ANSWER

PAYABLES CONTROL

	$		$
Bank payments	79,500	Balance b/f (balancing figure)	16,970
Discounts received	3,750	Purchases	83,200
Contra with receivables	4,000		
Balance c/f	12,920		
	100,170		100,170

QUESTION

The total of the balances in a company's receivables ledger is $800 more than the debit balance on its receivables control account. Which one of the following errors could by itself account for the discrepancy?

A The sales day book has been undercast by $800
B Settlement discounts totalling $800 have been omitted from the nominal ledger
C One receivables ledger account with a credit balance of $800 has been treated as a debit balance
D The cash receipts book has been undercast by $800

ANSWER

A The total of sales invoices in the day book is debited to the control account. If the total is understated by $800, the debits in the control account will also be understated by $800. Options B and D would have the opposite effect: credit entries in the control account would be understated. Option C would lead to a discrepancy of 2 × $800 = $1,600.

3.5 Summary of entries

It may help you to see how the receivables ledger and receivables control account are used, by means of a flow chart.

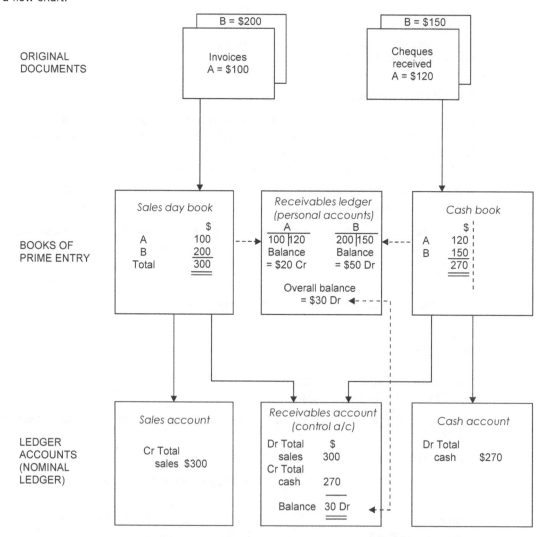

Notes

1   The receivables ledger is not part of the double entry system (it is not used to post the ledger accounts).

2   Nevertheless, the total balance on the receivables ledger (ie all the personal account balances added up) should equal the balance on the receivables control account.

See now whether you can do the following question yourself.

QUESTION   Receivables and payables control accounts

On examining the books of Exports Co, you ascertain that on 1 October 20X8 the receivables ledger balances were $8,024 debit and $57 credit, and the payables ledger balances on the same date $6,235 credit and $105 debit.

For the year ended 30 September 20X9 the following particulars are available.

	$
Sales	63,728
Purchases	39,974
Cash from trade accounts receivable	55,212
Cash to trade accounts payable	37,307
Discount received	1,475
Discount allowed	2,328
Returns inwards	1,002
Returns outwards	535
Irrecoverable debts written off	326
Cash received in respect of debit balances in payables ledger	105
Amount due from customer as shown by receivables ledger, offset against amount due to the same firm as shown by payables ledger (settlement by contra)	434
Allowances to customers on goods damaged in transit	212

On 30 September 20X9 there were no credit balances in the receivables ledger except those outstanding on 1 October 20X8, and no debit balances in the payables ledger.

Required

Write up the following accounts recording the above transactions bringing down the balances as on 30 September 20X9.

(a)   Receivables control account
(b)   Payables control account

ANSWER

(a)   RECEIVABLES CONTROL ACCOUNT

20X8		$	20X8		$
1 Oct	Balances b/f	8,024	1 Oct	Balances b/f	57
20X9			20X9		
30 Sep	Sales	63,728	30 Sep	Cash received from credit customers	55,212
	Balances c/f	57		Discount allowed	2,328
				Returns	1,002
				Irrecoverable debts written off	326
				Contra payables control account	434
				Allowances on goods damaged	212
				Balances c/f	12,238
		71,809			71,809

(b)

PAYABLES CONTROL ACCOUNT

20X8		$	20X8		$
1 Oct	Balances b/f	105	1 Oct	Balances b/f	6,235
20X9			20X9		
30 Sep	Cash paid to credit		30 Sep	Purchases	39,974
	suppliers	37,307		Cash	105
	Discount received	1,475			
	Returns outwards	535			
	Contra receivables				
	control account	434			
	Balances c/f	6,458			
		46,314			46,314

4 The purpose of control accounts

Cash books and day books are totalled periodically and the totals posted to the control accounts. At suitable intervals, the balances on the personal accounts are extracted and totalled. These balance totals should agree to the balance on the control account. In this way, errors can be located and corrected.

4.1 Reasons for having control accounts

The reasons for having control accounts are as follows.

(a) They provide a **check on the accuracy** of entries made in the personal accounts in the receivables ledger and payables ledger. It is very easy to make a mistake in posting entries, because there might be hundreds of entries to make. Figures can get transposed. Some entries might be omitted altogether, so that an invoice or a payment transaction does not appear in a personal account as it should. By comparing (i) and (ii) below, it is possible to identify the fact that errors have been made.

   (i) The total balance on the receivables control account with the total of individual balances on the personal accounts in the receivables ledger.

   (ii) The total balance on the payables control account with the total of individual balances on the personal accounts in the payables ledger.

(b) The control accounts also assist in the **location of errors**, where postings to the control accounts are made daily or weekly, or even monthly. If a clerk fails to record an invoice or a payment in a personal account, or makes a transposition error, it would be a formidable task to locate the error or errors at the end of a year, say, given the number of transactions. By using the control account, a comparison with the individual balances in the receivables or payables ledger can be made for every week or day of the month and the error found much more quickly than if control accounts did not exist.

(c) Where there is a separation of clerical (bookkeeping) duties, the control account provides an **internal check**. The person posting entries to the control accounts will act as a check on a different person(s) whose job it is to post entries to the receivables and payables ledger accounts.

(d) To provide total receivables and payables balances more quickly for producing a trial balance or statement of financial position. A single balance on a control account is obviously **extracted more simply and quickly** than many individual balances in the receivables or payables ledger. This also means that the number of accounts in the double entry bookkeeping system can be kept down to a manageable size, since the personal accounts are memorandum accounts only.

However, particularly in computerised systems, it may be feasible to use receivables and payables ledgers without the need for operating separate control accounts. In such a system, the receivables or payables ledger printouts produced by the computer constitute the list of individual balances as well as providing a total balance which represents the control account balance.

4.2 Balancing and agreeing control accounts with receivables and payables ledgers

The control accounts should be **balanced regularly** (at least monthly) and the balance on the account agreed with the sum of the individual debtors' or suppliers' balances extracted from the receivables or payables ledgers respectively. It is one of the sad facts of an accountant's life that more often than not the balance on the control account does not agree with the sum of balances extracted, for one or more of the following reasons.

(a)　An **incorrect amount** may be **posted** to the control account because of a **miscast** of the total in the book of original entry (ie adding up incorrectly the total value of invoices or payments). The nominal ledger debit and credit postings will then balance, but the control account balance will not agree with the sum of individual balances extracted from the (memorandum) receivables ledger or payables ledger. A **journal entry** must then be made in the nominal ledger to correct the control account and the corresponding sales or expense account.

(b)　A **transposition error** may occur in posting an individual's balance from the book of prime entry to the memorandum ledger, eg a sale to C Cloning of $250 might be posted to the account as $520. This means that the sum of balances extracted from the memorandum ledger must be corrected. **No accounting entry** would be required to do this, except to alter the figure in C Cloning's account.

(c)　A transaction may be **recorded in the control account** and *not* in the **memorandum ledger**, or vice versa. This requires an **entry in the ledger** that has been missed out which means a double posting if the control account has to be corrected, and a single posting if it is the individual's balance in the memorandum ledger that is at fault.

(d)　The sum of balances extracted from the memorandum ledger may be **incorrectly extracted or miscast**. This would involve simply **correcting the total of the balances**.

4.3 Example: agreeing control account balances with the receivables and payables ledgers

Reconciling the control account balance with the sum of the balances extracted from the (memorandum) receivables ledger or payables ledger should be done in two stages.

(a)　Correct the total of the balances extracted from the memorandum ledger. (The errors must be located first, of course.)

	$	$
Receivables ledger total		
Original total extracted		15,320
Add difference arising from transposition error ($95 written as $59)		36
		15,356
Less: credit balance of $60 extracted as a debit balance ($60 × 2)	120	
overcast of list of balances	90	
		210
		15,146

(b)　Bring down the balance before adjustments on the control account, and adjust or post the account with correcting entries.

RECEIVABLES CONTROL ACCOUNT

	$		$
Balance before adjustments	15,091	Petty cash: posting omitted	10
		Returns inwards: individual posting omitted from Control Account	35
		Balance c/d (now in agreement with the corrected total of individual balances	
Undercast of total invoices issued		in (a))	
in sales day book	100		15,146
	15,191		15,191
Balance b/d	15,146		

QUESTION

Receivables control account

April Showers sells goods on credit to most of its customers. In order to control its receivables collection system, the company maintains a receivables control account. In preparing the accounts for the year to 30 October 20X3 the accountant discovers that the total of all the personal accounts in the receivables ledger amounts to $12,802, whereas the balance on the receivables control account is $12,550.

Upon investigating the matter, the following errors were discovered.

(a) Sales for the week ending 27 March 20X3 amounting to $850 had been omitted from the control account.

(b) A customer's account balance of $300 had not been included in the list of balances.

(c) Cash received of $750 had been entered in a personal account as $570.

(d) Discounts allowed totalling $100 had not been entered in the control account.

(e) A personal account balance had been undercast by $200.

(f) A contra item of $400 with the payables ledger had not been entered in the control account.

(g) An irrecoverable debt of $500 had not been entered in the control account.

(h) Cash received of $250 had been debited to a personal account.

(i) Discounts received of $50 had been debited to Bell's receivables ledger account.

(j) Returns inwards valued at $200 had not been included in the control account.

(k) Cash received of $80 had been credited to a personal account as $8.

(l) A cheque for $300 received from a customer had been dishonoured by the bank, but no adjustment had been made in the control account.

Required

(a) Prepare a corrected receivables control account, bringing down the amended balance as at 1 November 20X3.

(b) Prepare a statement showing the adjustments that are necessary to the list of personal account balances so that it reconciles with the amended receivables control account balance.

ANSWER

(a)

RECEIVABLES CONTROL ACCOUNT

	$		$
Uncorrected balance b/d	12,550	Discounts omitted (d)	100
Sales omitted (a)	850	Contra entry omitted (f)	400
Bank: cheque dishonoured (l)	300	Irrecoverable debt omitted (g)	500
		Returns inwards omitted (j)	200
		Amended balance c/d	12,500
	13,700		13,700
Balance b/d	12,500		

Note. Items (b), (c), (e), (h), (i) and (k) are matters affecting the personal accounts of customers. They have no effect on the control account.

(b)   STATEMENT OF ADJUSTMENTS TO LIST OF PERSONAL ACCOUNT BALANCES

		$	$
Original total of list of balances			12,802
Add	debit balance omitted (b)	300	
	debit balance understated (e)	200	
			500
			13,302
Less	transposition error (c): understatement of cash received	180	
	cash debited instead of credited (2 × $250) (h)	500	
	discounts received wrongly debited to Bell (i)	50	
	understatement of cash received (k)	72	
			802
			12,500

QUESTION

ABC has a payables control account balance of $12,500 at 31 December 20X6. However, the extract of balances from the payables ledger totals $12,800. Investigation finds the following errors: purchases for week 52 of $1,200 had been omitted from the control account; a supplier account of $900 had been omitted from the list of balances.

What is the correct payables balance at 31 December 20X6?

A $12,500
B $13,400
C $12,800
D $13,700

ANSWER

D

PAYABLES CONTROL ACCOUNT

	$		$
		Bal b/d	12,500
Bal c/d	13,700	Purchases – week 52	1,200
	13,700		13,700

Corrected list of balances:

	$
Original	12,800
Omitted account	900
	13,700

QUESTION

XYZ has a payables control account balance of $17,250 at 31 December 20X9. However, the extract of balances from the payables ledger totals $14,500. Investigation finds the following errors: a contra entry of $750 had been omitted from the control account; an account with a balance of $500 debit had been included as $500 credit in the list of balances; and payments totalling $3,000 had been posted to the individual accounts but the double entry postings had not yet been made.

Required

(a)   Prepare a corrected payables control account, bringing down the amended balance as at 31 December 20X9.

(b)   Prepare a statement showing the adjustments that are necessary to the list of personal account balances so that it reconciles with the amended payables control account balance.

ANSWER

(a)
PAYABLES CONTROL ACCOUNT

	$		$
Contra entry omitted	750	Bal b/d	17,250
Payment omitted	3,000		
Bal c/d	13,500		
	17,250		
		Bal b/d	

(b)   STATEMENT OF ADJUSTMENTS TO LIST OF PERSONAL ACCOUNT BALANCES

	$
Original	14,500
Less debit balance entered as credit (2 × $500)	1,000
Amended total	13,500

EXAM FOCUS POINT

The ACCA examining team has highlighted control accounts as one of the areas poorly answered in recent exams.

The key to carrying out reconciliations is to ask yourself the following questions:

- What is the correct entry?
- What entries were actually made?

One of the requirements of performance objective PO6 Record and process transactions and events, is to 'verify, input, and process routine financial accounting data within the accounting system'. This chapter of the Text will help you fulfil this requirement.

CHAPTER ROUNDUP

- A **control account** keeps a total record of a number of individual items. It is an **impersonal** account which is part of the double entry system.

- Discounts can be defined as follows.

  - A **trade discount** is a reduction in the list price of an article, given by a wholesaler or manufacturer to a retailer. It is often given in return for bulk purchase orders.

  - A **cash (or settlement) discount** is a reduction in the amount payable in return for payment in cash, or within an agreed period.

- **Trade discounts received** are deducted from the cost of purchases. **Cash discounts received** are included as 'other income' of the period. **Trade discounts allowed** are deducted from sales and **cash discounts allowed** are shown as expenses of the period.

- The two most important **control accounts** are those for **receivables** and **payables**. They are part of the double entry system.

- Cash books and day books are totalled periodically and the totals posted to the control accounts. At suitable intervals, the balances on the personal accounts are extracted and totalled. These balance totals should agree to the balance on the control account. In this way, errors can be located and corrected.

QUICK QUIZ

1   Which of the following accounting items may have control accounts in the nominal ledger?

    1   Receivables and payables
    2   Inventories
    3   Cash
    4   Salaries and wages

    A   1 and 2
    B   1, 2 and 4
    C   1, 2 and 3
    D   1, 2, 3 and 4

2   Sales of $4,000 have been omitted from the receivables control account. What is the entry to correct this?

    A   DEBIT RCA $4,000
    B   CREDIT RCA $4,000

3   During a period, A Co has the following transactions on receivables control account: sales $125,000, cash received $50,000, discounts allowed $2,000. The balance carried forward is $95,000. What was the opening balance at the beginning of the period?

    A $22,000 debit
    B $22,000 credit
    C $18,000 debit
    D $20,000 debit

4   An invoice amount has been incorrectly posted to the sales day book. The memorandum accounts are posted direct from the invoices. A receivables control account reconciliation will reveal this error. True or false?

5   A transaction for $10,000 of sales offers 2% trade discount and 5% cash discount. If both discounts are claimed, how much is posted to discounts allowed?

    A $490
    B $500
    C $690
    D $700

1 D (i), (ii), (iii) and (iv)

2 A DEBIT RCA $4,000

3 A

RECEIVABLES CONTROL

	$		$
Bal b/d (bal. figure)	22,000	Cash	50,000
Sales	125,000	Discounts allowed	2,000
		Bal c/d	95,000
	147,000		147,000

If you had answer B, you reversed the double entry and so produced a payables control account. In answer D, you omitted the discounts allowed figure; while in answer C you put discounts allowed on the debit instead of the credit side of the control account.

4 True. However, if the memorandum accounts were posted from the sales day book, then the answer would be false.

5 A The sale is recorded as $9,800 ($10,000 – $200 trade discount).
Discount allowed is then 5% × $9,800 = $490.

Now try ...

Attempt the questions below from the **Practice Question Bank**

Number

Qs 55 – 59

Bank reconciliations

It is very likely that you will have had to do a bank reconciliation at work. If not, you will probably have done one on your own bank account without even being aware of it.

The first two sections of this chapter explain why we need a bank reconciliation, and the sort of differences that need to be reconciled.

The third section takes you through some examples of increasing complexity.

1   Bank statement and cash book

In theory, the entries appearing on a business's **bank statement** should be exactly the same as those in the business **cash book**. The balance shown by the bank statement should be the same as the cash book balance on the same date.

The cash book of a business is the record of **how much cash the business believes** that it **has in the bank**. In the same way, you might keep a private record of how much you think you have in your own bank account, perhaps by making a note in your cheque book of income received and the cheques you write. If you do keep such a record, you will probably agree that your bank statement balance is rarely exactly the same as your own figure.

Why might your own estimate of your bank balance be different from the amount shown on your bank statement? There are three common explanations.

(a)   **Error**. Errors in calculation, or recording income and payments, are more likely to have been made by you than by the bank, but it is conceivable that the bank has made a mistake too.

(b)   **Bank charges or bank interest**. The bank might deduct charges for interest on an overdraft or for its services, which you are not informed about until you receive the bank statement.

(c)   **Timing differences**

     (i)   There might be some cheques that you have received and paid into the bank, but which have not yet been '**cleared**' and added to your account. So although your own records show that some cash has been added to your account, it has not yet been acknowledged by the bank – although it will be soon once the cheque has cleared.

     (ii)   Similarly, you might have made some payments by cheque, and reduced the balance in your account in the record that you keep, but the person who receives the cheque might not bank it for a while. Even when it is banked, it takes a day or two for the banks to process it and for the money to be deducted from your account.

If you keep a personal record of your cash position at the bank, and if you check your periodic bank statements against what you think you should have in your account, you will be doing a bank reconciliation.

A bank reconciliation is a comparison of a bank statement (sent monthly, weekly or even daily by the bank) with the cash book. Differences between the balance on the bank statement and the balance in the cash book will be errors or timing differences, and they should be identified and satisfactorily explained.

2 The bank reconciliation

Differences between the cash book and the bank statement arise for three reasons.

- Errors – usually in the cash book
- Omissions – such as bank charges not posted in the cash book
- Timing differences – such as unpresented cheques

2.1 The bank statement

A bank statement is sent by a bank to its customers itemising the balance on the account at the beginning of the period, receipts into the account and payments from the account during the period, and the balance at the end of the period.

It is necessary to remember, however, that if a customer has money in their account, the bank owes them that money, and the customer is therefore a **payable** of the bank (hence the phrase 'to be in credit' means to have money in your account). This means that if a business has $8,000 cash in the bank, it will have a debit balance in its own cash book, but the bank statement, if it reconciles exactly with the cash book, will state that there is a credit balance of $8,000. **(The bank's records are a 'mirror image' of the customer's own records, with debits and credits reversed.)**

2.2 Why is a bank reconciliation necessary?

A bank reconciliation is needed to identify and account for the differences between the cash book and the bank statement.

QUESTION   Differences

These differences fall into three categories. What are they?

ANSWER

Look back to the beginning of this section.

2.3 What to look for when doing a bank reconciliation

The cash book and bank statement will rarely agree at a given date. If you are doing a bank reconciliation, you may have to look for the following items.

(a) **Corrections and adjustments to the cash book**

    (i)   Payments made into the bank account or from the bank account by way of standing order or direct debit, which have not yet been entered in the cash book

    (ii)   Dividends received (on investments held by the business), paid direct into the bank account but not yet entered in the cash book

    (iii) Bank interest and bank charges, not yet entered in the cash book

    (iv) Errors in the cash book that need to be corrected

         The **corrected cash book** balance is the balance that is shown in the statement of financial position.

(b) **Items reconciling the corrected cash book balance to the bank statement**

    (i)   Cheques drawn (ie paid) by the business and credited in the cash book, which have not yet been presented to the bank, or 'cleared', and so do not yet appear on the bank statement. These are commonly known as unpresented cheques or outstanding cheques.

(ii)   Cheques received by the business, paid into the bank and debited in the cash book, but which have not yet been cleared and entered in the account by the bank, and so do not yet appear on the bank statement. These are commonly known as outstanding lodgements or deposits credited after date.

(iii)   Electronic payments that have not yet been cleared.

EXAM FOCUS POINT

You are highly likely to have a bank reconciliation question in your exam. You may have to adjust the cash book, the bank balance or both. Make sure you pay particular attention to the next section.

The ACCA examining team reported that in the December 2013 exam, students scored highly on the question on bank reconciliations.

3 Worked examples

When the differences between the bank statement and the cash book are identified, the cash book must be corrected for any errors or omissions. Any remaining difference can then be shown to be due to timing differences.

3.1 Example: bank reconciliation

At 30 September 20X6, the balance in the cash book of Wordsworth Co was $805.15 debit. A bank statement on 30 September 20X6 showed Wordsworth Co to be in credit by $1,112.30.

On investigation of the difference between the two sums, it was established that:

(a)   The cash book had been undercast by $90.00 on the debit side*

(b)   Cheques paid in not yet credited by the bank amounted to $208.20, called outstanding lodgements

(c)   Cheques drawn not yet presented to the bank amounted to $425.35 called unpresented cheques

* **Note**. 'Casting' is an accountant's term for adding up.

Required

(a)   Show the correction to the cash book.

(b)   Prepare a statement reconciling the balance per bank statement to the balance per cash book.

Solution

(a)   CORRECTED CASH BOOK

	$
Cash book balance brought forward	805.15
Add	
Correction of undercast	90.00
Corrected balance	895.15

(b)   BANK RECONCILIATION

	$
Balance per bank statement	1,112.30
Add outstanding lodgements	208.20
	1,320.50
Less unpresented cheques	(425.35)
Balance per cash book	895.15

QUESTION
Reconciliation

On 31 January 20X8 a company's cash book showed a credit balance of $150 on its current account which did not agree with the bank statement balance. In performing the reconciliation the following points came to light.

	$
Not recorded in the cash book	
Bank charges	36
Transfer from deposit account to current account	500
Not recorded on the bank statement	
Unpresented cheques	116
Outstanding lodgements	630

It was also discovered that the bank had debited the company's account with a cheque for $400 in error. What was the original balance on the bank statement?

ANSWER

CASH ACCOUNT

	$		$
		Balance b/d	150
Transfer from deposit a/c	500	Charges	36
		Balance c/d	314
	500		500

	$
Balance per corrected cash book	314
Add unpresented cheques	116
Less outstanding lodgements	(630)
Less error by bank*	(400)
Balance per bank statement	(600)

* Note that, on the bank statement, a debit is a payment out of the account.

EXAM FOCUS POINT

You may well be asked to reconstruct opening figures in the exam. If so, then you may need to reverse the usual workings, as illustrated in the example above.

QUESTION
Bank statement

A company's bank statement shows $715 direct debits and $353 investment income not recorded in the cash book. The bank statement does not show a customer's cheque for $875 entered in the cash book on the last day of the accounting period. If the cash book shows a credit balance of $610, what balance appears on the bank statement?

A $1,847 debit
B $1,847 credit
C $972 credit
D $972 debit

Handwritten working:
DR / CR
−610 (715) / 610
353
(362)
(972)
(875)
(1,847) Bal on Bank Statement

ANSWER

A

	$	$
Balance per cash book		(610)
Items on statement, not in cash book		
Direct debits	(715)	
Investment income	353	
		(362)
Corrected balance per cash book		(972)
Item in cash book, not on statement		
Customer's cheque		(875)
Balance per bank statement		(1,847)

As the balance is overdrawn, this is a debit on the bank statement.

QUESTION

Bank balance

Given the facts in the question above, what is the figure for the bank balance to be reported in the final accounts?

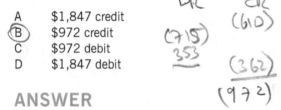

A $1,847 credit
B $972 credit
C $972 debit
D $1,847 debit

ANSWER

B   The figure to go in the statement of financial position is the **corrected cash book figure**. This is $972 credit (or overdrawn). So the bank figure will appear in liabilities.

3.2 Example: more complicated bank reconciliation

On 30 June 20X0, Cook's cash book showed that he had an overdraft of $300 on his current account at the bank. A bank statement as at the end of June 20X0 showed that Cook was in credit with the bank by $65.

On checking the cash book with the bank statement you find the following.

(a)   Cheques drawn, amounting to $500, had been entered in the cash book but had not been presented.

(b)   Cheques received, amounting to $400, had been entered in the cash book, but had not been credited by the bank.

(c)   On instructions from Cook the bank had transferred interest received on his deposit account amounting to $60 to his current account, recording the transfer on 5 July 20X0. However, this amount had been credited in the cash book as on 30 June 20X0.

(d)   Bank charges of $35 shown in the bank statement had not been entered in the cash book.

(e)   The payments side of the cash book had been undercast by $10.

(f)   Dividends received amounting to $200 had been paid direct to the bank and not entered in the cash book.

(g)   A cheque for $50 drawn on deposit account had been shown in the cash book as drawn on current account.

(h)   A cheque issued to Jones for $25 was replaced when out of date. It was entered again in the cash book, no other entry being made. Both cheques were included in the total of unpresented cheques shown above.

Required

(a)   Indicate the appropriate adjustments in the cash book.

(b)   Prepare a statement reconciling the corrected cash book balance with that shown in the bank statement.

Solution

(a)   The errors to correct are given in notes (c), (e), (f), (g) and (h) of the question. Bank charges (note (d)) also call for an adjustment.

(Note that debit entries **add** to the cash balance and credit entries are **deductions** from the cash balance.)

Items		Adjustments in cash book	
		Debit	*Credit*
		$	$
(c)	Cash book incorrectly credited with interest on 30 June; should have been debited with the receipt	60	
(c)	Debit cash book (current a/c) with transfer of interest from deposit a/c (note 1)	60	
(d)	Bank charges		35
(e)	Undercast on payments (credit) side of cash book		10
(f)	Dividends received should be debited in the cash book	200	
(g)	Cheque drawn on deposit account, not current account Add cash back to current account	50	
(h)	Cheque paid to Jones is out of date and so cancelled Cash book should now be debited, since previous credit entry is no longer valid (note 2)	25	
		395	45

		$	$
Cash book: balance on current account as at 30 June 20X0			(300)
Adjustments and corrections:			
Debit entries (adding to cash)		395	
Credit entries (reducing cash balance)		(45)	
Net adjustments			350
Corrected balance in the cash book			50

Notes

1   Item (c) is rather complicated. The transfer of interest from the deposit to the current account was presumably given as an instruction to the bank on or before 30 June 20X0. Since the correct entry is to debit the current account (and credit the deposit account) the correction in the cash book should be to debit the current account with 2 × $60 = $120, ie to cancel out the incorrect credit entry in the cash book and then to make the correct debit entry. However, the bank does not record the transfer until 5 July, and so it will not appear in the bank statement.

2   Item (h). Two cheques have been paid to Jones, but one is now cancelled. Since the cash book is credited whenever a cheque is paid, it should be debited whenever a cheque is cancelled. The amount of cheques paid but not yet presented should be reduced by the amount of the cancelled cheque.

(b)   BANK RECONCILIATION STATEMENT AT 30 JUNE 20X0

	$	$
Balance per bank statement		65
Add outstanding lodgements	400	
deposit interest not yet credited	60	
		460
		525
Less: unpresented cheques	500	
less cheque to Jones cancelled	(25)	
		475
Balance per corrected cash book		50

EXAM FOCUS POINT

Notice that in preparing a bank reconciliation it is good practice to begin with the balance shown by the bank statement and end with the balance shown by the cash book. It is this corrected cash book balance which will appear in the statement of financial position as 'cash at bank'. However, examination questions sometimes ask for the reverse order: as always, read the question carefully.

You might be interested to see the adjustments to the cash book in part (a) of the problem presented in the T-account format, as follows.

CASH BOOK

20X0		$	20X0		$
Jun 30	Bank interest – reversal of		Jun 30	Balance brought down	300
	incorrect entry	60		Bank charges	35
	Bank interest account	60		Correction of undercast	10
	Dividends paid direct to bank	200		Balance carried down	50
	Cheque drawn on deposit				
	account written back	50			
	Cheque issued to Jones				
	cancelled	25			
		395			395

QUESTION   Bank reconciliation

From the information given below relating to PWW Co you are required to:

(a)   Make such additional entries in the cash at bank account of PWW Co as you consider necessary to show the correct balance at 31 October 20X2.

(b)   Prepare a statement reconciling the correct balance in the cash at bank account as shown in (a) above with the balance at 31 October 20X2 that is shown on the bank statement from Z Bank Co.

CASH AT BANK ACCOUNT IN THE LEDGER OF PWW CO

20X2 October		$	20X2 October		$
1	Balance b/f	274	1	Wages	3,146✓
8	Q Manufacturing	3,443✓	1	Petty cash	55✓
8	R Cement	1,146✓	8	Wages	3,106✓
11	S Co	638✓	8	Petty cash	39✓
11	T & Sons	512✓	15	Wages	3,029✓
11	U & Co	4,174✓	15	Petty cash	78✓
15	V Co	1,426✓	22	A & Sons	929✓
15	W Electrical	887✓	22	B Co	134✓
22	X and Associates	1,202✓	22	C & Company	77✓
26	Y Co	2,875✓	22	D & E	263✓
26	Z Co	982✓	22	F Co	1,782✓
29	ABC Co	1,003✓	22	G Associates	230✓
29	DEE Corporation	722✓	22	Wages	3,217✓
29	GHI Co	2,461✓	22	Petty cash	91✓
31	Balance c/f	14	25	H & Partners	26✓
			26	J Sons & Co	(868)
			26	K & Co	(107)
			26	L, M & N	666✓
			28	O Co	(112)
			29	Wages	3,191✓
			29	Petty cash	52✓
			29	P & Sons	(561)
		21,759			21,759

Z BANK CO – STATEMENT OF ACCOUNT WITH PWW CO

20X2 October		Payments $	Receipts $	Balance $	
1				1,135	
1	cheque	55✓			
1	cheque	3,146✓			
1	cheque	(421)		2,487	O/D
2	cheque	(73)			
2	cheque	(155)		2,715	O/D
6	cheque	(212)		2,927	O/D
8	sundry credit		4,589✓		
8	cheque	3,106✓			
8	cheque	39✓		1,483	O/D
11	sundry credit		5,324✓	3,841	
15	sundry credit		2,313✓		
15	cheque	78✓			
15	cheque	3,029✓		3,047	
22	sundry credit		1,202✓		
22	cheque	3,217✓			
22	cheque	91✓		941	
25	cheque	1,782✓			
25	cheque	134✓		975	O/D
26	cheque	929✓			
26	sundry credit		3,857✓		
26	cheque	230✓		1,723	
27	cheque	263✓			
27	cheque	77✓		1,383	
29	sundry credit		4,186✓		
29	cheque	52✓			
29	cheque	3,191✓			
29	cheque	26✓			

2,300

20X2 October		Payments $	Receipts $	Balance $
29	dividends on investments		2,728	
29	cheque	666		4,362
31	bank charges	936		3,426

ANSWER

(a)

CASH BOOK

		$				$
31 Oct	Dividends received	2,728	31 Oct	Unadjusted balance b/f (overdraft)		14
			31 Oct	Bank charges		936
			31 Oct	Adjusted balance c/f		1,778
		2,728				2,728

(b)   BANK RECONCILIATION STATEMENT
AT 31 OCTOBER 20X2

	$	$
Corrected balance as per cash book		1,778
Cheques paid out but not yet presented	1,648	
Cheques paid in but not yet cleared by bank	0	
		1,648
Balance as per bank statement		3,426

Workings

1	*Payments shown on bank statement but not in cash book** $(421 + 73 + 155 + 212)$ * Presumably recorded in cash book before 1 October 20X2 but not yet presented for payment as at 30 September 20X2	$861
2	*Payments in the cash book and on the bank statement* $(3,146 + 55 + 3,106 + 39 + 78 + 3,029 + 3,217 + 91 + 1,782 +$ $134 + 929 + 230 + 263 + 77 + 52 + 3,191 + 26 + 666)$	$20,111
3	*Payments in the cash book but not on the bank statement* = Total payments in cash book $21,759 minus $20,111 =	$1,648

		$
Alternatively:	J & Sons	868
	K & Co	107
	O Co	112
	P & Sons	561
		1,648

4	*Bank charges, not in the cash book*	$936
5	*Receipts recorded by bank statement but not in cash book:* dividends on investments	$2,728
6	*Receipts in the cash book and also bank statement* (8 Oct $4,589; 11 Oct $5,324; 15 Oct $2,313; 22 Oct $1,202; 26 Oct $3,857; 29 Oct $4,186)	$21,471
7	*Receipts recorded in cash book but not bank statement*	None

One of the requirements of performance objective PO6 Record and process transactions and events, is to 'prepare reconciliations and other accounting controls and review those performed by others'. This chapter of the Text will help you fulfil this requirement.

CHAPTER ROUNDUP

↳ In theory, the entries appearing on a business's **bank statement** should be exactly the same as those in the business **cash book**. The balance shown by the bank statement as on a particular date should be the same as the cash book balance at the same date.

↳ Differences between the cash book and the bank statement arise for three reasons.

– Errors – usually in the cash book
– Omissions – such as bank charges not posted in the cash book
– Timing differences – such as unpresented cheques

↳ When the differences between the bank statement and the cash book are identified, the cash book must be corrected for any errors or omissions. Any remaining difference can then be shown to be due to timing differences.

QUICK QUIZ

1 Which of the following are common reasons for differences between the cash book and the bank statements?

1 Timing differences
2 Errors
3 Omissions
4 Contra entries

A 1 and 2
B 1 and 4
C 2, 3 and 4
D 1, 2 and 3

2 A cash book and a bank statement will never agree.

Is this statement true or false?

A True
B False

3 A bank statement shows a balance of $1,200 in credit. An examination of the statement shows a $500 cheque paid in per the cash book but not yet on the bank statement and a $1,250 cheque paid out but not yet on the statement. In addition, the cash book shows deposit interest received of $50 but this is not yet on the statement. What is the balance per the cash book?

A $1,900 overdrawn
B $500 overdrawn
C $1,900 in hand
D $500 in hand

4 Comparing the cash book with the bank statement is called a ....(complete the blanks).

5 Why is it necessary to compare the cash book and bank statement?

ANSWERS TO QUICK QUIZ

1   D   Contra entries only occur between the receivables and payables control account.

2   B   False. In very small businesses, with few transactions, the cash book and bank statement could well agree.

3   D

	$	$
Balance per bank statement		1,200
Add outstanding lodgements	500	
deposit interest not yet credited	50	
		550
		1,750
Less unpresented cheques		(1,250)
Balance per cash book		500

4   Bank reconciliation

5   It highlights errors and omissions in the cash book and helps to prevent fraud. It also checks the bank figure and helps to spot any bank errors.

Now try ...

Attempt the questions below from the **Practice Question Bank**

Number

Qs 60 – 63

Correction of errors

This chapter continues the subject of errors in accounts. You have already learned about errors which arise in the context of the cash book or the receivables and payables ledgers and control accounts.

Here we deal with errors that may be corrected by means of the journal or a suspense account.

By the end of this chapter you should be able to prepare a set of final accounts for a sole trader from a trial balance after incorporating adjustments to profits for errors.

TOPIC LIST	SYLLABUS REFERENCE
1 Types of error in accounting	E2(a),(b)
2 The correction of errors	E2(c)–(d), E5(a)–(d), E2(d)

Study Guide	Intellectual level
E **Preparing a trial balance**	
2 **Correction of errors**	
(a) Identify the types of error which may occur in bookkeeping systems.	K
(b) Identify errors which would be highlighted by the extraction of a trial balance.	K
(c) Prepare journal entries to correct errors.	S
(d) Calculate and understand the impact of errors on the statement of profit or loss and other comprehensive income and statement of financial position.	S
5 **Suspense accounts**	
(a) Understand the purpose of a suspense account.	K
(b) Identify errors leading to the creation of a suspense account.	K
(c) Record entries in a suspense account.	S
(d) Make journal entries to clear a suspense account.	S

EXAM FOCUS POINT

The ACCA examining team has highlighted suspense accounts and errors as areas that students find particularly difficult. You need to use a methodical approach as highlighted in this chapter.

1 Types of error in accounting

There are five main types of error. Some can be corrected by journal entry; some require the use of a suspense account.

It is not really possible to draw up a complete list of all the errors which might be made by bookkeepers and accountants. Even if you tried, it is more than likely that as soon as you finished, someone would commit a completely new error that you had never even dreamed of! However, it is possible to describe **five frequent types of error**. They are as follows.

- Errors of **transposition**
- Errors of **omission**
- Errors of **principle**
- Errors of **commission**
- **Compensating errors**

Once an error has been detected, it needs to be put right.

(a) If the correction **involves a double entry** in the ledger accounts, then it is done by using a **journal entry**.

(b) When the error **breaks the rule of double entry**, then it is corrected by the use of a **suspense account** as well as a journal entry.

1.1 Errors of transposition

An error of transposition is when two digits in a figure are accidentally recorded the wrong way round.

For example, suppose that a sale is recorded in the sales account as $6,843, but it has been incorrectly recorded in the total receivables account as $6,483. The error is the transposition of the 4 and the 8. The consequence is that total debits will not be equal to total credits. You can often detect a transposition error by checking whether the difference between debits and credits can be divided exactly by 9. For example, $6,843 − $6,483 = $360; $360 ÷ 9 = 40.

1.2 Errors of omission

An error of omission means failing to record a transaction at all, or making a debit or credit entry, but not the corresponding double entry.

Here is an example.

(a)   If a business receives an invoice from a supplier for $250, the transaction might be omitted from the books entirely. As a result, both the total debits and the total credits of the business will be incorrect by $250.

(b)   If a business receives an invoice from a supplier for $300, the payables control account might be credited, but the debit entry in the purchases account might be omitted. In this case, the total credits would not equal total debits (because total debits are $300 less than they ought to be).

1.3 Errors of principle

An error of principle involves making a double entry in the belief that the transaction is being entered in the correct accounts, but subsequently finding out that the accounting entry breaks the 'rules' of an accounting principle or concept.

A typical example of such an error is to treat certain revenue expenditure incorrectly as capital expenditure.

(a)   For example, repairs to a machine costing $150 should be treated as revenue expenditure, and debited to a repairs account. If, instead, the repair costs are added to the cost of the non-current asset (capital expenditure) an error of principle would have occurred. As a result, although total debits still equal total credits, the repairs account is $150 less than it should be and the cost of the non-current asset is $150 greater than it should be.

(b)   Similarly, suppose that the proprietor of the business sometimes takes cash out of the till for their personal use and during a certain year these withdrawals on account of profit amount to $280. The bookkeeper states that they have reduced cash sales by $280 so that the cash book could be made to balance. This would be an error of principle, and the result of it would be that the withdrawal account is understated by $280, and so is the total value of sales in the sales account.

1.4 Errors of commission

Errors of commission are where the bookkeeper makes a mistake in carrying out their task of recording transactions in the accounts.

Here are two common types of errors of commission.

(a)   **Putting a debit entry or a credit entry in the wrong account**. For example, if telephone expenses of $540 are debited to the electricity expenses account, an error of commission would have occurred. The result is that although total debits and total credits balance, telephone expenses are understated by $540 and electricity expenses are overstated by the same amount.

(b)   **Errors of casting (adding up).** The total daily credit sales in the sales day book should be $28,425, but are incorrectly added up as $28,825. The total sales in the sales day book are then used to credit total sales and debit total receivables in the ledger accounts. Although total debits and total credits are still equal, they are incorrect by $400.

1.5 Compensating errors

Compensating errors are errors which are, coincidentally, equal and opposite to one another.

For example, although unlikely, in theory two transposition errors of $540 might occur in extracting ledger balances, one on each side of the double entry. In the administration expenses account, $2,282 might be written instead of $2,822 while, in the sundry income account, $8,391 might be written instead of $8,931. Both the debits and the credits would be $540 too low, and the mistake would not be apparent when the trial balance is cast. Consequently, compensating errors hide the fact that there are errors in the trial balance.

1.6 Summary: errors that can be detected by a trial balance

- Errors of transposition
- Errors of omission (if the omission is one-sided)
- Errors of commission (if one-sided, or two debit entries are made, for example)

Other errors will not be detected by extracting a trial balance, but may be spotted by other controls (such as bank and control account reconciliations).

2 | The correction of errors

Errors which leave total debits and credits in the ledger accounts in balance can be corrected by using **journal entries**. Otherwise a suspense account has to be opened first, and later cleared by a journal entry.

2.1 Journal entries

Some errors can be corrected by journal entries. To remind you, the format of a journal entry is:

Date	Debit	Credit
	$	$
Account to be debited	X	
Account to be credited		X
(Narrative to explain the transaction)		

The journal requires a debit and an equal credit entry for each 'transaction', ie for each correction. This means that if total debits equal total credits before a journal entry is made then they will still be equal after the journal entry is made. This would be the case if, for example, the original error was a debit wrongly posted as a credit and vice versa.

Similarly, if total debits and total credits are unequal before a journal entry is made, then they will still be unequal (by the same amount) after it is made.

For example, a bookkeeper accidentally posts a bill for $40 to the local taxes account instead of to the electricity account. A trial balance is drawn up, and total debits are $40,000 and total credits are $40,000. A journal entry is made to correct the misposting error as follows.

1.7.20X7

DEBIT	Electricity account	$40
CREDIT	Local taxes account	$40

To correct a misposting of $40 from the local taxes account to electricity account.

After the journal has been posted, total debits will still be $40,000 and total credits will be $40,000. Total debits and totals credits are still equal.

Now suppose that, because of some error which has not yet been detected, total debits were originally $40,000 but total credits were $39,900. If the same journal correcting the $40 is put through, total debits will remain $40,000 and total credits will remain $39,900. Total debits were different by $100 **before** the journal, and they are still different by $100 **after** the journal.

This means that journals can only be used to correct errors which require both a credit and (an equal) debit adjustment.

2.2 Example: journal entries

Listed below are five errors which were used as examples earlier in this chapter. Write out the journal entries which would correct these errors.

(a)   A business receives an invoice for $250 from a supplier which was omitted from the books entirely.

(b)   Repairs worth $150 were incorrectly debited to the non-current asset (machinery) account instead of the repairs account.

(c)   The bookkeeper of a business reduces cash sales by $280 because they were not sure what the $280 represented. In fact, it was a withdrawal on account of profit.

(d)   Telephone expenses of $540 were incorrectly debited to the electricity account.

(e)   A page in the sales day book has been added up to $28,425 instead of $28,825.

Solution

(a)
DEBIT	Purchases	$250
CREDIT	Trade accounts payable	$250

A transaction previously omitted

(b)
DEBIT	Repairs account	$150
CREDIT	Non-current asset (machinery) a/c	$150

The correction of an error of principle: repairs costs incorrectly added to non-current asset costs

(c)
DEBIT	Withdrawals on account	$280
CREDIT	Sales	$280

An error of principle, in which sales were reduced to compensate for cash withdrawals not accounted for

(d)
DEBIT	Telephone expenses	$540
CREDIT	Electricity expenses	$540

Correction of an error of commission: telephone expenses wrongly charged to the electricity account

(e)
DEBIT	Trade accounts receivable	$400
CREDIT	Sales	$400

The correction of a casting error in the sales day book
($28,825 – $28,425 = $400)

2.3 Use of journal entries in examinations

Occasionally an examination question might ask you to 'journalise' a transaction (ie select one of two, three or four journal entries), even though the transaction is perfectly normal and nothing to do with an error. This is just the examiner's way of finding out whether you know your debits and credits. For example:

QUESTION
Journal

A business sells $500 of goods on credit. What is the correct journal to reflect this transaction?

A   DEBIT sales $500, CREDIT trade receivables $500
B   DEBIT trade receivables $500, CREDIT sales $500

ANSWER

B	DEBIT	Trade receivables	$500	
	CREDIT	Sales		$500

No error has occurred here, just a normal credit sale of $500. By asking you to select a journal, the examining team can see that you understand the double entry bookkeeping.

2.4 Suspense accounts

Suspense accounts, as well as being used to correct some errors, are also opened when it is not known immediately where to post an amount. When the mystery is solved, the suspense account is closed and the amount correctly posted using a journal entry.

A suspense account is an account showing a balance equal to the difference in a trial balance.

A suspense account is a **temporary** account which can be opened for a number of reasons. The most common reasons are as follows.

(a)   A trial balance is drawn up which does not balance (ie total debits do not equal total credits).

(b)   The bookkeeper of a business knows where to post the credit side of a transaction, but does not know where to post the debit (or vice versa). For example, a cash payment might be made and must obviously be credited to cash. But the bookkeeper may not know what the payment is for, and so will not know which account to debit.

In both these cases, a temporary suspense account is opened up until the problem is sorted out. The next few paragraphs explain exactly how this works.

2.5 Use of suspense account: when the trial balance does not balance

When an error has occurred which results in an imbalance between total debits and total credits in the ledger accounts, the first step is to open a suspense account. For example, an accountant draws up a trial balance and finds that total debits exceed total credits by $162.

They know that there is an error somewhere, but for the time being they open a suspense account and enter a credit of $162 in it. This serves two purposes.

(a)   As the suspense account now exists, the accountant will not forget that there is an error (of $162) to be sorted out.

(b)   Now that there is a credit of $162 in the suspense account, the trial balance balances.

When the cause of the $162 discrepancy is tracked down, it is corrected by means of a journal entry. For example, the credit of $162 should be to purchases. The journal entry would be:

DEBIT	Suspense a/c	$162
CREDIT	Purchases	$162

To close off suspense a/c and correct error

Three more examples are given below.

2.6 Example: transposition error

The bookkeeper of Mixem Gladly Co made a transposition error when entering an amount for sales in the sales account. Instead of entering the correct amount of $37,453.60 they entered $37,543.60, transposing the 4 and 5. The trade accounts receivable were posted correctly, and so when total debits and credits on the ledger accounts were compared it was found that credits exceeded debits by $(37,543.60 − 37,453.60) = $90.

The initial step is to equalise the total debits and credits by posting a debit of $90 to a suspense account.

When the cause of the error is discovered, the double entry to correct it should be logged in the journal as:

DEBIT	Sales	$90
CREDIT	Suspense a/c	$90

To close off suspense a/c and correct transposition error

2.7 Example: error of omission

When Guttersnipe Builders paid the monthly salary cheques to its office staff, the payment of $5,250 was correctly entered in the cash account, but the bookkeeper omitted to debit the office salaries account. As a consequence, the total debit and credit balances on the ledger accounts were not equal, and credits exceeded debits by $5,250.

The initial step in correcting the situation is to debit $5,250 to a suspense account in order to equalise the total debits and total credits.

When the cause of the error is discovered, the double entry to correct it should be logged in the journal as:

DEBIT	Office salaries account	$5,250
CREDIT	Suspense a/c	$5,250

To close off suspense account and correct error of omission

Note. Most accounting software will have controls to prevent you from posting a one-sided entry, or a double entry that does not balance.

2.8 Example: error of commission

A bookkeeper might make a mistake by entering what should be a debit entry as a credit, or vice versa. For example, a credit customer pays $460 of the $660 they owe to Ashdown Tree Felling Contractors, but Ashdown's bookkeeper debits $460 on the receivables account in the nominal ledger by mistake instead of crediting the payment received.

The total debit balances in Ashdown's ledger accounts would now exceed the total credits by 2 × $460 = $920. The initial step in correcting the error would be to make a credit entry of $920 in a suspense account. When the cause of the error is discovered, it should be corrected as follows.

DEBIT	Suspense a/c	$920
CREDIT	Trade receivables	$920

To close off suspense account and correct error of commission

In the receivables control account in the nominal ledger, the correction would therefore appear as follows.

RECEIVABLES CONTROL ACCOUNT

	$		$
Balance b/d	660	Suspense a/c: error corrected	920
Payment incorrectly debited	460	Balance c/d	200
	1,120		1,120

2.9 Use of suspense account: not knowing where to post a transaction

Another use of suspense accounts occurs when a bookkeeper does not know where to post one side of a transaction. Until the mystery is sorted out, the entry can be recorded in a suspense account. A typical example is when the business receives cash through the post from a source which cannot be determined. The double entry in the accounts would be a debit in the cash book, and a credit to a suspense account.

2.10 Example: not knowing where to post a transaction

Windfall Garments received a cheque in the post for $620. The name on the cheque is R J Beasley, but Windfall Garments have no idea who this person is, nor why they should be sending $620. The bookkeeper decides to open a suspense account, so that the double entry for the transaction is:

DEBIT	Cash	$620	
CREDIT	Suspense a/c		$620

Eventually, it transpires that the cheque was in payment for a debt owed by the Haute Couture Corner Shop and paid out of the proprietor's personal bank account. The suspense account can now be cleared, as follows.

DEBIT	Suspense a/c	$620	
CREDIT	Trade receivables		$620

2.11 Suspense accounts might contain several items

If more than one error or unidentifiable posting to a ledger account arises during an accounting period, they will all be merged together in the same suspense account. Indeed, until the causes of the errors are discovered, the bookkeepers are unlikely to know exactly how many errors there are. An examination question might give you a balance on a suspense account, together with enough information to make the necessary corrections, leaving a nil balance on the suspense account and correct balances on various other accounts. In practice, of course, finding these errors is far from easy!

EXAM FOCUS POINT

For each error, apply the following method.

- What is the correct entry?
- What entry has been made (if any)?
- What is the entry needed to correct the error?
- The other side of the entry then goes to the suspense account (eg if the entry above is a debit, then the entry in the suspense account will be a credit)

2.12 Suspense accounts are temporary

Suspense accounts are only temporary. None should exist when it comes to drawing up the financial statements at the end of the accounting period.

It must be stressed that a **suspense account can only be temporary**. Postings to a suspense account are only made when the bookkeeper doesn't yet know what to do, or when an error has occurred. Mysteries

must be solved, and errors must be corrected. **Under no circumstances should there still be a suspense account when it comes to preparing the statement of financial position of a business. The suspense account must be cleared and all the correcting entries made before the final accounts are drawn up.**

This question is quite comprehensive. See if you can tackle it.

QUESTION

Errors

At the year end of T Down & Co, an imbalance in the trial balance was revealed which resulted in the creation of a suspense account with a credit balance of $1,040.

Investigations revealed the following errors.

(i) A sale of goods on credit for $1,000 had been omitted from the sales account.

(ii) Delivery and installation costs of $240 on a new item of plant had been recorded as a revenue expense.

(iii) Cash discount of $150 on paying a supplier, JW, had been taken, even though the payment was made outside the time limit.

(iv) Inventory of stationery at the end of the period of $240 had been ignored.

(v) A purchase of raw materials of $350 had been recorded in the purchases account as $850.

(vi) The purchase returns day book included a sales credit note for $230 which had been entered correctly in the account of the customer concerned, but included with purchase returns in the nominal ledger.

Required

(a) Prepare journal entries to correct **each** of the above errors. Narratives are **not** required.

(b) Open a suspense account and show the corrections to be made.

(c) Prior to the discovery of the errors, T Down & Co's gross profit was calculated at $35,750 and the profit for the year at $18,500.

Calculate the revised gross profit and profit for the year figures after the correction of the errors.

ANSWER

(a)

				Dr $	Cr $
(i)	DEBIT	Suspense a/c		1,000	
	CREDIT	Sales			1,000
(ii)	DEBIT	Plant		240	
	CREDIT	Delivery cost			240
(iii)	DEBIT	Cash discount received		150	
	CREDIT	JW a/c			150
(iv)	DEBIT	Inventory of stationery		240	
	CREDIT	Stationery expense			240
(v)	DEBIT	Suspense a/c		500	
	CREDIT	Purchases			500
(vi)	DEBIT	Purchase returns		230	
	DEBIT	Sales returns		230	
	CREDIT	Suspense a/c			460

(b)

SUSPENSE A/C

		$			$
(i)	Sales	1,000		End of year balance	1,040
(v)	Purchases	500	(vi)	Purchase returns/sales returns	460
		1,500			1,500

(c)

	$
Gross profit originally reported	35,750
Sales omitted	1,000
Plant costs wrongly allocated	240
Incorrect recording of purchases	500
Sales credit note wrongly allocated	(460)
Adjusted gross profit	37,030
Profit for the year originally reported	18,500
Adjustments to gross profit $(37,030 − 35,750)	1,280
Cash discount incorrectly taken	(150)
Stationery inventory	240
Adjusted profit for the year	19,870

Note. It has been assumed that the delivery and installation costs on plant have been included in purchases.

EXAM FOCUS POINT

If you are asked in an exam question to calculate the balance remaining on the suspense account after certain errors have been adjusted, the key is to first recognise which errors affect the suspense account, and then to put the adjustments through correctly, as in the above example.

2.13 Effect of corrections of errors on profit for the year and total assets

In the exam, questions on errors often ask you to give the effect of the correction of the error on profit for the year or the statement of financial position total. Work through the following questions to make sure you understand how to do this.

QUESTION

Effect on the financial statements I

A company's statement of profit or loss for the year ended 31 December 20X5 showed a profit for the year of $65,000. It was later found that $18,000 paid for maintenance to motor vehicles had been debited to the motor vehicles at cost account and had been depreciated as if it was a new motor vehicle. It is the company's policy to depreciate motor vehicles at 25% per year on the straight line basis, with a full year's charge in the year of acquisition.

What would the profit for the year be after adjusting for this error?

A $78,500
B $47,000
C $83,000
D $51,500

ANSWER

D $51,500

Maintenance costs should be debited to the repairs and maintenance account in the statement of profit or loss, not to the motor vehicles at cost account. In order to calculate the revised profit for the year, we need to first calculate how much depreciation has been incorrectly charged, add this back to profit for the year and then deduct the full amount of maintenance charge, as follows.

	$
Profit for the year before correction of errors	65,000
Add back depreciation charge (18,000 × 25%)	4,500
Less maintenance	(18,000)
Corrected profit for the year	51,500

QUESTION

Beta Co has total assets of $555,000 and profit for the year of $160,000 recorded in the financial statements for the year ended 31 December 20X3. Inventory costing $45,000, which was received into the warehouse on 2 January 20X4, was included in the financial statements at 31 December 20X3 in error.

What would be the profit for the year and total assets after adjusting for this error?

	Profit for the year	Total assets
A	$205,000	$600,000
B	$115,000	$600,000
C	$205,000	$510,000
D	$115,000	$510,000

ANSWER

D   Profit for the year $115,000   Total assets $510,000

The inventory received on 2 January 20X4 should not be included in the financial statements at 31 December 20X3, as it relates to the following year. The inventory value should be deducted from total assets. To work out the effect on profit for the year, remember that cost of sales is calculated as follows.

	$
Cost of sales	
Opening inventory	X
Plus purchases	X
Less closing inventory	(X)
	X

So if closing inventory is overstated, cost of sales will be understated, and gross profit will be overstated. Therefore we need to deduct the value of the inventory included in error from profit for the year.

QUESTION

Rogitts Co purchased goods on credit with a list price of $75,000 from Bodean Co and received a trade discount of 10%. Rogitts Co paid the full amount due to Bodean Co within 25 days and received a settlement discount of 5% for prompt payment. The trainee accountant at Rogitts Co recorded the purchase of goods in the purchases account net of both discounts. At the year end all these goods had been sold.

What is the effect on gross profit and profit for the year of correcting the trainee accountant's mistake?

	Gross profit	Profit for the year
A	decrease by $3,375	no effect
B	decrease by $3,375	decrease by $3,375
C	increase by $10,875	increase by $10,875
D	decrease by $10,875	no effect

ANSWER

A   Gross profit – decrease by $3,375   profit for the year – no effect

Purchases should be recorded net of trade discounts received only. Settlement discounts received are shown as other income in the statement of profit or loss. So in this question, the correction will increase the cost of purchases and increase other income by $3,375 ($75,000 × 90% = $67,500, $67,500 × 5% = $3,375):

DEBIT purchases $3,375
CREDIT other income $3,375

The effect on gross profit is therefore to decrease it by $3,375 (because the value of purchases has increased). The effect on profit for the year is nil, as the correction just moves the settlement discount received from one part of the statement of profit or loss (purchases) to another part (other income).

CHAPTER ROUNDUP

↳ There are five main types of error. Some can be corrected by journal entry; some require the use of a suspense account.

↳ Errors which leave total debits and credits in the ledger accounts in balance can be corrected by using **journal entries**. Otherwise a suspense account has to be opened first, and later cleared by a journal entry.

↳ **Suspense accounts**, as well as being used to correct some errors, are also opened when it is not known immediately where to post an amount. When the mystery is solved, the suspense account is closed and the amount correctly posted using a journal entry.

↳ **Suspense accounts are only temporary**. None should exist when it comes to drawing up the financial statements at the end of the accounting period.

QUICK QUIZ

1 List five types of error made in accounting.

2 What is a journal most commonly used for?

A Correct errors
B Correct errors and post unusual transactions
C Correct errors and clear suspense account
D Make adjustments to the double entry

3 A suspense account is a temporary account to make the trial balance.

4 What must be done with a suspense account before preparing a statement of financial position?

A Include it in assets
B Clear it to nil
C Include it in liabilities
D Write it off to capital

5 Sales returns of $460 have inadvertently been posted to the purchase returns, although the correct entry has been made to the accounts receivable control. A suspense account needs to be set up for how much?

A $460 debit
B $460 credit
C $920 debit
D $920 credit

1   Transposition, omission, principle, commission and compensating errors

2   D   Although A, B and C are correct as far as they go, they don't cover everything. D is the most comprehensive answer.

3   True

4   B   All errors must be identified and the suspense account cleared to nil.

5   C   The sales returns of $460 have been credited to accounts receivable and also $460 has been credited to purchase returns. Therefore the trial balance needs a debit of 2 × $460 = $920 to balance.

Now try ...

Attempt the questions below from the **Practice Question Bank**

Number

Qs 64 – 66

^{part}

F

Preparing basic financial statements

Incomplete records

So far we have assumed that sole traders keep a full set of records. In practice, many sole traders do not keep a complete set of records and you must apply certain techniques to arrive at the figures that are missing.

Incomplete records questions are a very good test of your understanding of the way in which a set of accounts is built up.

In most countries, limited liability companies are obliged by national laws to keep proper accounting records.

TOPIC LIST	SYLLABUS REFERENCE
1 Incomplete records questions	F6(a)
2 The accounting and business equations	F6(a)
3 Credit sales and trade receivables	F6(a)
4 Purchases and trade payables	F6(a)
5 Establishing cost of sales	F6(a)
6 Stolen goods or goods destroyed	F6(a)
7 The cash book	F6(a)
8 Accruals and prepayments	F6(a)

Study Guide

Intellectual level

F   Preparing basic financial statements

6   Incomplete records

(a)   Understand and apply techniques used in incomplete record situations.   S

    (i)   Use of accounting equation

    (ii)   Use of ledger accounts to calculate missing figures

    (iii)   Use of cash and/or bank summaries

    (iv)   Use of profit percentages to calculate missing figures

1   Incomplete records questions

Incomplete records questions may test your ability to prepare accounts in the following situations.

- A trader **does not maintain a ledger** and therefore has no continuous double entry record of transactions.
- Accounting records are **destroyed** by accident, such as fire.
- Some essential figure is **unknown** and must be calculated as a balancing figure. This may occur as a result of inventory being damaged or destroyed, or because of misappropriation of assets.

Incomplete records problems occur when a business does not have a full set of accounting records for one of the following reasons.

- The proprietor of the business does not keep a full set of accounts.
- Some of the business accounts are accidentally lost or destroyed.

The problem for the accountant is to prepare a set of year-end accounts for the business; ie a statement of profit or loss and a statement of financial position. Since the business does not have a full set of accounts, preparing the final accounts is not a simple matter of closing off accounts and transferring balances to the profit or loss account, or showing outstanding balances in the statement of financial position. The task of preparing the final accounts involves the following.

(a)   Establishing the **cost of purchases** and other expenses

(b)   Establishing the **total amount of sales**

(c)   Establishing the amount of **accounts payable, accruals, accounts receivable and prepayments** at the end of the year

Examination questions often take incomplete records problems a stage further by introducing an 'incident', such as fire and burglary, which leaves the owner of the business uncertain about how much inventory has been destroyed or stolen.

The great merit of incomplete records problems is that they focus attention on the relationship between cash received and paid, sales and accounts receivable, purchases and accounts payable, and inventory, as well as calling for the preparation of final accounts from basic principles.

To understand what incomplete records are about, we need to look at what exactly might be incomplete. The items we shall consider in turn are:

(a)   The accounting and business equations
(b)   Credit sales and trade receivables
(c)   Purchases and trade payables
(d)   Purchases, inventory and the cost of sales
(e)   Stolen goods or goods destroyed

(f)   The cash book

(g)   Accruals and prepayments

EXAM FOCUS POINT

Incomplete records questions are a good test of whether you have a really thorough grasp of double entry. The ACCA examining team is fond of them because they really test your understanding. With practice they become easier!

2   The accounting and business equations

Two equations are very useful in incomplete records calculations.

*   The accounting equation:

    assets = capital + liabilities

*   The business equation:

    closing net assets = opening net assets + capital introduced + profit – drawings

2.1 The accounting equation

In practice, there should not be any missing item in the opening statement of financial position of the business, because it should be available from the preparation of the previous year's final accounts. However, an exam question might provide information about the assets and liabilities of the business at the beginning of the period under review, but then leave the balancing figure (ie the proprietor's business capital) unspecified. If you remember the accounting equation (Assets = Capital + Liabilities), the problem is quite straightforward.

2.2 Example: opening statement of financial position

Suppose Joe Han's business has the following assets and liabilities as at 1 January 20X3.

	$
Fixtures and fittings at cost	7,000
Provision for depreciation, fixtures and fittings	4,000
Motor vehicles at cost	12,000
Provision for depreciation, motor vehicles	6,800
Inventory	4,500
Trade receivables	5,200
Cash at bank and in hand	1,230
Trade payables	3,700
Prepayment	450
Accrued rent	2,000

Required

Prepare a statement of financial position for the business, inserting a balancing figure for proprietor's capital.

Solution

STATEMENT OF FINANCIAL POSITION AS AT 1 JANUARY 20X3

	$	$
Assets		
Non-current assets		
Fixtures and fittings at cost	7,000	
Less accumulated depreciation	4,000	
		3,000
Motor vehicles at cost	12,000	
Less accumulated depreciation	6,800	
		5,200
Current assets		
Inventory	4,500	
Trade receivables	5,200	
Prepayment	450	
Cash	1,230	
		11,380
Total assets		19,580
Capital and liabilities		
Proprietor's capital as at 1 January 20X3 (balancing figure)*		13,880
Current liabilities		
Trade payables	3,700	
Accrual	2,000	
		5,700
Total capital and liabilities		19,580

* Calculated as follows:

Assets	=	Capital	+	Liabilities
19,580	=	Capital	+	5,700
Capital	=	19,580	–	5,700
Capital	=	$13,880		

2.3 The business equation

The business equation is simply an extension of the accounting equation.

Closing net assets = opening net assets + capital introduced + profit – drawings

So, if we are able to establish the trader's net assets at the beginning and end of the period, we can compute profits as follows.

Profit/(loss) = movement in net assets – capital introduced + drawings

We want to eliminate any movement caused by money paid in or taken out for personal use by the trader. So we take out capital introduced and add back in drawings.

The most obvious incomplete records situation is that of a sole trader who has kept no trading records. It may not be possible to reconstruct their whole statement of profit or loss, but it will be possible to compute his profit for the year using the business equation.

2.4 Example: business equation

Joe starts up his camera shop on 1 January 20X1, from rented premises, with $5,000 inventory and $3,000 in the bank. All his sales are for cash. He keeps no record of his takings.

At the end of the year he has inventory worth $6,600 and $15,000 in the bank. He owes $3,000 to suppliers. He had paid in $5,000 he won on the lottery and drawn out $2,000 to buy himself a motorbike. The motorbike is not used in the business. He has been taking drawings of $100 per week. What is his profit at 31 December 20X1?

Solution

	$
Opening net assets	
Inventory	5,000
Cash	3,000
	8,000
Closing net assets	
Inventory	6,600
Cash	15,000
Payables	(3,000)
	18,600
Movement in capital (net assets)	10,600
Less capital paid in	(5,000)
Plus drawings ((100 × 52) + 2,000)	7,200
Profit	12,800

QUESTION

Net assets at the beginning of 20X7 were $101,700. The proprietor injected new capital of $8,000 during the year and took drawings of $2,200. Net assets at the end of 20X7 were $180,000.

What was the profit earned by the business in 20X7?

A $72,500 profit
B $88,300 profit
C $84,300 profit
D $(84,100) loss

ANSWER

A $72,500 profit

Profit = movement in net assets – capital introduced + drawings

Profit = (180,000 – 101,700) – 8,000 + 2,200

Profit = $72,500

2.5 Drawings

Drawings often feature as the missing item in an incomplete records problem. The trader has been drawing money but does not know how much.

Drawings would normally represent no particular problem at all in preparing a set of final accounts from incomplete records, but it is not unusual for exam questions to contain complicating situations.

(a) The business owner may pay income into their bank account which has nothing whatever to do with the business operations. For example, the owner might pay dividend income, or other income from investments into the bank, from stocks and shares which they own personally, separate from the business itself. (In other words, there are no investments in the business statement of financial position, and so income from investments cannot possibly be income of the business.) These amounts will be **credited to their drawings**.

(b) The business owner may pay money out of the business bank account for items which are not business expenses, such as life insurance premiums and a payment for their family's holidays. These will be **treated as drawings**.

Remember that the **business entity concept** means that the personal transactions of the trader should be kept separate from the transactions of the business. Where such **personal items of receipts or payments** are made, the following adjustments should be made.

(a)   Receipts should be set off against drawings. For example, if a business owner receives $600 in dividend income from investments not owned by the business and pays it into their business bank account, then the accounting entry is:

DEBIT   Cash
CREDIT   Drawings

(b)   Payments should be charged to drawings on account; ie:

DEBIT   Drawings
CREDIT   Cash

Another situation that may arise is that the trader has taken goods from inventory for personal use. When a trader does this, the transaction is treated in the same way as cash drawings. The goods should be taken out of purchases and not included in inventories. The double entry to record the transaction is:

DEBIT   Drawings
CREDIT   Purchases

The value of the goods taken is recorded at cost to the business, not at sale price.

EXAM FOCUS POINT

Beware of the wording in an exam question.

You should note that:

(a)   If a question states that a proprietor's drawings during a given year are 'approximately $40 per week' then you should assume that drawings for the year are 40×52 weeks = $2,080.

(b)   However, if a question states that drawings in the year are 'between $35 and $45 per week', do not assume that the drawings average $40 per week and so amount to $2,080 for the year. You could not be certain that the actual withdrawals did average $40, and so you should treat the withdrawals figure as a missing item that needs to be calculated.

3   Credit sales and trade receivables

The approach to incomplete records questions is to build up the information given so as to complete the necessary **double entry**. This may involve reconstructing **control accounts** for:

*   Cash and bank
*   Trade receivables and payables

If a business does not keep a record of its sales on credit, the value of these sales can be derived from the opening balance of trade receivables, the closing balance of trade receivables, and the payments received from customers during the period.

FORMULA TO LEARN

	$
Payments from trade receivables	X
Plus closing balance of trade receivables (since these represent sales in the current period for which cash payment has not yet been received)	X
Less opening balance of trade receivables (these represent credit sales in a previous period)	(X)
Credit sales in the period	X

For example, suppose that Joe Han's business had trade receivables of $1,750 on 1 April 20X4 and trade receivables of $3,140 on 31 March 20X5. If payments received from receivables during the year to 31 March 20X5 were $28,490, and if there are no bad debts, then credit sales for the period would be:

	$
Cash from receivables	28,490
Plus closing receivables	3,140
Less opening receivables	(1,750)
Credit sales	29,880

If there are irrecoverable debts during the period, the value of sales will be increased by the amount of irrecoverable debts written off, no matter whether they relate to opening receivables or credit sales during the current period.

QUESTION
Calculating sales

The calculation above could be made in a T-account, with credit sales being the balancing figure to complete the account. Prepare the T-account.

ANSWER

TRADE RECEIVABLES

	$		$
Opening balance b/f	1,750	Cash received	28,490
Credit sales (balancing figure)	29,880	Closing balance c/f	3,140
	31,630		31,630

The same interrelationship between credit sales, cash from receivables, and opening and closing receivables balances can be used to derive a missing figure for cash from receivables, or opening or closing receivables, given the values for the three other items. For example, if we know that opening receivables are $6,700, closing receivables are $3,200 and credit sales for the period are $69,400, then cash from receivables during the period would be as follows.

TRADE RECEIVABLES

	$		$
Opening balance	6,700	Cash received (balancing figure)	72,900
Sales (on credit)	69,400	Closing balance c/f	3,200
	76,100		76,100

An alternative way of presenting the same calculation would be:

	$
Opening balance of receivables	6,700
Credit sales during the period	69,400
Total money owed to the business	76,100
Less closing balance of receivables	(3,200)
Equals cash received during the period	72,900

4 Purchases and trade payables

A similar relationship exists between purchases of inventory during a period, the opening and closing balances for trade payables, and amounts paid to suppliers during the period.

If we wish to calculate an unknown amount for purchases, the amount would be derived as follows.

FORMULA TO LEARN

	$
Payments to trade payables during the period	X
Plus closing balance of trade payables (since these represent purchases in the current period for which payment has not yet been made)	X
Less opening balance of trade payables (these debts, paid in the current period, relate to purchases in a previous period)	(X)
Purchases during the period	X

For example, suppose that Joe Han's business had trade payables of $3,728 on 1 October 20X5 and trade payables of $2,645 on 30 September 20X6. If payments to trade payables during the year to 30 September 20X6 were $31,479, then purchases during the year would be:

	$
Payments to trade payables	31,479
Plus closing balance of trade payables	2,645
Less opening balance of trade payables	(3,728)
Purchases	30,396

QUESTION

Calculating purchases I

Again, the calculation above could be made in a T-account, with purchases being the balancing figure to complete the account. Prepare the T-account.

ANSWER

TRADE PAYABLES

	$		$
Cash payments	31,479	Opening balance b/d	3,728
Closing balance c/d	2,645	Purchases (balancing figure)	30,396
	34,124		34,124

QUESTION

Calculating purchases II

Mr Harmon does not keep full accounting records, but the following information is available in respect of his accounting year ended 31 December 20X9.

	$
Cash purchases in year	3,900
Cash paid for goods supplied on credit	27,850
Trade payables at 1 January 20X9	970
Trade payables at 31 December 20X9	720

In his trading account for 20X9, what will be Harmon's figure for purchases?

ANSWER

Credit purchases = $(27,850 + 720 – 970) = $27,600. Therefore total purchases = $(27,600 + 3,900) = $31,500.

5 Establishing cost of sales

> Where inventory, sales or purchases is the unknown figure, it will be necessary to use information on **gross profit percentages** to construct a working for gross profit in which the unknown figure can be inserted as a balance.

When the value of purchases is not known, a different approach might be required to find out what they were, depending on the nature of the information given to you.

One approach would be to use information about the cost of sales, and opening and closing inventory rather than trade payables to find the cost of purchases.

π FORMULA TO LEARN

		$
Since	opening inventory	X
	plus purchases	X
	less closing inventory	(X)
	equals the cost of goods sold	X
Then	the cost of goods sold	X
	plus closing inventory	X
	less opening inventory	(X)
	equals purchases	X

Suppose that the inventory of Joe Han's business on 1 July 20X6 has a value of $8,400, and an inventory count at 30 June 20X7 showed inventory to be valued at $9,350. Sales for the year to 30 June 20X7 are $80,000, and the business makes a mark-up of $33^1/3\%$ on cost for all the items that it sells. What were the purchases during the year?

The cost of goods sold can be derived from the value of sales, as follows.

		$
Sales	($133^1/3\%$)	80,000
Gross profit (mark-up)	($33^1/3\%$)	20,000
Cost of goods sold	(100%)	60,000

The cost of goods sold is 75% ($100/133^1/3$) of sales value.

	$
Cost of goods sold	60,000
Plus closing inventory	9,350
Less opening inventory	(8,400)
Purchases	60,950

Two different terms may be given to you in the exam for the calculation of profit.

- Mark-up is the profit as a percentage of **cost**.
- Gross profit margin is the profit as a percentage of **sales**.

Looking at the above example:

(a) The mark-up on cost is $33^1/3\%$

		$
Sales	($133^1/3\%$)	80,000
Cost of goods sold	(100%)	(60,000)
Gross profit	($33^1/3\%$)	20,000

(b)   The gross profit margin is 25% (ie $33^{1}/_{3}/133^{1}/_{3} \times 100\%$)

		$
Sales	(100%)	80,000
Cost of goods sold	(75%)	(60,000)
Gross profit	(25%)	20,000

QUESTION

Calculating purchases III

Harry has budgeted sales for the coming year of $175,000. He achieves a constant mark-up of 40% on cost. He plans to reduce his inventory level by $13,000 over the year.

What will Harry's purchases be for the year?

ANSWER

Cost of sales   = 100/140 × $175,000
            = $125,000

Since the inventory level is being allowed to fall, it means that purchases will be $13,000 less than $125,000 = $112,000.

QUESTION

Calculating purchases IV

Using the same facts as in the question above, calculate Harry's purchases for the year if he achieves a constant **margin** of 40% on sales.

ANSWER

Gross profit = 40% of sales, so cost of sales = 60% of sales.

Cost of sales $= \dfrac{60}{100} \times \$175,000$

            $= \$105,000$

Since the inventory level is being allowed to fall, it means purchases will be $13,000 less than $105,000 = $92,000.

6 Stolen goods or goods destroyed

A similar type of calculation might be required to derive the value of goods stolen or destroyed. When an unknown quantity of goods is lost, whether they are stolen, destroyed in a fire, or lost in any other way such that the quantity lost cannot be counted, then the cost of the goods lost is the difference between (a) and (b).

(a)   The **cost of goods sold**

(b)   **Opening inventory of the goods** (at cost) plus **purchases** less **closing inventory of the goods** (at cost)

In theory, (a) and (b) should be the same. However, if (b) is a larger amount than (a), it follows that the difference must be the cost of the goods purchased and neither sold nor remaining in inventory, ie the cost of the goods lost.

6.1 Example: cost of goods destroyed

Orlean Flames is a shop which sells fashion clothes. On 1 January 20X5, it had trade inventory which cost $7,345. During the 9 months to 30 September 20X5, the business purchased goods from suppliers costing $106,420. Sales during the same period were $154,000. The shop makes a gross profit of 40% on cost for everything it sells. On 30 September 20X5, there was a fire in the shop which destroyed most of the inventory in it. Only a small amount of inventory, known to have cost $350, was undamaged and still fit for sale.

How much of the inventory was lost in the fire?

Solution

(a)

	$
Sales (140%)	154,000
Gross profit (40%)	44,000
Cost of goods sold (100%)	110,000

(b)

	$
Opening inventory, at cost	7,345
Plus purchases	106,420
	113,765
Less closing inventory, at cost	350
Equals cost of goods sold and goods lost	113,415

(c)

	$
Cost of goods sold and lost	113,415
Cost of goods sold	110,000
Cost of goods lost	3,415

6.2 Example: cost of goods stolen

Beau Gullard runs a jewellery shop on the high street. On 1 January 20X9, his trade inventory, at cost, amounted to $4,700 and his trade payables were $3,950.

During the 6 months to 30 June 20X9, sales were $42,000. Beau Gullard makes a gross profit of $33^1/_3$% on the sales value of everything he sells.

On 30 June, there was a burglary at the shop, and all the inventory was stolen.

In trying to establish how much inventory had been taken, Beau Gullard was only able to say that:

(a) He knew from his bank statements that he had paid $28,400 to trade account payables in the 6 month period to 30 June 20X9.

(b) He currently had payables due of $5,550.

Required

(a) Calculate the amount of inventory stolen.
(b) Calculate gross profit for the 6 months to 30 June 20X9.

Solution

Step 1 The first 'unknown' is the amount of purchases during the period. This is established as follows.

TRADE PAYABLES

	$		$
Payments to trade payables	28,400	Opening balance b/d	3,950
Closing balance c/d	5,550	Purchases (balancing figure)	30,000
	33,950		33,950

Step 2 The cost of goods sold is also unknown, but this can be established from the gross profit margin and the sales for the period.

		$
Sales	(100%)	42,000
Gross profit	(33^1/$_3$%)	14,000
Cost of goods sold	(66^2/$_3$%)	28,000

Step 3 The cost of the goods stolen is:

	$
Opening inventory at cost	4,700
Purchases	30,000
	34,700
Less closing inventory (after burglary)	0
Cost of goods sold and goods stolen	34,700
Cost of goods sold (see (b) above)	28,000
Cost of goods stolen	6,700

Step 4 The cost of the goods stolen will not be included in cost of sales, and so the gross profit for the period is as follows.

BEAU GULLARD
GROSS PROFIT FOR THE SIX MONTHS TO 30 JUNE 20X9

		$	$
Sales			42,000
Less	cost of goods sold		
	opening inventory	4,700	
	purchases	30,000	
		34,700	
	less inventory stolen	6,700	
			28,000
Gross profit			14,000

6.3 Accounting for inventory destroyed, stolen or otherwise lost

When inventory is stolen, destroyed or otherwise lost, the loss must be accounted for somehow. The procedure was described briefly in the earlier chapter on inventory accounting. Since the loss is not a trading loss, the cost of the goods lost is not included in the cost of sales, as the previous example showed.

The account that is to be debited is one of two possibilities, depending on whether or not the lost goods were insured against the loss.

(a) If the lost goods were not insured, the business must bear the loss, and the loss is shown in the statement of profit or loss, ie:

DEBIT   Expenses (eg administrative expenses)
CREDIT   Cost of sales

(b) If the lost goods were insured, the business will not suffer a loss, because the insurance will pay back the cost of the lost goods. This means that there is no charge at all in the statement of profit or loss, and the appropriate double entry is:

DEBIT   Insurance claim account (receivable account)
CREDIT   Cost of sales

with the cost of the loss. The insurance claim will then be a current asset, and shown in the statement of financial position of the business as such. When the claim is paid, the account is then closed by:

DEBIT   Cash
CREDIT   Insurance claim account

7 The cash book

The construction of a cash book, largely from bank statements showing receipts and payments of a business during a given period, is often an important feature of incomplete records problems.

We have already seen that information about cash receipts or payments might be needed to establish:

(a)   The amount of purchases during a period

(b)   The amount of credit sales during a period

Other items of receipts or payments might be relevant to establishing:

(a)   The amount of cash sales

(b)   The amount of certain expenses in the statement of profit or loss

(c)   The amount of withdrawals on account of profit by the business proprietor

It might therefore be helpful, if a business does not keep a cash book day to day, to construct a cash book at the end of an accounting period. A business which typically might not keep a day to day cash book is a shop, because:

(a)   Many sales, if not all sales, are cash sales (ie with payment by notes and coins, cheques, or credit cards at the time of sale).

(b)   Some payments are made in notes and coins out of the till rather than by payment out of the business bank account by cheque.

Where there appears to be a sizeable volume of receipts and payments in cash (ie notes and coins), then it is also helpful to construct a two column cash book.

A two column cash book is a cash book with one column for cash receipts and payments, and one column for money paid into and out of the business bank account.

An example will illustrate the technique and the purpose of a two column cash book.

7.1 Example: two column cash book

Jonathan Slugg owns and runs a shop selling fishing tackle, making a gross profit of 25% on the cost of everything he sells. He does not keep a cash book.

On 1 January 20X7 the statement of financial position of his business was as follows.

	$	$
Current assets		
Inventory	10,000	
Cash in the bank	3,000	
Cash in the till	200	
		13,200
Net long-term assets		20,000
		33,200
Trade payables		1,200
Proprietor's capital		32,000
		33,200

In the year to 31 December 20X7:

(a)   There were no sales on credit.

(b) $41,750 in receipts were banked.

(c)   The bank statements of the period show the payments:

		$
(i)	To trade payables	36,000
(ii)	For sundry expenses	5,600
(iii)	To drawings	4,400

(d)   Payments were also made in cash out of the till:

		$
(i)	To trade payables	800
(ii)	For sundry expenses	1,500
(iii)	To drawings	3,700

At 31 December 20X7, the business had cash in the till of $450 and trade payables of $1,400. The cash balance in the bank was not known and the value of closing inventory has not yet been calculated. There were no accruals or prepayments. No further long-term assets were purchased during the year. The depreciation charge for the year is $900.

Required

(a)   Prepare a two column cash book for the period.

(b)   Prepare the statement of profit or loss for the year to 31 December 20X7 and the statement of financial position as at 31 December 20X7.

7.2 Discussion and solution

A two column cash book is completed as follows.

Step 1	Enter the opening cash balances.
Step 2	Enter the information given about cash payments (and any cash receipts, if there had been any such items given in the problem).
Step 3	The cash receipts banked are a 'contra' entry, being both a debit (bank column) and a credit (cash in hand column) in the same account.

Step 4   Enter the closing cash in hand (cash in the bank at the end of the period is not known).

CASH BOOK

	Cash in hand $	Bank $		Cash in hand $	Bank $
Balance b/f	200	3,000			
Cash receipts banked (contra)		41,750	Trade payables	800	36,000
Sales*	48,000		Sundry expenses	1,500	5,600
			Drawings	3,700	4,400
			Cash receipts banked (contra)	41,750	
Balance c/f		*1,250	Balance c/f	450	
	48,200	46,000		48,200	46,000

* Balancing figure

Step 5	The closing balance of money in the bank is a balancing figure.
Step 6	Since all sales are for cash, a balancing figure that can be entered in the cash book is sales, in the cash in hand (debit) column.

It is important to notice that since not all receipts from cash sales are banked, the value of cash sales during the period is:

	$
Receipts banked	41,750
Plus expenses and withdrawals paid out of the till in cash	
$(800 + 1,500 + 3,700)	6,000
Plus any cash stolen (here there is none)	0
Plus the closing balance of cash in hand	450
	48,200
Less the opening balance of cash in hand	(200)
Equals cash sales	48,000

The cash book constructed in this way has enabled us to establish both the closing balance for cash in the bank and also the volume of cash sales. The statement of profit or loss and the statement of financial position can also be prepared once a value for purchases has been calculated.

TRADE PAYABLES

	$		$
Cash book: payments from bank	36,000	Balance b/f	1,200
Cash book: payments in cash	800	Purchases (balancing figure)	37,000
Balance c/f	1,400		
	38,200		38,200

The gross profit margin of 25% on cost indicates that the cost of the goods sold is $38,400, ie:

	$
Sales (125%)	48,000
Gross profit (25%)	9,600
Cost of goods sold (100%)	38,400

The closing inventory is now a balancing figure in the trading account.

JONATHAN SLUGG
STATEMENT OF PROFIT OR LOSS FOR THE YEAR ENDED 31 DECEMBER 20X7

	$	$
Revenue		48,000
Cost of sales		
Opening inventory	10,000	
Purchases	37,000	
	47,000	
Closing inventory (balancing figure)	8,600	
		38,400
Gross profit (25/125 × $48,000)		9,600
Expenses		
Sundry $(1,500 + 5,600)	7,100	
Depreciation	900	
		8,000
Profit for the year		1,600

JONATHAN SLUGG
STATEMENT OF FINANCIAL POSITION AS AT 31 DECEMBER 20X7

	$	$
Assets		
Current assets		
Inventory	8,600	
Cash in the till	450	
		9,050
Net long-term assets $(20,000 − 900)		19,100
Total assets		28,150

	$	$
Capital and liabilities		
Proprietor's capital		
Balance b/f	32,000	
Profit for the year	1,600	
Withdrawals on account $(3,700 + 4,400)$	(8,100)	
Balance c/f		25,500
Current liabilities		
Bank overdraft	1,250	
Trade payables	1,400	
		2,650
Total capital and liabilities		28,150

7.3 Theft of cash from the till

When cash is stolen from the till, the amount stolen will be a credit entry in the cash book, and a debit in either the expenses section of the statement of profit or loss or insurance claim account, depending on whether the business is insured. The missing figure for cash sales, if this has to be calculated, must not ignore cash received but later stolen – see above.

7.4 Using trade receivables to calculate both cash sales and credit sales

A final point which needs to be considered is how a missing value can be found for cash sales and credit sales, when a business has both, but takings banked by the business are not divided between takings from cash sales and takings from credit sales.

7.5 Example: using trade receivables

Suppose, for example, that a business had, on 1 January 20X8, trade receivables of $2,000, cash in the bank of $3,000 and cash in hand of $300.

During the year to 31 December 20X8 the business banked $95,000 in takings.

It also paid out the following expenses in cash from the till.

	$
Drawings	1,200
Sundry expenses	800

On 29 August 20X8 a thief broke into the shop and stole $400 from the till.

At 31 December 20X8 trade receivables amounted to $3,500, cash in the bank $2,500 and cash in the till $150.

What was the value of sales during the year?

Solution

If we tried to prepare a trade receivables account and a two column cash book, we would have insufficient information, in particular about whether the takings which were banked related to cash sales or credit sales.

TRADE RECEIVABLES

	$		$
Balance b/f	2,000	Cash from receivables (credit sales)	Unknown
Credit sales	Unknown		
		Balance c/f	3,500

CASH BOOK

	Cash $	Bank $		Cash $	Bank $
Balance b/f	300	3,000	Drawings	1,200	
			Sundry expenses	800	
Cash from receivables		Unknown	Cash stolen	400	
Cash sales	Unknown		Balance c/f	150	2,500

All we know is that the combined sums from trade receivables and cash takings banked is $95,000.

The value of sales can be found by using the trade receivables account, which should be used to record cash takings banked as well as payments from receivables. The balancing figure in the receivables account will then be a combination of credit sales and some cash sales. The cash book only needs to be a single column.

TRADE RECEIVABLES

	$		$
Balance b/f	2,000	Cash banked	95,000
Sales: to trading account (bal. fig.)	96,500	Balance c/f	3,500
	98,500		98,500

CASH (EXTRACT)

	$		$
Balance in hand b/f	300	*Payments in cash*	
Balance in bank b/f	3,000	Drawings	1,200
Trade receivables a/c	95,000	Expenses	800
		Cash stolen	400
		Balance in hand c/f	150
		Balance at bank c/f	2,500

The remaining 'undiscovered' amount of cash sales is now found as follows.

	$	$
Payments in cash out of the till		
Drawings	1,200	
Expenses	800	
		2,000
Cash stolen		400
Closing balance of cash in hand		150
		2,550
Less opening balance of cash in hand		(300)
Further cash sales		2,250

(This calculation is similar to the one described above for calculating cash sales.)

Total sales for the year are:

	$
From trade receivables	96,500
From cash book	2,250
Total sales	98,750

8 Accruals and prepayments

Where there is an accrued expense or a prepayment, the charge to be made in the statement of profit or loss for the item concerned should be found from the opening balance b/f, the closing balance c/f and cash payments for the item during the period. The charge in the statement of profit or loss is perhaps most easily found as the balancing figure in a T-account.

For example, suppose that on 1 April 20X6 a business had prepaid rent of $700 which relates to the next accounting period. During the year to 31 March 20X7 it pays $9,300 in rent, and at 31 March 20X7 the prepayment of rent is $1,000. The cost of rent in the P/L account for the year to 31 March 20X7 would be the balancing figure in the following T-account. (Remember that a prepayment is a current asset, and so is a debit balance b/f.)

RENT

	$		$
Prepayment: balance b/d	700	P/L a/c (balancing figure)	9,000
Cash	9,300	Prepayment: balance c/d	1,000
	10,000		10,000
Balance b/f	1,000		

Similarly, if a business has accrued telephone expenses as at 1 July 20X6 of $850, pays $6,720 in telephone bills during the year to 30 June 20X7, and has accrued telephone expenses of $1,140 as at 30 June 20X7, then the telephone expense to be shown in the statement of profit or loss for the year to 30 June 20X7 is the balancing figure in the following T-account. (Remember that an accrual is a current liability, and so is a credit balance b/d.)

TELEPHONE EXPENSES

	$		$
Cash	6,720	Balance b/d (accrual)	850
Balance c/d (accrual)	1,140	P/L a/c (balancing figure)	7,010
	7,860		7,860
		Balance b/f	1,140

EXAM FOCUS POINT

Questions on incomplete records in your exam will usually be based on short scenarios. However, it is well worth attempting the longer question below, as it will help you to really understand what is going on in a set of financial statements. You may also need to use these techniques in one of the 15 mark questions, either on this topic or on accounts preparation.

QUESTION

Incomplete records

Mary Grimes, wholesale fruit and vegetable merchant, does not keep a full set of accounting records. However, the following information has been produced from the business's records.

(a)   *Summary of the bank account for the year ended 31 August 20X8*

	$		$
1 Sept 20X7 balance b/d	1,970	Payments to suppliers	72,000
Cash from trade receivables	96,000	Purchase of motor van (E471 KBR)	13,000
Sale of private yacht	20,000	Rent and local taxes	2,600
Sale of motor van (A123 BWA)	2,100	Wages	15,100
		Motor vehicle expenses	3,350
		Postage and stationery	1,360
		Drawings	9,200
		Repairs and renewals	650
		Insurance	800
		31 Aug 20X8 balance c/d	2,010
	120,070		120,070
1 Sep 20X8 balance b/f	2,010		

(b)   *Assets and liabilities, other than balance at bank*

		1 Sep 20X7	31 Aug 20X8
		$	$
Trade payables		4,700	2,590
Trade receivables		7,320	9,500
Rent and local taxes accrued		200	260
Motor vans:			
A123 BWA:	At cost	10,000	–
	Accumulated depreciation	8,000	–
E471 KBR:	At cost	–	13,000
	Accumulated depreciation	–	To be determined
Inventory		4,900	5,900
Insurance prepaid		160	200

(c) All receipts are banked and all payments are made from the business bank account.

(d) A trade debt of $300 owing by John Blunt and included in the trade receivables at 31 August 20X8 (see (b) above) is to be written off as an irrecoverable debt.

(e) Mary Grimes provides depreciation at the rate of 20% on the cost of motor vans held at the end of each financial year. No depreciation is provided in the year of sale or disposal of a motor van.

(f) Discounts received during the year ended 31 August 20X8 from trade payables amounted to $1,100.

Required

(a) Prepare Mary Grimes' statement of profit or loss for the year ended 31 August 20X8.

(b) Prepare Mary Grimes' statement of financial position as at 31 August 20X8.

ANSWER

(a) STATEMENT OF PROFIT OR LOSS
FOR THE YEAR ENDED 31 AUGUST 20X8

	$	$
Revenue (W1)		98,180
Opening inventory	4,900	
Purchases (W2)	70,990	
	75,890	
Less closing inventory	5,900	
		69,990
Gross profit		28,190
Discounts received		1,100
Profit on sale of motor vehicle ($2,100 – $(10,000 – 8,000))		100
		29,390
Rent and local taxes (W3)	2,660	
Wages	15,100	
Motor vehicle expenses	3,350	
Postage and stationery	1,360	
Repairs and renewals	650	
Insurance (W4)	760	
Irrecoverable debt	300	
Depreciation of van (20% × $13,000)	2,600	
		26,780
Profit for the year		2,610

(b) STATEMENT OF FINANCIAL POSITION AS AT 31 AUGUST 20X8

	$	$
Assets		
Non-current assets		
Motor van: cost	13,000	
depreciation	2,600	
		10,400
Current assets		
Inventory	5,900	
Trade receivables ($9,500 – $300 irrecoverable debt)	9,200	
Prepayment	200	
Cash at bank	2,010	
		17,310
Total assets		27,710

	$	$
Capital and liabilities		
Capital account		
Balance at 1 September 20X7 (W5)	11,450	
Additional capital: proceeds on sale of yacht	20,000	
Profit for the year	2,610	
Less drawings	(9,200)	
Balance at 31 August 20X8		24,860
Current liabilities		
Trade payables	2,590	
Accrual	260	
		2,850
Total capital and liabilities		27,710

Workings

1   Revenue (sales)

	$
Cash received from customers	96,000
Add trade receivables at 31 August 20X8	9,500
	105,500
Less trade receivables at 1 September 20X7	7,320
Sales in year	98,180

2   Purchases

	$	$
Payments to suppliers		72,000
Add trade payables at 31 August 20X8	2,590	
discounts granted by suppliers	1,100	
		3,690
		75,690
Less trade payables at 1 September 20X7		4,700
		70,990

3   Rent and local taxes

	$
Cash paid in year	2,600
Add accrual at 31 August 20X8	260
	2,860
Less accrual at 1 September 20X7	200
Charge for the year	2,660

4   Insurance

	$
Cash paid in year	800
Add prepayment at 1 September 20X7	160
	960
Less prepayment at 31 August 20X8	200
	760

Workings 1 to 4 could also be presented in ledger account format as follows.

TRADE RECEIVABLES

	$		$
Balance b/d	7,320	Bank	96,000
∴ Sales	98,180	Balance c/d	9,500
	105,500		105,500

TRADE PAYABLES

	$		$
Bank	72,000	Balance b/d	4,700
Discounts received	1,100	∴ Purchases	70,990
Balance c/d	2,590		
	75,690		75,690

RENT AND LOCAL TAXES

	$		$
Bank	2,600	Balance b/d	200
Balance c/d	260	∴ P/L charge	2,660
	2,860		2,860

INSURANCE

	$		$
Balance b/d	160	∴ P/L charge	760
Bank	800	Balance c/d	200
	960		960

5   *Capital at 1 September 20X7*

	$	$
Assets		
Bank balance		1,970
Trade receivables		7,320
Motor van $(10,000 – 8,000)		2,000
Inventory		4,900
Prepayment		160
		16,350
Liabilities		
Trade payables	4,700	
Accrual	200	
		4,900
		11,450

↳ **Incomplete records** questions may test your ability to prepare accounts in the following situations.

– A trader **does not maintain a ledger** and therefore has no continuous double entry record of transactions.

– Accounting records are **destroyed** by accident, such as fire.

– Some essential figure is **unknown** and must be calculated as a balancing figure. This may occur as a result of inventory being damaged or destroyed, or because of misappropriation of assets.

↳ Two equations are very useful in incomplete records calculations.

– The accounting equation:
assets = capital + liabilities

– The business equation:
closing net assets = opening net assets + capital introduced + profit – drawings

↳ **Drawings** often feature as the missing item in an incomplete records problem. The trader has been drawing money but does not know how much.

↳ The approach to incomplete records questions is to build up the information given so as to complete the necessary **double entry**. This may involve reconstructing **control accounts** for:

– Cash and bank
– Trade receivables and payables

↳ Where inventory, sales or purchases is the unknown figure it will be necessary to use information on **gross profit percentages** to construct a working for gross profit in which the unknown figure can be inserted as a balance.

↳ The construction of a cash book, largely from bank statements showing receipts and payments of a business during a given period, is often an important feature of incomplete records problems.

1   In the absence of a sales account or sales day book, how can a figure of sales for the year be computed?

2   A business has opening payables of $75,000 and closing payables of $65,000. Cash paid to suppliers was $65,000 and discounts received were $3,000. What is the figure for purchases?

     A $58,000
     B $78,000
     C $52,000
     D $55,000

3   What is the difference between 'mark-up' and 'gross profit percentage'?

4   What is the accounting double entry to record the loss of inventory by fire or burglary?

     A   DEBIT P/L a/c   CREDIT cost of sales
     B   DEBIT cost of sales   CREDIT P/L a/c

5   In what circumstances is a two column cash book useful?

6   If a business proprietor pays their personal income into the business bank account, what is the accounting double entry to record the transaction?

     A   DEBIT drawings   CREDIT cash
     B   DEBIT cash   CREDIT drawings

7   A business has net assets of $70,000 at the beginning of the year and $80,000 at the end of the year. Drawings were $25,000 and a lottery win of $5,000 was paid into the business during the year. What was the profit for the year?

     A $10,000 loss
     B $30,000 profit
     C $10,000 profit
     D $30,000 loss

8   A business usually has a mark-up of 20% on cost of sales. During a year, its sales were $90,000. What was cost of sales?

     A $15,000
     B $72,000
     C $18,000
     D $75,000

1 By using the trade receivables control account to calculate sales as a balancing figure.

2 A

PAYABLES CONTROL

	$		$
Bank	65,000	Opening payables	75,000
Discounts received	3,000	Purchases (bal. fig.)	58,000
Closing payables	65,000		
	133,000		133,000

3
- Mark-up is the profit as a percentage of cost
- Gross profit percentage is the profit as a percentage of sales

4 A DEBIT P/L a/c
         CREDIT Cost of sales

Assuming that the goods were not insured.

5 Where a large amount of receipts and payments are made in cash.

6 B DEBIT Cash
         CREDIT Drawings

7 B Profit = movement in net assets – capital introduced + drawings
         = (80,000 – 70,000) – 5,000 + 25,000
         = 30,000

8 D

	$
Sales	90,000
Cost of sales (bal. fig.)	75,000
Profit $\left(\dfrac{20}{120} \times 90,000\right)$	15,000

Now try ...

Attempt the questions below from the **Practice Question Bank**

Number

Qs 68 – 72

Preparation of financial statements for sole traders

We have now reached our goal of preparing the final accounts of a sole trader!

We will deal with the preparation of a trial balance and then making adjustments to produce final accounts.

This chapter also acts as a revision of what we have covered to date. Use this period to review all the work covered to date. If you have any problems with the examples and questions, thoroughly revise the appropriate chapter before proceeding to the next part.

TOPIC LIST	SYLLABUS REFERENCE
1 Preparation of final accounts	F1(d), F2(a)

F   Preparing basic financial statements

1   Statements of financial position

(d)   Prepare a statement of financial position or extracts as   S
applicable from given information.

**2   Statements of profit or loss and other comprehensive
income**

(a)   Prepare a statement of profit or loss and other   S
comprehensive income or extracts as applicable from given
information.

---

1   Preparation of final accounts

You should now be able to prepare a set of final accounts for a sole trader from a trial balance after incorporating period-end adjustments for depreciation, inventory, prepayments, accruals, irrecoverable debts, and allowances for receivables.

1.1 Adjustments to accounts

You should now use what you have learned to produce a solution to the following exercise, which involves preparing a statement of profit or loss and statement of financial position. We have met Newbegin Tools before, but now we add a lot more information.

QUESTION   Adjustments to accounts

The financial affairs of Newbegin Tools prior to the commencement of trading were as follows.

NEWBEGIN TOOLS
STATEMENT OF FINANCIAL POSITION AS AT 1 AUGUST 20X5

	$	$
Non-current assets		
Motor vehicle		2,000
Shop fittings		3,000
		5,000
Current assets		
Inventories		12,000
Cash		1,000
		18,000
Capital		12,000
Current liabilities		
Bank overdraft	2,000	
Trade payables	4,000	
		6,000
		18,000

At the end of six months the business had made the following transactions.

(a)   Goods were purchased on credit at a list price of $10,000.

(b)   Trade discount received was 2% on list price and there was a settlement discount received of 5% on settling debts to suppliers of $8,000. These were the only payments to suppliers in the period.

(c)   Closing inventories of goods were valued at $5,450.

(d)   All sales were on credit and amounted to $27,250.

(e)   Outstanding receivables balances at 31 January 20X6 amounted to $3,250, of which $250 were to be written off. An allowance for receivables is to be made amounting to 2% of the remaining outstanding receivables.

(f)   Cash payments were made in respect of the following expenses.

		$
(i)	Stationery, postage and wrapping	500
(ii)	Telephone charges	200
(iii)	Electricity	600
(iv)	Cleaning and refreshments	150

(g)   Cash drawings by the proprietor, Alf Newbegin, amounted to $6,000.

(h)   The outstanding overdraft balance as at 1 August 20X5 was paid off. Interest charges and bank charges on the overdraft amounted to $40.

Prepare the statement of profit or loss of Newbegin Tools for the 6 months to 31 January 20X6 and a statement of financial position as at that date. Ignore depreciation.

ANSWER

STATEMENT OF PROFIT OR LOSS
FOR THE SIX MONTHS ENDED 31 JANUARY 20X6

	$	$
Revenue		27,250
Cost of sales		
Opening inventory	12,000	
Purchases (Note 1)	9,800	
	21,800	
Closing inventory	5,450	
		16,350
Gross profit		10,900
Other income – discounts received (Note 2)		400
		11,300
Expenses		
Electricity (Note 3)	600	
Stationery, postage and wrapping	500	
Irrecoverable debts written off	250	
Allowance for receivables (Note 4)	60	
Telephone charges	200	
Cleaning and refreshments	150	
Interest and bank charges	40	
		1,800
Profit for the period		9,500

Notes

1   Purchases at cost $10,000 less 2% trade discount.

2   5% of $8,000 = $400.

3   Expenses are grouped into sales and distribution expenses (here assumed to be electricity, stationery and postage, bad debts and allowance for receivables), administration expenses (here assumed to be telephone charges and cleaning) and finance charges.

4   2% of $3,000 = $60.

The preparation of a statement of financial position is not so easy, because we must calculate the value of payables and cash in hand.

(a)   Payables as at 31 January 20X6

The amount owing to payables is the sum of the amount owing at the beginning of the period, plus the cost of purchases during the period (net of all discounts), less the payments already made for purchases.

		$
	Payables as at 1 August 20X5	4,000
	Add purchases during the period, net of trade discount	9,800
		13,800
	Less settlement discounts received	(400)
		13,400
	Less payments to payables during the period*	(7,600)
		5,800

* $8,000 less cash discount of $400.

(b) Cash at bank and in hand as at 31 January 20X6

You need to identify cash payments received and cash payments made.

		$
(i)	*Cash received from sales*	
	Total sales in the period	27,250
	Add receivables as at 1 August 20X5	0
		27,250
	Less unpaid debts as at 31 January 20X6	3,250
	Cash received	24,000

		$
(ii)	*Cash paid*	
	Trade payables (see (a))	7,600
	Stationery, postage and wrapping	500
	Telephone charges	200
	Electricity	600
	Cleaning and refreshments	150
	Bank charges and interest	40
	Bank overdraft repaid	2,000
	Drawings by proprietor	6,000
		17,090

Note. It is easy to forget some of these payments, especially drawings.

		$
(iii)	Cash in hand as at 1 August 20X5	1,000
	Cash received in the period	24,000
		25,000
	Cash paid in the period	(17,090)
	Cash at bank and in hand as at 31 January 20X6	7,910

(c) When irrecoverable debts are written off, the value of outstanding receivables must be reduced by the amount written off. Receivables will be valued at $3,250 less bad debts $250 and the allowance for receivables of $60 – ie at $2,940.

(d) Non-current assets should be depreciated. However, in this exercise depreciation has been ignored.

NEWBEGIN TOOLS
STATEMENT OF FINANCIAL POSITION AS AT 31 JANUARY 20X6

	$	$
Non-current assets		
Motor vehicles	2,000	
Shop fittings	3,000	
		5,000
Current assets		
Inventories	5,450	
Receivables, less allowance for receivables	2,940	
Cash	7,910	
		16,300
		21,300

	$	$
Capital		
Capital as at 1 August 20X5		12,000
Profit for the period		9,500
		21,500
Less drawings		6,000
Capital as at 31 January 20X6		15,500
Current liabilities		
Trade payables		5,800
		21,300

The opening bank overdraft was repaid during the year and is therefore not shown at the year end.

EXAM FOCUS POINT

You may not be asked to prepare a full statement of profit or loss or statement of financial position in your exam. However, the 15 mark format questions are likely to ask you to prepare extracts from these statements.

In addition, the ACCA examining team has stated that it is essential that you practise preparing full financial statements so that you fully understand the concepts and principles involved. If you are moving on to study F7, practising full questions now is vital.

1.2 Example: accounts preparation from a trial balance

The following trial balance was extracted from the ledger of Stephen Chee, a sole trader, as at 31 May 20X1 – the end of his financial year.

STEPHEN CHEE
TRIAL BALANCE AS AT 31 MAY 20X1

	Dr	Cr
	$	$
Property, at cost	120,000	
Equipment, at cost	80,000	
Provisions for depreciation (as at 1 June 20X0)		
– on property		20,000
– on equipment		38,000
Purchases	250,000	
Sales		402,200
Inventory, as at 1 June 20X0	50,000	
Discounts allowed	18,000	
Discounts received		4,800
Returns out		15,000
Wages and salaries	58,800	
Irrecoverable debts	4,600	
Loan interest	5,100	
Other operating expenses	17,700	
Trade payables		36,000
Trade receivables	38,000	
Cash in hand	300	
Bank	1,300	
Drawings	24,000	
Allowance for receivables		500
17% long-term loan		30,000
Capital, as at 1 June 20X0		121,300
	667,800	667,800

The following additional information as at 31 May 20X1 is available.

(a)   Inventory as at the close of business has been valued at cost at $42,000.

(b)   Wages and salaries need to be accrued by $800.

(c)   Other operating expenses are prepaid by $300.

(d)   The allowance for receivables is to be adjusted so that it is 2% of trade receivables.

(e)   Depreciation for the year ended 31 May 20X1 has still to be provided for as follows.

    (i)   Property: 1.5% per annum using the straight line method
    (ii)   Equipment: 25% per annum using the reducing balance method

Required

Prepare Stephen Chee's statement of profit or loss for the year ended 31 May 20X1 and his statement of financial position as at that date.

Tutorial note. Again, you have met a simplified form of Stephen Chee before. However, this version contains a lot more information for you to deal with before you can prepare the accounts.

Solution

STEPHEN CHEE
STATEMENT OF PROFIT OR LOSS FOR THE YEAR ENDED 31 MAY 20X1

	$	$
Revenue		402,200
Cost of sales		
Opening inventory	50,000	
Purchases	250,000	
Purchases returns	(15,000)	
	285,000	
Closing inventory	42,000	
		243,000
Gross profit		159,200
Other income – discounts received		4,800
		164,000
Expenses		
Operating expenses		
Wages and salaries ($58,800 + $800)	59,600	
Discounts allowed	18,000	
Irrecoverable debts (W1)	4,860	
Loan interest	5,100	
Depreciation (W2)	12,300	
Other operating expenses ($17,700 – $300)	17,400	
		117,260
Profit for the year		46,740

STEPHEN CHEE
STATEMENT OF FINANCIAL POSITION AS AT 31 MAY 20X1

	Cost $	Accumulated depn. $	Carrying value $
Non-current assets			
Property	120,000	21,800	98,200
Equipment	80,000	48,500	31,500
	200,000	70,300	129,700
Current assets			
Inventory		42,000	
Trade receivables net of allowance for receivables ($38,000 – 760 (W1))		37,240	
Prepayments		300	
Bank		1,300	
Cash in hand		300	
			81,140
			210,840
Capital			
Balance as at 1 June 20X0			121,300
Profit for the year			46,740
			168,040
Drawings			24,000
			144,040
Non-current liabilities			
17% loan			30,000
Current liabilities			
Trade payables		36,000	
Accruals		800	
			36,800
			210,840

Workings

1	Irrecoverable debts	$
	Previous allowance	500
	New allowance (2% × 38,000)	760
	Increase	260
	Per trial balance	4,600
	Statement of profit or loss	4,860

2	Depreciation	
	Property	
	Opening provision	20,000
	Provision for the year (1.5% × 120,000)	1,800
	Closing provision	21,800
	Equipment	
	Opening provision	38,000
	Provision for the year (25% × 42,000)	10,500
	Closing provision	48,500
	Total charge in SPL	12,300

QUESTION

Final accounts

Donald Brown, a sole trader, extracted the following trial balance on 31 December 20X0.

TRIAL BALANCE AS AT 31 DECEMBER 20X0

	Debit $	Credit $
Capital as at 1 January 20X0		26,094
Receivables	42,737	
Cash in hand	1,411	
Payables		35,404
Fixtures and fittings at cost	42,200	
Discounts allowed	1,304	
Discounts received		1,175
Inventory as at 1 January 20X0	18,460	
Sales		491,620
Purchases	387,936	
Motor vehicles at cost	45,730	
Lighting and heating	6,184	
Motor expenses	2,862	
Rent	8,841	
General expenses	7,413	
Bank overdraft		19,861
Provision for depreciation		
Fixtures and fittings		2,200
Motor vehicles		15,292
Drawings	26,568	
	591,646	591,646

The following information as at 31 December is also available.

(a) $218 is owing for motor expenses.

(b) $680 has been prepaid for rent.

(c) Depreciation is to be provided for the year as follows.

- Motor vehicles: 20% on cost
- Fixtures and fittings: 10% reducing balance method

(d) Inventory at the close of business was valued at $19,926.

Required

(a)   Prepare Donald Brown's statement of profit or loss for the year ended 31 December 20X0.

(7 marks)

(b)   Which of the following formulas correctly describes the figure to be entered as capital in Donald Brown's statement of financial position?

    A   Balance b/f + gross profit for the year – drawings
    B   Balance b/f – gross profit for the year + drawings
    C   Balance b/f + profit for the year – drawings
    D   Balance b/f – profit for the year + drawings   **(2 marks)**

(c)   What is the net effect on profit of the adjustments in notes (a) to (c) above?   **(6 marks)**

    Total marks for the question   **(15 marks)**

ANSWER

Tutorial notes

1   Discounts allowed are an expense of the business and should be shown as a deduction from gross profit. Similarly, discounts received is a revenue item and should be added to gross profit.

2   The figure for depreciation in the trial balance represents accumulated depreciation up to and including 20W9. You have to calculate the charge for the year 20X0 for the statement of profit or loss.

(a)   DONALD BROWN
        STATEMENT OF PROFIT OR LOSS FOR THE YEAR ENDED 31 DECEMBER 20X0

	$	$
Revenue		491,620
Cost of sales		
Opening inventory	18,460	
Purchases	387,936	
	406,396	
Closing inventory	19,926	
		386,470
Gross profit		105,150
Other income – discounts received		1,175
		106,325
Expenses		
Discounts allowed	1,304	
Lighting and heating	6,184	
Motor expenses (2,862 + 218)	3,080	
Rent (8,841 – 680)	8,161	
General expenses	7,413	
Depreciation (W)	13,146	
		39,288
Profit for the year		67,037

Working: Depreciation charge

Motor vehicles: $45,730 \times 20\% = \$9,146$
Fixtures and fittings: $10\% \times \$(42,200 - 2,200) = \$4,000$
Total: $\$4,000 + \$9,146 = \$13,146$

(b)   C   The correct answer is: Balance b/f + profit for the year – drawings

(c)   The effects are as follows.

    (i)   Motor expenses accrual – $218 additional expense, so reduction in profit.

    (ii)   Rent prepayment – $680 reduction in expense, so increase in profit.

    (iii)   Depreciation – total charge $13,146 (9,146 + 4,000) additional expense, so reduction in profit.

Total effect on profit for the year   = + 680 – 218 – 13,146
                                    = 12,684 reduction

Although you were not asked to prepare the statement of financial position, this is shown on the next page for completeness. **You may like to have an attempt at the statement yourself before checking the answer.**

DONALD BROWN
STATEMENT OF FINANCIAL POSITION AS AT 31 DECEMBER 20X0

	Cost $	Depreciation $	Carrying value $
Non-current assets			
Fixtures and fittings	42,200	6,200	36,000
Motor vehicles	45,730	24,438	21,292
	87,930	30,638	57,292
Current assets			
Inventory		19,926	
Receivables		42,737	
Prepayments		680	
Cash in hand		1,411	
			64,754
			122,046
Capital			
Balance b/f			26,094
Profit for the year			67,037
			93,131
Less drawings			26,568
			66,563
Current liabilities			
Payables		35,404	
Accruals		218	
Bank overdraft		19,861	
			55,483
			122,046

EXAM FOCUS POINT

There is an article on adjustments to financial statements on the ACCA website:
www.accaglobal.com/gb/en/student/exam-support-resources/fundamentals-exams-study-resources/f3/technical-articles/adjustments-financial-statements.html

CHAPTER ROUNDUP

↻ You should now be able to prepare a set of final accounts for a sole trader from a trial balance after incorporating period-end adjustments for depreciation, inventory, prepayments, accruals, irrecoverable debts and allowances for receivables.

QUICK QUIZ

1   Which of the following is the correct formula for cost of sales?

    A   Opening inventory – purchases + closing inventory
    B   Purchases – closing inventory + sales
    C   Opening inventory + closing inventory – purchases
    D   Opening inventory – closing inventory + purchases

2   If an owner takes goods out of inventory for their own use, how is this dealt with?

    A   Credited to drawings at cost
    B   Credited to drawings at selling price
    C   Debited to drawings at cost
    D   Debited to drawings at selling price

3   A business starts trading on 1 September 20X0. During the year, it has sales of $500,000, purchases of $250,000 and closing inventory of $75,000. What is the gross profit for the year?

    A $175,000
    B $250,000
    C $325,000
    D $675,000

4   Mario's trial balance includes the following items: non-current assets $50,000, inventory $15,000, payables $10,000, receivables $5,000, bank $110,000, allowance for receivables $1,000.

    What is the figure for current assets?

    A $180,000
    B $170,000
    C $129,000
    D $134,000

5   Using the information in Question 4 above, what is the figure for total assets?

1   D   Correct, this is a version of the more normal formula: opening inventory + purchases – closing inventory.

   A   Incorrect

   B   Incorrect. Sales should never form part of cost of sales.

   C   Incorrect

2   C   Although we have not specifically covered this point, you should have realised that goods for own use must be treated as drawings (and so debited to drawings). If the goods were transferred at selling price, the business would show a profit on the sale of the goods that it has not made. So the transaction must be shown at cost. (Now think about where the credit entry goes before trying the question from the EQB.)

3   C

		$
Sales		500,000
Purchases	250,000	
Closing inventory	(75,000)	
Cost of sales		175,000
Gross profit		325,000

4   C

	$
Current assets	
Inventory	15,000
Receivables (5,000 – 1,000)	4,000
Bank	110,000
	129,000

5   Total assets   = non-current assets + current assets
   = 50,000 + 129,000
   = 179,000

Now try ...

Attempt the question below from the **Practice Question Bank**

Number

Q 67

Introduction to company accounting

We begin this chapter by considering the **status of limited liability** companies and the type of accounting records they maintain in order to prepare financial statements.

Then we will look at those accounting entries unique to limited liability companies: share capital, reserves, and bonus and rights issues.

This chapter provides the grounding for Chapter 20, where you will learn to prepare company financial statements.

TOPIC LIST	SYLLABUS REFERENCE
1 Limited liability and accounting records	A1(d)
2 Share capital	D10(a)
3 Reserves	D10(b),(c),(h), F1(b)
4 Bonus and rights issues	D10(d)–(g)
5 Ledger accounts and limited liability companies	D10(h),(i)

Study Guide

Intellectual level

A THE CONTEXT AND PURPOSE OF FINANCIAL REPORTING

1 The scope and purpose of, financial statements for external reporting

(d) Identify the advantages and disadvantages of operating as a limited liability company, sole trader or partnership   K

D Recording transactions and events

10 Capital structure and finance costs

(a) Understand the capital structure of a limited liability company, including: K

    (i) Ordinary shares

    (ii) Preference shares (redeemable and irredeemable)

    (iii) Loan notes

(b) Record movements in the share capital and share premium accounts.   S

(c) Identify and record the other reserves which may appear in the company statement of financial position.   S

(d) Define a bonus (capitalisation) issue and its advantages and disadvantages.   K

(e) Define a rights issue and its advantages and disadvantages.   K

(f) Record and show the effects of a bonus (capitalisation) issue in the statement of financial position.   S

(g) Record and show the effects of a rights issue in the statement of financial position.   S

(h) Record dividends in ledger accounts and the financial statements.   S

(i) Calculate and record finance costs in ledger accounts and the financial statements.   S

F Preparing basic financial statements

1 Statements of financial position

(b) Understand the nature of reserves.   K

1 Limited liability and accounting records

> There are some important differences between the accounts of a **limited liability company** and those of sole traders or partnerships.

So far, this Text has dealt mainly with the accounts of businesses in general. In this chapter we shall turn our attention to the accounts of **limited liability companies**. The accounting rules and conventions for recording the business transactions of limited liability companies and then preparing their final accounts are much the same as for sole traders. For example, companies will have a cash book, sales day book, purchase day book, journal, receivables ledger, payables ledger and nominal ledger. They will also prepare a statement of profit or loss annually and a statement of financial position at the end of the accounting year.

There are, however, some **fundamental differences** in the accounts of limited liability companies, of which the following are perhaps the most significant.

(a) The **national legislation** governing the activities of limited liability companies tends to be very extensive. Among other things, such legislation may define certain minimum accounting records which must be maintained by companies. They may specify that the annual accounts of a company must be filed with a government bureau and so be available for public inspection. They often contain detailed requirements on the minimum information which must be disclosed in a company's accounts. Businesses which are not limited liability companies (non-incorporated businesses) often enjoy comparative freedom from statutory regulation.

(b) The **owners of a company** (its **members** or **shareholders**) may be **very numerous**. Their capital is shown differently from that of a sole trader. Similarly, the 'appropriation account' of a company is different.

1.1 Unlimited and limited liability

Unlimited liability means that if the business runs up debts that it is unable to pay, the proprietors will become personally liable for the unpaid debts and would be required, if necessary, to sell their private possessions to repay them.

It is worth recapping on the relative **advantages and disadvantages** of limited liability (which we have mentioned in earlier parts of the Text). Sole traders and partnerships are, with some significant exceptions, generally fairly small concerns. The amount of capital involved may be modest, and the proprietors of the business usually participate in managing it. Their liability for the debts of the business is unlimited. This means that if the business runs up debts that it is unable to pay, the proprietors will become personally liable for the unpaid debts and would be required, if necessary, to sell their private possessions in order to repay them. For example, if a sole trader has some capital in their business, but the business now owes $40,000 which it cannot repay, the trader might have to sell their house to raise the money to pay off their business debts.

Limited liability companies offer limited liability to their owners.

Limited liability means that the maximum amount that an owner stands to lose, in the event that the company becomes insolvent and cannot pay off its debts, is their share of the capital in the business.

Thus limited liability is a **major advantage** of turning a business into a limited liability company. However, in practice, banks will normally seek personal guarantees from shareholders before making loans or granting an overdraft facility and so the advantage of limited liability is lost to a small owner-managed business.

1.1.1 Disadvantages

(a) Compliance with national legislation
(b) Compliance with national accounting standards and/or International Financial Reporting Standards
(c) Formation and annual registration costs

These are needed to avoid the privilege of limited liability being abused.

As a business grows, it needs **more capital** to finance its operations, and probably significantly more than the people managing the business can provide themselves. One way of obtaining more capital is to invite investors from outside the business to invest in the ownership or equity of the business. These new co-owners would not usually be expected to help with managing the business. To such investors, limited liability is very attractive, as the worst case scenario is that they only lose the amount they've invested.

Investments are always risky undertakings, but with limited liability the investor knows the maximum amount that they stand to lose when they put some capital into a company.

1.2 The accounting records of limited companies

Companies are normally required by law to keep accounting records which are sufficient to show and explain the company's transactions. To be sufficient, the records would normally have the following qualities.

(a) Disclose the company's current financial position at any time

(b) Contain:

    (i) Day to day entries of money received and spent

    (ii) A record of the company's assets and liabilities

    (iii) Where the company deals in goods:

        (1) A statement of inventories held at the year end, and supporting inventory count records

        (2) With the exception of retail sales, statements of goods bought and sold which identify the sellers and buyers of those goods

(c) Enable the managers of the company to ensure that the final accounts of the company give a true and fair view of the company's profit or loss and statement of financial position

The detailed requirements of accounting records which must be maintained will vary from country to country.

QUESTION

Companies

How are limited liability companies regulated in your country?

---

2 Share capital

In preparing a statement of financial position you must be able to deal with:

- Ordinary and preference share capital
- Reserves
- Loan stock

2.1 The capital of limited liability companies

The proprietors' capital in a limited liability company consists of **share capital**. When a company is set up for the first time, it issues shares, which are paid for by investors, who then become shareholders of the company. Shares are denominated in units of 25 cents, 50 cents, $1 or whatever seems appropriate. The 'face value' of the shares is called their **par value** or **legal value** (or sometimes the **nominal value**).

For example, when a company is set up with a share capital of, say, $100,000, it may be decided to issue:

(a) 100,000 shares of $1 each par value;
(b) 200,000 shares of 50c each;
(c) 400,000 shares of 25c each; or
(d) 250,000 shares of 40c each, etc.

The amount at which the shares are issued may exceed their par value. For example, a company might issue 100,000 $1 shares at a price of $1.20 each. Subscribers will then pay a total of $120,000. The issued share capital of the company would be shown in its accounts at par value, $100,000. The excess of $20,000 is described not as share capital, but as **share premium** or **capital paid-up in excess of par value**.

2.2 Authorised, issued, called-up and paid-up share capital

A distinction must be made between authorised, issued, called-up and paid-up share capital.

(a) **Authorised (or legal) capital** is the maximum amount of share capital that a company is empowered to issue. The amount of authorised share capital varies from company to company, and can change by agreement.

For example, a company's authorised share capital might be 5,000,000 ordinary shares of $1 each. This would then be the maximum number of shares it could issue, unless the maximum were to be changed by agreement.

(b) **Issued capital** is the par amount of share capital that has been issued to shareholders. The amount of issued capital cannot exceed the amount of authorised capital.

Continuing the example above, the company with authorised share capital of 5,000,000 ordinary shares of $1 might have issued 4,000,000 shares. This would leave it the option to issue 1,000,000 more shares at some time in the future.

When share capital is issued, shares are allotted to shareholders. The term 'allotted' share capital means the same thing as issued share capital.

(c) **Called-up capital**. When shares are issued or allotted, a company does not always expect to be paid the full amount for the shares at once. It might instead call up only a part of the issue price, and wait until a later time before it calls up the remainder.

For example, if a company allots 400,000 ordinary shares of $1, it might call up only, say, 75 cents per share. The issued share capital would be $400,000, but the called-up share capital would only be $300,000.

(d) **Paid-up capital**. Like everyone else, investors are not always prompt or reliable payers. When capital is called up, some shareholders might delay their payment (or even default on payment). Paid-up capital is the amount of called-up capital that has been paid.

For example, if a company issues 400,000 ordinary shares of $1 each, calls up 75 cents per share, and receives payments of $290,000, we would have:

	$
Allotted or issued capital	400,000
Called-up capital	300,000
Paid-up capital	290,000
Capital not yet paid-up	10,000

The statement of financial position of the company would appear as follows.

	$
Assets	
Called-up capital not paid	10,000
Cash (called-up capital paid)	290,000
	300,000
Equity	
Called-up share capital	
(400,000 ordinary shares of $1, with 75c per share called up)	300,000

Notice that in a limited liability company's statement of financial position the owners' capital is called **equity**. In business and in your wider reading, shares may be called **equities**.

2.3 Ordinary shares and preference shares

At this stage we need to distinguish between the two types of shares most often encountered: **preference shares** and **ordinary shares**.

2.3.1 Preference shares

Preference shares are shares which confer certain preferential rights on their holder.

Preference shares carry the right to a final dividend which is expressed as a percentage of their par value: eg a 6% $1 preference share carries a right to an annual dividend of 6c. Preference dividends have priority over ordinary dividends. In other words, if the managers of a company wish to pay a dividend (which they are not obliged to do) they must pay any preference dividend first. Otherwise, no ordinary dividend may be paid.

The rights attaching to preference shares are set out in the company's constitution. They may vary from company to company and country to country, but typically:

(a) Preference shareholders have a **priority right** to a return of their capital over ordinary shareholders if the company goes into liquidation.

(b) Preference shares do not **carry a right to vote**.

(c) If the preference shares are **cumulative**, it means that before a company can pay an ordinary dividend it must not only pay the current year's preference dividend but must also make good any arrears of preference dividends unpaid in previous years.

2.3.2 Classification of preference shares

Preference shares may be classified in one of two ways.

- Redeemable
- Irredeemable

Redeemable preference shares mean that the company will redeem (repay) the nominal value of those shares at a later date. For example, 'redeemable 5% $1 preference shares 20X9' means that the company will pay these shareholders $1 for every share they hold on a certain date in 20X9. The shares will then be cancelled and no further dividends paid. Redeemable preference shares are treated like loans and are included as non-current liabilities in the statement of financial position. Remember to reclassify them as current liabilities if the redemption is due within 12 months. Dividends paid on redeemable preference shares are treated like interest paid on loans and are included in financial costs in the statement of profit or loss.

Irredeemable preference shares are treated just like other shares. They form part of equity and their dividends are treated as appropriations of profit.

QUESTION

Preference shares

How would you classify redeemable preference shares 20X9 in the financial statements for the year ended 30 June 20X8, if the shares are due to be redeemed in September 20X9?

A As part of equity
B A long-term liability
C A current liability

ANSWER

B The preference shares are not due to be redeemed until 15 months after the year end and so form part of non-current liabilities.

EXAM FOCUS POINT

In the exam, the question will specifically state whether the shares are redeemable or irredeemable preference shares.

2.3.3 Ordinary shares

Ordinary shares are by far the most common type of share. They carry no right to a fixed dividend but are entitled to all profits left after payment of any preference dividend. Generally, however, only a part of such remaining profits is distributed, the rest being kept in reserve (see below).

Ordinary shares are shares which are not preferred with regard to dividend payments. Thus a holder only receives a dividend after fixed dividends have been paid to preference shareholders.

The amount of ordinary dividends normally fluctuates, although it is often expected that it will increase from year to year. Should the company be wound up, any surplus not distributed is shared between the ordinary shareholders. Ordinary shares normally carry voting rights.

Ordinary shareholders are thus the effective **owners** of a company. They own the 'equity' of the business, and any reserves of the business (described later) belong to them. Ordinary shareholders are sometimes referred to as **equity shareholders**. Preference shareholders are in many ways more like payables of the company (although legally they are members, not payables). It should be emphasised, however, that the precise rights attached to preference and ordinary shares may vary; the distinctions noted above are generalisations.

2.4 Example: dividends on ordinary shares and preference shares

Garden Gloves Co has issued 50,000 ordinary shares of 50 cents each and 20,000 7% preference shares of $1 each. Its profits after taxation for the year to 30 September 20X5 were $8,400. The management board has decided to pay an ordinary dividend (ie a dividend on ordinary shares) which is 50% of profits after tax and preference dividend.

Required

Show the amount in total of dividends and of retained profits, and calculate the dividend per share on ordinary shares.

Solution

	$
Profit after tax	8,400
Preference dividend (7% of $1 × 20,000)	1,400
Earnings (profit after tax and preference dividend)	7,000
Ordinary dividend (50% of earnings)	3,500
Retained earnings (also 50% of earnings)	3,500

The ordinary dividend is 7 cents per share ($3,500 ÷ 50,000 ordinary shares).

The appropriation of profit would be as follows.

	$	$
Profit after tax		8,400
Dividends: preference	1,400	
ordinary	3,500	
		4,900
Retained earnings		3,500

As we will see later, appropriations of profit do not appear in the statement of profit or loss, but are shown as movements on reserves.

2.5 The market value of shares

The par value of shares will be different from their market value, which is the price at which someone is prepared to purchase shares in the company from an existing shareholder. If Mr A owns 1,000 $1 shares in Z Co he may sell them to Mr B for $1.60 each.

This transfer of existing shares does not affect Z Co's own financial position in any way whatsoever. Apart from changing the register of members, Z Co does not have to bother with the sale by Mr A to Mr B at all. There are certainly no accounting entries to be made for the share sale.

Shares in private companies do not change hands very often; hence their market value often being hard to estimate. Companies listed on a stock exchange are quoted, ie it is the market value of the shares which is quoted.

2.6 Loan stock or bonds

Limited liability companies may issue loan stock or bonds. These are long-term liabilities. In some countries they are described as **loan capital** because they are a means of raising finance, in the same way as issuing share capital raises finance. They are different from share capital in the following ways.

(a)   **Shareholders** are **members** of a company, while **providers of loan capital** are **creditors**.

(b)   **Shareholders** receive **dividends** (appropriations of profit) whereas the **holders of loan capital** are entitled to a **fixed rate of interest** (an expense charged against revenue).

(c)   Loan capital holders can take legal action against a company if their interest is not paid when due, whereas **shareholders cannot enforce the payment of dividends**.

(d)   Loan stock is **often secured on company assets**, whereas shares are not.

The holder of loan capital is generally in a less risky position than the shareholder. They have greater security, although their income is fixed and cannot grow, unlike ordinary dividends. As remarked earlier, preference shares are in practice very similar to loan capital, not least because the preference dividend is normally fixed.

Interest is calculated on the par or legal value of loan capital, regardless of its market value. If a company has $700,000 (par value) 12% loan stock in issue, interest of $84,000 will be charged in the statement of profit or loss per year. Interest is usually paid half-yearly; examination questions often require an accrual to be made for interest due at the year end.

For example, if a company has $700,000 of 12% loan stock in issue, pays interest on 30 June and 31 December each year, and ends its accounting year on 30 September, there would be an accrual of 3 months' unpaid interest (3/12 × $84,000) = $21,000 at the end of each accounting year that the loan stock is still in issue.

QUESTION   Share capital

Distinguish between authorised, issued, called-up and paid-up capital.

ANSWER

Authorised share capital: the maximum amount of share capital that a company is empowered to issue

Issued share capital: the amount of share capital that has been issued to shareholders

Called-up share capital: the amount the company has asked shareholders to pay, for the time being, on shares issued to them

Paid-up share capital: the amounts actually paid by shareholders on shares issued to them

3   Reuerves

Share capital and reserves are 'owned' by the shareholders. They are known collectively as 'shareholders' equity'.

Shareholders' equity consists of the following.

(a)   The par value of issued capital (minus any amounts not yet called up on issued shares)
(b)   Other equity

The share capital itself might consist of both ordinary shares and preference shares. All reserves, however, are owned by the ordinary shareholders, who own the 'equity' in the company. We looked at share capital in detail above.

'Other equity' consists of four elements.

(a)   Capital paid-up in excess of par value (share premium)
(b)   Revaluation surplus
(c)   Reserves
(d)   Retained earnings

We will look at each in turn.

3.1 The share premium account

In this context, 'premium' means the difference between the issue price of the share and its par value. The account is sometimes called 'capital paid-up in excess of par value'. When a company is first incorporated (set up) the issue price of its shares will probably be the same as their par value and so there would be no share premium. If the company does well, the market value of its shares will increase, but not the par value. The price of any new shares issued will be approximately their market value.

The difference between cash received by the company and the par value of the new shares issued is transferred to the **share premium account**. For example, if X Co issues 1,000 $1 ordinary shares at $2.60 each the book entry will be:

		$	$
DEBIT	Cash	2,600	
CREDIT	Ordinary shares		1,000
	Share premium account		1,600

A share premium account only comes into being when a company issues shares at a price in excess of their par value. The market price of the shares, once they have been issued, has no bearing at all on the company's accounts, and so if their market price goes up or down, the share premium account would remain unaltered.

A share premium account is an account into which sums received as payment for shares in excess of their nominal value must be placed.

Once established, the share premium account constitutes capital of the company which cannot be paid out in dividends, ie it is a capital reserve. The share premium account will increase in value if and when new shares are issued at a price above their par value. The share premium account can be 'used' – and so decrease in value – only in certain very limited ways, which are largely beyond the scope of your basic financial accounting syllabus. One common use of the share premium account, however, is to 'finance' the issue of bonus shares. Other uses of this account may depend on national legislation.

EXAM FOCUS POINT

The share premium account cannot be distributed as a dividend under any circumstances.

The reason for creating such non-distributable reserves is to maintain the capital of the company. This capital 'base' provides some security for the company's creditors, bearing in mind that the liability of shareholders is limited in the event that the company cannot repay its debts. It would be most unjust – and illegal – for a company to pay its shareholders a dividend out of its base capital when it is not even able to pay back its debts.

QUESTION

Share issue

AB Co issues 5,000 50c shares for $6,000. What are the entries for share capital and share premium in the statement of financial position?

	Share capital	Share premium
A	$5,000	$1,000
B	$1,000	$5,000
C	$3,500	$3,500
D	$2,500	$3,500

ANSWER

Did you notice that the shares are 50c each, not $1? The shares were issued for $1.20 each ($6,000/5,000 shares). Of this, 50c is share capital and 70c is share premium. Therefore option D is the correct answer.

3.2 Revaluation surplus

The result of an upward revaluation of a non-current asset is a '**revaluation surplus**'. This reserve is **non-distributable**, as it represents unrealised profits on the revalued assets. It is another capital reserve. The relevant part of a revaluation surplus can only become realised if the asset in question is sold, thus realising the gain. The revaluation surplus may fall, however, if an asset which had previously been revalued upwards suffered a fall in value in the next revaluation.

3.3 Reserves

In most countries, a distinction must be made between the following.

(a)   **Statutory reserves**, which are reserves which a company is required to set up by law, and which are not available for the distribution of dividends.

(b)   **Non-statutory reserves**, which are reserves consisting of profits which are distributable as dividends, if the company so wishes.

Statutory reserves are capital reserves (share premium, revaluation) and non-statutory reserves are revenue reserves.

We are concerned here with the latter type, which the company managers may choose to set up. These may have a specific purpose (eg plant and machinery replacement reserve) or not (eg general reserve). The creation of these reserves usually indicates a general intention not to distribute the profits involved at any future date, although legally any such reserves, being non-statutory, remain available for the payment of dividends.

Profits are transferred to these reserves by making an appropriation out of profits, usually profits for the year. Typically, you might come across the following.

	$	$
Profit after taxation		100,000
Appropriations of profit		
Dividend	60,000	
Transfer to general reserve	10,000	
		70,000
Retained earnings for the year		30,000
Retained earnings b/f		250,000
Retained earnings c/f		280,000

3.3.1 Dividends

Dividends are appropriations of profit after tax.

Shareholders who are also managers of their company will receive a salary as a manager. They are also entitled to a share of the profits made by the company.

Many companies pay dividends in two stages during the course of their accounting year.

(a)   In mid-year, after the half-year financial results are known, the company might pay an **interim dividend**.

(b)   At the end of the year, the company might propose a further **final dividend**.

The total dividend to be included in the financial statements for the year is the sum of the dividends actually paid in the year. (Not all companies by any means pay an interim dividend. Interim dividends are, however, commonly paid out by larger limited liability companies.)

At the end of an accounting year, a company's managers may have proposed a final dividend payment, but this will not yet have been paid. The proposed dividend **does not appear in the accounts** but will be disclosed in the notes in accordance with IAS 10 *Events after the reporting period* (see Chapter 21).

EXAM FOCUS POINT

Dividends which have been **paid** are shown in the statement of changes in equity (see chapter 20). They are not shown in the statement of profit or loss, although they are deducted from retained earnings in the statement of financial position. **Proposed** dividends are not adjusted for, they are simply disclosed by note.

The terminology of dividend payments can be confusing, since they may be expressed either in the form, of 'x cents per share' or of 'y%'. In the latter case, the meaning is always 'y% of the **par value** of the shares in issue'. For example, suppose a company's issued share capital consists of 100,000 50c ordinary shares which were issued at a premium of 10c per share. The company's statement of financial position would include the following.

		$
Ordinary shares:	100,000 50c ordinary shares	50,000
Share premium account:	(100,000 × 10c)	10,000

If the managers wish to pay a dividend of $5,000, they may propose either of the following.

(a)   A dividend of 5c per share (100,000 × 5c = $5,000)

(b)   A dividend of 10% (10% × $50,000 = $5,000)

Not all profits are distributed as dividends; some will be retained in the business to finance future projects.

QUESTION   Dividend

A company has authorised share capital of 1,000,000 50c ordinary shares and an issued share capital of 800,000 50c ordinary shares. If an ordinary dividend of 5% is declared, what is the amount payable to shareholders?

A $50,000
B $20,000
C $40,000
D $25,000

ANSWER

B   800,000 × 50c × 5% = $20,000.

3.4 Retained earnings

This is the **most significant reserve** and is variously described as:

(a)   Revenue reserve
(b)   Retained earnings
(c)   Accumulated profits
(d)   Undistributed profits
(e)   Unappropriated profits

These are **profits** earned by the company and not appropriated by dividends, taxation or transfer to another reserve account.

Provided that a company is earning profits, this reserve generally increases from year to year, as most companies do not distribute all their profits as dividends. Dividends can be paid from it: even if a loss is made in one particular year, a dividend can be paid from previous years' retained earnings.

For example, if a company makes a loss of $100,000 in one year, yet has unappropriated profits from previous years totalling $250,000, it can pay a dividend not exceeding $150,000. One reason for retaining some profit each year is to enable the company to pay dividends even when profits are low (or non-existent). Another reason is usually shortage of cash.

Very occasionally, you might come across a debit balance on the retained earnings account. This would indicate that the company has accumulated losses.

3.5 Distinction between reserves and provisions

A reserve is an appropriation of distributable profits for a specific purpose (eg plant replacement) while a provision is an amount charged against revenue as an expense. A provision relates to a diminution in the value of either an asset or a known liability (eg audit fees), the amount of which cannot be established with any accuracy.

Provisions or allowances (for depreciation etc) are dealt with in company accounts in the same way as in the accounts of other types of business.

---

4 Bonus and rights issues

A company can increase its share capital by means of a **bonus issue** or a **rights issue**.

4.1 Bonus (capitalisation) issues

A company may wish to increase its share capital without wishing to raise additional finance by issuing new shares. For example, a profitable company might expand from modest beginnings over a number of years. Its profitability would be reflected in large balances on its reserves, while its original share capital might look like that of a much smaller business.

It is open to such a company to **reclassify some of its reserves as share capital**. This is purely a paper exercise which raises no funds. Any reserve may be reclassified in this way, including a share premium account or other reserve. Such a reclassification increases the capital base of the company and gives creditors greater protection.

4.1.1 Advantages

- Increases capital without diluting current shareholders' holdings
- Capitalises reserves, so they cannot be paid as dividends

4.1.2 Disadvantages

- Does not raise any cash
- Could jeopardise payment of future dividends if profits fall

4.2 Example: bonus issue

BUBBLES CO
STATEMENT OF FINANCIAL POSITION (EXTRACT)

	$'000	$'000
Shareholders' equity		
Share capital		
$1 ordinary shares (fully paid)		1,000
Reserves		
Share premium	500	
Retained earnings	2,000	
		2,500
		3,500

Bubbles decided to make a '3 for 2' bonus issue (ie 3 new shares for every 2 already held).

The double entry is:		$'000	$'000
DEBIT	Share premium	500	
	Retained earnings	1,000	
CREDIT	Ordinary share capital		1,500

After the issue the statement of financial position is as follows.

	$'000
Share capital: $1 ordinary shares (fully paid)	2,500
Retained earnings	1,000
Shareholders' equity	3,500

1,500,000 new ('bonus') shares are issued to existing shareholders, so that if Mr X previously held 20,000 shares he will now hold 50,000. However, the total value of his holding should theoretically remain the same, since the net assets of the company remain unchanged and his share of those net assets remains at 2% (ie 50,000/2,500,000; previously 20,000/1,000,000).

QUESTION

Bonus issue

CLARKE FRINGLAND CO
STATEMENT OF FINANCIAL POSITION AS AT 31 DECEMBER 20X3 (EXTRACT)

	$
Share capital (50c)	10,000
Share premium	7,000
Retained earnings	8,000
	25,000

Clarke Fringland Co has decided on a bonus issue of shares of 1 for 4 and will use the share premium account for this purpose.

Required

What is the double entry to record the bonus issue of shares and what is the adjusted financial position extract after the bonus issue?

ANSWER

There are 20,000 ($10,000 ÷ 50c) shares before the bonus issue. Each shareholder will receive 1 share for every 4 held, so 5,000 (20,000 ÷ 4 × 1) new shares will be issued.

The double entry is:

DEBIT	Share premium	$2,500	($5,000 × 50c)
CREDIT	Share capital	$2,500	

ADJUSTED STATEMENT OF FINANCIAL POSITION

	$
Share capital (50c)	12,500
Share premium	4,500
Retained earnings	8,000
	25,000

4.3 Rights issues

A **rights issue** (unlike a bonus issue) is **an issue of shares for cash**. The 'rights' are offered to existing shareholders, who can sell them if they wish. This is beneficial for existing shareholders in that the shares are usually issued at a **discount** to the **current market price**.

4.3.1 Advantages

- Raises cash for the company
- Keeps reserves available for future dividends

4.3.2 Disadvantage

- Dilutes shareholders' holdings if they do not take up rights issue

4.4 Example: rights issue

Bubbles Co (above) decides to make a rights issue, shortly after the bonus issue. The terms are '1 for 5 @ $1.20' (ie 1 new share for every 5 already held, at a price of $1.20). Assuming that all shareholders take up their rights (which they are not obliged to), the double entry is:

		$'000	$'000
DEBIT	Cash (2,500 ÷ 5 × $1.20)	600	
CREDIT	Ordinary share capital		500
	Share premium		100

Mr X, who previously held 50,000 shares, will now hold 60,000. The value of his holding should increase (all other things being equal) because the net assets of the company will increase. The new statement of financial position will show:

	$'000
$1 ordinary shares	3,000
Share premium	100
Retained earnings	1,000
Shareholders' equity	4,100

The increase in funds of $600,000 represents the cash raised from the issue of 500,000 new shares at a price of $1.20 each.

Rights issues are a popular way of raising cash by issuing shares and they are cheap to administer. In addition, shareholders retain control of the business, as their holding is not diluted.

QUESTION

CLARKE FRINGLAND CO
STATEMENT OF FINANCIAL POSITION AS AT 31 DECEMBER 20X3 (EXTRACT)

	$
Share capital (50c)	8,000
Share premium	7,000
Retained earnings	10,000
	25,000

Clarke Fringland Co decides on a rights issue of 1 for 4 at $1.20.

Required

What is the double entry to record the issue of shares and what is the adjusted financial position extract after the issue?

ANSWER

The double entry is:

DEBIT	Bank	$4,800	($8,000 ÷ 50c × ¼ × $1.20)
CREDIT	Share capital	$2,000	($8,000 ÷ 50c × ¼ × 50c)
CREDIT	Share premium	$2,800	

ADJUSTED STATEMENT OF FINANCIAL POSITION

	$
Share capital (50c)	10,000
Share premium	9,800
Retained earnings	10,000
	29,800

QUESTION

Bonus and rights issue

X Co has the following capital structure.

	$
400,000 ordinary shares of 50c	200,000
Share premium account	70,000
Retained earnings	230,000
Shareholders' equity	500,000

Show its capital structure following:

(a)   A '1 for 2' bonus issue
(b)   A rights issue of '1 for 3' at 75c following the bonus issue, assuming all rights taken up

ANSWER

(a)

	$
600,000 ordinary shares of 50c	300,000
Retained earnings	200,000
Shareholders' equity	500,000

(b)

	$
800,000 ordinary shares of 50c	400,000
Share premium account	50,000
Retained earnings	200,000
Shareholders' equity	650,000

The bonus issue was financed by the whole of the share premium account and $30,000 retained earnings. The share premium account has funds again following the rights issue. Note that the bonus issue leaves shareholders' equity unchanged. The rights issue will have brought in cash of $150,000 (200,000 × 75c) and shareholders' equity is increased by this amount.

EXAM FOCUS POINT

The ACCA examining team highlighted bonus and rights issues as an area poorly answered in the December 2013 exam. Some students confused bonus issues with rights issues and failed to understand that rights issues are offered at a discount to the **market value** and not the **nominal value**.

5 Ledger accounts and limited liability companies

Limited companies keep ledger accounts. The only difference between the ledger accounts of companies and sole traders is the nature of some of the transactions, assets and liabilities for which accounts need to be kept.

For example, there will be an account for each of the following items.

(a) **Taxation**

    (i)   Tax charged against profits will be accounted for by:

        DEBIT   SPL
        CREDIT   Taxation account

    (ii)   The outstanding balance on the taxation account will be a liability in the statement of financial position, until eventually paid, when the accounting entry would be:

        DEBIT   Taxation account
        CREDIT   Cash

(b) **Dividends**

A separate account will be kept for the dividends for each different class of shares (eg unredeemable preference, ordinary).

    (i)   Dividends declared out of profits will be disclosed in the notes if they are unpaid at the year end.

    (ii)   When dividends are paid, we have:

        DEBIT   Dividends paid account
        CREDIT   Cash

(c) **Loan stock**

Loan stock being a long-term liability will be shown as a credit balance in a loan stock account.

Interest payable on such loans is not credited to the loan account, but is credited to a separate payables account for interest until it is eventually paid: ie

DEBIT   Interest account (an expense, chargeable against profits)
CREDIT   Interest payable (a current liability until eventually paid)

(d) **Share capital and reserves**

There will be a separate account for:

    (i)   Each different class of share capital (always a credit balance b/d)
    (ii)   Each different type of reserve (nearly always a credit balance b/d)

(e) **Finance costs**

Finance costs mean interest paid. They include interest on bank loans, the loan stock interest in (c) above and the dividend paid on redeemable preference shares. The entries are exactly the same.

DEBIT   Interest account (an expense, chargeable against profits)
CREDIT   Interest payable (a current liability until eventually paid)

CHAPTER ROUNDUP

↳ There are some important differences between the accounts of a **limited liability company** and those of sole traders or partnerships.

↳ In preparing a statement of financial position you must be able to deal with:

– Ordinary and preference share capital
– Reserves
– Loan stock

↳ Share capital and reserves are 'owned' by the shareholders. They are known collectively as 'shareholders' equity'.

↳ A company can increase its share capital by means of a **bonus issue** or a **rights issue**.

QUICK QUIZ

1 Limited liability means the shareholders are responsible for the company's debts only up to the amount paid on the shares. True or false?

2 Fill in the blanks.

.... share capital is the par value of shares issued to shareholders. .... share capital is the amount payable to date by the shareholders.

3 What are the differences between ordinary shares and preference shares?

4 What are the differences between loan stock and share capital?

5 A company issues 50,000 $1 shares at a price of $1.25 per share. How much should be posted to the share premium account?

A $50,000
B $12,500
C $62,500
D $60,000

6 Distinguish between a bonus (capitalisation) issue and a rights issue.

7 A company has a balance on share premium account of $50,000 and on retained earnings of $75,000. Issued share capital is 400,000 25c shares. The company decides to make a bonus issue of 1 for 1. What are the closing balances on share premium and retained earnings?

	Share premium	Retained earnings
A	$25,000	Nil
B	$10,000	$15,000
C	Nil	$25,000
D	Nil	$(275,000)

ANSWERS TO QUICK QUIZ

1   True. The maximum amount that a shareholder has to pay is the amount paid on their shares.

2   **Issued** share capital is the par value of shares issued to shareholders. **Called-up** share capital is the amount payable to date by the shareholders.

3   Ordinary shares can be paid any or no dividend. The dividend attaching to preference shares is set from the start.

4   Loan stock are long-term loans, and so loan stock holders are long-term payables. Equity shareholders own the company.

5   B   (50,000 × 25c)

6   A bonus issue is financed by capitalising reserves. A rights issue is paid for by the shareholders taking up the shares.

7   C   Capitalisation of 1:1 means a further 400,000 25c shares are issued. This represents $100,000. This $100,000 is taken from share premium account first ($50,000) and the balance of $50,000 is taken from retained earnings, leaving (75,000 – 50,000) = $25,000.

Now try ...

Attempt the questions below from the **Practice Question Bank**

Number

Qs 73 – 76

CHAPTER

20

Preparation of financial statements for companies

You have now come to the point in your studies for F3/FFA when you can look at the form and content of the financial statements of **limited liability companies**. Your later financial accounting studies will be concerned almost entirely with company accounts so it is vital that you acquire a sound understanding of the basic concepts now.

The financial statements of limited liability companies are usually governed by national legislation and accounting standards. From an international standpoint, however, the **general content** of financial statements is governed by IAS 1 *Presentation of financial statements*. We will look at the standard and explain those items in the financial statements which have not yet appeared in the Text.

We will look at another IAS which has a significant impact on the content and form of company accounts, IAS 18 *Revenue*.

All these standards are concerned with financial statements produced for external reporting purposes (ie to external users). However, companies also produce financial accounts for internal purposes, and we will look at the different approach in preparing accounts for internal as well as external use.

TOPIC LIST	SYLLABUS REFERENCE
1 IAS 1: *Presentation of financial statements*	F1(d), F2(a),(g)
2 The statement of financial position	F1(a),(d), D8(l)
3 The statement of profit or loss and other comprehensive income	F1(e), F2(a)–(g)
4 Statement of changes in equity	D10(j), F1(c)
5 Notes to the financial statements	F3(a),(b)
6 Company accounts for internal purposes	F1(d), F2(a),(c)
7 IAS 18 *Revenue*	F2(b)
8 Practice question	F1(d), F2(a),(c),(d)

Study Guide	Intellectual level

D **Recording transactions and events**

8 **Receivables and payables**

(l) Classify items as current or non-current liabilities in the statement of financial position. | S

10 **Capital structure and finance costs**

(j) Identify the components of the statement of changes in equity. | K

F **Preparing basic financial statements**

1 **Statements of financial position**

(a) Recognise how the accounting equation, accounting treatments as stipulated within sections D and E and the examinable documents, and business entity convention underlie the statement of financial position. | K

(c) Identify and report reserves in a company statement of financial position. | S

(d) Prepare a statement of financial position or extracts as applicable from given information using accounting treatments as stipulated within sections D and E and the examinable documents. | S

(e) Understand why the heading retained earnings appears in a company statement of financial position. | K

2 **Statements of profit or loss and other comprehensive income**

(a) Prepare a statement of profit or loss and other comprehensive income or extracts as applicable from given information using accounting treatments as stipulated within sections D and E and the examinable documents. | S

(b) Understand how accounting concepts apply to revenue and expenses. | K

(c) Calculate revenue, cost of sales, gross profit, profit for the year and total comprehensive income from given information. | S

(d) Disclose items of income and expenditure in the statement of profit or loss. | S

(e) Record income tax in the statement of profit or loss of a company, including the under- and overprovision of tax in the prior year. | S

(f) Understand the interrelationship between the statement of financial position and the statement of profit or loss and other comprehensive income. | K

(g) Identify items requiring separate disclosure on the face of the statement of profit or loss. | K

Study Guide	Intellectual level

3   Disclosure notes

(a)   Explain the purpose of disclosure notes.

K

(b)   Draft the following disclosure notes:

S

   (i)   Non-current assets including tangible and intangible
      assets

   (ii)   Provisions

   (iii) Events after the reporting period

   (iv)   Inventory

1   IAS 1: *Presentation of financial statements*

> IAS 1 lists the required contents of a company's financial statements. It also gives guidance on how items
> should be presented in the financial statements.
>
> A complete set of financial statements includes a statement of financial position, a statement of profit or
> loss and other comprehensive income, a statement of changes in equity, a statement of cash flows and
> disclosure notes.

As well as covering accounting policies and other general considerations governing financial statements,
IAS 1 *Presentation of financial statements* gives substantial guidance on the form and content of
published financial statements.

A complete set of financial statements includes the following.

- Statement of financial position

- Statement of profit or loss and other comprehensive income (either as a single statement or as
  two separate statements: the statement of profit or loss and the statement of other comprehensive
  income)

- Statement of changes in equity

- Statement of cash flows

- Notes, including a summary of significant accounting policies and other explanatory information

IAS 1 gives guidance on the format and content of all of these, apart from the statement of cash flows,
which is covered by IAS 7. We will consider each of these in turn in this chapter. First of all, though,
some general points are made about financial statements.

1.1 How items are disclosed

IAS 1 specifies disclosures of certain items in certain ways.

- Some items must appear on the **face of the statement of financial position or statement of profit
  or loss**

- Other items can appear in a **note to the financial statements** instead

- **Recommended formats** are given which entities may or may not follow, depending on their
  circumstances

Obviously, disclosures specified by **other standards** must also be made. Disclosures in both IAS 1 and
other standards must be made either on the face of the statement or in the notes unless otherwise
stated, ie disclosures cannot be made in an accompanying commentary or report.

1.2 Identification of financial statements

As a result of the above point, it is most important that entities **distinguish the financial statements** very clearly from any other information published with them. This is because all International Financial Reporting Standards (IFRSs) apply **only** to the financial statements (ie the main statements and related notes), so readers of the annual report must be able to differentiate between the parts of the report which are prepared under IFRSs, and other parts which are not.

The entity should **identify each component** of the financial statements very clearly. IAS 1 also requires disclosure of the following information in a prominent position. If necessary it should be repeated wherever it is felt to be of use to the readers in their understanding of the information presented.

- **Name** of the reporting entity (or other means of identification)
- Whether the accounts cover the **single entity** only or a **group** of entities
- The **reporting date** or the period covered by the financial statements (as appropriate)
- The **reporting currency** used in presenting the figures in the financial statements

Judgement must be used to determine the best method of presenting this information. In particular, the standard suggests that the approach to this will be very different when the financial statements are communicated electronically.

The **level of precision** is important, as presenting figures in thousands or millions of units makes the figures more understandable. The level of precision must be disclosed, however, and it should not obscure necessary details or make the information less relevant.

1.3 Reporting period

Entities normally present financial statements **annually**. IAS 1 states that they should be prepared at least as often as this.

EXAM FOCUS POINT

In the July to December 2014 examining team's report, the examining team commented that in section B where students are required to prepare various financial statements, many students were unsure of the format in which to present their answer and how to apply various accounting techniques.

Study the following sections carefully and use the format provided.

2 The statement of financial position

IAS 1 specifies what should be included in a statement of financial position and includes a suggested format. It also provides guidance on the current/non-current distinction.

2.1 Statement of financial position

IAS 1 gives the following suggested format for a statement of financial position.

ABC CO
STATEMENT OF FINANCIAL POSITION AS AT 31 DECEMBER 20X2

	20X2 $'000	20X2 $'000	20X1 $'000	20X1 $'000
Assets				
Non-current assets				
Property, plant and equipment	X		X	
Goodwill	X		X	
Other intangible assets	X̲		X̲	
		X		X
Current assets				
Inventories	X		X	
Trade receivables	X		X	
Other current assets	X		X	
Cash and cash equivalents	X̲		X̲	
		X̲		X̲
Total assets		X̳		X̳
Equity and liabilities				
Equity				
Share capital	X		X	
Retained earnings	X		X	
Other components of equity	X̲		X̲	
		X		X
Non-current liabilities				
Long-term borrowings	X		X	
Long-term provisions	X̲		X̲	
		X		X
Current liabilities				
Trade and other payables	X		X	
Short-term borrowings	X		X	
Current portion of long-term borrowings	X		X	
Current tax payable	X		X	
Short-term provisions	X̲		X̲	
		X̲		X̲
Total equity and liabilities		X̳		X̳

2.1.1 Concepts

The statement of financial position makes use of the accounting equation concept that:

Assets = Capital + Liabilities

The statement of financial position is also prepared according to the **business entity** convention, that a business is separate from its owners.

2.1.2 Assets

The assets are exactly the same as those we would expect to find in the accounts of a sole trader. The only difference is that the detail is given in notes. Only the totals are shown on the face of the statement of financial position.

2.1.3 Equity

We looked at share capital and reserves in detail in the previous chapter. Movements in equity must be reported in the statement of changes in equity, which we will consider below.

Capital reserves usually have to be set up by law, whereas revenue reserves are appropriations of profit. With a sole trader, profit was added to capital. However, in a limited company, share capital and profit have to be **disclosed separately**, because profit is distributable as a dividend but share capital cannot be distributed. Therefore any retained profits are kept in the retained earnings reserve.

2.1.4 Liabilities

Liabilities are split between current and non-current. This is dealt with next.

2.2 The current/non-current distinction

Current assets and current liabilities of various types have been discussed in earlier parts of this Text. Users of financial statements need to be able to identify current assets and current liabilities in order to determine the company's financial position. Where current assets are greater than current liabilities, the net excess is often called 'working capital' or 'net current assets'.

2.3 Alternative views of current assets and current liabilities

IAS 1 lays down rules for entities which choose to show the current/non-current distinction. It also states what should happen if they do not do so.

Each entity should decide whether it wishes to present current/non-current assets and current/non-current liabilities as **separate classifications** in the statement of financial position. This decision should be based on the nature of the entity's operations. Where an entity does **not** choose to make this classification, it should present assets and liabilities broadly **in order of their liquidity**.

In either case, the entity should disclose any portion of an asset or liability which is expected to be recovered or settled **after more than 12 months**. For example, for an amount receivable which is due in instalments over 18 months, the portion due after more than 12 months must be disclosed.

2.4 Current assets

An asset should be classified as a current asset when it is:

- Expected to be realised in, or is held for sale or consumption in, the entity's normal operating cycle

- Held primarily for the purpose of being traded

- Expected to be realised within 12 months after the reporting date

- Cash or a cash equivalent which is not restricted in its use

All other assets should be classified as non-current assets.   IAS 1)

Non-current includes tangible, intangible operating and financial assets of a long-term nature. Other terms with the same meaning can be used (eg 'fixed', 'long-term').

The term 'operating cycle' is defined by the standard as follows.

The operating cycle of an entity is the time between the acquisition of assets for processing and their realisation in cash or cash equivalents.   (IAS 1)

Current assets therefore include assets (such as inventories and trade receivables) that are sold or realised as part of the normal operating cycle. **This is the case even where they are not expected to be realised within 12 months**.

2.5 Current liabilities

A liability should be classified as a current liability when it is:

- Expected to be settled in the entity's normal operating cycle
- Due to be settled within 12 months of the reporting date
- Held primarily for the purpose of being traded

All other liabilities should be classified as non-current liabilities.   (IAS 1)

The categorisation of current liabilities is very similar to that of current assets. Thus, some current liabilities are part of the **working capital** used in the normal operating cycle of the business (ie trade payables and accruals for employee and other operating costs). Such items will be classed as current liabilities **even where they are due to be settled more than 12 months after the reporting date**.

There are also current liabilities which are not settled as part of the normal operating cycle, but which are due to be settled within 12 months of the reporting date. These include bank overdrafts, income taxes, other non-trade payables and the current portion of interest-bearing liabilities. Any interest-bearing liabilities that are used to finance working capital on a long-term basis, and that are not due for settlement within 12 months, should be classed as **non-current liabilities**.

3 The statement of profit or loss and other comprehensive income

IAS 1 specifies what should be included in a statement of profit or loss and other comprehensive income and includes a suggested format. Some items must be disclosed on the face of the statement.

3.1 Statement of profit or loss and other comprehensive income

So far in this Text, we have considered just the statement of profit or loss. However, IAS 1 requires entities to include a **statement of profit or loss and other comprehensive income**, either as a single statement or as two separate statements: a statement of profit or loss and a statement of other comprehensive income.

The statement of profit or loss and other comprehensive income takes the statement of profit or loss and adjusts it for certain gains and losses. At F3/FFA level, this just means gains on revaluations of property, plant and equipment. The idea is to present all gains and losses, both those recognised in profit or loss (in the statement of profit or loss) as well as those recognised directly in equity, such as the revaluation surplus (in other comprehensive income).

IAS 1 gives the following suggested format for a statement of profit or loss and other comprehensive income.

ABC CO

STATEMENT OF PROFIT OR LOSS AND OTHER COMPREHENSIVE INCOME
FOR THE YEAR ENDED 31 DECEMBER 20X2
Illustrating the classification of expenses by function

	20X2	20X1
	$'000	$'000
Revenue	X	X
Cost of sales	(X)	(X)
Gross profit	X	X
Other income	X	X
Distribution costs	(X)	(X)
Administrative expenses	(X)	(X)
Other expenses	(X)	(X)
Finance cost	(X)	(X)
Profit before tax	X	X
Income tax expense	(X)	(X)
Profit for the year	X	X
Other comprehensive income:		
Gains on property revaluation	X	X
Total comprehensive income for the year	X	X

EXAM FOCUS POINT

Questions in the exam may refer to a statement of profit or loss: this means the entries from revenue to profit for the year. A reference to **other comprehensive income** means the last three lines in the statement above. However, a reference to **statement of profit or loss and other comprehensive income** means the whole statement shown above.

As a minimum, IAS 1 requires the following items to be disclosed on the face of the statement of profit or loss and other comprehensive income.

(a) Revenue

(b) Finance costs

(c) Share of profits and losses of associates and joint ventures accounted for using the equity method (Note 1)

(d) Pre-tax gain or loss attributable to discontinued operations (note 2)

(e) Tax expense

(f) Profit or loss

(g) Each component of other comprehensive income classified by nature (note 3)

(h) Share of the other comprehensive income of associates and joint ventures (note 1)

(i) Total comprehensive income

Notes

1   These items relate to group accounts which are covered later in this Text. Note that joint ventures are not included in the F3/FFA syllabus.

2   Discontinued operations are not included in the F3/FFA syllabus.

3   At F3/FFA level, the only items of other comprehensive income are gains on revaluations of property, plant and equipment.

IAS 1 also requires that any other line items, headings or subtotals be shown in the statement of profit or loss and other comprehensive income when it is necessary for an understanding of the entity's financial position or if another IFRS requires it.

Management must decide whether to present additional items separately. They should consider factors including materiality and the nature and function of the items of income and expense when making this decision.

3.2 Revenue

There are important rules on revenue recognition and these are the subject of IAS 18 *Revenue*. We will look at this in detail in later in this chapter.

3.3 Cost of sales

This represents the summary of the detailed workings we have used in a sole trader's financial statements.

3.4 Expenses

Notice that expenses are gathered under a number of headings. Any detail needed will be given in the notes to the financial statements.

3.4.1 Managers' salaries

The salary of a sole trader or a partner in a partnership is not a charge to the statement of profit or loss but is an appropriation of profit. The **salary of a manager or member of management board of a limited liability company**, however, is an **expense in the statement of profit or loss**, even when the manager is a shareholder in the company. Management salaries are included in **administrative expenses**.

3.5 Finance cost

This is interest **payable** during the period. Remember (from the previous chapter) that this may include accruals for interest payable on loan stock.

3.6 Income tax expense

This represents taxation as detailed in Section 3.7 below. Once again, this will include accruals for the tax due on the current year's profits. However, it may also include adjustments for any over- or underprovision for prior periods (see example 3.7.1 below).

3.7 Taxation

Taxation affects both the statement of financial position and the statement of profit or loss.

All companies pay some kind of corporate taxation on the profits they earn, which we will call **income tax** in line with the terminology in IAS 1, but which you may find called 'corporation tax'. The rate of income tax will vary from country to country. There may be variations in rate within individual countries for different types or size of company.

Note that because a company has a **separate legal personality, its tax is included in its accounts**. An unincorporated business would not show personal income tax in its accounts, as it would not be a business expense but the personal affair of the proprietors.

(a)   The **charge for income tax on profits for the year** is shown as a **deduction from profit for the year**.

(b)   In the statements of financial position, **tax payable** to the Government is generally shown as a **current liability**, as it is usually due within 12 months of the year end.

(c)   For various reasons, the tax on profits in the statement of profit or loss and the tax payable in the statement of financial position are not normally the same amount.

3.7.1 Example: taxation

A company has a tax liability brought forward of $15,000. The liability is finally agreed at $17,500 and this is paid during the year. The company estimates that the tax liability based on the current year's profits will be $20,000. Prepare the tax liability account for the year.

Solution

TAX LIABILITY ACCOUNT

	$		$
Cash paid	17,500	Balance b/f	15,000
Balance c/f	20,000	Statement of profit or loss	22,500
	37,500		37,500

Notice that the statement of profit or loss charge consists of the following.

	$
Underprovision for prior year (17,500 – 15,000)	2,500
Provision for current year	20,000
	22,500

Notice also that the balance carried forward consists solely of the provision for the current year.

3.8 Interrelationship of statement of profit or loss and statement of financial position

When we were dealing with the financial statements of sole traders, we transferred the profit for the year to the capital account. In the case of limited liability companies, the profit for the year is transferred to **retained earnings** in the statement of changes in equity. The closing balance of the accounts in the statement of changes in equity are then transferred to the statement of financial position.

3.9 Gains on property revaluation

Gains on property revaluation arise when a property is revalued. The revaluation is recognised in the **other comprehensive income** part of the statement of profit or loss and other comprehensive income and shown in the statement of changes in equity as a movement in the revaluation surplus.

For example, an asset originally cost $10,000 and was revalued to $15,000. The gain on the revaluation is recognised in the statement of profit or loss and other comprehensive income (in the other comprehensive income section) and then shown as a movement in the revaluation surplus in the statement of changes in equity, as shown below.

STATEMENT OF PROFIT OR LOSS AND OTHER COMPREHENSIVE INCOME
FOR THE YEAR ENDED 31 DECEMBER 20X8 – EXTRACT

	20X8 $'000
Gross profit	20
Profit before tax	
Income tax expense	(3)
Profit for the year	12
Other comprehensive income:	
Gains on property revaluation	5
Total comprehensive income for the year	17

STATEMENT OF CHANGES IN EQUITY – EXTRACT

	Revaluation surplus $'000	Retained earnings $'000	Total $'000
Balance at 1.1.X8	–	10	10
Changes in equity for 20X8			
Total comprehensive income for the year*	5	12	17
Balance at 31.12.X8	5	22	27

* The total comprehensive income for the year is split into the gains on revaluation of property, which is credited to the revaluation surplus, and the profit for the year, which is credited to retained earnings.

4 Statement of changes in equity

IAS 1 requires an entity to provide a statement of changes in equity. The statement of changes in equity shows the movements in the entity's equity for the period.

4.1 Statement of changes in equity

The statement of profit or loss and other comprehensive income is a straightforward measure of the **financial performance** of the entity, in that it shows all items of income and expense recognised in a period. It is then necessary to link this result with the results of **transactions with owners** of the business, such as share issues and dividends. The statement making the link is the **statement of changes in equity**.

The statement of changes in equity simply takes the equity section of the statement of financial position and shows the movements during the year. The bottom line shows the amounts for the current statement of financial position. As we saw above, the **total comprehensive income** for the year is split between the gains on revaluation of property, which is credited to the revaluation surplus, and the profit for the year, which is credited to retained earnings.

An example statement of changes in equity is shown below.

ABC CO
STATEMENT OF CHANGES IN EQUITY FOR THE YEAR ENDED 31 DECEMBER 20X2

	Share capital	Share premium	Revaluation surplus	Retained earnings	Total
Balance at 1.1.X2	X	X	X	X	X
Changes in accounting policy	–	–	–	(X)	(X)
Restated balance	X̄	X̄	X̄	X̄	X̄
Changes in equity for 20X2					
Dividends	–	–	–	(X)	(X)
Total comprehensive income for the year	–	–	X	X	X
Issue of share capital	X	X	–	–	X
Balance at 31.12.X2	X̄	X̄	X̄	X̄	X̄

Dividends paid during the year are not shown on the statement of profit or loss; they are shown in the statement of changes in equity.

5 Notes to the financial statements

Disclosure notes are included in a set of financial statements to give users extra information.

EXAM FOCUS POINT

The ACCA examining team has reported that questions on this topic were not very well answered in the last assessment round. In particular, students did not know the purpose or content of the notes. You should expect to see a question on this area in your exam. You are expected to have a detailed knowledge of the disclosures given below, so make sure you learn these.

Notes to the financial statements provide **more detail** for the users of the accounts about the information in the statement of profit or loss and other comprehensive income, the statement of financial position, the statement of cash flows and the statement of changes in equity. For example, the statement of financial position shows just the total carrying amount of property, plant and equipment owned by an entity. The notes to the financial statements then break down this total into the different categories of assets, the cost, any revaluation, the accumulated depreciation and the depreciation charge for the year.

For your exam, you need to know the following disclosure requirements in detail.

(a) **Tangible non-current assets** (Chapter 8)

A reconciliation of the opening and closing amounts at the beginning and end of the period, as shown below.

PROPERTY, PLANT AND EQUIPMENT NOTE

	Total $	Land and buildings $	Plant and equipment $
Cost or valuation			
At 1 January 20X4	50,000	40,000	10,000
Revaluation surplus	12,000	12,000	–
Additions in year	4,000	–	4,000
Disposals in year	(1,000)	–	(1,000)
At 31 December 20X4	65,000	52,000	13,000

	Total $	Land and buildings $	Plant and equipment $
Depreciation			
At 1 January 20X4	16,000	10,000	6,000
Charge for year	4,000	1,000	3,000
Eliminated on disposals	(500)	–	(500)
At 31 December 20X4	19,500	11,000	8,500
Carrying amount			
At 31 December 20X4	45,500	41,000	4,500
At 1 January 20X4	34,000	30,000	4,000

As well as the reconciliation above, the financial statements should disclose the following.

(i)   An accounting policy note should disclose the **measurement bases** used for determining the amounts at which depreciable assets are stated, along with the other accounting policies.

(ii)   For each class of **property, plant and equipment**:

- Depreciation methods used

- Useful lives or the depreciation rates used

- Total depreciation allocated for the period

- Gross amount of depreciable assets and the related accumulated depreciation at the beginning and end of the period

(iii)   For **revalued assets**:

- **Basis** used to revalue the assets

- **Effective date** of the revaluation

- Whether an **independent valuer** was involved

- **Carrying amount** of each class of property, plant and equipment that would have been included in the financial statements had the assets been carried at cost less depreciation

- **Revaluation surplus**, indicating the movement for the period and any restrictions on the distribution of the balance to shareholders

(b)   **Intangible non-current assets** (Chapter 9)

A **reconciliation of the carrying amount** of intangible assets at the beginning and end of the period, as shown below.

INTANGIBLE ASSETS NOTE

	Total $	Development costs $	Patents $
Cost			
At 1 January 20X4	40,000	30,000	10,000
Additions in year	19,000	15,000	4,000
Disposals in year	(1,000)	–	(1,000)
At 31 December 20X4	58,000	45,000	13,000
Amortisation			
At 1 January 20X4	11,000	5,000	6,000
Charge for year	4,000	1,000	3,000
Eliminated on disposals	(500)	–	(500)
At 31 December 20X4	14,500	6,000	8,500
Carrying amount			
At 31 December 20X4	43,500	39,000	4,500
At 1 January 20X4	29,000	25,000	4,000

As well as the reconciliation above, the financial statements should disclose the following.

(i)   The **accounting policies** for intangible assets that have been adopted

(ii)   For **each class of intangible assets** (including development costs), disclosure is required of the following.

- The method of amortisation used

- The useful life of the assets or the amortisation rate used

- The gross carrying amount, the accumulated amortisation and the accumulated impairment losses as at the beginning and end of the period

- The carrying amount of internally generated intangible assets

- The line item(s) of the statement of profit or loss in which any amortisation of intangible assets is included

(c)   **Provisions** (Chapter 11)

Disclosures required in the financial statements for **provisions** fall into two parts.

(a)   Disclosure of details of the change in carrying amount of a provision from the beginning to the end of the year, including additional provisions made, amounts used and other movements.

(b)   For each class of provision, disclosure of the background to the making of the provision and the uncertainties affecting its outcome, including:

(i)   A brief description of the nature of the provision and the expected timing of any resulting outflows relating to the provision

(ii)   An indication of the uncertainties about the amount or timing of those outflows and, where necessary to provide adequate information, the major assumptions made concerning future events.

(iii)   The amount of any expected reimbursement relating to the provision and whether any asset has been recognised for that expected reimbursement

Example: disclosure in the financial statements

Below is an example of how a **warranty provision** might be disclosed in the notes to the financial statements.

Note X: Provisions

	Warranty provision $'000
At 1 April 20X6	150
Increase in the provision during the year	60
Amounts used during the year	(75)
At 31 March 20X7	135

The warranty provision relates to estimated claims on those products sold in the year ended 31 March 20X7 which come with a three year warranty. The expected value method is used to provide a best estimate. It is expected that the expenditure will be incurred in the next three years.

Contingent liabilities (Chapter 11)

Unless remote, disclose for each contingent liability:

(i)   A brief description of its nature; and where practicable
(ii)   An estimate of the financial effect
(iii)   An indication of the uncertainties relating to the amount or timing of any outflow
(iv)   The possibility of any reimbursement

Contingent assets (Chapter 11)

Where an inflow of economic benefits is **probable**, an entity should disclose:

(i)   A brief description of its nature; and where practicable
(ii)   An estimate of the financial effect.

(d)   **Events after the reporting period** (Chapter 21)

In respect of **non-adjusting events** after the reporting period disclose:

(i)   The nature of the event

(ii)   An estimate of its financial effect (or a statement that an estimate cannot be made)

Example: disclosure in financial statements

Below is an example of how a material non-adjusting event may be disclosed in the financial statements for a company with a year end of 31 December 20X8.

Note X: Events after the reporting period

On 22 January 20X9, there was a fire at the company's warehouse. As a result, inventories costing a total of $250,000 were destroyed. These inventories are included in assets at the reporting date.

(e)   **Inventory** (Chapter 7)

The financial statements should disclose the following.

(i)   **Accounting policies** adopted in measuring inventories, including the cost formula used

(ii)   **Total carrying amount of inventories** and the carrying amount in classifications appropriate to the entity

(iii) **Carrying amount** of inventories carried at net realisable value (NRV).

Example disclosure

An example of disclosure for inventories is given below.

Accounting policies

Inventories

Inventories are valued at the lower of cost and NRV. Cost is determined using the first in, first out (FIFO) method. NRV is the estimated selling price in the ordinary course of business, less the costs estimated to make the sale.

Note X: Inventories

	20X1	20X0
	$'000	$'000
Raw materials	31	28
Work in progress	23	25
Finished goods	25	15
	79	68

Included in the carrying value presented above was $8,000 (20X0: $10,000) of inventories held at NRV.

6   Company accounts for internal purposes

The large amount of information in this chapter so far has really been geared towards the financial statements companies produce for external reporting purposes. In particular, the IFRSs discussed here are all concerned with external disclosure. **However, companies do produce financial accounts for internal purposes.**

It will often be the case that financial accounts used internally look very similar to those produced for external reporting for various reasons.

(a)   The information required by internal users is similar to that required by external users. Any additional information for managers is usually provided by **management accounts**.

(b)   Financial accounts produced for internal purposes can be used for external reporting with very little further adjustment.

It remains true, nevertheless, that **financial accounts for internal use can follow whichever format managers wish**. They may be more detailed in some areas than external financial accounts (perhaps giving breakdown of sales and profits by region or by product), but may also exclude some items. For example, the taxation charge and dividend may be missed out of the statement of profit or loss.

You should always read question requirements carefully to discover whether you are being asked to produce accounts for external or internal purposes. Even when producing the latter, however, it is a good idea to stick to the external statement formats, as these show best practice.

Now try this exercise.

EXAM FOCUS POINT

Please note that this question is not intended to represent a 15 mark question in the exam. It is far more detailed. However, the ACCA examining team has suggested that it is useful for students to work through an exercise like this one, which shows how the various statements are linked together.

QUESTION

Internal accounts

The accountant of Zabit Co has prepared the following trial balance as at 31 December 20X7.

	$'000
50c ordinary shares (fully paid)	350
7% $1 preference shares (fully paid)	100
10% loan stock (secured)	200
Retained earnings 1.1.X7	242
General reserve 1.1.X7	171
Land and buildings 1.1.X7 (cost)	430
Plant and machinery 1.1.X7 (cost)	830
Accumulated depreciation	
Buildings 1.1.X7	20
Plant and machinery 1.1.X7	222
Inventory 1.1.X7	190
Sales	2,695
Purchases	2,152
Preference dividend	7
Ordinary dividend (interim)	8
Loan interest	10
Wages and salaries	254
Light and heat	31
Sundry expenses	113
Suspense account	135
Trade accounts receivable	179
Trade accounts payable	195
Cash	126

Notes

1 Sundry expenses include $9,000 paid in respect of insurance for the year ending 1 September 20X8. Light and heat does not include an invoice of $3,000 for electricity for the 3 months ending 2 January 20X8, which was paid in February 20X8. Light and heat also includes $20,000 relating to salespeople's commission.

2 The suspense account is in respect of the following items.

	$'000
Proceeds from the issue of 100,000 ordinary shares	120
Proceeds from the sale of plant	300
	420
Less consideration for the acquisition of Mary & Co	285
	135

3   The net assets of Mary & Co were purchased on 3 March 20X7. Assets were valued as follows.

	$'000
Investments	231
Inventory	34
	265

All the inventory acquired was sold during 20X7. The investments were still held by Zabit at 31.12.X7.

4   The property was acquired some years ago. The buildings element of the cost was estimated at $100,000 and the estimated useful life of the assets was 50 years at the time of purchase. As at 31 December 20X7 the property is to be revalued at $800,000.

5   The plant which was sold had cost $350,000 and had a carrying amount of $274,000 as at 1.1.X7. $36,000 depreciation is to be charged on plant and machinery for 20X7.

6   The loan stock has been in issue for some years. The 50c ordinary shares all rank for dividends at the end of the year.

7   The management wish to provide for:

(i)   Loan stock interest due
(ii)   A transfer to general reserve of $16,000
(iii)   Audit fees of $4,000

8   Inventory as at 31 December 20X7 was valued at $220,000 (cost).

9   Taxation is to be ignored.

Required

Prepare the financial statements of Zabit Co as at 31 December 20X7, including the statement of changes in equity. No other notes are required.

ANSWER

(a)   Normal adjustments are needed for accruals and prepayments (insurance, light and heat, loan interest and audit fees). The loan interest accrued is calculated as follows.

	$'000
Charge needed in statement of profit or loss (10% × $200,000)	20
Amount paid so far, as shown in list of account balances	10
Accrual: presumably 6 months' interest now payable	10

The accrued expenses shown in the statement of financial position comprise:

	$'000
Loan interest	10
Light and heat	3
Audit fee	4
	17

(b)   The misposting of $20,000 to light and heat is also adjusted, by reducing the light and heat expense, but charging $20,000 to salespeople's commission.

(c)   Depreciation on the building is calculated as $\dfrac{\$100,000}{50} = \$2,000$

The carrying value of the property is then $430,000 – $20,000 – $2,000 = $408,000 at the end of the year. When the property is revalued a reserve of $800,000 – $408,000 = $392,000 is then created.

(d)   The profit on disposal of plant is calculated as proceeds $300,000 (per suspense account) less carrying value $274,000, ie $26,000. The cost of the remaining plant is calculated at $830,000 – $350,000 = $480,000. The depreciation allowance at the year end is:

	$'000
Balance 1.1.X7	222
Charge for 20X7	36
Less depreciation on disposals (350 – 274)	(76)
	182

(e) Goodwill arising on the purchase of Mary & Co is:

	$'000
Consideration (per suspense account)	285
Assets at valuation	265
Goodwill	20

This is shown as an asset on the statement of financial position. The investments, being owned by Zabit at the year end, are also shown on the statement of financial position, whereas Mary's inventory, acquired and then sold, is added to the purchases figure for the year.

(f) The other item in the suspense account is dealt with as follows.

	$'000
Proceeds of issue of 100,000 ordinary shares	120
Less nominal value 100,000 × 50c	50
Excess of consideration over par value (= share premium)	70

(g) The transfer to general reserve increases it to $171,000 + $16,000 = $187,000.

We can now prepare the financial statements.

ZABIT CO
STATEMENT OF PROFIT OR LOSS AND OTHER COMPREHENSIVE INCOME
FOR THE YEAR ENDED 31 DECEMBER 20X7

	$'000	$'000	$'000
Revenue			2,695
Cost of sales			
Opening inventory		190	
Purchases (2,152 + 34)		2,186	
		2,376	
Closing inventory		220	
			2,156
Gross profit			539
Profit on disposal of plant			26
			565
Expenses			
Wages, salaries and commission		274	
Sundry expenses (113 – 6)		107	
Light and heat (31 – 20 + 3)		14	
Depreciation: buildings		2	
plant		36	
Audit fees		4	
Loan interest		20	
			457
Profit for the year			108
Other comprehensive income:			
Revaluation of non-current assets			392
Total comprehensive income for the year			500

ZABIT CO
STATEMENT OF CHANGES IN EQUITY FOR THE YEAR ENDED 31 DECEMBER 20X7

	Share capital	Share premium	Revaluation surplus	General reserve	Retained earnings	Total
	$'000	$'000	$'000	$'000	$'000	$'000
Balance at 1.1.X7	450	–	–	171	242	863
Total comprehensive income for the year	–	–	392	–	108	500
Issue of shares	50	70	–	–	–	120
Dividends paid	–	–	–	–	(15)	(15)
Transfer to general reserve	–	–	–	16	(16)	–
Balance at 1.12.X7	500	70	392	187	319	1,468

ZABIT CO
STATEMENT OF FINANCIAL POSITION AS AT 31 DECEMBER 20X7

	$'000	$'000
ASSETS		
Non-current assets		
Property, plant land and equipment		
Property at valuation		800
Plant: cost	480	
depreciation	182	
		298
Goodwill		20
Investments		231
Current assets		
Inventory	220	
Trade accounts receivable	179	
Prepayments	6	
Cash	126	
		531
Total assets		1,880
EQUITY AND LIABILITIES		
Equity		
50c ordinary shares (350 + 50)	400	
7% $1 preference shares	100	
Share premium	70	
Revaluation surplus	392	
General reserve	187	
Retained earnings	319	
		1,468
Non-current liabilities		
10% loan stock (secured)		200
Current liabilities		
Trade accounts payable	195	
Accrued expenses	17	
		212
Total equity and liabilities		1,880

Tutorial note. A lot of information has been shown on the face of the statement of profit or loss and other comprehensive income and the statement of financial position. However, for external purposes, most of this would be hidden in the notes.

7 IAS 18 *Revenue*

EXAM FOCUS POINT

A new standard on revenue, IFRS 15 *Revenue from contracts with customers*, was issued in May 2014 and is effective for reporting periods beginning on or after 1 January 2018. However ACCA has decided to continue to examine IAS 18 and not to examine IFRS 15 in F3/FFA until September 2017 at the earliest.

IAS 18 *Revenue* is concerned with the recognition of revenues arising from fairly common transactions.

- The sale of goods
- The rendering of services
- The use by others of assets of the entity yielding interest, royalties and dividends

Generally, revenue is recognised when the entity has transferred to the buyer the **significant risks and rewards** of ownership and when the revenue can be **measured reliably**.

7.1 Introduction

Accruals accounting is based on the **matching of costs with the revenue they generate**. It is crucially important under this convention that we establish the point at which revenue is recognised, so that the correct treatment can be applied to the related costs. For example, the costs of producing an item of finished goods should be carried as an asset in the statement of financial position until such time as it is sold; they should then be written off as a charge to the trading account. Which of these two treatments should be applied cannot be decided until it is clear at what moment the sale of the item takes place.

The decision has a **direct impact on profit** since it would not be prudent to recognise the profit on sale until a sale has taken place, in accordance with the criteria of revenue recognition.

Revenue is generally recognised as **earned at the point of sale**, because at that point four criteria will generally have been met.

(a)   The product or service has been **provided for the buyer**.

(b)   The buyer has **recognised their liability** to pay for the goods or services provided. The converse of this is that the seller has recognised that ownership of goods has passed from themselves to the buyer.

(c)   The buyer has indicated their **willingness to hand over cash** or other assets in settlement of their liability.

(d)   The **monetary value** of the goods or services has been established.

At earlier points in the business cycle there will not in general be **firm evidence** that the above criteria will be met. Until work on a product is complete, there is a risk that some flaw in the manufacturing process will necessitate writing it off. Even when the product is complete there is no guarantee that it will find a buyer.

At later points in the business cycle, for example when cash is received for a credit sale, the recognition of revenue may occur in a period later than that in which the related costs were charged. Revenue recognition then depends on fortuitous circumstances, such as the cash flow of a company's receivables, and can fluctuate misleadingly from one period to another.

However, there are times when revenue is **recognised at other times than at the completion of a sale**; for example, in the recognition of profit on long-term construction contracts. Under IAS 11 *Construction contracts* (not in the F3/FFA syllabus) contract revenue and contract costs are recognised by reference to the stage of completion of the contract activity at the reporting date.

7.2 IAS 18 Revenue

IAS 18 governs the recognition of revenue in specific (common) types of transaction. Generally, recognition occurs when it is probable that **future economic benefits** will flow to the entity and when these benefits can be **measured reliably**.

Income, as defined by the IASB's *Conceptual Framework*, includes both revenues and gains. Revenue is income arising in the ordinary course of an entity's activities, such as sales, fees, interest, dividends and royalties.

7.3 Scope

IAS 18 covers the revenue from specific types of transaction or events.

- **Sale of goods** (manufactured products and items purchased for resale)
- **Rendering of services**
- Use by others of entity assets yielding **interest, royalties and dividends**

Interest, royalties and dividends are included as income because they arise from the use of an entity's assets by other parties.

Interest is the charge for the use of cash or cash equivalents or amounts due to the entity.

Royalties are charges for the use of long-term assets of the entity, eg patents, computer software and trademarks.

Dividends are distributions of profit to holders of equity investments, in proportion with their holdings, of each relevant class of capital.

The standard specifically **excludes** various types of revenue arising from leases, insurance contracts, changes in value of financial instruments or other current assets, natural increases in agricultural assets and mineral ore extraction.

7.4 Definitions

The following definitions are given in the standard.

Revenue is the gross inflow of economic benefits during the period arising in the course of the ordinary activities of an entity when those inflows result in increases in equity, other than increases relating to contributions from equity participants. *(IAS 18)*

Fair value is the price that would be received to sell an asset or paid to transfer a liability in an orderly transaction between market participants at the measurement date. *(IFRS 13)*

Revenue **does not include** sales taxes, value-added taxes or goods and service taxes which are only collected for third parties, because these do not represent economic benefits flowing to the entity. The same is true for revenues collected by an agent on behalf of a principal. Revenue for the agent is only the commission received for acting as agent.

7.5 Measurement of revenue

When a transaction takes place, the amount of revenue is usually decided by the **agreement of the buyer and seller**. The revenue is actually measured, however, as the **fair value of the consideration received**, which will take account of any trade discounts and volume rebates.

QUESTION
Revenue and prudence

Discuss under what circumstances, if any, revenue might be recognised at the following stages of a sale.

(a)   Goods are acquired by the business which it confidently expects to resell very quickly
(b)   A customer places a firm order for the goods
(c)   The goods are delivered to the customer

(d) The customer is invoiced for the goods
(e) The customer pays for the goods
(f) The customer's cheque in payment for the goods is cleared by the bank

ANSWER

(a) A sale must never be recognised before the goods have even been ordered by a customer. There is no certainty about the value of the sale, nor when it will take place, even if it is virtually certain that goods will be sold.

(b) A sale must never be recognised when the customer places an order. Even though the order will be for a specific quantity of goods at a specific price, it is not yet certain that the sale transaction will go through. The customer may cancel the order, the supplier may be unable to deliver the goods as ordered or it may be decided that the customer is not a good credit risk.

(c) A sale will be recognised when delivery of the goods is made only when:

(i) The sale is for cash, and so the cash is received at the same time.
(ii) The sale is on credit and the customer accepts delivery (eg by signing a delivery note).

(d) The critical event for a credit sale is usually the despatch of an invoice to the customer. There is then a legally enforceable debt, payable on specified terms, for a completed sale transaction.

(e) The critical event for a cash sale is when delivery takes place and when cash is received; both take place at the same time.

It would be too cautious or 'prudent' to await cash payment for a credit sale transaction before recognising the sale, unless the customer is a high credit risk and there is a serious doubt about their ability or intention to pay. But in that case, why would the business risk despatching the goods?

(f) It would again be overcautious to wait for clearance of the customer's cheques before recognising sales revenue. Such a precaution would only be justified in cases where there is a very high risk of the bank refusing to honour the cheque.

8 Practice question

Now work through this example to give you practice in preparing financial statements in accordance with IAS 1.

Note that very little detail appears in the statement of profit or loss – all items of income and expenditure are accumulated under the standard headings. Write out the standard proformas and then go through the workings, inserting figures as you go.

QUESTION

USB, a limited liability company, has the following trial balance at 31 December 20X9.

	Debit $'000	Credit $'000
Cash at bank	100	
Inventory at 1 January 20X9	2,400	
Administrative expenses	2,206	
Distribution costs	650	
Non-current assets at cost:		
Buildings	10,000	
Plant and equipment	1,400	
Motor vehicles	320	
Suspense		1,500
Accumulated depreciation		
Buildings		4,000
Plant and equipment		480
Motor vehicles		120
Retained earnings		560
Trade receivables	876	
Purchases	4,200	
Dividend paid	200	

	Debit $'000	Credit $'000
Sales revenue		11,752
Sales tax payable		1,390
Trade payables		1,050
Share premium		500
$1 ordinary shares		1,000
	22,352	22,352

The following additional information is relevant.

(a) Inventory at 31 December 20X9 was valued at $1,600,000. While doing the inventory count, errors in the previous year's inventory count were discovered. The inventory brought forward at the beginning of the year should have been $2.2m, not $2.4m as above.

(b) Depreciation is to be provided as follows.

  (i) Buildings at 5% straight line, charged to administrative expenses
  (ii) Plant and equipment at 20% on the reducing balance basis, charged to cost of sales
  (iii) Motor vehicles at 25% on the reducing balance basis, charged to distribution costs

(c) No final dividend is being proposed.

(d) A customer has gone bankrupt owing $76,000. This debt is not expected to be recovered and an adjustment should be made. An allowance for receivables of 5% is to be set up.

(e) 1m new ordinary shares were issued at $1.50 on 1 December 20X9. The proceeds have been left in a suspense account.

Required

Prepare the following.

(a) Statement of profit or loss for the year ended 31 December 20X9 **(3 marks)**
(b) Statement of changes in equity for the year ended 31 December 20X9 **(4 marks)**
(c) Statement of financial position as at 31 December 20X9 **(8 marks)**

All statements are to be prepared in accordance with the requirements of IFRSs. Ignore taxation.

Total marks for the question **(15 marks)**

ANSWER

(a) USB
STATEMENT OF PROFIT OR LOSS FOR THE YEAR ENDED 31 DECEMBER 20X9

	$'000
Revenue	11,752
Cost of sales (W2)	4,984
Gross profit	6,768
Administrative expenses (W3)	2,822
Distribution costs (650 + 50 (W1))	700
Profit for the year	3,246

(b) USB
STATEMENT OF CHANGES IN EQUITY FOR THE YEAR ENDED 31 DECEMBER 20X9

	Share capital $'000	Share premium $'000	Retained earnings $'000	Total $'000
Balance at 1 January 20X9	1,000	500	560	2,060
Prior period adjustment	–	–	(200)	(200)
Restated balance	1,000	500	360	1,860
Total comprehensive income for the year	–	–	3,246	3,246
Dividend paid	–	–	(200)	(200)
Share issue	1,000	500	–	1,500
Balance at 31 December 20X9	2,000	1,000	3,406	6,406

(c) USB
STATEMENT OF FINANCIAL POSITION AS AT 31 DECEMBER 20X9

	$'000	$'000
Non-current assets		
Property, plant and equipment (W4)		6,386
Current assets		
Inventory	1,600	
Trade receivables (876 – 76 – 40)	760	
Cash	100	
		2,460
Total assets		8,846
Equity and liabilities		
Equity		
Share capital (1000 + 1000)		2,000
Share premium (500 + 500)		1,000
Retained earnings (W5)		3,406
Current liabilities		
Sales tax payable	1,390	
Trade payables	1,050	
		2,440
Total equity and liabilities		8,846

Workings

1 *Depreciation*

	$'000
Buildings (10,000 × 5%)	500
Plant (1,400 – 480) × 20%	184
Motor vehicles (320 – 120) × 25%	50

2 *Cost of sales*

	$'000
Opening inventory	2,200
Purchases	4,200
Depreciation (W1)	184
Closing inventory	(1,600)
	4,984

3   *Administrative expenses*

	$'000
Per T/B	2,206
Depreciation (W1)	500
Irrecoverable debt	76
Receivables allowance ((876 − 76) × 5%)	40
	2,822

4   *Property, plant and equipment*

	Cost	Acc. dep	Dep. chg	Carrying value
	$'000	$'000	$'000	$'000
Buildings	10,000	4,000	500	5,500
Plant	1,400	480	184	736
Motor vehicles	320	120	50	150
	11,720	4,600	734	6,386

5   *Retained earnings*

	$'000
B/f per T/B	560
Prior period adjustment (inventory)	(200)
Profit for period	3,246
Dividend paid	(200)
	3,406

This section of the Text will help fulfil performance objective PO7 of the PER: Prepare external financial reports.

CHAPTER ROUNDUP

↳ IAS 1 lists the required contents of a company's financial statements. It also gives guidance on how items should be presented in the financial statements.

↳ A complete set of financial statements includes a statement of financial position, a statement of profit or loss and other comprehensive income, a statement of changes in equity, a statement of cash flows and disclosures notes.

↳ IAS 1 specifies what should be included in a statement of financial position and includes a suggested format. It also provides guidance on the current/non-current distinction.

↳ IAS 1 specifies what should be included in a statement of profit or loss and other comprehensive income and includes a suggested format. Some items must be disclosed on the face of the statement.

↳ IAS 1 requires an entity to provide a statement of changes in equity. The statement of changes in equity shows the movements in the entity's equity for the period.

↳ Disclosure notes are included in a set of financial statements to give users extra information.

↳ IAS 18 *Revenue* is concerned with the recognition of revenues arising from fairly common transactions.

- The sale of goods
- The rendering of services
- The use by others of assets of the entity yielding interest, royalties and dividends

↳ Generally revenue is recognised when the entity has transferred to the buyer the **significant risks** and **rewards** of ownership and when the revenue can be **measured reliably**.

1 According to IAS 1, which of the following items must appear on the face of the statement of profit or loss and other comprehensive income?

1   Tax expense
2   Revenue
3   Cost of sales
4   Profit or loss

A   4 only
B   2 and 4 only
C   1, 2 and 4 only
D   2 and 3 only

2 According to IAS 1, which of the following items make up a complete set of financial statements?

1   Statement of changes in equity
2   Statement of cash flows
3   Notes to the accounts
4   Statement of financial position
5   Statement of profit or loss and other comprehensive income
6   Chairman's report

A   All of the items
B   1, 2, 4 and 5 only
C   1, 2, 3, 4 and 5 only
D   3, 4 and 5 only

3 Which of the following items are non-current assets?

1   Land
2   Machinery
3   Bank loan
4   Inventory

A   1 only
B   1 and 2 only
C   1, 2 and 3 only
D   2, 3 and 4 only

4 How is a bank overdraft classified in the statement of financial position?

A   Non-current asset
B   Current asset
C   Current liability
D   Non-current liability

5 In the published accounts of XYZ Co, the profit for the period is $3,500,000. The balance of retained earnings at the beginning of the year is $500,000. If dividends of $2,500,000 were paid, what is the closing balance of retained earnings?

A $4,000,000
B $1,500,000
C $500,000
D $1,000,000

1 C See Paragraph 3.1 for a complete list of items that must be disclosed on the face of the statement of profit or loss and other comprehensive income.

2 C The chairman's report does not form part of the financial statements required by IAS 1, although it often accompanies a company's financial statements.

3 B Item (3) is a liability and item (4) is a current asset.

4 C A bank overdraft is strictly payable on demand and so it is a current liability.

5 B

	$'000
Retained earnings	
Opening balance	500
Profit for the period	3,500
	4,000
Dividends paid	(2,500)
Closing balance	1,500

Now try ...

Attempt the questions below from the **Practice Question Bank**

Number

Qs 77 – 80

Events after the reporting period

We will now examine a standard that applies very much to limited liability companies, IAS 10 *Events after the reporting period*.

You will see in IAS 10 whether or not events after the reporting period give rise to adjustments in the financial statements, and the disclosures that are required.

TOPIC LIST	SYLLABUS REFERENCE
1 IAS 10 *Events after the reporting period*	F3(b), F4(a)–(c)

1   IAS 10 *Events after the reporting period*

> **Events after the reporting period** which provide **additional evidence** of conditions existing at the reporting date will cause **adjustments** to be made to the assets and liabilities in the financial statements.

The financial statements are significant indicators of a company's success or failure. It is important, therefore, that they include all the information necessary for an understanding of the company's position.

IAS 10 *Events after the reporting period* requires the provision of additional information in order to facilitate such an understanding. IAS 10 deals with events **after** the reporting date which may **affect the position at** the reporting date.

1.1 Definitions

The standard gives the following definition.

Events after the reporting period: An event which could be favourable or unfavourable, that occurs between the reporting period and the date that the financial statements are authorised for issue. *(IAS 10)*

Adjusting event: An event after the reporting period that provides further evidence of conditions that existed at the reporting period.   *(IAS 10)*

1.2 Events after the reporting period

Between the reporting date and the date the financial statements are authorised (ie for issue outside the organisation), events may occur which show that assets and liabilities at the reporting date should be adjusted, or that disclosure of such events should be given.

Adjusting event: An event after the reporting period that provides further evidence of conditions that existed at the reporting period.   *(IAS 10)*

1.3 Events requiring adjustment

Events that provide **further evidence** of **conditions that existed at the reporting date** should be **adjusted** for in the financial statements.

The standard requires adjustment of assets and liabilities in certain circumstances: 'An entity shall adjust the amounts recognised in its financial statements to reflect adjusting events after the reporting period.' *(IAS 10)*

An **example** of additional evidence which becomes available after the reporting date is where a **customer goes bankrupt, thus confirming that the trade account receivable balance at the year end is uncollectable**.

The standard states that, where operating results and the financial position have deteriorated after the reporting date, it may be necessary to reconsider whether the **going concern assumption** is appropriate in the preparation of the financial statements.

Other examples of adjusting events are:

- Evidence of a permanent diminution in property value prior to the year end
- Sale of inventory after the end of the reporting period for less than its carrying value at the year end
- Insolvency of a customer with a balance owing at the year end
- Amounts received or paid in respect of legal or insurance claims which were in negotiation at the year end
- Determination after the year end of the sale or purchase price of assets sold or purchased before the year end
- Evidence of a permanent diminution in the value of a long-term investment prior to the year end
- Discovery of fraud or errors that show that the financial statements are incorrect

1.4 Events not requiring adjustment

Events which do not affect the situation at the reporting date should not be adjusted for, but should be **disclosed** in the financial statements.

Non-adjusting event: An event after the reporting period that is indicative of a condition that arose after the end of the reporting period. *(IAS 10)*

The standard then looks at events which do **not** require adjustment:

'An entity shall not adjust the amounts recognised in its financial statements to reflect non-adjusting events after the reporting period.' *(IAS 10)*

The **example** given by the standard of such an event is where the **value of an investment falls between the reporting date and the date the financial statements are authorised** for issue. The fall in value represents circumstances during the current period, not conditions existing at the previous reporting date, so it is not appropriate to adjust the value of the investment in the financial statements. Disclosure is an aid to users, however, indicating 'unusual changes' in the state of assets and liabilities after the reporting date.

Other examples of non-adjusting events include the following.

- Acquisition, or disposal, of a subsidiary after the year end
- Announcement of a plan to discontinue an operation
- Major purchases and disposals of assets
- Destruction of a production plant by fire after the end of the reporting period
- Announcement or commencing implementation of a major restructuring
- Share transactions after the end of the reporting period
- Litigation commenced after the end of the reporting period

But note that, while they may be non-adjusting, events that are **material** should be disclosed in the notes to the financial statements.

1.5 Dividends

Dividends proposed or declared after the end of the reporting period are not recognised as a liability in the accounts at the reporting date, but are disclosed in the notes to the accounts.

1.6 Disclosures

The following **disclosure requirements** are given for material events which occur after the reporting period which do **not** require adjustment. If disclosure of events occurring after the reporting period is required by this standard, the following information should be provided.

(a)   The nature of the event
(b)   An estimate of the financial effect, or a statement that such an estimate cannot be made

EXAM FOCUS POINT

Expect to be asked whether an item is adjusting or non-adjusting. You may well be asked to adjust for an adjusting item.

QUESTION

Events after the reporting period

State whether the following events occurring after the reporting period require an adjustment to the assets and liabilities of the financial statements.

(a)   Purchase of an investment
(b)   A change in the rate of tax, applicable to the previous year
(c)   An increase in pension benefits
(d)   Losses due to fire
(e)   An irrecoverable debt suddenly being paid
(f)   The receipt of proceeds of sales or other evidence concerning the net realisable value of inventory
(g)   A sudden decline in the value of property held as a long-term asset

ANSWER

(b), (e) and (f) require adjustment.

Of the other items, (a) would not need to be disclosed at all. Item (c) could need a disclosure if the cost to the company is likely to be material. Item (d) again would be disclosed if material, as would (g) if material.

Assuming that item (d) is material, it would be disclosed by way of the following note to the accounts. (The company year end is 31 December 20X8.)

Events after the reporting period

On 22 January 20X9, there was a fire at the company's warehouse. As a result, inventories costing a total of $250,000 were destroyed. These inventories are included in assets at the reporting date.

↳ **Events after the reporting period** which provide **additional evidence** of conditions existing at the reporting date will cause **adjustments** to be made to the assets and liabilities in the financial statements.

↳ Events that provide **further evidence** of **conditions that existed at the reporting date** should be **adjusted** for in the financial statements.

↳ Events which do not affect the situation at the reporting date should not be adjusted for, but should be **disclosed** in the financial statements.

1 When does an event after the reporting period require changes to the financial statements?

2 What disclosure is required when it is not possible to estimate the financial effect of an event not requiring adjustment?

   A No disclosure
   B A note to the accounts giving what information is available

3 Which of the following items are adjusting events?

   1 Inventory found to have deteriorated
   2 Dividends proposed at the year end
   3 A building destroyed by fire after the reporting date

   A 1 only
   B 2 only
   C 3 only
   D None of the above

4 Which of the following items are non-adjusting events?

   1 Inventory destroyed by flood two days before the reporting date

   2 A customer goes bankrupt

   3 Fall in value of an investment between the reporting date and the date the financial statements are finalised

   A 1 only
   B 2 only
   C 3 only
   D None of the above

5 A receivable has been written off as irrecoverable. However, the customer suddenly pays the written-off amount after the reporting date. This event is a non-adjusting event. True or false?

1   Assets and liabilities should be adjusted for events after the reporting period when these provide additional evidence for estimates existing at the reporting date.

2   B   A statement of the nature of the event and the fact that a financial estimate of the event cannot be made

3   A   1 only

4   C   3 only

5   False. It is an adjusting event.

Now try ...

Attempt the questions below from the **Practice Question Bank**

Number

Qs 81 – 83

Statements of cash flows

In the long run, a profit will result in an increase in the company's cash balance. In the short run, **the making of a profit will not necessarily result in an increased cash balance**. The observation leads us to two questions. The first relates to the importance of the distinction between cash and profit. The second is concerned with the usefulness of the information provided by the statement of financial position and statement of profit or loss in the problem of deciding whether the company has, or will be able to generate, sufficient cash to finance its operations.

The importance of the **distinction between cash and profit** and the lack of information about actual cash flows in the statement of profit or loss has resulted in the development of statements of cash flows.

This chapter adopts a systematic approach to the preparation of statements of cash flows in examinations. You should learn this method and you will then be equipped for any problems in the exam itself.

TOPIC LIST	SYLLABUS REFERENCE
1 IAS 7 *Statement of cash flows*	F5(a)–(h)
2 Preparing a statement of cash flows	F5(g)

F   Preparing basic financial statements

5   Statements of cash flows (excluding partnerships)

(a) Differentiate between profit and cash flow.   K

(b) Understand the need for management to control cash flow.   K

(c) Recognise the benefits and drawbacks to users of the financial statements of a statement of cash flows.   K

(d) Classify the effect of transactions on cash flows.   S

(e) Calculate the figures needed for the statement of cash flows, including: S

    (i)   Cash flows from operating activities
    (ii)   Cash flows from investing activities
    (iii) Cash flows from financing activities

(f) Calculate the cash flow from operating activities using the indirect and direct methods.   S

(g) Prepare statements of cash flows and extracts from statements of cash flows from given information.   S

(h) Identify the treatment of given transactions in a company's statement of cash flows.   K

EXAM FOCUS POINT

The ACCA examining team has repeatedly highlighted statements of cash flows as an area that students struggle with. The ACCA examining team recommend practising full questions on this topic, as they will help you gain a better understanding of the individual parts of the statement of cash flows, and how it links with the statement of financial position and the statement of profit or loss and other comprehensive income.

In the July to December 2014 ACCA examining team's report, the examining team also provided the following comments which may help students to improve their performance:

Have a thorough understanding of how to prepare a statement of cash flows in accordance with IAS 7:

*   Use the appropriate headings for example 'Cash flow from operating activities'.

*   Use the correct notation to indicate the movements in cash eg state an increase or decrease and use brackets where necessary.

*   Understand how to calculate the tax paid during the year.

*   Remember to adjust the profit before tax for depreciation and any profit on the disposal of an asset.

*   For the paper exam, always prepare workings that support figures in the statement. If you have a wrong final answer the markers will always carefully scrutinise workings to identify if any credit can be given for method.

1   IAS 7 *Statement of cash flows*

Statements of cash flows are a useful addition to the financial statements of a company because accounting profit is not the only indicator of performance. They concentrate on the sources and uses of cash and are a useful indicator of a company's **liquidity and solvency**.

It has been argued that 'profit' does not always give a useful or meaningful picture of a company's operations. Readers of a company's financial statements might even be **misled by a reported profit figure**.

(a)   Shareholders might believe that if a company makes a profit after tax of, say, $100,000 then this is the amount that it could afford to **pay as a dividend**. Unless the company has **sufficient cash** available to stay in business and also to pay a dividend, the shareholders' expectations would be wrong.

(b)   Employees might believe that if a company makes profits, it can afford to **pay higher wages** next year. This opinion may not be correct: the ability to pay wages depends on the **availability of cash**.

(c)   Survival of a business entity depends not so much on profits as on its **ability to pay its debts when they fall due**. Such payments might include 'profit and loss' items, such as material purchases, wages, interest and taxation, but also capital payments for new non-current assets and the repayment of loan capital when this falls due (for example on the redemption of loan stock).

From these examples, it seems that a company's performance and prospects depend not so much on the 'profits' earned in a period, but more realistically on liquidity or **cash flows**.

1.1 Funds flow and cash flow

Some countries have required the disclosure of additional statements based on **funds flow** rather than cash flow. However, the definition of 'funds' can be very vague. Such statements often simply require a rearrangement of figures already provided in the statement of financial position and statement of profit or loss. By contrast, a statement of cash flows is unambiguous and provides information which is additional to that provided in the rest of the accounts. It also lends itself to organisation by activity and not by statement of financial position classification.

Statements of cash flows are frequently given as an **additional statement**, supplementing the statement of financial position, statement of profit or loss and related notes. The group aspects of statements of cash flows (and certain complex matters) have been excluded, as they are beyond the scope of your syllabus.

1.2 Objective of IAS 7

The aim of IAS 7 is to provide information for users of financial statements about an entity's **ability to generate cash and cash equivalents**, as well as indicating the cash needs of the entity. The statement of cash flows provides **historical** information about cash and cash equivalents, classifying cash flows between operating, investing and financing activities.

1.3 Scope

A statement of cash flows should be presented as an **integral part** of an entity's financial statements. All types of entity can provide useful information about cash flows, as the need for cash is universal, whatever the nature of their revenue-producing activities. Therefore **all entities are required by the standard to produce a statement of cash flows**.

1.4 Benefits of cash flow information

The use of statements of cash flows is very much **in conjunction** with the rest of the financial statements. Users can gain further appreciation of the change in net assets, of the entity's financial position (liquidity and solvency) and the entity's ability to adapt to changing circumstances by adjusting the amount and timing of cash flows. Statements of cash flows **enhance comparability**, as they are not affected by differing accounting policies used for the same type of transactions or events.

Cash flow information of a historical nature can be used as an indicator of the amount, timing and certainty of future cash flows. Past forecast cash flow information can be **checked for accuracy** as actual figures emerge. The relationship between profit and cash flows can be analysed, as can changes in prices over time. All this information helps management to control costs by controlling cash flow.

1.5 Definitions

The standard gives the following definitions, the most important of which are **cash** and **cash equivalents**.

- Cash comprises cash on hand and demand deposits.

- Cash equivalents are short-term, highly liquid investments that are readily convertible to known amounts of cash and which are subject to an insignificant risk of changes in value.

- Cash flows are inflows and outflows of cash and cash equivalents.

- Operating activities are the principal revenue-producing activities of the enterprise and other activities that are not investing or financing activities.

- Investing activities are the acquisition and disposal of non-current assets and other investments not included in cash equivalents.

- Financing activities are activities that result in changes in the size and composition of the equity capital and borrowings of the entity. *(IAS 7)*

1.6 Cash and cash equivalents

The standard expands on the definition of cash equivalents: they are not held for investment or other long-term purposes, but rather to meet short-term cash commitments. To fulfil the above definition, an investment's **maturity date should normally be three months from its acquisition date**. Usually equity investments (ie shares in other companies) are **not** cash equivalents. An exception would be where redeemable preference shares were acquired with a very close redemption date.

Loans and other borrowings from banks are classified as financing activities. In some countries, however, **bank overdrafts** are repayable on demand and are treated as part of an enterprise's total cash management system. In these circumstances an overdrawn balance will be included in cash and cash equivalents. Such banking arrangements are characterised by a balance which fluctuates between overdrawn and credit.

Movements between different types of cash and cash equivalent are not included in cash flows. The investment of surplus cash in cash equivalents is part of cash management, not part of operating, investing or financing activities.

1.7 Presentation of a statement of cash flows

IAS 7 requires statements of cash flows to report cash flows during the period classified by **operating, investing and financing activities**.

The manner of presentation of cash flows from operating, investing and financing activities **depends on the nature of the enterprise**. By classifying cash flows between different activities in this way, users can see the impact on cash and cash equivalents of each one, and their relationships with each other. We can look at each in more detail.

1.7.1 Operating activities

This is perhaps the key part of the statement of cash flows because it shows whether, and to what extent, companies can **generate cash from their operations**. It is these operating cash flows which must, in the end, pay for all cash outflows relating to other activities, ie paying loan interest, dividends and so on.

Most of the components of cash flows from operating activities will be those items which **determine the net profit or loss of the enterprise**, ie they relate to the main revenue-producing activities of the enterprise. The standard gives the following as examples of cash flows from operating activities.

(a) Cash receipts from the sale of goods and the rendering of services
(b) Cash receipts from royalties, fees, commissions and other revenue
(c) Cash payments to suppliers for goods and services
(d) Cash payments to and on behalf of employees

Certain items may be included in the net profit or loss for the period which do **not** relate to operational cash flows; for example, the profit or loss on the sale of a piece of plant will be included in net profit or loss, but the cash flows will be classed as **investing**.

1.7.2 Investing activities

The cash flows classified under this heading show the extent of new investment in **assets which will generate future profit and cash flows**. The standard gives the following examples of cash flows arising from investing activities.

(a)   Cash payments to acquire property, plant and equipment, intangibles and other non-current assets, including those relating to capitalised development costs and self-constructed property, plant and equipment

(b)   Cash receipts from sales of property, plant and equipment, intangibles and other non-current assets

(c)   Cash payments to acquire shares or debentures of other enterprises

(d)   Cash receipts from sales of shares or debentures of other enterprises

(e)   Cash advances and loans made to other parties

(f)   Cash receipts from the repayment of advances and loans made to other parties

1.7.3 Financing activities

This section of the statement of cash flows shows the share of cash which the enterprise's capital providers have claimed during the period. This is an indicator of **likely future interest and dividend payments**. The standard gives the following examples of cash flows which might arise under these headings.

(a)   Cash proceeds from issuing shares

(b)   Cash payments to owners to acquire or redeem the enterprise's shares

(c)   Cash proceeds from issuing debentures, loans, notes, bonds, mortgages and other short- or long-term borrowings

(d)   Cash repayments of amounts borrowed

1.8 Reporting cash flows from operating activities

The standard offers a choice of method for this part of the statement of cash flows.

(a)   **Direct method**: disclose major classes of gross cash receipts and gross cash payments

(b)   **Indirect method**: net profit or loss is adjusted for the effects of transactions of a non-cash nature, any deferrals or accruals of past or future operating cash receipts or payments, and items of income or expense associated with investing or financing cash flows

The **direct method** discloses information not available elsewhere in the financial statements, which could be of use in estimating future cash flows. However, the **indirect method** is simpler, more widely used and more likely to be examined.

1.8.1 Using the direct method

There are different ways in which the **information about gross cash receipts and payments** can be obtained. The most obvious way is simply to extract the information from the accounting records.

A proforma for the direct method is given below.

	$'000	$'000
Cash flows from operating activities		
Cash receipts from customers	X	
Cash paid to suppliers and employees	(X)	
Cash generated from operations	X	
Interest paid	(X)	
Income taxes paid	(X)	
Net cash from operating activities		X

1.8.2 Example: the direct method

Boggis Co had the following transactions during the year.

(a)   Purchases from suppliers were $19,500, of which $2,550 was unpaid at the year end. Brought forward payables were $1,000.

(b)   Wages and salaries amounted to $10,500, of which $750 was unpaid at the year end. The accounts for the previous year showed an accrual for wages and salaries of $1,500.

(c)   Interest of $2,100 on a long-term loan was paid in the year.

(d)   Sales revenue was $33,400, including $900 receivables at the year end. Brought forward receivables were $400.

(e)   Interest on cash deposits at the bank amounted to $75.

Calculate the cash flow from operating activities using the direct method.

Solution

	$	$
Cash flows from operating activities		
Cash received from customers ($400 + $33,400 – $900)	32,900	
Cash paid to suppliers ($1,000 + $19,500 – $2,550)	(17,950)	
Cash paid to employees ($1,500 + $10,500 – $750)	(11,250)	
Interest paid	(2,100)	
Interest received	75	
Net cash flow from operating activities		1,675

This may be a laborious task, however, and the indirect method described below may be easier.

1.8.3 Using the indirect method

This method is undoubtedly **easier** from the point of view of the preparer of the statement of cash flows. The net profit or loss for the period is adjusted for the following.

(a)   Changes during the period in inventories, operating receivables and payables
(b)   Non-cash items, eg depreciation, provisions, profits/losses on the sales of assets
(c)   Other items, the cash flows from which should be classified under investing or financing activities

A **proforma** of such a calculation is as follows and this method may be more common in the exam.

	$
Profit before tax (statement of profit or loss)	X
Add depreciation	X
interest expense	X
Loss (profit) on sale of non-current assets	X
(Increase)/decrease in inventories	(X)/X
(Increase)/decrease in receivables	(X)/X
Increase/(decrease) in payables	X/(X)
Cash generated from operations	X
Interest (paid)/received	(X)
Income taxes paid	(X)
Net cash flows from operating activities	X

It is important to understand why **certain items are added and others subtracted**. Note the following points.

(a)   Depreciation is not a cash expense, but is deducted in arriving at the profit figure in the statement of profit or loss. It makes sense, therefore, to eliminate it by adding it back.

(b)   By the same logic, a loss on a disposal of a non-current asset (arising through underprovision of depreciation) needs to be added back and a profit deducted.

(c)   An increase in inventories means less cash – you have spent cash on buying inventory.

(d)   An increase in receivables means the company's receivables have not paid as much, and therefore there is less cash.

(e)   If we pay off payables, causing the figure to decrease, again we have less cash.

1.8.4 Indirect versus direct

The direct method is encouraged where the necessary information is not too costly to obtain, but IAS 7 does not demand it. In practice, therefore, the direct method is rarely used. It could be argued that companies ought to monitor their cash flows carefully enough to be able to use the direct method at minimal extra cost.

1.9 Interest and dividends

Cash flows from interest and dividends received and paid should each be **disclosed separately**. Each should be classified in a consistent manner from period to period.

(a)   Interest paid should be classified as an **operating cash flow** or a **financing cash flow**.

(b)   Interest received and dividends received should be classified as **operating cash flows** or, more usually, as **investing cash flows**.

(c)   Dividends paid by the enterprise should be classified as an **operating cash flow**, so that users can assess the enterprise's ability to pay dividends out of operating cash flows or, more usually, as a **financing cash flow**, showing the cost of obtaining financial resources.

1.10 Taxes on income

Cash flows arising from taxes on income should be **separately disclosed** and should be classified as cash flows from operating activities **unless** they can be specifically identified with financing and investing activities.

Taxation cash flows are often **difficult to match** to the originating underlying transaction, so most of the time all tax cash flows are classified as arising from operating activities.

1.11 Components of cash and cash equivalents

The components of cash and cash equivalents should be disclosed and a **reconciliation** should be presented, showing the amounts in the statement of cash flows reconciled with the equivalent items reported in the statement of financial position.

It is also necessary to disclose the **accounting policy** used in deciding the items included in cash and cash equivalents, in accordance with IAS 1 *Presentation of financial statements*, but also because of the wide range of cash management practices worldwide.

1.12 Other disclosures

All enterprises should disclose, together with a **commentary by management**, any other information likely to be of importance, for example:

(a)   Restrictions on the use of, or access to, any part of cash equivalents

(b)   The amount of undrawn borrowing facilities which are available

(c)   Cash flows which increased operating capacity compared with cash flows which merely maintained operating capacity

1.13 Example of a statement of cash flows

In the next section we will look at the procedures for preparing a statement of cash flows. First, look at this **example**, adapted from the example given in IAS 7.

1.13.1 Direct method

STATEMENT OF CASH FLOWS (DIRECT METHOD)
YEAR ENDED 20X7

	$m	$m
Cash flows from operating activities		
Cash receipts from customers	30,330	
Cash paid to suppliers and employees	(27,600)	
Cash generated from operations	2,730	
Interest paid	(270)	
Income taxes paid	(900)	
Net cash from operating activities		1,560
Cash flows from investing activities		
Purchase of property, plant and equipment	(900)	
Proceeds from sale of equipment	20	
Interest received	200	
Dividends received	200	
Net cash used in investing activities		(480)
Cash flows from financing activities		
Proceeds from issuance of share capital	250	
Proceeds from long-term borrowings	250	
Dividends paid*	(1,290)	
		(790)
Net cash used in financing activities		
Net increase in cash and cash equivalents		290
Cash and cash equivalents at beginning of period		120
Cash and cash equivalents at end of period		410

* This could also be shown as an operating cash flow.

1.13.2 Indirect method

STATEMENT OF CASH FLOWS (INDIRECT METHOD)
YEAR ENDED 20X7

	$m	$m
Cash flows from operating activities		
Net profit before taxation	3,570	
Adjustments for:		
Depreciation	450	
Investment income	(500)	
Interest expense	400	
Operating profit before working capital changes	3,920	
Increase in trade and other receivables	(500)	
Decrease in inventories	1,050	
Decrease in trade payables	(1,740)	
Cash generated from operations	2,730	
Interest paid	(270)	
Income taxes paid	(900)	
Net cash from operating activities		1,560
Cash flows from investing activities		
Purchase of property, plant and equipment	(900)	
Proceeds from sale of equipment	20	
Interest received	200	
Dividends received	200	
Net cash used in investing activities		(480)
Cash flows from financing activities		
Proceeds from issuance of share capital	250	
Proceeds from long-term borrowings	250	
Dividends paid*	(1,290)	

	$m	$m
Net cash used in financing activities		(790)
Net increase in cash and cash equivalents		290
Cash and cash equivalents at beginning of period (Note)		120
Cash and cash equivalents at end of period (Note)		410

* This could also be shown as an operating cash flow.

The following note is required to both versions of the statement.

Note. *Cash and cash equivalents*

Cash and cash equivalents consist of cash on hand and balances with banks, and investments in money market instruments. Cash and cash equivalents included in the statement of cash flows comprise the following statement of financial position amounts.

	20X7	20X6
	$m	$m
Cash on hand and balances with banks	40	25
Short-term investments	370	95
Cash and cash equivalents	410	120

The company has undrawn borrowing facilities of $2,000, of which only $700 may be used for future expansion.

2 Preparing a statement of cash flows

You need to be aware of the **format** of the statement as laid out in IAS 7. Setting out the format is the first step. Then follow the **step by step preparation procedure**.

> ### EXAM FOCUS POINT
>
> In essence, preparing a statement of cash flows is very straightforward. You should therefore simply learn the format (the ACCA examining team emphasised the need to learn the format in a recent ACCA Conference) and apply the steps noted in the example below. Although you may not have to prepare a full statement of cash flows in your exam, the ACCA examining team has highlighted the importance of practising full questions so that you fully understand the underlying principles.
>
> The ACCA examining team has advised students to think of the cash effect of transactions. Students also need to be aware of what goes where, a common error being to confuse investing and financing cash flows.

Note that the following items are treated in a way that might seem confusing, but the treatment is logical if you **think in terms of cash**.

(a) **Increase in inventory** is treated as **negative** (in brackets). This is because it represents a cash **outflow**; cash is being spent on inventory.

(b) An **increase in receivables** would be treated as **negative** for the same reasons; more receivables means less cash.

(c) By contrast, an **increase in payables is positive** because cash is being retained and not used to settle accounts payable. There is therefore more of it.

2.1 Example: preparation of a statement of cash flows

Colby Co's statement of profit or loss for the year ended 31 December 20X2 and statements of financial position at 31 December 20X1 and 31 December 20X2 were as follows.

COLBY CO
STATEMENT OF PROFIT OR LOSS FOR THE YEAR ENDED 31 DECEMBER 20X2

	$'000	$'000
Revenue		720
Raw materials consumed	70	
Staff costs	94	
Depreciation	118	
Loss on disposal of non-current asset	18	
		(300)
		420
Interest payable		(28)
Profit before tax		392
Taxation		(124)
Profit for the year		268

COLBY CO
STATEMENT OF FINANCIAL POSITION AS AT 31 DECEMBER

	20X2		20X1	
	$'000	$'000	$'000	$'000
Assets				
Property, plant and equipment				
Cost	1,596		1,560	
Depreciation	318		224	
		1,278		1,336
Current assets				
Inventory	24		20	
Trade receivables	76		58	
Bank	48		56	
		148		134
Total assets		1,426		1,470
Equity and liabilities				
Capital and reserves				
Share capital	360		340	
Share premium	36		24	
Retained earnings	716		514	
		1,112		878
Non-current liabilities				
Non-current loans		200		500
Current liabilities				
Trade payables	12		6	
Taxation	102		86	
		114		92
		1,426		1,470

During the year, the company paid $90,000 for a new piece of machinery.

Dividends paid during 20X2 totalled $66,000 and interest paid was $28,000.

Required

Prepare a statement of cash flows for Colby Co for the year ended 31 December 20X2 in accordance with the requirements of IAS 7, using the indirect method.

Solution

Step 1	**Set out the proforma statement of cash flows** with the headings required by IAS 7. You should leave plenty of space. Ideally, use three or more sheets of paper, one for the main statement, one for the notes and one for your workings. It is obviously essential to know the formats very well.
Step 2	Begin with the **reconciliation of profit before tax to net cash from operating activities** as far as possible. When preparing the statement from statements of financial position, you will usually have to calculate such items as depreciation, loss on sale of non-current assets, profit for the year and tax paid (see Step 4). Note that you may not be given the tax charge in the statement of profit or loss. You will then have to assume that the tax paid in the year is last year's year-end provision and calculate the charge as the balancing figure.
Step 3	Calculate the cash flow figures for **dividends paid, purchase or sale of non-current assets, issue of shares and repayment of loans** if these are not already given to you (as they may be).
Step 4	If you are not given the profit figure, open up a **working for the trading, income and expense account**. Using the opening and closing balances, the taxation charge and dividends paid and proposed, you will be able to calculate profit for the year as the balancing figure to put as the net profit in the net cash flow from operating activities section.
Step 5	You will now be able to **complete the statement** by slotting in the figures given or calculated.

COLBY CO
STATEMENT OF CASH FLOWS FOR THE YEAR ENDED 31 DECEMBER 20X2

	$'000	$'000
Net cash flow from operating activities		
Profit before tax	392	
Depreciation charges	118	
Loss on sale of property, plant and equipment	18	
Interest expense	28	
Increase in inventories	(4)	
Increase in receivables	(18)	
Increase in payables	6	
Cash generated from operations	540	
Interest paid	(28)	
Dividends paid	(66)	
Tax paid (86 + 124 – 102)	(108)	
Net cash flow from operating activities		338
Cash flows from investing activities		
Payments to acquire property, plant and equipment	(90)	
Receipts from sales property, plant and equipment (W)	12	
Net cash outflow from investing activities		(78)

	$'000	$'000
Cash flows from financing activities		
Issues of share capital (360 + 36 – 340 – 24)	32	
Long-term loans repaid (500 – 200)	(300)	
Net cash flows from financing		(268)
Decrease in cash and cash equivalents		(8)
Cash and cash equivalents at 1.1.X2		56
Cash and cash equivalents at 31.12.X2		48

Working: property, plant and equipment

COST

	$'000		$'000
At 1.1.X2	1,560	At 31.12.X2	1,596
Purchases	90	Disposals (balance)	54
	1,650		1,650

ACCUMULATED DEPRECIATION

	$'000		$'000
At 31.12.X2	318	At 1.1.X2	224
Depreciation on disposals		Charge for year	118
(balance)	24		
	342		342

	$'000
Carrying value of disposals (54 – 24)	30
Net loss reported	(18)
Proceeds of disposals	12

QUESTION

Statement of cash flows

Set out below are the financial statements of Shabnum Co. You are the financial controller, faced with the task of implementing IAS 7 *Statement of cash flows*.

SHABNUM CO
STATEMENT OF PROFIT OR LOSS FOR THE YEAR ENDED 31 DECEMBER 20X2

	$'000
Revenue	2,553
Cost of sales	(1,814)
Gross profit	739
Distribution costs	(125)
Administrative expenses	(264)
	350
Interest received	25
Interest paid	(75)
Profit before taxation	300
Taxation	(140)
Profit for the year	160

SHABNUM CO
STATEMENTS OF FINANCIAL POSITION AS AT 31 DECEMBER

	20X2	20X1
	$'000	$'000
Assets		
Non-current assets		
Property, plant and equipment	380	305
Intangible assets	250	200
Investments	–	25

	20X2 $'000	20X1 $'000
Current assets		
Inventories	150	102
Receivables	390	315
Short-term investments	50	–
Cash in hand	2	1
Total assets	1,222	948
Equity and liabilities		
Equity		
Share capital ($1 ordinary shares)	200	150
Share premium account	160	150
Revaluation surplus	100	91
Retained earnings	260	180
Non-current liabilities		
Loan	170	50
Current liabilities		
Trade payables	127	119
Bank overdraft	85	98
Taxation	120	110
Total equity and liabilities	1,222	948

The following information is available.

(a)   The proceeds of the sale of non-current asset investments amounted to $30,000.

(b)   Fixtures and fittings, with an original cost of $85,000 and a carrying amount of $45,000, were sold for $32,000 during the year.

(c)   The following information relates to property, plant and equipment.

	31.12.20X2 $'000	31.12.20X1 $'000
Cost	720	595
Accumulated depreciation	340	290
Carrying amount	380	305

(d)   50,000 $1 ordinary shares were issued during the year at a premium of 20c per share.

(e)   Dividends totalling $80,000 were paid during the year.

Required

(a)   Prepare the net cash flows from operating activities for the year to 31 December 20X2 using the format laid out in IAS 7.   **(6 marks)**

(b)   Prepare the net cash flows from investing activities for the year to 31 December 20X2 using the format laid out in IAS 7.   **(4 marks)**

(c)   Which one of the following options gives the net cash flows from financing activities for the year?

A $180k inflow
B $189k outflow
C $350k outflow
D $360k inflow

(2marks)

(d)   Prepare the note to the statement of cash flows for the year to 31 December 20X2 using the format laid out in IAS 7.   **(3 marks)**

Total marks for the question   **(15 marks)**

ANSWER

(a) **Net cash flows from operating activities**

	$'000	$'000
Net cash flows from operating activities		
Profit before tax	300	
Depreciation charge (W1)	90	
Interest expense	50	
Loss on sale of property, plant and equipment (45 – 32)	13	
Profit on sale of non-current asset investments (30 – 25)	(5)	
(Increase)/decrease in inventories	(48)	
(Increase)/decrease in receivables	(75)	
Increase/(decrease) in payables	8	
Cash generated from operating activities	333	
Interest received	25	
Interest paid	(75)	
Dividends paid	(80)	
Tax paid (W3)	(130)	
Net cash flow from operating activities		73

(b) **Net cash flows from investing activities**

	$'000	$'000
Cash flows from investing activities		
Payments to acquire property, plant and equipment (W2)	(201)	
Payments to acquire intangible non-current assets (250 – 200)	(50)	
Receipts from sales of property, plant and equipment	32	
Receipts from sale of non-current asset investments	30	
Net cash flows from investing activities		(189)

(c) **Net cash flows from financing activities**

A $180k inflow

	$'000	$'000
Cash flows from financing activities		
Issue of share capital (200 + 160 – 150 – 150)	60	
Long-term loan (170 – 50)	120	
Net cash flows from financing		180

(d) **Note to the cash flow**

NOTES TO THE STATEMENT OF CASH FLOWS

Note. *Analysis of the balances of cash and cash equivalents as shown in the statement of financial position*

	20X2 $'000	20X1 $'000	Change in year $'000
Cash in hand	2	1	1
Short-term investments	50		50
Bank overdraft	(85)	(98)	13
	(33)	(97)	64

Workings

1 *Depreciation charge*

	$'000	$'000
Depreciation at 31 December 20X2		340
Depreciation at 31 December 20X1	290	
Depreciation on assets sold (85 – 45)	40	
		250
Charge for the year		90

2   Purchase of property, plant and equipment

PROPERTY, PLANT AND EQUIPMENT

	$'000		$'000
1.1.X2 Balance b/d	595	Disposals	85
Revaluation (100 – 91)	9		
Purchases (bal. fig.)	201	31.12.X2 Balance c/d	720
	805		805

3   Tax paid

TAX

	$'000		$'000
Tax paid (bal. fig.)	130	1.1.X2 Balance b/d	110
31.12.X2 Balance c/d	120		140
	250		250

Although you were not asked to prepare it, the full statement of cash flows follows so you can see where everything goes. **You may wish to prepare the full statement yourself as question practice, before looking at the answer.**

SHABNUM CO
STATEMENT OF CASH FLOWS FOR THE YEAR ENDED 31 DECEMBER 20X2

	$'000	$'000
Net cash flows from operating activities		
Profit before tax	300	
Depreciation charge (W1)	90	
Interest expense	50	
Loss on sale of property, plant and equipment (45 – 32)	13	
Profit on sale of non-current asset investments (30 – 25)	(5)	
(Increase)/decrease in inventories	(48)	
(Increase)/decrease in receivables	(75)	
Increase/(decrease) in payables	8	
Cash generated from operating activities	333	
Interest received	25	
Interest paid	(75)	
Dividends paid	(80)	
Tax paid (110 + 140 – 120)	(130)	
Net cash flow from operating activities		73
Cash flows from investing activities		
Payments to acquire property, plant and equipment (W2)	(201)	
Payments to acquire intangible non-current assets (250 – 200)	(50)	
Receipts from sales of property, plant and equipment	32	
Receipts from sale of non-current asset investments	30	
Net cash flows from investing activities		(189)
Cash flows from financing activities		
Issue of share capital (200 + 160 – 150 – 150)	60	
Long-term loan (170 – 50)	120	
Net cash flows from financing		180
Increase in cash and cash equivalents (Note)		64
Cash and cash equivalents at 1.1.X2 (Note)		(97)
Cash and cash equivalents at 31.12.X2 (Note)		(33)

NOTES TO THE STATEMENT OF CASH FLOWS

Note. *Analysis of the balances of cash and cash equivalents as shown in the statement of financial position*

	20X2 $'000	20X1 $'000	Change in year $'000
Cash in hand	2	1	1
Short-term investments	50		50
Bank overdraft	(85)	(98)	13
	(33)	(97)	64

2.2 The advantages of cash flow accounting

The advantages of cash flow accounting are as follows.

(a) Survival in business depends on the **ability to generate** cash. Cash flow accounting directs attention towards this critical issue.

(b) Cash flow is **more comprehensive** than 'profit' which is dependent on accounting conventions and concepts.

(c) **Creditors** of the business (both long and short term) are more interested in an enterprise's ability to repay them than in its profitability. While 'profits' might indicate that cash is likely to be available, cash flow accounting gives clearer information.

(d) Cash flow reporting provides a better means of **comparing the results** of different companies than traditional profit reporting.

(e) Cash flow reporting **satisfies the needs of all users** better.

    (i) For **management**, it provides the sort of information on which decisions should be taken (in management accounting, 'relevant costs' to a decision are future cash flows). Traditional profit accounting does not help with decision making.

    (ii) For **shareholders and auditors**, cash flow accounting can provide a satisfactory basis for stewardship accounting.

    (iii) As described previously, the information needs of **creditors and employees** will be better served by cash flow accounting.

(f) Cash flow forecasts are **easier to prepare**, as well as more useful, than profit forecasts.

(g) They can in some respects be **audited more easily** than accounts based on the accruals concept.

(h) The accruals concept is confusing, and cash flows are **more easily understood**.

(i) Cash flow information can be retrospective and can also include a forecast for the future. This is of **great information value** to all users of accounting information.

(j) **Forecasts** can subsequently be **monitored** by the publication of variance statements which compare actual cash flows against the forecast.

QUESTION

Cash flow accounting

Can you think of some possible disadvantages of cash flow accounting?

ANSWER

The main disadvantages of cash accounting are essentially the advantages of accruals accounting (proper matching of related items). There is also the practical problem that few businesses keep historical cash flow information in the form needed to prepare a historical statement of cash flows and so extra recordkeeping is likely to be necessary.

2.3 Criticisms of IAS 7

The inclusion of **cash equivalents** has been criticised because it does not reflect the way in which businesses are managed. In particular, the requirement that to be a cash equivalent an investment's maturity date has to be within three months of its acquisition date is considered **unrealistic**.

The management of assets similar to cash (ie 'cash equivalents') is not distinguished from other investment decisions.

EXAM FOCUS POINT

In the exam, you could be asked to consider the usefulness of a statement of cash flows as well as having to calculate extracts from one.

Performance Objective PO8 of the PER is 'Analyse and interpret financial reports'. You can apply the knowledge you obtain from this chapter to help to achieve this objective.

⊊ **Statements of cash flows** are a useful addition to the financial statements of companies because it is recognised that accounting profit is not the only indicator of a company's performance. They concentrate on the sources and uses of cash and are a useful indicator of a company's **liquidity and solvency**.

⊊ You need to be aware of the **format** of the statement as laid out in IAS 7. Setting out the format is the first step. Then follow the **step by step preparation procedure**.

1 Fill in the blanks.

The objective of IAS 7 is to provide information for ...... about the company's ability to generate .... and ....

2 What are the benefits of cash flow information according to IAS 7?

3 Define cash and cash equivalents according to IAS 7 in no more than 40 words.

4 Which of the following headings is not a classification of cash flows in IAS 7?

A Operating
B Investing
C Administration
D Financing

5 A company has the following information about property, plant and equipment.

	20X7	20X6
	$'000	$'000
Cost	750	600
Accumulated depreciation	250	150
Carrying amount	500	450

Plant with a carrying amount of $75,000 (original cost $90,000) was sold for $30,000 during the year.

What is the cash flow from investing activities for the year?

A $95,000 inflow
B $210,000 inflow
C $210,000 outflow
D $95,000 outflow

6 A company has the following extract from a statement of financial position.

	20X7	20X6
	$'000	$'000
Share capital	2,000	1,000
Share premium	500	–
Loan stock	750	1,000

If there had been a bonus issue of 500,000 shares of $1 each during the year, what is the cash flow from financing activities for the year?

A $1,250 inflow
B $750 inflow
C $750 outflow
D $1,250 outflow

7 When adjusting profit before tax to arrive at cash generated from operations, a decrease in receivables is added to profit before tax. Is this statement true or false?

1   The objective of IAS 7 is to provide information for **users** about the company's ability to generate **cash** and **cash equivalents**.

2   Further information is available about liquidation and solvency, of the change in net assets, the ability to adapt to changing circumstances and comparability between entities.

3   **Cash** comprises cash on hand and demand deposits. **Cash equivalents** are short-term, highly liquid investments that are readily convertible to known amounts of cash and which are subject to an insignificant risk of changes in value.

4   C   Administration costs are a classification in the statement of profit or loss, not the statement of cash flows.

5   C

PROPERTY, PLANT AND EQUIPMENT

	$'000		$'000
Opening balance	600	Disposals	90
Purchases (balancing figure)	240	Closing balance	750
	840		840

Purchase of property, plant and equipment	240,000
Proceeds of sale of property, plant and equipment	(30,000)
Net cash outflow	210,000

6   B

	$'000
Issue of share capital for cash (2,000 + 500 – 1,000 – 500 bonus))	1,000
Repayment of loan stock (1,000 – 750)	(250)
Net cash inflow	750

7   True

Now try ...

Attempt the questions below from the **Practice Question Bank**

Number

Qs 84 – 86

part

G

Preparing simple consolidated financial statements

Introduction to consolidated financial statements

Preparing consolidated financial statements is an important area of your syllabus.

In this chapter we will look at the basic principles of consolidation and the definitions given in the relevant IFRSs. These matters are fundamental to your comprehension of consolidation, so make sure you go through this chapter carefully.

G Preparing simple consolidated financial statements

1 Subsidiaries

(a) Define and describe the following terms in the context of group accounting:

    (i) Parent
    (ii) Subsidiary
    (iii) Control
    (iv) Consolidated or group financial statements
    (v) Non-controlling interest
    (vi) Trade/simple investment

K

(b) Identify subsidiaries within a group structure.

K

2 Associates

(a) Define and identify an associate and significant influence and identify the situations where significant influence or participating interest exists.

K

(b) Describe the key features of a parent-associate relationship and be able to identify an associate within a group structure.

K

(c) Describe the principle of equity accounting.

K

1 Groups and consolidation: an overview

Consolidation means presenting the results, assets and liabilities of a group of companies as if they were **one company**.

EXAM FOCUS POINT

The ACCA examining team commented that answers to questions on simple consolidated financial statements and interpretations had improved in the December 2013 assessment round.

This is an important area so make sure you read carefully this and the following two chapters and attempt all the examples and questions. You should also make sure that you attempt the questions on this topic, including the long questions, in the Practice & Revision Kit for F3/FFA.

You will probably know that many large companies actually consist of several companies controlled by one central or administrative company. Together, these companies are called a **group**.

1.1 How does a group arise?

The central company, called a **parent**, generally owns most or all of the shares in the other companies, which are called **subsidiaries**.

The parent company usually **controls** the subsidiary by **owning most of the shares in that company**, but share ownership is not always the same as control, which can arise in other ways.

Businesses may operate as a group for all sorts of practical reasons. If you were going out for a pizza, you might go to Pizza Hut; if you wanted some fried chicken you might go to KFC. Both sound more appetising than 'Yum! Brands Inc', the parent company of these subsidiaries.

However, from the legal point of view, the **results of a group must be presented as a whole**. In other words, they need to be **consolidated**. Consolidation will be defined more formally later in the chapter. Basically, it means **presenting the results of a group of companies as if they were a single company**.

1.2 What does consolidation involve?

Before moving on to the formal definitions, think about what consolidation involves.

- Consolidation means **adding together**

- Consolidation means **cancellation of like items** internal to the group

- Consolidate as if you **owned everything** then **show** the **extent to which you do not** own everything

What does this mean? Consider the following example.

1.3 Example: basic principles of consolidation

Consolidate as if you owned everything, and then show the extent to which you do not.

There are two companies, Pleasant and Sweet. Pleasant owns 80% of the shares in Sweet. Pleasant has a head office building worth $100,000. Sweet has a factory worth $80,000. Remember that consolidation means presenting the results of two or more companies as if they were one.

Adding together

You add together the values of the head office building and the factory to get an asset, land and buildings, in the group accounts of $100,000 + $80,000 = $180,000. So far so good; this is what you would expect consolidation to mean.

Intra-group debts

Suppose Pleasant has receivables of $40,000 and Sweet has receivables of $30,000. Included in the receivables of Pleasant is $5,000 owed by Sweet. Remember again that consolidation means presenting the results of the two companies as if they were one.

Do we then simply add together $40,000 and $30,000 to arrive at the figure for consolidated receivables? We cannot simply do this, because $5,000 of the receivables is owed within the group. This amount is irrelevant when we consider what the group as a whole is owed.

Further, suppose that Pleasant has payables of $50,000 and Sweet has payables of $45,000. We already know that $5,000 of Sweet's payables is a balance owed to Pleasant. If we just added the figures together, we would not reflect fairly the amount the group owes to the outside world. The outside world does not care what these companies owe to each other – that is an internal matter for the group.

Cancellation of like items

To arrive at a fair picture we eliminate both the receivable of $5,000 in Pleasant's books and the payable of $5,000 in Sweet's books. Only then do we consolidate by adding together.

Consolidated receivables   = $40,000 + $30,000 – $5,000
                                   = $65,000

Consolidated payables   = $50,000 + $45,000 – $5,000
                                   = $90,000

So far we have established that consolidation means adding together any items that are not eliminated as internal to the group. Going back to the example, however, we see that Pleasant only owns 80% of Sweet. Should we not then add Pleasant's assets and liabilities to 80% of Sweet's?

Consolidate as if you owned everything

The answer is no. Pleasant **controls** Sweet, its subsidiary. The directors of Pleasant can visit **all** of Sweet's factory, if they wish, not just 80% of it. So the figure for consolidated land and buildings is $100,000 plus $80,000 as stated above.

Show the extent to which you do not own everything

However, if we just add the figures together, we are not telling the whole story. There may well be one or more shareholders who own the remaining 20% of the shares in Sweet Ltd. These shareholders cannot visit 20% of the factory or tell 20% of the workforce what to do, but they do have an **interest** in 20% of the net assets of Sweet. The answer is to show this **non-controlling interest** separately in the equity section of the consolidated statement of financial position.

Summary

- Consolidation means adding together (uncancelled items).
- Consolidation means cancellation of like items internal to the group.
- Consolidate as if you owned everything then show the extent to which you do not.

Keep these basic principles in mind as you work through the detailed techniques of consolidated financial statements.

Now try the following questions.

QUESTION

Consolidated non-current assets

Apple Co owns 60% of Pear Co. Apple has non-current assets of $80,000 and Pear has non-current assets of $50,000.

Consolidated non-current assets is calculated as:

	$
Apple	80,000
Pear 60% × $50,000	30,000
	110,000

True or false? Explain your answer.

ANSWER

False. The correct calculation is:

	$
Apple	80,000
Pear	50,000
	130,000

Pear is a subsidiary of Apple, which controls **all** its non-current assets, not just 60%. The 40% non-controlling interest is accounted for separately.

QUESTION

Consolidated receivables

Apple Co owns 60% of Pear Co. Apple has receivables of $60,000 and Pear has receivables of $40,000. Pear owes Apple $10,000. What are consolidated receivables?

A $74,000
B $84,000
C $90,000
D $100,000

ANSWER

C   *Consolidated receivables*

	$
Apple	60,000
Less intra-group	(10,000)
	50,000
Pear	40,000
Consolidated	90,000

QUESTION

Consolidated payables

Apple Co owns 60% of Pear Co. Pear has payables of $90,000, of which $10,000 is owed to Apple. Apple has payables of $120,000.

Required

Calculate the consolidated payables balance.

ANSWER

Consolidated payables

	$	$
Apple		120,000
Pear	90,000	
Less intra-group	(10,000)	
		80,000
		200,000

2 Subsidiaries

A **subsidiary** is an entity **controlled** by another entity.

Now you know what a group is in general terms and what consolidation means in principle, you are ready to learn some more formal definitions.

The relevant IFRSs for consolidation are:

- IAS 27 *Separate financial statements*
- IAS 28 *Investments in associates and joint ventures*
- IFRS 3 *Business combinations*
- IFRS 10 *Consolidated financial statements*

In this and the next two chapters we will consider the principles of IAS 27/IFRS 10 and IFRS 3. IAS 27 was previously issued as IAS 27 *Consolidated and separate financial statements*. Effective from 1 January 2013, it was superseded by IAS 27 *Separate financial statements*. The consolidation requirements in the old IAS 27 are now contained in IFRS 10 *Consolidated financial statements*. IAS 28 is considered in Section 3 below. First of all, however, we will look at all the important definitions, which **determine how to treat each particular type of investment** in consolidated financial statements.

EXAM FOCUS POINT

All the definitions relating to group accounts are extremely important. You must **learn them** and **understand** their meaning and application. The ACCA examining team has stated that students need to be able to identify the nature of an investment, using the definitions of control and significant influence. So questions in your exam may require you to apply these definitions to scenarios.

2.1 Definitions

We will look at some of these definitions in more detail later, but they are useful here in that they give you an overview of all aspects of consolidation.

- **Control.** An investor controls an investee when the investor is exposed, or has rights, to variable returns from its involvement with the investee and has the ability to affect those returns through its power over the investee.

- **Power.** Existing rights that give the current ability to direct the relevant activities.

- **Subsidiary.** An entity that is controlled by another entity (known as the parent).

- **Parent.** An entity that controls one or more entities.

- **Group.** A parent and all its subsidiaries.

- **Consolidated financial statements.** The financial statements of a group in which the assets, liabilities, equity, income, expenses and cash flows of the parent and its subsidiaries are presented as those of a single economic entity.

- **Non-controlling interest.** The equity in a subsidiary not attributable, directly or indirectly, to a parent.

- A **trade** (or 'simple') **investment.** An investment in the shares of another entity, that is held for the accretion of wealth, and is not an associate or a subsidiary.

2.2 Investments in subsidiaries

You should be able to tell from the definitions given above that the important point here is **control**. In most cases, this will involve the holding company or parent owning a majority of the ordinary shares in the subsidiary (to which normal voting rights are attached). There are circumstances, however, when the parent may own only a minority of the voting power in the subsidiary, **but** the parent still has control.

Control can usually be assumed to exist when the parent **owns more than half (ie over 50%) of the voting power** of an entity **unless** it can be clearly shown that **such ownership does not constitute control** (these situations will be very rare).

What about situations where this ownership criterion does not exist? The following situations show where control exists, even when the parent owns only 50% or less of the voting power of an entity.

(a) The parent has power over more than 50% of the voting rights by virtue of **agreement with other investors**.

(b) The parent has power to **govern the financial and operating policies** of the entity by statute or under an agreement.

(c) The parent has the power to appoint or remove a majority of members of the board of directors (or equivalent governing body).

(d) The parent has power to cast a majority of votes at meetings of the board of directors.

EXAM FOCUS POINT

You may be asked to work out whether a parent has control over another entity in your exam.

2.3 Accounting treatment of subsidiaries in consolidated financial statements

IFRS 10 requires a parent to present consolidated financial statements (also referred to as **group accounts**) in which the accounts of the parent and subsidiary (or subsidiaries) are combined and presented **as a single entity**. This presentation means that the **substance**, rather than the legal form, of the relationship between parent and subsidiaries will be presented.

Consolidated financial statements **ignore the legal boundaries** of the separate legal entities. But why are they considered necessary? They are important because the users of the parent's financial statements need to know about the financial position, results of operations and changes in financial position of the **group as a whole**.

IFRS 10 requires that, when a parent issues consolidated financial statements, it should consolidate **all subsidiaries**, both foreign and domestic, except in certain circumstances, but this is beyond the scope of the F3/FFA syllabus.

We will consider the mechanics of preparing consolidated accounts in the next two chapters.

QUESTION

Subsidiaries

Socket Co has 100,000 shares of $1 each. On 1 January 20X3, Power Co acquired 45,000 of these shares. In addition, Power Co is able to appoint 4 out of the 5 directors of Socket Co, thus exercising control over their activities.

How should Socket Co be treated in the consolidated financial statements of Power Co?

ANSWER

Power holds **less than 50%** of the ordinary shares of Socket. Nevertheless, Socket is a **subsidiary** of Power because its status is determined by a number of factors other than percentage of shares held. The key point is **control** rather than share ownership.

Socket will be treated as a subsidiary if any of the following apply.

(a) It holds more than half the voting power.

(b) It has power over more than half the voting rights by virtue of an agreement with other investors.

(c) It has power to govern the financial and operating policies of the entity under a statute or agreement.

(d) It has power to appoint or remove the majority of the members of the board of directors.

(e) It has power to cast the majority of votes at meetings of the board of directors.

Socket should be treated as a **subsidiary** on the grounds that Power is able to appoint four out of the five directors (criterion (d)). Assuming that the other criteria do not apply, if Power did not have such a power, consolidation would not be appropriate because Socket would not be a subsidiary.

---

3 | Associates and trade investments

An **associate** is an entity over which another entity exerts **significant influence**. Associates are accounted for in the consolidated statements of a group using the equity method.

3.1 Investments in associates

This type of investment is something less than a subsidiary, but more than a simple trade investment. The key criterion here is **significant influence**. This is the 'power to participate', but **not** to 'control' (which would make the investment a subsidiary).

- Associate. An entity over which the investor has significant influence.
- Significant influence. The power to participate in the financial and operating policy decisions of the investee but which is not control or joint control of those policies. *(IAS 28)*

As with control, significant influence can be determined by the holding of voting rights (usually attached to ordinary shares) in the entity. IAS 28 states that if an investor holds **20% or more** of the voting power of the entity, it can be presumed that the investor has significant influence over the entity, **unless** it can be clearly shown that this is not the case.

Significant influence can be presumed **not** to exist if the investor holds **less than 20%** of the voting power of the entity, unless it can be demonstrated otherwise.

The **existence of significant influence** is usually evidenced in one or more of the following ways.

(a) Representation on the **board of directors** (or equivalent) of the investee
(b) Participation in the **policy making process**
(c) **Material transactions** between investor and investee
(d) Interchange of **management personnel**
(e) Provision of **essential technical information**

EXAM FOCUS POINT

In your exam, you may be asked to define significant influence or to determine whether an entity is an associate. The ACCA examining team has commented that students need to be able to describe the principle of equity accounting. A question on the identification of associates and describing the principle of equity accounting was one of the three questions with the lowest pass rates in the December 2012 exam.

Furthermore, in the January to June 2015 ACCA examining team's report, the ACCA examining team's re-iterated that students need to have an understanding of IAS 28, in particular the application of equity accounting.

3.2 Equity method

IAS 28 requires the use of the **equity method** of accounting (or 'equity accounting') for investments in associates.

3.2.1 Consolidated statement of profit or loss

The basic principle of equity accounting is that the investing company (P Co) should take account of its **share of the earnings** of the associate, A Co, whether or not A Co distributes the earnings as dividends. P Co achieves this by adding to consolidated profit the **group's share of A Co's profit after tax**.

Notice the difference between this treatment and the **consolidation** of a subsidiary company's results. If A Co were a 100% owned subsidiary, P Co would take credit for the whole of its sales revenue, cost of sales etc.

Under equity accounting, the associate's sales revenue, cost of sales and so on are *not* **amalgamated** with those of the group. Instead, only the group share of the associate's profit after tax is added to the group profit.

3.2.2 Other comprehensive income

The 'other comprehensive income' element of consolidated financial statements has been removed from the F3/FFA syllabus with effect from the September 2016 sitting.

3.2.3 Consolidated statement of financial position

A figure for **investment in associates** is shown in the consolidated statement of financial position which must be stated at cost at the time of the acquisition of the associate. This amount will increase (or decrease) each year by **the amount of the group's share of the associated company's increase (or decrease) in post-acquisition retained reserves**.

3.2.4 Example: equity accounting

P Co acquires 25,000 of the 100,000 $1 ordinary shares in A Co for $60,000 on 1 January 20X8. In the year to 31 December 20X8, A Co earns profits after tax of $24,000, from which it pays a dividend of $6,000.

How will A Co's results be accounted for in the individual and consolidated accounts of P Co for the year ended 31 December 20X8?

Solution

In the **individual accounts** of P Co, the investment will be recorded on 1 January 20X8 at cost. Unless there is an impairment in the value of the investment, this amount will remain in the individual statement of financial position of P Co permanently. The only entry in P Co's **individual statement of profit or loss** will be to record dividends received. For the year ended 31 December 20X8, P Co will:

DEBIT	Cash	$1,500	
CREDIT	Dividends received (6,000 × 25%)		$1,500

In the **consolidated accounts** of P Co, equity accounting principles will be used to account for the investment in A Co.

Instead of showing the dividend received, the consolidated statement of profit or loss will include the group's share of A Co's net profit for the year (25% × $24,000 = $6,000), which is shown before group profit before tax.

The consolidated statement of financial position will include the asset 'Investment in associate', calculated as follows.

	$
Cost of investment in associate	60,000
Share of A's profit for the year	6,000
Less dividend received	(1,500)
Investment in associate	64,500

In the following year, the share of A's profit is $6,500 and no dividend is received. The figure for 'Investment in associate' in the consolidated financial statements will be calculated as follows.

	$
Investment in associate b/f	64,500
Share of A's profit for the year	6,500
Investment in associate c/f	71,000

3.2.5 No consolidated accounts

Equity accounting is only applied in the consolidated accounts. A company only has to prepare consolidated accounts if it has one or more subsidiaries. If a company has no subsidiaries, then it is not required to prepare consolidated accounts and so any investments in associates will be treated as a simple investment in the parent company's individual accounts.

EXAM FOCUS POINT

The F3/FFA syllabus requires you to understand the **principle** of equity accounting, but you will not be expected to perform calculations using equity accounting techniques in your exam.

3.3 Trade investments

A **trade investment** is a simple investment in the shares of another entity that is not an associate or a subsidiary.

A trade investment is a simple investment in the shares of another entity, that is held for the accretion of wealth, and is not an associate or a subsidiary.

Trade investments are simply shown as **investments** under non-current assets in the consolidated statement of financial position of the group.

QUESTION

Associates

Which **two** of the following investments would be treated as an associate in the consolidated financial statements of Smith Co?

A   Smith Co owns 15% of the ordinary shares of Red Co and has significant influence over Red Co.

B   Smith Co owns 45% of the ordinary shares of Pink Co and can appoint 4 out of 5 directors to the board of directors of Pink Co.

C   Smith co owns 40% of the preference shares (non-voting) and 15% of the ordinary shares of Yellow Co.

D   Smith Co owns 60% of the preference shares (non-voting) and 40% of the ordinary shares of Aquamarine Co.

ANSWER

The correct answers are A and D.

Red Co is an **associate** of Smith Co, as Smith Co has significant influence over Red Co.

Pink Co is a **subsidiary** of Smith Co, as Smith Co's ability to appoint 4 out of 5 directors gives it **control** over Pink Co.

Yellow Co is a trade investment of Smith Co, as Smith Co holds less than 20% of the voting rights of Yellow Co, so is assumed not to have significant influence. Note that the preference shares do not have voting rights so do not have any influence over the running of the company. Remember that shareholdings are not the only way of demonstrating control or significant influence. If it could be shown in another way that Smith Co does have significant influence over Yellow Co, Yellow Co would be classified as an associate.

Aquamarine Co is an **associate** of Smith Co, as Smith Co holds more than 20% of the voting rights of Aquamarine Co and is therefore presumed to have significant influence over Aquamarine Co.

4 Content of consolidated financial statements

Consolidated financial statements present the results of the group; they do not replace the separate financial statements of the individual group companies.

It is important to note at this point that consolidated financial statements are an **additional** set of financial statements that are produced. They do not replace the individual financial statements of the parent or its subsidiaries. The group itself has no legal form, the group accounts are produced to satisfy accounting standards and, in some countries, legal requirements.

Consolidated financial statements are issued to the shareholders of the parent and provide information for those shareholders on all the companies controlled by the parent.

Most parent companies present their own individual accounts and their group accounts in a single **package**. The package typically comprises the following.

- **Parent company financial statements**, which will include 'investments in subsidiary undertakings' as an asset in the statement of financial position, and income from subsidiaries (dividends) in the statement of profit or loss and other comprehensive income

- **Consolidated statement of financial position**

- **Consolidated statement of profit or loss and other comprehensive income** (the other comprehensive income element of consolidated financial statements is beyond the scope of the F3/FFA syllabus)

- **Consolidated statement of cash flows** (this is beyond the scope of the F3/FFA syllabus)

QUESTION
Consolidated financial statements

Companies with subsidiaries are required to publish consolidated financial statements.

Required

State why you feel the preparation of consolidated financial statements is necessary and outline their limitations, if any.

ANSWER

The object of financial statements is to help shareholders exercise control over their company by providing information about how its affairs have been conducted. The shareholders of a parent company would not be given sufficient information from the financial statements of the parent company on its own, because not enough would be known about the nature of the assets, income and profits of all the subsidiary companies in which the parent company has invested. The primary purpose of consolidated financial statements is to provide a true and fair view of the position and earnings of the parent company group as a whole, from the standpoint of the shareholders in the parent company.

A number of arguments have been put forward, however, which argue that consolidated financial statements have certain limitations.

(a) Consolidated financial statements may be misleading.

    (i)   The solvency (liquidity) of one company may hide the insolvency of another

    (ii)   The profit of one company may conceal the losses of another

    (iii)   They imply that group companies will meet each others' debts (this is certainly not true: a parent company may watch creditors of an insolvent subsidiary go unpaid without having to step in)

(b) There may be some difficulties in defining the group or 'entity' of companies, although IFRS 10 has removed many of the grey areas here.

(c) Where a group consists of widely diverse companies in different lines of business, a set of consolidated financial statements may obscure much important detail unless supplementary information about each part of the group's business is provided.

One of the competences you require to fulfil performance objective PO7 of the PER is the ability to 'prepare drafts or review primary financial statements in accordance with relevant accounting standards and policies and legislation'. You can apply the knowledge you obtain from this chapter and the following two chapters on consolidated financial statements to help demonstrate this competence.

CHAPTER ROUNDUP

- Consolidation means presenting the results, assets and liabilities of a group of companies as if they were **one company**.

- Consolidate as if you owned everything, and then show the extent to which you do not.

- A **subsidiary** is an entity **controlled** by another entity.

- An **associate** is an entity over which another entity exerts **significant influence**. Associates are accounted for in the consolidated statements of a group using the equity method.

- A **trade investment** is a simple investment in the shares of another entity that is not an associate or a subsidiary.

- Consolidated financial statements present the results of the group; they do not replace the separate financial statements of the individual group companies.

QUICK QUIZ

1 Fill in the blank.

   A .... is an entity controlled by another entity.

2 When the parent owns over 50% of the voting power of an entity, control can be assumed. True or false?

3 What accounting treatment does IFRS 10 require of a parent company?

4 What is a non-controlling interest?

5 Define an associate in no more than 25 words.

6 How should trade investments be accounted for in the consolidated financial statements of the investor?

   A They should be consolidated on a line by line basis.

   B They should be equity accounted for.

   C A percentage of the investment's profits and assets and liabilities should be consolidated on a line by line basis.

   D The amount paid for the investment at cost should be shown in the statement of financial position.

ANSWERS TO QUICK QUIZ

1   A **subsidiary** is an entity controlled by another entity.

2   True

3   To prepare consolidated financial statements

4   That part of the equity or preference capital not owned by the parent

5   An entity in which an investor has a significant influence, but which is not a subsidiary or a joint venture of the investor

6   D   A trade investment is simply shown as an investment in the statement of financial position. The investor will only produce consolidated accounts if they also have subsidiaries.

Now try ...

Attempt the questions below from the **Practice Question Bank**

Number

Qs 87 – 89

The consolidated statement of financial position

This chapter introduces the basic procedures required to produce a consolidated statement of financial position.

There are plenty of questions and examples in this chapter – work through **all** of them carefully.

G   Preparing simple consolidated financial statements

1   Subsidiaries

(c)   Describe the components of and prepare a consolidated   S
        statement of financial position or extracts thereof, including:

   (i)   Fair value adjustments at acquisition on land and
           buildings (excluding depreciation adjustments)

   (ii)   Fair value of consideration transferred from cash and
           shares (excluding deferred and contingent consideration)

   (iii) Elimination of intra-group trading balances
           (excluding cash and goods in transit)

   (iv)   Removal of unrealised profit arising on intra-group trading

   (v)   Acquisition of subsidiaries part way through the financial
           year

(d)   Calculate goodwill (excluding impairment of goodwill) using the   S
        full goodwill method only as follows:

Fair value of consideration	X
Fair value of non-controlling interest	X
Less fair value of net assets at acquisition	(X)
Goodwill at acquisition	X

1   Summary of consolidation procedures

> Basic consolidation consists of two procedures.
>
> * Cancelling out items which appear as an asset in one company and a liability in another
> * Then adding together all the uncancelled assets and liabilities on a line by line basis
>
> The asset 'investment in subsidiaries' in the parent company accounts always cancels with the share capital of the subsidiary companies. The only share capital in the consolidated accounts is that of the parent company.

How are consolidated financial statements prepared? We will consider the basic procedures in the rest of this chapter.

1.1 Basic consolidation procedure

The preparation of a consolidated statement of financial position, in a very simple form, consists of two procedures.

(a)   Take the individual accounts of the parent company and each subsidiary and **cancel out items** which appear as an asset in one company and a liability in another.

(b)   **Add together** all the uncancelled assets and liabilities throughout the group on a line by line basis.

Items requiring cancellation may include the following.

(a)   The asset 'investment in subsidiary companies' which appears in the parent company's accounts will be matched with the liability 'share capital' in the subsidiaries' accounts.

(b)   There may be intra-group trading within the group. For example, Subsidiary Co may sell goods on credit to Parent Co. Parent Co would then be a receivable in the accounts of Subsidiary Co, while Subsidiary Co would be a payable in the accounts of Parent Co.

1.2 Example: cancellation

Parent Co has just bought 100% of the shares of Subsidiary Co. Below are the statements of financial position of both companies just before consolidation.

PARENT CO STATEMENT OF FINANCIAL POSITION	$'000	SUBSIDIARY CO STATEMENT OF FINANCIAL POSITION	$'000
Assets			
Investment in subsidiary*	50	Receivables	20
Receivables	30	Cash	30
	80		50
Equity and liabilities			
Share capital	80	Share capital*	50
	80		50

* Cancelling items

The consolidated statement of financial position will appear as follows.

PARENT AND SUBSIDIARY
CONSOLIDATED STATEMENT OF FINANCIAL POSITION

	$'000
Receivables (30 + 20)	50
Cash	30
	80
Share capital**	80
	80

****Note**. This is the parent company's share capital only. The subsidiary's has been cancelled.

1.3 Example: cancellation with intra-group trading

P Co regularly sells goods to its one subsidiary company, S Co. The statements of financial position of the two companies on 31 December 20X6 are given below.

STATEMENTS OF FINANCIAL POSITION AS AT 31 DECEMBER 20X6

	P Co $	S Co $
Assets		
Non-current assets		
Property, plant and equipment	35,000	45,000
Investment in 40,000 $1 shares in S Co at cost	40,000	–
	75,000	45,000
Current assets		
Inventories	16,000	12,000
Receivables: S Co	2,000	–
Other	6,000	9,000
Cash at bank	1,000	–
	25,000	21,000
Total assets	100,000	66,000
Equity and liabilities		
Equity		
$1 ordinary shares	70,000	40,000
Retained earnings	16,000	19,000
	86,000	59,000
Current liabilities		
Bank overdraft	–	3,000
Payables: P Co	–	2,000
Payables: other	14,000	2,000
	14,000	7,000
Total equity and liabilities	100,000	66,000

Required

Prepare the consolidated statement of financial position of P Co.

1.4 Solution

The cancelling items are as follows.

(a)   P Co's asset 'investment in shares of S Co' ($40,000) cancels with S Co's liability 'share capital' ($40,000).

(b)   P Co's asset 'receivables: S Co' ($2,000) cancels with S Co's liability 'payables: P Co' ($2,000).

The remaining assets and liabilities are added together to produce the following consolidated statement of financial position.

P CO
CONSOLIDATED STATEMENT OF FINANCIAL POSITION AS AT 31 DECEMBER 20X6

	$	$
Assets		
Non-current assets		
Property, plant and equipment (35 + 45)		80,000
Current assets		
Inventories (16 + 12)		28,000
Receivables (6 + 9)		15,000
Cash at bank		1,000
		44,000
Total assets		124,000
Equity and liabilities		
Equity		
$1 ordinary shares (P Co only)	70,000	
Retained earnings (16 + 19)	35,000	
		105,000
Current liabilities		
Bank overdraft	3,000	
Payables (14 + 2)	16,000	
		19,000
Total equity and liabilities		124,000

Notes

1   P Co's bank balance is **not netted off** with S Co's bank overdraft. To offset one against the other would be less informative and would conflict with the principle that assets and liabilities should not be netted off.

2   The share capital in the consolidated statement of financial position is the **share capital of the parent company alone**. This must **always** be the case, no matter how complex the consolidation, because the share capital of subsidiary companies must **always** be a wholly cancelling item.

1.5 Part cancellation

An item may appear in the statements of financial position of a parent company and its subsidiary, but not at the same amounts.

(a)   The parent company may have acquired **shares in the subsidiary** at a price **greater or less than their face (or 'par') value**. The asset will appear in the parent company's accounts at cost, while the equity will appear in the subsidiary's accounts at par value. This raises the issue of **goodwill**, which we will deal with next.

(b)   Even if the parent company acquired shares at par value, it **may not** have **acquired all the shares of the subsidiary** (so the subsidiary may be only partly owned). This raises the issue of **non-controlling interests**, which we will deal with later in the chapter.

2 | Goodwill arising on consolidation

Goodwill arising on consolidation is recognised as an intangible asset in the consolidated statement of financial position.

In the examples we have looked at so far the cost of shares acquired by the parent company has always been equal to the par value of those shares. This is seldom the case in practice and we must now consider some more complicated examples. We will do this through the following example.

2.1 Example: goodwill arising on consolidation

P Co purchased all of the share capital (40,000 $1 shares) of S Co for $60,000 in cash. The statements of financial position of P Co and S Co prior to the acquisition are as follows.

STATEMENTS OF FINANCIAL POSITION AS AT 31.12.X1

	P Co	S Co
Non-current assets	$'000	$'000
Property, plant and equipment	100	40
Cash at bank	60	–
Total assets	160	40
Equity and liabilities		
Share capital	160	40
Total equity and liabilities	160	40

Firstly we will examine the entries made by the parent company in its own statement of financial position when it acquires the shares.

The entries in P Co's books would be:

DEBIT	Investment in S Co	$60,000	
CREDIT	Bank		$60,000

So P Co's individual statement of financial position will look as follows.

	P Co
Non-current assets	$'000
Property, plant and equipment	100
Investment in S Co	60
Total assets	160
Equity and liabilities	
Share capital	160
Total equity and liabilities	160

Next we will look at the group financial statements.

Now when the directors of P Co agree to pay $60,000 for a 100% investment in S Co they must believe that, in addition to its non-current assets of $40,000, S Co must also have **intangible assets** worth $20,000. This amount of $20,000 paid over and above the value of the tangible assets acquired is called the **goodwill arising on consolidation** (or sometimes **premium on acquisition**).

Following the normal cancellation procedure, the $40,000 share capital in S Co's statement of financial position could be cancelled against $40,000 of the 'investment in S Co' in the statement of financial position of P Co. This would leave a $20,000 debit uncancelled in the parent company's accounts. This $20,000 would appear in the consolidated statement of financial position under the caption 'Intangible non-current assets: goodwill arising on consolidation', as follows.

CONSOLIDATED STATEMENT OF FINANCIAL POSITION OF P GROUP AS AT 31.12.X1

	$'000
Non-current assets	
Property, plant and equipment (100 + 40)	140
Intangible non-current assets: goodwill arising on consolidation	20
Total assets	160
Equity and liabilities	
Share capital	160
Total equity and liabilities	160

2.2 Goodwill and pre-acquisition profits

Up to now we have assumed that S Co was owned by P Co from incorporation, and therefore we have not had to deal with any profits made by S Co before P Co took ownership of it. Assuming instead that S Co was purchased sometime after incorporation and had earned profits of $8,000 in the period before acquisition, its statement of financial position just before the purchase would look as follows.

	$'000
Total assets	48
Share capital	40
Retained earnings	8
Total equity and liabilities	48

If P Co now purchases all the shares in S Co it will acquire total assets worth $48,000 at a cost of $60,000. Clearly in this case S Co's intangible assets (goodwill) are being valued at $12,000. It should be apparent that any earnings retained by the subsidiary **prior to its acquisition** by the parent company must be **incorporated in the cancellation** process so as to arrive at a figure for goodwill arising on consolidation. In other words, not only S Co's share capital but also its **pre-acquisition** retained earnings must be cancelled against the asset 'investment in S Co' in the accounts of the parent company. The uncancelled balance of $12,000 appears in the consolidated statement of financial position.

The consequence of this is that **any pre-acquisition retained earnings of a subsidiary company are not aggregated with the parent company's retained earnings** in the consolidated statement of financial

position. The figure of consolidated retained earnings comprises the retained earnings of the parent company plus the **post-acquisition retained earnings only of subsidiary companies**. The post-acquisition retained earnings are simply retained earnings now **less** retained earnings at acquisition.

Other reserves, such as the **revaluation surplus**, are treated in the same way as retained earnings.

EXAM FOCUS POINT

If you're confused by this, think of it another way, from the point of view of group reserves. Only the profits earned **by the group** should be consolidated. Profits earned by the subsidiary before it became part of the group are not group profits. They reflect what the parent company is getting for its money on acquisition.

2.2.1 Example: goodwill and pre-acquisition profits

Sing Co acquired the ordinary shares of Wing Co on 31 March 20X1 when the draft statements of financial position of each company were as follows.

SING CO
STATEMENT OF FINANCIAL POSITION AS AT 31 MARCH 20X1

	$
Assets	
Non-current assets	
Investment in 50,000 shares of Wing Co at cost	80,000
Current assets	40,000
Total assets	120,000
Equity and liabilities	
Equity	
Ordinary shares	75,000
Retained earnings	45,000
Total equity and liabilities	120,000

WING CO
STATEMENT OF FINANCIAL POSITION AS AT 31 MARCH 20X1

	$
Current assets	60,000
Equity	
50,000 ordinary shares of $1 each	50,000
Retained earnings	10,000
	60,000

Prepare the consolidated statement of financial position as at 31 March 20X1.

2.2.2 Solution

The technique to adopt here is to produce a new working: *Goodwill*. A proforma working is set out below.

Goodwill	$	$
Consideration transferred		X
Less value of identifiable assets acquired and liabilities assumed*:		
Ordinary share capital	X	
Share premium	X	
Retained earnings at acquisition	X	
		(X)
Goodwill		X

* We use this wording because it best reflects the wording IFRS 3 uses. Don't let it confuse you; remember that that: assets – liabilities = capital, so the value of assets acquired and liabilities assumed is equal to the share capital and reserves of the company.

Applying this to our example, the working will look like this.

	$	$
Consideration transferred*		80,000
Less value of identifiable assets acquired and liabilities assumed:		
Ordinary share capital	50,000	
Retained earnings at acquisition	10,000	
		(60,000)
Goodwill		20,000

* This is the cost of the investment in Sing Co's statement of financial position.

SING CO
CONSOLIDATED STATEMENT OF FINANCIAL POSITION AS AT 31 MARCH 20X1

	$
Assets	
Non-current assets	
Goodwill arising on consolidation	20,000
Current assets	100,000
	120,000
Capital and reserves	
Ordinary shares	75,000
Retained earnings	45,000
	120,000

2.2.3 Example: goodwill and pre-acquisition profits continued

Suppose that a year has passed, and you now wish to prepare the consolidated statement of financial position for the Sing group as at 31 March 20X2. The individual statements of financial position are as follows.

SING CO
STATEMENT OF FINANCIAL POSITION AS AT 31 MARCH 20X2

	$
Assets	
Non-current assets	
Investment in 50,000 shares of Wing Co at cost	80,000
Current assets	50,000
Total assets	130,000
Equity and liabilities	
Equity	
Ordinary shares	75,000
Retained earnings	55,000
Total equity and liabilities	130,000

WING CO
STATEMENT OF FINANCIAL POSITION AS AT 31 MARCH 20X2

	$
Current assets	80,000
Equity	
50,000 ordinary shares of $1 each	50,000
Retained earnings	30,000
	80,000

Prepare the consolidated statement of financial position as at 31 March 20X2.

Solution

We can see from the individual statements of financial position that Wing Co has generated profits of $20,000 since being owned by Sing Co, as the retained earnings balance has increased from $10,000 on acquisition to $30,000 at 31 March 20X2. These profits belong to the group and should be consolidated. The technique to adopt here is to produce a new working: *Retained earnings.* A proforma working is set out below.

Retained earnings

	P Co $	S Co $
Per question	X	X
Pre-acquisition retained earnings		(X)
		X
Post-acquisition retained earnings of S Co	X	
Group retained earnings	X	

Applying this to our example, the working will look like this.

Retained earnings

	Sing Co $	Wing Co $
Per question	55,000	30,000
Pre-acquisition retained earnings		(10,000)
		20,000
Post-acq'n ret'd earnings of Wing Co	20,000	
Group retained earnings	75,000	

The goodwill calculation will be the same as before, as it is based on the net assets of Wing Co, which includes retained earnings, at the **acquisition date**.

SING GROUP
CONSOLIDATED STATEMENT OF FINANCIAL POSITION AS AT 31 MARCH 20X2

	$
Assets	
Non-current assets	
Goodwill arising on consolidation	20,000
Current assets (50,000 + 80,000)	130,000
	150,000
Equity and liabilities	
Ordinary shares (Sing only)	75,000
Retained earnings (see working above)	75,000
	150,000

2.3 Fair value of net assets at acquisition

The land and buildings of the subsidiary may be worth more than their carrying amount at acquisition. If this is the case, it must be taken into account in the consolidated financial statements, as follows.

(a)   The subsidiary's land and buildings must be included in the consolidated statement of financial position at their fair value.

(b)   The difference between the fair value of the subsidiary's land and buildings and the carrying value of those land and buildings must be taken into account in the goodwill calculation. This is known as a **fair value adjustment**. The proforma for goodwill will now look as follows.

	$	$
Goodwill		
Consideration transferred		X
Less net **acquisition-date fair value** of identifiable assets acquired and liabilities assumed:		
Ordinary share capital	X	
Share premium	X	
Retained earnings at acquisition	X	
Fair value adjustments at acquisition	**X**	
		(X)
Goodwill		X

QUESTION

Fair value of assets on acquisition

P Co acquired 100% of the ordinary shares of S Co on 1 September 20X5. At that date the fair value of S Co's land and buildings was $23,000 greater than their carrying value and retained earnings were $21,000. The statements of financial position of both companies at 31 August 20X6 are given below.

P CO
STATEMENT OF FINANCIAL POSITION AS AT 31 AUGUST 20X6

	$	$
Assets		
Non-current assets		
Land and buildings	63,000	
Investment in S Co at cost	67,000	
		130,000
Current assets		82,000
Total assets		212,000
Equity and liabilities		
Equity		
Ordinary shares of $1 each	80,000	
Retained earnings	112,000	
		192,000
Current liabilities		20,000
Total equity and liabilities		212,000

S CO
STATEMENT OF FINANCIAL POSITION AS AT 31 AUGUST 20X6

	$	$
Assets		
Land and buildings		28,000
Current assets		43,000
Total assets		71,000
Equity and liabilities		
Equity		
Ordinary shares of $1 each	20,000	
Retained earnings	41,000	
		61,000
Current liabilities		10,000
Total equity and liabilities		71,000

Required

Prepare P Co's consolidated statement of financial position as at 31 August 20X6.

ANSWER

P CO
CONSOLIDATED STATEMENT OF FINANCIAL POSITION AS AT 31 AUGUST 20X6

	$	$
Non-current assets		
Land and buildings (63,000 + 28,000 + 23,000*)	114,000	

	$	$
Goodwill (W1)	3,000	
		117,000
Current assets (82,000 + 43,000)		125,000
		242,000
Equity and liabilities		
Equity		
Ordinary shares of $1 each (P Co only)	80,000	
Retained earnings (W2)	132,000	
		212,000
Current liabilities (20,000 + 10,000)		30,000
		242,000

* The $23,000 fair value adjustment is added to the land and buildings balance, so that the consolidated statement of financial position shows the fair value of land and buildings acquired.

Workings

1   Goodwill

	$	$
Consideration transferred		67,000
Less net acquisition-date fair value of identifiable assets acquired and liabilities assumed:		
Ordinary share capital	20,000	
Retained earnings	21,000	
Fair value adjustment at acquisition	23,000	
		(64,000)
Goodwill		3,000

2   Retained earnings

	P Co $	S Co $
Per question	112,000	41,000
Pre-acquisition retained earnings		(21,000)
		20,000
Post-acq'n ret'd earnings of S Co	20,000	
Group retained earnings	132,000	

2.4 Types of consideration transferred

The consideration paid by the parent for the shares in the subsidiary can take different forms. For example, the parent could pay cash for the subsidiary, as we have assumed so far. However, the parent could pay a combination of cash as well as shares in itself, or perhaps just shares in itself to acquire the subsidiary.

IMPORTANT

The calculation of goodwill must be based on the **fair value** of the consideration transferred. For cash, this is straightforward; it is simply the amount of cash paid. But what about shares? The fair value of shares is their **market price** on the **date of acquisition**.

The following example shows the effect of consideration in the form of shares on the consolidated statement of financial position.

2.4.1 Example: consideration in the form of shares

P Co has acquired all of the share capital of S Co (12,000 $1 shares) by issuing 5 of its own $1 shares for every 4 shares in S Co. The market value of P Co's shares was $6 at the date of acquisition. The fair value of the net assets of S Co at the date of acquisition was $75,000.

The fair value of the consideration transferred for the acquisition is:

	$
12,000 × 5/4 × $6	90,000

This is credited to the share capital and share premium of P Co as follows.

	Dr	Cr
Investment in subsidiary	90,000	
Share capital ($12,000 × 5/4)		15,000
Share premium ($12,000 × 5/4 × 5)		75,000

Goodwill on acquisition is calculated in the usual way as follows.

	$
Fair value of consideration transferred	90,000
Less net acquisition-date fair value of identifiable assets acquired and liabilities assumed	(75,000)
Goodwill	15,000

3 Non-controlling interests

The non-controlling interest (NCI) shows the extent to which net assets controlled by the group are owned by other parties.

Let's recap on the general principles of consolidation.

- Consolidation means adding together
- Consolidation means cancellation of items internal to the group
- Consolidate as if you owned everything and then show the extent to which you do not

It is this third point with which we are now concerned.

Following the above principle, the total assets and liabilities of subsidiary companies are included in the consolidated statement of financial position, even in the case of subsidiaries which are only partly owned, by which we mean where the parent doesn't own 100% of the share capital of the subsidiary. A proportion of the net assets of such subsidiaries in fact belongs to investors from outside the group which we call the **non-controlling interests (NCI)**.

IFRS 10 defines non-controlling interest as the equity in a subsidiary not attributable, directly or indirectly, to a parent.

NCI is shown in the equity section of the consolidated statement of financial position and is included in the consolidated financial statements at its **fair value plus the NCI's share of post-acquisition retained earnings and other reserves**.

Non-controlling interest

	$
Fair value of NCI at acquisition	X
Plus NCI's share of post-acquisition retained earnings (and other reserves)	**X**
NCI at reporting date	X̄

EXAM FOCUS POINT

In the exam there are a couple of ways that you could be given the fair value of the NCI at acquisition.

(a) The question could simply provide you with the figure.

(b) You could be told the subsidiary's share price just before the acquisition. You would then need to multiply the share price by the number of shares held by the NCI.

The existence of a NCI also has an impact on the calculation of group retained earnings as some of the retained earnings are owned by the NCI, as we have seen in the calculation above. Group retained earnings should only reflect the **group's share** of the post-acquisition retained earnings of the subsidiary. The proforma for group retained earnings working is amended as follows.

Retained earnings

	P Co	S Co
	$	$
Per question	X	X
Pre-acquisition retained earnings		(X)
		Y
Group share of post-acquisition retained earnings:		
S Co (Y × %)	X	
Group retained earnings	X	

3.1 Goodwill and NCIs

In the calculations of goodwill we have looked at so far, the parent company has acquired 100% of the shares in the subsidiary.

Where there is a NCI, the **consolidated accounts show 100% of goodwill** even though the group does not 'own' all of it. This is consistent with the treatment of other assets and the concept of control. Because this is the case, we need to include the fair value of the NCI in our goodwill calculation.

The proforma for goodwill will now look as follows.

Goodwill	$	$
Fair value of consideration transferred		X
Plus fair value of NCI at acquisition		X
Less net acquisition-date fair value of identifiable assets acquired and liabilities assumed:		
Ordinary share capital	X	
Share premium	X	
Retained earnings at acquisition	X	
Fair value adjustments at acquisition	X	
		(X)
Goodwill		X

3.1.1 Example

P Co acquires 90% of S Co for $10,000,000. At this date the fair value of S Co's net assets are $8,000,000 and the fair value of the NCI is $1,000,000. Calculate goodwill.

Goodwill	$'000
Fair value of consideration transferred	10,000
Fair value of NCI at acquisition	1,000
	11,000
Less net acquisition-date fair value of identifiable assets acquired and liabilities assumed	(8,000)
Total goodwill	3,000

3.1.2 Goodwill attributable to NCI

Total goodwill is recognised in the statement of financial position, as the group controls 100% of it. However, we can calculate goodwill attributable to the NCI as follows.

	$'000
Fair value of NCI	1,000
NCI in net assets at acquisition (10% × 8,000)	(800)
Goodwill	200

3.2 Example: NCIs

P Co purchased 75% of the share capital of S Co on 1 January 20X1 for $60,000 when the retained earnings of S Co were $5,000. The fair value of the NCI in S Co at that date was $15,000. The statements of financial position of P Co and S Co as at 31 December 20X1 are given below.

P CO
STATEMENT OF FINANCIAL POSITION

	$	$
Assets		
Non-current assets		
Tangible assets	50,000	
30,000 $1 ordinary shares in S Co at cost	60,000	
		110,000
Current assets		45,000
Total assets		155,000
Equity and liabilities		
Equity		
80,000 $1 ordinary shares		80,000
Retained earnings		55,000
		135,000
Current liabilities		20,000
Total equity and liabilities		155,000

S CO
STATEMENT OF FINANCIAL POSITION

	$
Assets	
Tangible non-current assets	35,000
Current assets	40,000
Total assets	75,000
Equity and liabilities	
Equity	
40,000 $1 ordinary shares	40,000
Retained earnings	15,000
	55,000
Current liabilities	20,000
Total equity and liabilities	75,000

Required

Prepare the consolidated statement of financial position at 31 December 20X1.

3.3 Solution

All of S Co's net assets are consolidated despite the fact that the company is only 75% owned. NCI is included in the statement of financial position at its fair value plus its share of post-acquisition retained earnings.

P GROUP
CONSOLIDATED STATEMENT OF FINANCIAL POSITION

	$	$
Assets		
Non-current assets		
Tangible non-current assets (50,000 + 35,000)	85,000	
Goodwill (W1)	30,000	
		115,000
Current assets (45,000 + 40,000)		85,000
Total assets		200,000

	$	$
Equity and liabilities		
Equity attributable to owners of the parent		
Share capital (P Co only)	80,000	
Retained earnings (W2)	62,500	
		142,500
NCI (W3)		**17,500**
Total equity		160,000
Current liabilities (20,000 + 20,000)		40,000
Total equity and liabilities		200,000

Workings

1   *Goodwill*

	$	$
Fair value of consideration transferred		60,000
Plus fair value of NCI at acquisition		15,000
Less net acquisition-date fair value of identifiable assets acquired and liabilities assumed:		
Ordinary share capital	40,000	
Retained earnings at acquisition	5,000	
		(45,000)
Goodwill		30,000

2   *Retained earnings*

	P Co $	S Co $
Per question	55,000	15,000
Pre-acquisition retained earnings		(5,000)
		10,000
Group share of post-acq ret'd earnings:		
S Co (75% × 10,000)	7,500	
Group retained earnings	62,500	

3   *NCI at reporting date*

	$
Fair value of NCI at acquisition	15,000
Plus NCI's share of post-acquisition retained earnings (25% × 10,000)	2,500
NCI at reporting date	17,500

QUESTION

Goodwill

On 31 December 20X8 Pandora Co acquired 4m of the 5m $1 ordinary shares of Sylvester Co, paying $10m cash. On that date the fair value of Sylvester's net assets was $7.5m.

The market price of the shares held by the non-controlling shareholders just before the acquisition was $2.00. What is goodwill in the consolidated statement of financial position?

	$'000
A	2,000
B	2,500
C	4,000
D	4,500

ANSWER

D

	$'000
Fair value of consideration transferred	10,000
Fair value of NCI ($2 × 1m)	2,000
	12,000
Less net acquisition-date fair value of identifiable assets acquired and liabilities assumed	(7,500)

Goodwill	4,500

4 Intra-group trading

A consolidation adjustment is required to remove **unrealised profit** on intra-group trading.

We have already come across cases where one company in a group engages in trading with another group company. Any receivable/payable balances outstanding between the companies are cancelled on consolidation. No further problem arises if all such intra-group transactions are **undertaken at cost**, without any mark-up for profit.

However, each company in a group is a separate trading entity and may wish to treat other group companies in the same way as any other customer. In this case, a company (say A Co) may buy goods at one price and sell them at a higher price to another group company (B Co). The accounts of A Co will quite properly include the profit earned on sales to B Co. Similarly, B Co's statement of financial position will include inventories at their cost to B Co, ie at the amount at which they were purchased from A Co.

This gives rise to two problems.

(a)   Although A Co makes a profit as soon as it sells goods to B Co, the group does not make a sale or achieve a profit until an outside customer buys the goods from B Co.

(b)   Any purchases from A Co which remain unsold by B Co at the year end will be included in B Co's inventory. Their statement of financial position value will be their cost to B Co, which is not the same as their cost to the group.

The objective of consolidated accounts is to present the financial position of several connected companies as that of a **single entity**, the group. This means that **in a consolidated statement of financial position the only profits recognised should be those earned by the group** in providing goods or services for outsiders. Similarly, inventory in the consolidated statement of financial position should be valued at cost to the group.

4.1 Example: intra-group trading and unrealised profits

Suppose that a holding company P Co buys goods for $1,600 and sells them to a wholly owned subsidiary S Co for $2,000. The goods are all still in S Co's inventory at the year end and appear in S Co's statement of financial position at $2,000. In this case, P Co will record a profit of $400 in its individual accounts, but from the group's point of view the figures are:

Cost	$1,600
External sales	nil
Closing inventory at cost	$1,600
Profit/loss	nil

If we add together the figures for retained reserves and inventory in the individual statements of financial position of P Co and S Co, the resulting figures for consolidated reserves and consolidated inventory will each be overstated by $400. A **consolidation adjustment** is therefore necessary as follows.

DEBIT   Group reserves
CREDIT   Group inventory (statement of financial position)

with the amount of **profit unrealised** by the group. We call this the '**provision for unrealised profit**' or PUP, as it is a provision against inventory for the unrealised profit generated by the intra-group sale.

QUESTION   Consolidated financial statements

P Co acquired all the shares in S Co one year ago when the retained earnings of S Co stood at $10,000. Draft statements of financial position for each company are as follows.

	P Co		S Co	
	$	$	$	$
Assets				
Non-current assets				

	$			$
Tangible assets	80,000			40,000
Investment in S Co at cost	46,000			
		126,000		
Current assets				
Trade receivables	30,000		25,000	
Inventories	10,000		5,000	
		40,000		30,000
Total assets		166,000		70,000
Equity and liabilities				
Equity				
Ordinary shares of $1 each	100,000		30,000	
Retained earnings	45,000		22,000	
		145,000		52,000
Current liabilities				
Trade payables		21,000		18,000
Total equity and liabilities		166,000		70,000

During the year S Co sold goods to P Co for $50,000, the profit to S Co being 20% of selling price. At the period end, 25% of these goods remained unsold in the inventories of P Co. At the same date, P Co owed S Co $12,000 for goods bought and this debt is included in the trade payables of P Co and the trade receivables of S Co.

Required

Prepare a draft consolidated statement of financial position for P Co.

ANSWER

P CO
CONSOLIDATED STATEMENT OF FINANCIAL POSITION

	$	$
Assets		
Non-current assets		
Tangible assets	120,000	
Goodwill (W1)	6,000	
		126,000
Current assets		
Trade receivables (30,000 + 25,000 – 12,000*)	43,000	
Inventories (10,000 + 5,000 – 2,500**(W2))	12,500	
		55,500
Total assets		181,500
Equity and liabilities		
Equity		
Ordinary shares of $1 each	100,000	
Retained earnings (W3)	54,500	
		154,500
Current liabilities		
Trade payables (21,000 + 18,000 – 12,000*)		27,000
Total equity and liabilities		181,500

* To cancel the intra-group receivable and payable

** To remove the unrealised profit on items still in inventories

Workings

1   *Goodwill*

	$	$
Fair value of consideration transferred		46,000
Less net acquisition-date fair value of identifiable assets acquired and liabilities assumed:		
Share capital	30,000	
Retained earnings at acquisition	10,000	
		40,000
Goodwill		6,000

2   *Provision for unrealised profit*

	$
Profit on intra-group sales (20% × $50,000)	10,000
Unrealised profit (25% × 10,000)*	2,500

* 25% of the inventories from the intra-group sales remain in inventories at the year end, therefore the unrealised profit is 25% of the overall profit made on the intra-group sales. The rest of the profit from the intra-group sales is now realised as the inventories have been sold outside the group.

3   *Retained earnings*

	P Co	S Co
	$	$
Per question	45,000	22,000
Adjustment (unrealised profit (W2))		**(2,500)**
Pre-acquisition retained earnings		(10,000)
		9,500
Group share of post-acq'n ret'd earnings:		
S Co (12,000 × 100%)	9,500	
Group retained earnings	54,500	

EXAM FOCUS POINT

You will probably have to calculate the unrealised profit given either a gross profit margin or a mark-up on cost. Remember that:

- **Mark-up** is the profit as a percentage of **cost**.
- **Gross profit margin** is the profit as a percentage of **sales**.

4.2 NCIs and intra-group trading

A further problem occurs where a subsidiary company which is **not wholly owned is involved in intra-group trading** within the group.

For example, P Co owns 75% of the equity of S Co. S Co sells goods to P Co for $20,000 ($16,000 cost plus $4,000 profit). If these items are unsold by P Co at the period end, then there will be unrealised profit of $4,000 earned by S Co and charged to P Co. However, P Co only owns 75% of S Co, so this unrealised profit will be partly owned by the NCI of S Co. However, from the perspective of the NCI, their share of the profit of the sale of the goods (25% of $4,000 = $1,000) would appear to have been fully realised, as the NCI is external to the group. It is only the group that has not yet made a profit on the sale.

To account for this in the group accounts, we remove the whole profit, charging the NCI with their proportion.

DEBIT	Group retained earnings
DEBIT	NCI
CREDIT	Group inventory (statement of financial position)

Note that the adjustment to the NCI only occurs when the sale is from the subsidiary to the parent (where the unrealised profit is in the subsidiary). If the sale was from the parent to the subsidiary, then there is no adjustment to the NCI.

4.3 Example: NCIs and intra-group trading

P Co acquired 75% of the shares in S Co on 1 January 20X2 when the retained earnings of S Co stood at $10,000. The fair value of the NCI at the date of acquisition was $15,000. During the year to 31 December 20X2, S Co sold goods to P Co for $20,000 at a mark-up of 25%. 50% of these goods were still unsold by P Co at the end of the year. At the same date, P Co owed S Co $12,000 for goods bought and this debt is included in the trade payables of P Co and the trade receivables of S Co.

Draft statements of financial position of each company at 31 December 20X2 were as follows.

	P Co		S Co	
	$	$	$	$
Assets				
Non-current assets				
Tangible assets	80,000			40,000
Investment in S Co at cost	46,000			
		126,000		
Current assets				
Trade receivables	30,000		25,000	
Inventories	10,000		5,000	
		40,000		30,000
Total assets		166,000		70,000
Equity and liabilities				
Equity				
Ordinary shares of $1 each	100,000		30,000	
Retained earnings	45,000		22,000	
		145,000		52,000
Current liabilities				
Trade payables		21,000		18,000
Total equity and liabilities		166,000		70,000

Required

Prepare a draft consolidated statement of financial position for P Co.

Solution

P CO
CONSOLIDATED STATEMENT OF FINANCIAL POSITION AS AT 31 DECEMBER 20X2

	$	$
Assets		
Non-current assets		
Tangible assets (80,000 + 40,000)		120,000
Goodwill (W1)		21,000
Current assets		
Trade receivables (30,000 + 25,000 – 12,000)	43,000	
Inventories (10,000 + 5,000 – 2,000 (W2))	13,000	
		56,000
Total assets		197,000
Equity and liabilities		
Equity attributable to owners of the parent		
Ordinary shares of $1 each	100,000	
Retained earnings (W3)	52,500	
		152,000
NCI (W4)		17,500
		170,000
Current liabilities (21,000 + 18,000 – 12,000)		27,000
Total equity and liabilities		197,000

Workings

1   Goodwill

	$	$
Fair value of consideration transferred		46,000
Plus fair value of NCI at acquisition		15,000
Less net acquisition-date fair value of identifiable assets acquired and liabilities assumed:		
Share capital	30,000	
Retained earnings	10,000	
		40,000
Goodwill		21,000

2   *Provision for unrealised profit*

		$
Sale price	125%	20,000
Cost price	100%	(16,000)
Gross profit	25%	4,000

	$
Unrealised profit (4,000 × 50%)	2,000
Unrealised profit attributable to group (2,000 × 75%)	1,500
Unrealised profit attributable to NCI (2,000 × 25%)	500

3   *Retained earnings*

	P Co $	S Co $
Per question	45,000	22,000
Adjustments (unrealised profit attributable to P (W2))	(1,500)	–
Pre-acquisition retained earnings		(10,000)
		12,000
Group share of post-acq'n ret'd earnings:		
S Co (75% × 12,000)	9,000	
Group retained earnings	52,500	

4   *NCI at reporting date*

	$
Fair value of NCI at acquisition	15,000
Plus NCI's share of post-acquisition retained earnings (25% × 12,000)	3,000
Less unrealised profit attributable to NCI (W2)	(500)
NCI at reporting date	17,500

5   Acquisition of a subsidiary part way through the year

> When a parent acquires a subsidiary part way through the year, the profits for the period need to be apportioned between pre- and post-acquisition. Only post-acquisition profits are included in the group's consolidated statement of financial position.

In the examples we have looked at already in this chapter, the subsidiary was conveniently purchased on the first day of the accounting period. However, in practice this will probably not be the case!

If a parent purchases a subsidiary company during the year, as we have already seen, at the end of the accounting year it will be necessary to prepare consolidated accounts.

The subsidiary's accounts to be consolidated will show the subsidiary's profit or loss for the whole year. For consolidation purposes, however, it will be necessary to distinguish between:

(a)   Profits earned before acquisition – so that we can calculate goodwill
(b)   Profits earned after acquisition – so that we can calculate group retained earnings

To do this, we usually assume that the subsidiary's **profits accrue evenly** over the year. Then we can take the profit for the year and calculate the pre- and post-acquisition profits based on the number of months the parent has owned the subsidiary.

QUESTION   Acquisition during the year

Hinge Co acquired 80% of the ordinary shares of Singe Co on 1 April 20X5. On 31 December 20X4 Singe Co's accounts showed a revaluation surplus of $4,000 and retained earnings of $15,000. The fair value of the NCI at acquisition was $7,000. The statements of financial position of the two companies at 31 December 20X5 are set out below.

HINGE CO
STATEMENT OF FINANCIAL POSITION AS AT 31 DECEMBER 20X5

	$	$

Assets
Non-current assets
   Property, plant and equipment 32,000
   16,000 ordinary shares of 50c each in Singe Co 50,000

		82,000
Current assets		85,000
Total assets		167,000

Equity and liabilities
Equity
Ordinary shares of $1 each 100,000
Revaluation surplus 7,000
Retained earnings 40,000

		147,000
Current liabilities		20,000
Total equity and liabilities		167,000

SINGE CO
STATEMENT OF FINANCIAL POSITION AS AT 31 DECEMBER 20X5

	$	$
Assets		
Property, plant and equipment		30,000
Current assets		43,000
Total assets		73,000
Equity and liabilities		
Equity		
20,000 ordinary shares of 50c each	10,000	
Revaluation surplus	4,000	
Retained earnings	39,000	
		53,000
Current liabilities		20,000
Total equity and liabilities		73,000

Required

Prepare the consolidated statement of financial position of Hinge Co at 31 December 20X5. You should assume that profits have accrued evenly over the year to 31 December 20X5.

(15 marks)

EXAM FOCUS POINT

We have allocated 15 marks to the above question, as an indication of the type of question that could arise in the exam. However, the ACCA examining team has indicated that a 15 mark consolidation question could include a small amount of interpretation, which is covered in Chapter 26. A combined consolidation and interpretation question is included in the Practice Question Bank.

ANSWER

Singe Co has made a profit of $24,000 ($39,000 − $15,000) for the year. This is assumed to have arisen evenly over the year; $6,000 in the 3 months to 31 March and $18,000 in the 9 months after acquisition. The company's pre-acquisition retained earnings are therefore as follows.

	$
Balance at 31 December 20X4	15,000
Profit for three months to 31 March 20X5 ($^3/_{12} \times 24,000$)	6,000
Pre-acquisition retained earnings	21,000

The balance of $4,000 on the revaluation surplus is all pre-acquisition.

HINGE CO

431

CONSOLIDATED STATEMENT OF FINANCIAL POSITION AS AT 31 DECEMBER 20X5

	$	$
Assets		
Non-current assets		
Property, plant and equipment (32,000 + 30,000)	62,000	
Goodwill (W1)	22,000	
		84,000
Current assets (85,000 + 43,000)		128,000
Total assets		212,000
Equity and liabilities		
Equity attributable to owners of the parent		
Ordinary shares of $1 each	100,000	
Revaluation surplus (W3)	7,000	
Retained earnings (W2)	54,400	
		161,400
NCI (W4)		10,600
Total equity		172,000
Current liabilities (20,000 + 20,000)		40,000
Total equity and liabilities		212,000

Workings

1   *Goodwill*

	$	$
Fair value of consideration transferred		50,000
Fair value of NCI		7,000
Less net acquisition-date fair value of identifiable assets acquired and liabilities assumed:		
Ordinary share capital	10,000	
Retained earnings at acquisition (as above)	21,000	
Revaluation surplus	4,000	
		(35,000)
Goodwill		22,000

2   *Retained earnings*

	Hinge Co $	Singe Co $
Per question	40,000	39,000
Pre-acquisition retained earnings (W2)		(21,000)
		18,000
Group share of post-acq'n ret'd earnings		
Singe Co: $18,000 × 80%	14,400	
	54,400	

3   *Revaluation surplus*

	$
Hinge Co	7,000
Group share of post-acq'n revaluation surplus: Singe Co	–
	7,000

4   *NCI at reporting date*

	$
Fair value of NCI at acquisition date	7,000
NCI share of post-acquisition retained earnings (20% × 18,000)	3,600
NCI	10,600

6 Summary: consolidated statement of financial position

Purpose	To show the net assets which P controls and the ownership of those assets
Net assets	Always 100% P plus 100% S
Share capital	P only
Reason	Simply reporting to the parent company's shareholders in another form
Retained earnings	100% P plus group share of post-acquisition retained earnings of S less consolidation adjustments
Reason	To show the extent to which the group actually owns total assets less liabilities
Non-controlling interest	Fair value at acquisition plus share of post-acquisition retained earnings and other resources
Reason	To show the equity in a subsidiary not attributable to the parent

EXAM FOCUS POINT

In the January to June 2015 ACCA examining team's report, the ACCA examining team provided the following comments on the consolidated statement of financial position, which may help students to improve their performance:

- In the paper version of the exam, use the correct format for a consolidated statement of financial position.

- Give the statement its correct title ie 'Consolidated statement of financial position at (year-end date)'

- The assets and liabilities of the parent and the subsidiary are added together on a line-by-line basis.

- The investment in the subsidiary (shown in the parent's SoFP) is replaced with a goodwill figure. Where necessary, show clearly your workings for the goodwill figure.

- The share capital and share premium balances are not added together; only the balances related to the parent are used in the consolidation.

- The group share of the subsidiary's profit is calculated and added to the groups retained earnings. Where necessary, clearly show workings for the calculation of retained earnings.

- If there is intra-group trading then adjust the receivables and payables that cancel each other out.

- Any dividends paid by the subsidiary to the parent should be adjusted, as the net effect to the group is zero.

- Adjust for any unrealised profits on sales of inventory between the parent and the subsidiary.

CHAPTER ROUNDUP

ↄ Basic consolidation consists of two procedures.

– Cancelling out items which appear as an asset in one company and a liability in another
– Then adding together all the uncancelled assets and liabilities on a line by line basis.

ↄ The asset 'investment in subsidiaries' in the parent company accounts always cancels with the share capital of the subsidiary companies. The only share capital in the consolidated accounts is that of the parent company.

ↄ Goodwill arising on consolidation is recognised as an intangible asset in the consolidated statement of financial position.

ↄ The non-controlling interest (NCI) shows the extent to which net assets controlled by the group are owned by other parties.

ↄ A consolidation adjustment is required to remove **unrealised profit** on intra-group trading.

ↄ When a parent acquires a subsidiary part way through the year, the profits for the period need to be apportioned between pre- and post-acquisition. Only post-acquisition profits are included in the group's consolidated statement of financial position.

QUICK QUIZ

1 Fill in the blanks.

Goodwill is the excess of .... plus fair value of ....-.............. .... over fair value of net assets acquired. It should be included in the consolidated statement of financial position as an ....

2 Pretty Co owns 80% of Ugly Co. Ugly Co sells goods to Pretty Co at cost plus 50%. The total invoiced sales to Pretty Co by Ugly Co in the year ended 31 December 20X9 were $120,000 and, of these sales, 50% were held in inventory by Pretty Co at 31 December 20X9. What is the provision for unrealised profit?

3 Major Co, which makes up its accounts to 31 December, has an 80% owned subsidiary Minor Co. Minor Co sells goods to Major Co at a margin of 30%. At 31 December 20X8, Major had $12,000 of such goods in its inventory. What is the provision for unrealised profit?

4 Complete the equation for calculating the NCI figure in the statement of financial position below.

Non-controlling interest	$
Fair value of NCI at acquisition	X
Plus	X
NCI at reporting date	X̲

5 The summarised statements of financial position of Falcon and Kestrel at 31 December 20X8 were as follows.

	Falcon	Kestrel
	$m	$m
Net assets	68̲	25̲
Share capital	10	10
Reserves	58	15
	68̲	25̲

On 1 January 20X8 Falcon purchased 80% of the equity share capital of Kestrel for $28m. The fair value of the net assets of Kestrel was $30m at that date. The fair value of the NCI at the acquisition date was $5m.

Calculate the goodwill arising on consolidation.

1 Goodwill is the excess of **consideration paid** plus fair value of **non-controlling interest** over fair value of net assets acquired. It should be included in the consolidated statement of financial position as an **intangible asset**.

2

Provision for unrealised profit

		$
Sale price	150%	120,000
Cost price	100%	(80,000)
Gross profit	50%	40,000
Unrealised profit (40,000 × 50%)		20,000

3

Provision for unrealised profit

		$
Sale price	100%	12,000
Cost price	70%	(8,400)
Gross profit	30%	3,600
Unrealised profit		3,600

4

	$
Non-controlling interest	
Fair value of NCI at acquisition	X
Plus **NCI's share of post-acquisition retained earnings (and other reserves)**	X
NCI at reporting date	X̲

5

Goodwill	$	$
Fair value of consideration transferred		28
Fair value of NCI at acquisition		5
Less net acquisition-date fair value of identifiable assets acquired and liabilities assumed:		
Ordinary share capital	10	
Retained earnings at acquisition	15	
Fair value adjustments at acquisition	5	
		(30)
Goodwill		3

Now try ...

Attempt the questions below from the **Practice Question Bank**

Number

Qs 90 – 93

The consolidated statement of profit or loss

This chapter introduces the basic procedures required to produce a consolidated statement of profit or loss.

We begin by looking at a basic consolidated statement of profit or loss, including the impact of a non-controlling interest. We then move on to look at the effects of intra-group trading and acquisitions of subsidiaries part way through the year.

There are plenty of questions and examples in this chapter – work through **all** of them carefully.

G   Preparing simple consolidated financial statements

1   Subsidiaries

(e)   Describe the components of and prepare a consolidated
      statement of profit or loss or extracts thereof, including: S

   (i)   Elimination of intra-group trading balances (excluding
         cash and goods in transit)

   (ii) Removal of unrealised profit arising on intra-group
         trading

   (iii) Acquisition of subsidiaries part way through the financial
         year

1   Introduction to the consolidated statement of profit or loss

The consolidated statement of profit or loss is prepared by combining the statements of profit or loss of each group company on a line by line basis.

EXAM FOCUS POINT

In the July to December 2014 ACCA examining team's report, the ACCA examining team provided the following comments which may help students to improve their performance:

Know the format for a consolidated statement of profit or loss and understand consolidation techniques. Some questions may require you to calculate key figures such as a profit figure when given a mark-up percentage, before you can calculate unrealised profit. Some of the common errors when preparing the consolidated statement of profit or loss include NOT:

- Adjusting the revenue figure and cost of sales figure for the intra-group transactions
- Adjusting the cost of sales for the goods remaining unsold at the year end
- Clearly showing the profit attributable to the parent company and the non-controlling interest
- Adjusting the subsidiary profit for unrealised profit
- Showing workings for the calculation of the non-controlling interest

How are consolidated financial statements prepared? IFRS 10 lays out the basic procedures and we will consider these in the rest of this chapter.

The consolidated statement of profit or loss summarises the revenue and expenses of the group as if it was a single entity. As with the consolidated statement of financial position, the source of the consolidated statement of profit or loss is the individual accounts of the separate companies in the group. The consolidation procedure is also the same: consolidate as if you owned everything, then show the extent to which you do not.

Consider the following example.

1.1 Example: consolidated statement of profit or loss

P Co acquired 75% of the ordinary shares of S Co on that company's incorporation in 20X3. The summarised statements of profit or loss of the two companies for the year ending 31 December 20X6 are set out below.

	P Co $	S Co $
Revenue	75,000	38,000
Cost of sales	30,000	20,000
Gross profit	45,000	18,000
Administrative expenses	14,000	8,000
Profit before taxation	31,000	10,000
Income taxes	10,000	2,000
Profit for the year	21,000	8,000
Note: Movement on retained earnings		
Retained earnings brought forward	87,000	17,000
Profit for the year	21,000	8,000
Retained earnings carried forward	108,000	25,000

Required

Prepare the consolidated statement of profit or loss and movement on retained earnings for the group.

Solution

P CO

CONSOLIDATED STATEMENT OF PROFIT OR LOSS FOR THE YEAR ENDED 31 DECEMBER 20X6

	$
Revenue (75 + 38)	113,000
Cost of sales (30 + 20)	50,000
Gross profit	63,000
Administrative expenses (14 + 8)	22,000
Profit before taxation	41,000
Income taxes (10 + 2)	12,000
Profit for the year	29,000
Profit attributable to:	
Owners of the parent (bal. fig.)	27,000
Non-controlling interest (25% × 8)	2,000
	29,000
Movement on retained earnings	
Group profit for year	27,000
Retained earnings brought forward (87 + (17 × 75%))	99,750
Retained earnings carried forward	126,750

Notice how the non-controlling interest (NCI) is dealt with.

(a)   Down to the line '**profit for the year**' the **whole** of S Co's results is included without reference to group share or NCI share. Profit for the year is then split between the group and the NCI.

(b)   The NCI's share ($17,000 × 25% = $4,250) of S Co's **retained earnings** brought forward is **excluded from group retained earnings**. This means that the carried forward figure of $126,750 is the figure which would appear in the statement of financial position for group retained earnings.

This last point may be clearer if we construct the working for group retained earnings.

Group retained earnings

	P Co $	S Co $
Per question	108,000	25,000
Pre-acquisition retained earnings		–
		25,000
Group share of post-acq'n ret'd earnings:		
S Co (75% × 25,000)	18,750	
Group retained earnings	126,750	

Notice that a consolidated statement of profit or loss **links up** with a consolidated statement of financial position exactly as in the case of an individual company's accounts. Now try the following question.

QUESTION

Consolidated statement of profit or loss

The following information relates to the Wheeler group for the year to 30 April 20X7.

	Wheeler Co $'000	Brookes Co $'000
Revenue	1,100	500
Cost of sales	630	300
Gross profit	470	200
Administrative expenses	105	150
Profit before tax	365	50
Income taxes	65	10
Profit for the year	300	40

Note.

Retained earnings brought forward	460	106
Retained earnings carried forward	760	146

Additional information

(a)   The issued share capital of the group was as follows.

Wheeler Co: 5,000,000 ordinary shares of $1 each
Brookes Co: 1,000,000 ordinary shares of $1 each

(b)   Wheeler Co purchased 80% of the issued share capital of Brookes Co in 20X0. At that time, the retained earnings of Brookes amounted to $56,000.

Required

Prepare the consolidated statement of profit or loss and the movement on retained earnings for the Wheeler group for the year to 30 April 20X7.

ANSWER

WHEELER GROUP
CONSOLIDATED STATEMENT OF PROFIT OR LOSS FOR THE YEAR TO 30 APRIL 20X7

	$'000
Revenue (1,100 + 500)	1,600
Cost of sales (630 + 300)	930
Gross profit	670
Administrative expenses (105 + 150)	255
Profit before taxation	415
Income taxes (65 + 10)	75
Profit for the year	340
Profit attributable to:	
Owners of the parent (bal fig)	332
NCI (20% × 40)	8
	340
Movement on retained earnings	
Group profit for year	332
Retained earnings brought forward (460 + 80% × (106 – 56*))	500
Retained earnings carried forward	832

* Retained earnings at acquisition

We will now look at the complications introduced by **intra-group trading** and **acquisitions part way through the year**.

2 Intra-group trading

Intra-group sales and purchases are eliminated from the consolidated statement of profit or loss.

EXAM FOCUS POINT

The treatment of intra-group trading is very likely to be tested in an exam question on the consolidated statement of profit or loss.

Like the consolidated statement of financial position, the consolidated statement of profit or loss should deal with the results of the group as those of a single entity. When one company in a group sells goods to another, an identical amount is added to the sales revenue of the first company and to the cost of sales of the second. Yet as far as the entity's dealings with outsiders are concerned, no sale has taken place.

The consolidated figures for sales revenue and cost of sales should represent **sales to**, and **purchases from, outsiders**. An adjustment is therefore necessary to reduce the sales revenue and cost of sales figures by the value of intra-group sales during the year.

We have also seen in the last chapter that any unrealised profits on intra-group trading should be excluded from the figure for group profits. This will occur whenever goods sold at a profit within the group remain in the inventory of the purchasing company at the year end. The best way to deal with this for the consolidated statement of profit or loss is to **calculate the unrealised profit on unsold inventories at the year end and reduce consolidated gross profit by this amount**. Cost of sales will be the balancing figure.

2.1 Example: intra-group trading

Suppose in our earlier example (Section 1.1) that S Co had recorded sales of $5,000 at a gross margin of 40% to P Co during 20X1. 50 per cent of the goods remained in P Co's inventories at 31 December 20X1. Prepare the revised consolidated statement of profit or loss.

Solution

The consolidated statement of profit or loss for the year ended 31 December 20X1 would now be as follows.

	$
Revenue (75 + 38 − 5*)	108,000
Cost of sales (30 + 20 − 5* + 1(W))	46,000
Gross profit (45 + 18 − 1(W))	62,000
Administrative expenses	22,000
Profit before taxation	40,000
Income taxes	12,000
Profit for the year	28,000
Profit attributable to:	
Owners of the parent (balancing figure)	26,250
NCI ((25% × 8,000) − 250(W))	1,750
	28,000
Movement on retained earnings	
Group profit for year	26,250
Retained earnings brought forward	99,750
Retained earnings carried forward	126,000

* to remove the intra-group sale

Working

Provision for unrealised profit

		$
Sale price	100%	5,000
Cost price	60%	(3,000)
Gross profit	40%	2,000
Unrealised profit (2,000 × 50%)		1,000
Unrealised profit attributable to NCI (1,000 × 25%)		250

As we saw in the last chapter, a provision will be made for the unrealised profit against the group inventories figure in the consolidated statement of financial position.

QUESTION

Intra-group trading I

Pumpkin has held 90% of the equity share capital of Squash for many years. Cost of sales for each entity for the year ended 31 December 20X3 was as follows.

	$
Pumpkin	100,000
Squash	80,000

During the year, Squash sold goods costing $5,000 to Pumpkin for $8,000. At the year end, all these goods remained in inventory.

(a) What figure should be shown as cost of sales in the consolidated statement of profit or loss of the Pumpkin group for the year ended 31 December 20X3?

	$
A	172,000
B	175,000
C	180,000
D	183,000

(b)   If Squash's profit for the year was $16,000, what is the profit attributable to the NCI?

ANSWER

(a)   B

	$
Pumpkin	100,000
Squash	80,000
	180,000
Less intra-group sales	(8,000)
Add unrealised profit	3,000
	175,000

(b)   Profit attributable to the NCI = (16,000 – 3,000 unrealised profit) × 10% = $1,300

QUESTION   Intra-group trading II

Percy has held 75% of the equity share capital of Mercy for many years.

Draft summarised statements of profit or loss for Percy and Mercy for the year ended 31 December 20X3 are below.

STATEMENTS OF PROFIT OR LOSS AT 31 DECEMBER 20X3

	Percy $	Mercy $
Revenue	500,000	300,000
Cost of sales	300,000	200,000
Gross profit	200,000	100,000
Administrative expenses	90,000	45,000
Profit before taxation	110,000	55,000
Income taxes	10,000	5,000
Profit for the year	100,000	50,000

During the year, Percy sold goods which cost $20,000 to Mercy at a margin of 20%. At the year end, all of these goods remained in inventory.

Required

Prepare the consolidated statement of profit or loss for the Percy group as at 31 December 20X3.

ANSWER

PERCY GROUP
CONSOLIDATED STATEMENT OF PROFIT OR LOSS AT 31 DECEMBER 20X3

	$
Revenue (500 + 300 – 25(W))	775,000
Cost of sales (300 + 200 – 25(W) + 5(W))	480,000
Gross profit (200 + 100 – 5(W))	295,000
Administrative expenses (90 + 45)	135,000
Profit before taxation	160,000
Income taxes (10 + 5)	15,000
Profit for the year	145,000
Profit attributable to:	
Owners of the parent (bal. fig.)	132,500
NCI (25% × 50)*	12,500
	145,000

Working

Intra-group sale

		$
Sale price	100%	25,000
Cost price	80%	(20,000)
Gross profit	20%	5,000

Unrealised profit	5,000

* Because the sale was made from the parent, Percy, to the subsidiary, Mercy, there is no unrealised profit attributable to the NCI.

3 Acquisitions part way through the year

If a subsidiary is acquired during the year, only the post-acquisition element of the statement of profit or loss balances is included on consolidation.

We have seen in the last chapter that retained earnings in the consolidated statement of financial position comprise:

(a)   The whole of the parent company's retained earnings
(b)   The **group's share of post-acquisition retained earnings** in the subsidiary

From the total retained earnings of the subsidiary we must therefore **exclude** both the **NCI's share** of total retained earnings and the **group's share of pre-acquisition** retained earnings.

A **similar procedure is necessary in the consolidated statement of profit or loss** if it is to link up with the consolidated statement of financial position.

As we have seen in the last chapter, if the subsidiary is **acquired part way through the accounting year**, it is necessary to split the profits earned between those earned pre-acquisition and those earned post-acquisition.

So we must first split the entire statement of profit or loss of the subsidiary between pre-acquisition and post-acquisition proportions. Only the post-acquisition figures are included in the consolidated statement of profit or loss. Try the following question.

EXAM FOCUS POINT

The December 2012 exam included a question on the consolidated statement of profit or loss where a subsidiary was acquired part way through the year. It was one of the three questions with the lowest pass rates on the paper, so make sure that you understand the answer to the following question.

QUESTION

P Co acquired 60% of the equity of S Co on 1 April 20X5. The statements of profit or loss of the two companies for the year ended 31 December 20X5 are set out below.

	P Co $	S Co $	S Co ($^9/_{12}$) $
Revenue	170,000	80,000	60,000
Cost of sales	65,000	36,000	27,000
Gross profit	105,000	44,000	33,000
Administrative expenses	43,000	12,000	9,000
Profit before tax	62,000	32,000	24,000
Income taxes	23,000	8,000	6,000
Profit for the year	39,000	24,000	18,000

Note.

Retained earnings brought forward	81,000	40,000
Retained earnings carried forward	108,000	58,000

Required

Prepare the consolidated statement of profit or loss and movements on retained earnings.

ANSWER

The shares in S Co were acquired three months into the year. Only the post-acquisition proportion (nine months' worth) of S Co's statement of profit or loss is included in the consolidated statement of profit or loss. This is shown above for convenience; in your exam, you will have to calculate the proportion to include.

P CO
CONSOLIDATED STATEMENT OF PROFIT OR LOSS FOR THE YEAR ENDED 31 DECEMBER 20X5

	$
Revenue (170 + 60)	230,000
Cost of sales (65 + 27)	92,000
Gross profit	138,000
Administrative expenses (43 + 9)	52,000
Profit before tax	86,000
Income taxes (23 + 6)	29,000
Profit for the year	57,000
Profit attributable to:	
Owners of the parent (bal. fig.)	49,800
NCI (40% × 18,000)	7,200
	57,000
Movement on retained earnings	
Group profit for year	49,800
Retained earnings brought forward*	81,000
Retained earnings carried forward	130,800

* All of S Co's retained earnings brought forward are pre-acquisition.

4 Summary: consolidated statement of profit or loss

The table below summarises the main points about the consolidated statement of profit or loss.

Purpose	To show the results of the group for an accounting period as if it were a single entity
Sales revenue to profit for year	100% P + 100% S (excluding adjustments for intra-group transactions)
Reason	To show the results of the group which were controlled by the parent company
Intra-group sales	Strip out intra-group activity from both sales revenue and cost of sales
Unrealised profit on intra-group sales	(a) Goods sold by P. Increase cost of sales by unrealised profit. (b) Goods sold by S. Increase cost of sales by full amount of unrealised profit and decrease NCI by their share of unrealised profit.
Non-controlling interests	S's profit after tax $\qquad\qquad\qquad\qquad$ X Less* unrealised profit $\qquad\qquad\qquad$ (X) $\qquad\qquad\qquad\qquad\qquad\qquad\qquad\qquad$ X NCI% $\qquad\qquad\qquad\qquad\qquad\qquad\qquad$ X * Only applicable if sales of goods made by subsidiary
Reason	To show the extent to which profits generated through P's control are in fact owned by other parties

QUICK QUIZ CHAPTER ROUNDUP

↳ The consolidated statement of profit or loss is prepared by combining the statements of profit or loss of each group company on a line by line basis.

↳ Intra-group sales and purchases are eliminated from the consolidated statement of profit or loss.

↳ If a subsidiary is acquired during the year, only the post-acquisition element of statement of profit or loss balances are included on consolidation.

1   Describe the preparation of a consolidated statement of profit or loss in its simplest form.

2   What adjustments are made to the consolidated statement of profit or loss in respect of intra-group trading?

The following information is relevant for questions 3 and 4

Hardy has a 90% subsidiary, Lawrence. During the year ended 31 December 20X2 Lawrence sold goods to Hardy for $25,000, which was at a mark-up of 25%. At 31 December 20X2 $10,000 of these goods remained unsold.

3   In the consolidated statement of profit or loss for the year ended 31 December 20X2, what will revenue be reduced by?

A $18,750   C $22,500
B $20,000   D $25,000

4   In the consolidated statement of profit or loss for the year ended 31 December 20X2, what will gross profit be reduced by?

A $1,800   C $2,250
B $2,000   D $2,500

5   Fill in the blank. Intra-group sales and purchases are .... from the consolidated statement of profit or loss.

ANSWERS TO QUICK QUIZ

1   The individual statements of profit or loss are totalled and certain adjustments made.

2   An adjustment is made to reduce the sales and cost of sales figures by the value of intra-group sales during the year. Thus the consolidated figures for sales and cost of sales should represent sales to and purchases from outsiders.

3   D   Revenue is reduced by the full amount of intra-group sales.

4   B   Gross profit is reduced by the element of unrealised profit which is $10,000 \times 25/125 = \$2,000$.

5   Intra-group sales and purchases are eliminated from the consolidated statement of profit or loss.

Now try ...

Attempt the questions below from the **Practice Question Bank**

Number

Qs 94 – 97

part

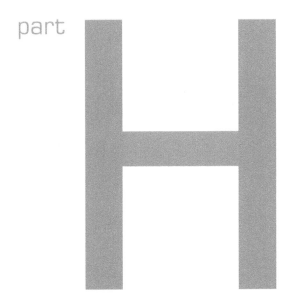

Interpretation of financial statements

Interpretation of financial statements

Interpretation of financial statements

If you were to look at a statement of financial position or statement of profit or loss, how would you decide whether the company was doing well or badly? Or whether it was financially strong or financially vulnerable? And what would you be looking at in the figures to help you to make your judgement?

The F3/FFA syllabus requires you to understand the importance and purpose of the interpretation and analysis of financial statements. It also requires you to be able to analyse financial statements, calculate key accounting ratios and draw conclusions about the information you are provided with.

Ratio analysis involves **comparing one figure against another** to produce a ratio, and assessing whether the ratio indicates a weakness or strength in the company's affairs, and is the main focus of this chapter.

H   Interpretation of financial statements

1   Importance and purpose of analysis of financial statements

(a)   Describe how the interpretation and analysis of financial   K
statements is used in a business environment.

(b)   Explain the purpose of interpretation of ratios.   K

2   Ratios

(a)   Calculate key accounting ratios: S

    (i)   Profitability
    (ii)   Liquidity
    (iii)   Efficiency
    (iv)   Position

(b)   Explain the interrelationships between ratios.   K

3   Analysis of financial statements

(a)   Calculate and interpret the relationship between the   S
elements of the financial statements with regard to
profitability, liquidity, efficient use of resources and financial
position.

(b)   Draw valid conclusions from the information contained within   S
the financial statements and present these to the
appropriate user of the financial statements.

1   Information required by users

Users of financial statements can gain a better understanding of the **significance** of the information in financial statements by comparing it with other relevant information.

The accounts of a business are designed to provide users with information about its performance and financial position. The bare figures, however, are not particularly useful and it is only through **comparisons** (usually in ratios) that their significance can be established. Comparisons may be made with previous financial periods, with other similar businesses or with averages for the particular industry. The choice will depend on the purpose for which the comparison is being made and the information that is available.

1.1 User groups

Various groups are interested in the performance and financial position of a company.

(a)   **Management** will use comparisons to ensure that the business is performing efficiently and according to plan.

(b)   **Employees**, trade unions and so on need information to be able to assess the employer's stability and profitability, and their ability to provide remuneration and other benefits.

(c)   **Governments** need to be able to assess taxation and regulate industries, as well as using information for statistical purposes.

(d)   Present and potential **investors** will assess the company with a view to judging whether it is a sound investment. They need information on risk and return on investment and the ability of the entity to pay dividends.

(e)   **Lenders** and **suppliers** will want to judge its creditworthiness, to assess whether loans and related interest and invoices will be paid when due.

(f)   **Customers** will want to judge whether the company will continue in existence, especially where they have a long-term involvement with the company or a dependence on their products.

This Text is concerned with financial rather than management accounting and the ratios discussed here are therefore likely to be calculated by external users. The following sources of information are readily available to external users.

- Published financial statements
- Documents filed as required by company legislation
- Statistics published by the Government
- Other published sources eg *Investor's Chronicle*, *The Economist, Wall Street Journal*

1.2 Financial analysis

The **lack of detailed information** available to the outsider is a considerable disadvantage in undertaking ratio analysis. The first difficulty is that there may simply be insufficient data to calculate all the required ratios. A second concerns the availability of a suitable average or standard with which the calculated ratios may be compared.

1.2.1 Trend analysis

Looking first at trend analysis (comparisons for the same business over time), some of the **problems** include the following.

- Changes in the nature of the business
- Unrealistic depreciation rates under historical cost accounting
- The changing value of the currency unit being reported
- Changes in accounting policies

Other factors will include changes in government incentive packages, changes from purchasing equipment to leasing and so on.

1.2.2 Comparisons across companies

When making comparisons with other companies, the position is even more difficult because of the problem of identifying companies that are comparable. **Comparability** between companies may be impaired due to the following reasons.

(a)   Different degrees of diversification

(b)   Different production and purchasing policies (if an investor was analysing the smaller car manufacturers, they would find that some of them buy in engines from one of the 'majors' while others develop and manufacture their own)

(c)   Different financing policies (eg leasing as opposed to buying)

(d)   Different accounting policies (one of the most serious problems particularly in relation to non-current assets and inventory valuation)

(e)   Different effects of government incentives

The major **intra-group comparison organisations** (whose results are intended for the use of participating companies and are not generally available) go to considerable length to adjust accounts to comparable bases. The external user will rarely be in a position to make such adjustments. Although the position is improved by increases in disclosure requirements, direct comparisons between companies will inevitably, on occasion, continue to give rise to misleading results.

1.3 Social and political considerations

Social considerations tend to be **short-lived** or 'fashionable' and therefore each set of statements can be affected by a different movement or fad. In recent years, the social aspect much in evidence has been

that of environmental issues. Companies have gone for a 'green' image, although this has been more in evidence in glossy pictures than in the accounts themselves.

Political considerations may be more far reaching. The regulatory regime may be instituted by statutes, but often self-regulation is encouraged through bodies such as the stock exchange.

1.4 Multinational companies

Multinational companies have great difficulties sometimes because of the need to comply with **legislation** in a large number of countries. As well as different reporting requirements, different rules of incorporation exist, as well as different directors' rules, tax legislation and so on. Sometimes the local rules can be so harsh that companies will avoid them altogether.

Different local reporting requirements will also make **consolidation** more difficult. The results of subsidiaries must be translated, not only to the company's base currency but also using the accounting rules used by head office. This is a requirement of IFRSs, as 'uniform accounting policies' are called for.

2 The broad categories of ratios

Ratios provide information through **comparison**.

Accounting ratios help to summarise and present financial information in a more understandable form. Broadly speaking, basic ratios can be grouped into five categories.

Broadly speaking, basic ratios can be grouped into five categories.

- Profitability and return
- Long-term solvency and stability
- Short-term solvency and liquidity
- Efficiency (turnover ratios)
- Shareholders' investment ratios

Shareholders' investment ratios are beyond the scope of the F3/FFA syllabus. Within the rest of this chapter, we will identify a number of **standard measures or ratios** that are normally calculated and generally accepted as meaningful indicators for the rest of these categories. Although these are standard measures, each individual business must be considered separately, because a ratio that is meaningful for a manufacturing company may be completely meaningless for a financial institution.

The key to obtaining meaningful information from ratio analysis is **comparison**. This may involve comparing ratios over time within the same business to establish whether things are improving or declining, and comparing ratios between similar businesses to see whether the company you are analysing is better or worse than average within its specific business sector.

It must be stressed that ratio analysis on its own is not sufficient for interpreting company accounts, and that there are **other items of information** which should be looked at, for example:

(a)   The content of any **accompanying commentary** on the accounts and other statements

(b)   The age and nature of the **company's assets**

(c)   **Current and future developments** in the company's markets, at home and overseas, recent acquisitions or disposals of a subsidiary by the company

(d)   Any other **noticeable features** of the financial statements, such as events after the reporting period, contingent liabilities and the company's taxation position

2.1 Example: calculating ratios

To illustrate the calculation of ratios, the following statement of financial position and statement of profit or loss figures will be used.

FURLONG CO STATEMENT OF PROFIT OR LOSS FOR THE YEAR ENDED 31 DECEMBER 20X8

	Notes	20X8 $	20X7 $
Revenue	1	3,095,576	1,909,051
Operating profit	1	359,501	244,229
Interest	2	17,371	19,127
Profit before tax		342,130	225,102
Income tax		74,200	31,272
Profit for the year		267,930	193,830

FURLONG CO STATEMENT OF FINANCIAL POSITION AS AT 31 DECEMBER 20X8

Bal Sheet

	Notes	20X8 $	20X8 $	20X7 $	20X7 $
Assets					
Non-current assets					
Tangible non-current assets			802,180		656,071
Current assets					
Inventories		64,422		86,550	
Receivables	3	1,002,701		853,441	
Cash at bank and in hand		1,327		68,363	
			1,068,450		1,008,354
Total assets			1,870,630		1,664,425
Equity and liabilities					
Equity					
Ordinary shares 10c each	5	210,000		210,000	
Share premium account		48,178		48,178	
Retained earnings		630,721		393,791	
			888,899		651,969
Non-current liabilities					
10% loan notes 20X4/20X9			100,000		100,000
Current liabilities	4		881,731		912,456
Total equity and liabilities			1,870,630		1,664,425

NOTES TO THE ACCOUNTS

		20X8 $	20X7 $
1	Sales revenue and profit		
	Sales revenue	3,095,576	1,909,051
	Cost of sales	2,402,609	1,441,950
	Gross profit	692,967	467,101
	Administration expenses	333,466	222,872
	Operating profit	359,501	244,229
	Depreciation charged	151,107	120,147
2	Interest		
	Payable on bank overdrafts and other loans	8,115	11,909
	Payable on loan notes	10,000	10,000
		18,115	21,909
	Receivable on short-term deposits	744	2,782
	Net payable	17,371	19,127
3	Receivables		
	Amounts falling due within one year		
	Trade receivables	884,559	760,252
	Prepayments and accrued income	97,022	45,729
		981,581	805,981
	Amounts falling due after more than one year		
	Trade receivables	21,120	47,460
	Total receivables	1,002,701	853,441

		20X8 $	20X7 $
4	*Current liabilities*		
	Trade payables	627,018	545,340
	Accruals and deferred income	81,279	280,464
	Income taxes	108,000	37,200
	Other taxes	65,434	49,452
		881,731	912,456
5	*Share capital*		
	Authorised ordinary shares of 10c each	1,000,000	1,000,000
	Issued and fully paid ordinary shares of 10c each	210,000	210,00

3 Profitability and return

Profitability ratios include:

- Return on capital employed
- Net profit as a percentage of sales
- Asset turnover ratio
- Gross profit as a percentage of sales

In our example, the company made a profit in both 20X8 and 20X7, and there was an increase in profit between one year and the next:

(a) Of 52% before taxation
(b) Of 39% after taxation

Profit before taxation is generally thought to be a better figure to use than profit after taxation, because there might be unusual variations in the tax charge from year to year which would not affect the underlying profitability of the company's operations.

Another profit figure that should be calculated is **PBIT**, **profit before interest and tax**. This is the amount of profit which the company earned before having to pay interest to the providers of loan capital. By providers of loan capital, we usually mean longer-term loan capital, such as loan notes and medium-term bank loans, which will be shown in the statement of financial position as non-current liabilities.

PBIT is therefore:

(a) The profit before taxation; **plus**
(b) Interest charges on long-term loans.

Published accounts do not always give sufficient detail on interest payable to determine how much is interest on long-term finance. We will assume in our example that the whole of the interest payable ($18,115, note 2) relates to long-term finance.

PBIT in our example is therefore:

	20X8 $	20X7 $
Profit before tax	342,130	225,102
Interest payable	18,115	21,909
PBIT	360,245	247,011

This shows a 46% growth between 20X7 and 20X8.

3.1 Return on capital employed (ROCE)

It is impossible to assess profits or profit growth properly without relating them to the **amount of funds (capital) that were employed in making the profits**. The most important profitability ratio is therefore **return on capital employed (ROCE)**, which states the profit as a percentage of the amount of capital employed. ROCE measures the overall **efficiency** of a company in employing the resources available to it.

FORMULA TO LEARN

ROCE $\quad = \quad \dfrac{\text{Profit before interest and taxation}}{\text{Capital employed}} \times 100\%$

Capital $\quad = \quad$ Shareholders' equity plus long-term liabilities
employed $\qquad\quad$ (**or** total assets less current liabilities)

The underlying principle is that we must **compare like with like**, and so if capital means share capital and reserves plus long-term liabilities and debt capital, profit must mean the profit earned by all this capital together. This is PBIT, since interest is the return for loan capital.

In our example, capital employed $\quad = \quad$ 20X8: $1,870,630 – $881,731 = $988,899

20X7: $1,664,425 – $912,456 = $751,969

These total figures are the total assets less current liabilities figures for 20X8 and 20X7 in the statement of financial position.

		20X8	20X7
ROCE	=	$\dfrac{\$360,245}{\$988,899}$	$\dfrac{\$247,011}{\$751,969}$
	=	36.4%	32.8%

What does a company's ROCE tell us? What should we be looking for? There are three comparisons that can be made.

(a) The **change in ROCE from one year to the next** can be examined. In this example, there has been an increase in ROCE by about 4% from its 20X7 level.

(b) The **ROCE being earned by other companies**, if this information is available, can be compared with the ROCE of this company. Here the information is not available.

(c) A comparison of the ROCE with **current market borrowing rates** may be made.

(i) What would be the cost of extra borrowing to the company if it needed more loans, and is it earning a ROCE that suggests it could make profits to make such borrowing worthwhile?

(ii) Is the company making a ROCE which suggests that it is getting value for money from its current borrowing?

(iii) Companies are in a risk business and commercial borrowing rates are a good independent benchmark against which company performance can be judged.

In this example, if we suppose that current market interest rates, say, for medium-term borrowing from banks, is around 10%, then the company's actual ROCE of 36% in 20X8 would not seem low. On the contrary, it might seem high.

However, it is easier to spot a low ROCE than a high one, because there is always a chance that the company's non-current assets, especially property, are **undervalued** in its statement of financial position, and so the capital employed figure might be unrealistically low. If the company had earned a ROCE not of 36% but of, say, only 6%, then its return would have been below current borrowing rates and so disappointingly low.

3.2 Return on equity (ROE)

Return on equity (ROE) gives a more restricted view of capital than ROCE, but it is based on the same principles.

FORMULA TO LEARN

ROE $= \dfrac{\text{Profit after tax and preference dividend}}{\text{Equity shareholders funds}}$

In our example, ROE is calculated as follows.

		20X8		20X7	
ROE =		$\dfrac{\$267{,}930}{\$888{,}899}$ = 30.1%		$\dfrac{\$193{,}830}{\$651{,}969}$ = 29.7%	

ROE is **not a widely used ratio**, however, because there are more useful ratios that give an indication of the return to shareholders, such as earnings per share, dividend per share, dividend yield and earnings yield, but these are beyond the scope of the F3/FFA syllabus.

3.3 Analysing profitability and return in more detail: the secondary ratios

We often sub-analyse ROCE, to find out more about why the ROCE is high or low, or better or worse than last year. There are two factors that contribute towards a return on capital employed, both related to sales revenue.

(a)   **Profit margin**. A company might make a high or low profit margin on its sales. For example, a company that makes a profit of 25c per $1 of sales is making a bigger return on its revenue than another company making a profit of only 10c per $1 of sales.

(b)   **Asset turnover**. Asset turnover is a measure of how well the assets of a business are being used to generate sales. For example, if two companies each have capital employed of $100,000 and Company A makes sales of $400,000 per annum whereas Company B makes sales of only $200,000 per annum, Company A is making a higher revenue from the same amount of assets (twice as much asset turnover as Company B) and this will help A to make a higher return on capital employed than B. Asset turnover is expressed as 'x times' so that assets generate x times their value in annual turnover. Here, Company A's asset turnover is four times and B's is two times.

Profit margin and asset turnover together explain the ROCE and if the ROCE is the primary profitability ratio, these other two are the secondary ratios. The relationship between the three ratios can be shown mathematically.

FORMULA TO LEARN

Profit margin × Asset turnover = ROCE

$$\therefore \quad \frac{\text{PBIT}}{\text{Sales}} \times \frac{\text{Sales}}{\text{Capital employed}} = \frac{\text{PBIT}}{\text{Capital employed}}$$

In our example:

		Profit margin		Asset turnover		ROCE
(a)	20X8	$\dfrac{\$360{,}245}{\$3{,}095{,}576}$	×	$\dfrac{\$3{,}095{,}576}{\$988{,}899}$	=	$\dfrac{\$360{,}245}{\$988{,}899}$
		11.64%	×	3.13 times	=	36.4%
(b)	20X7	$\dfrac{\$247{,}011}{\$1{,}909{,}051}$	×	$\dfrac{\$1{,}909{,}051}{\$751{,}969}$	=	$\dfrac{\$247{,}011}{\$751{,}969}$
		12.94%	×	2.54 times	=	32.8%

In this example, the company's improvement in ROCE between 20X7 and 20X8 is attributable to a higher asset turnover. Indeed, the profit margin has fallen a little, but the higher asset turnover has more than compensated for this.

It is also worth commenting on the change in sales revenue from one year to the next. You may already have noticed that Furlong achieved sales growth of over 60% from $1.9m to $3.1m between 20X7 and 20X8. This is very strong growth, and this is certainly one of the most significant items in the statement of profit or loss and statement of financial position.

3.4 A warning about comments on profit margin and asset turnover

It might be tempting to think that a high profit margin is good, and a low asset turnover means sluggish trading. In broad terms, this is so. But there is a trade-off between profit margin and asset turnover, and you cannot look at one without allowing for the other.

(a)   A **high profit margin** means a high profit per $1 of sales but, if this also means that sales prices are high, there is a strong possibility that sales turnover will be depressed, and so asset turnover lower.

(b)   A **high asset turnover** means that the company is generating a lot of sales, but to do this it might have to keep its prices down and so accept a low profit margin per $1 of sales.

Consider the following.

Company A		Company B	
Sales revenue	$1,000,000	Sales revenue	$4,000,000
Capital employed	$1,000,000	Capital employed	$1,000,000
PBIT	$200,000	PBIT	$200,000

These figures would give the following ratios.

$$\text{ROCE} = \frac{\$200,000}{\$1,000,000} = 20\% \qquad \text{ROCE} = \frac{\$200,000}{\$1,000,000} = 20\%$$

$$\text{Profit margin} = \frac{\$200,000}{\$1,000,000} = 20\% \qquad \text{Profit margin} = \frac{\$200,000}{\$4,000,000} = 5\%$$

$$\text{Asset turnover} = \frac{\$1,000,000}{\$1,000,000} = 1 \qquad \text{Asset turnover} = \frac{\$4,000,000}{\$1,000,000} = 4$$

The companies have the same ROCE, but it is arrived at in a very different fashion. Company A operates with a low asset turnover and a comparatively high profit margin whereas company B carries out much more business, but on a lower profit margin. Company A could be operating at the luxury end of the market, while company B is operating at the popular end of the market.

3.5 Gross profit margin, net profit margin and profit analysis

Depending on the format of the statement of profit or loss, you may be able to calculate the gross profit margin as well as the net profit margin. **Looking at the two together** can be quite informative.

For example, suppose that a company has the following summarised statements of profit or loss for two consecutive years.

	Year 1	Year 2
	$	$
Revenue	70,000	100,000
Cost of sales	42,000	55,000
Gross profit	28,000	45,000
Expenses	21,000	35,000
Profit for the year	7,000	10,000

Although the net profit margin is the same for both years at 10%, the gross profit margin is not.

$$\text{In year 1 it is:} \qquad \frac{\text{Gross profit}}{\text{Revenue}} = \frac{\$28,000}{\$70,000} = 40\%$$

$$\text{and in year 2 it is:} \qquad \frac{\text{Gross profit}}{\text{Revenue}} = \frac{\$45,000}{\$100,000} = 45\%$$

The improved gross profit margin has not led to an improvement in the net profit margin. This is because expenses as a percentage of sales have risen from 30% in year 1 to 35% in year 2.

4 Liquidity, gearing/leverage and working capital

Liquidity and working capital ratios include:

- Current ratio
- Quick ratio
- Receivables collection period
- Payables payment period
- Inventory turnover period

Debt and gearing/leverage ratios include:

- Debt ratios
- Gearing ratio/leverage
- Interest cover

handwritten: 341 CR, 342 QR
handwritten: Debt 376-7

4.1 Long-term solvency: debt and gearing ratios

Debt ratios are concerned with **how much the company owes in relation to its size**, whether it is getting into heavier debt or improving its situation, and whether its debt burden seems heavy or light.

(a) When a company is heavily in debt, banks and other potential lenders may be unwilling to advance further funds.

(b) When a company is earning only a modest profit before interest and tax, and has a heavy debt burden, there will be very little profit left over for shareholders after the interest charges have been paid. And so if interest rates were to go up (on bank overdrafts and so on) or the company were to borrow even more, it might soon be incurring interest charges in excess of PBIT. This might eventually lead to the liquidation of the company.

These are two big reasons why companies should keep their debt burden under control. There are three ratios that are particularly worth looking at: the debt ratio, gearing ratio and interest cover.

4.2 Debt ratio

The debt ratio is the ratio of a company's total debts to its total assets.

$$\text{Debt ratio} = \frac{\text{Total debts}}{\text{Total assets}}$$

(a) Assets consist of non-current assets at their statement of financial position value, plus current assets.

(b) Debts consist of all payables, whether they are due within one year or after more than one year.

You can ignore long-term provisions.

There is no absolute guide to the maximum safe debt ratio but, as a very general guide, you might regard 50% as a safe limit to debt. In practice, many companies operate successfully with a higher debt ratio than this, but 50% is nonetheless a helpful benchmark. In addition, if the debt ratio is over 50% and getting worse, the company's debt position will be worth looking at more carefully.

In the case of Furlong the debt ratio is as follows.

	20X8	20X7
$\frac{\text{Total debts}}{\text{Total assets}}=$	$\frac{\$(881,731+100,000)}{\$1,870,630}$	$\frac{\$(912,456+100,000)}{\$1,664,425}$
	= 52%	= 61%

In this case, the debt ratio is quite high, mainly because of the large amount of current liabilities. However, the debt ratio has fallen from 61% to 52% between 20X7 and 20X8, and so the company appears to be improving its debt position.

4.3 Gearing/leverage

Gearing or leverage is concerned with a company's **long-term capital structure**. We can think of a company as consisting of non-current assets and net current assets (ie working capital, which is current assets minus current liabilities). These assets must be financed by long-term capital of the company, which is either:

(a) Shareholders' equity
(b) Long-term debt

The **gearing ratio** can be calculated as follows.

FORMULA TO LEARN

$$\text{Gearing} = \frac{\text{Total long-term debt}}{\text{Shareholders' equity} + \text{total long-term debt}} \times 100\%$$

As with the debt ratio, there is **no absolute limit** to what a gearing ratio ought to be. A company with a gearing ratio of more than 50% is said to be highly geared, whereas low gearing means a gearing ratio of less than 50%. Many companies are highly geared, but if a highly geared company raises its level of gearing even more, it is likely to have problems borrowing in the future. However, it could lower its gearing by boosting its shareholders' capital, either with retained profits or by a new share issue.

Leverage is the term used to describe the converse of gearing, ie the proportion of total assets financed by equity, and which may be called the equity to assets ratio. It is calculated as follows.

FORMULA TO LEARN

$$\text{Leverage} = \frac{\text{Shareholders' equity}}{\text{Shareholders' equity plus total long - term debt}} \times 100\%$$

or

$$\frac{\text{Shareholders' equity}}{\text{Total assets less current liabilities}} \times 100\%$$

In the example of Furlong, we find that the company, although having a high debt ratio because of its current liabilities, has a low gearing ratio. Leverage is therefore high.

		20X8	20X7
Gearing ratio	=	$\dfrac{\$100,000}{\$988,899}$	$\dfrac{\$100,000}{\$751,969}$
		= 10%	= 13%
Leverage	=	$\dfrac{\$888,899}{\$988,899}$	$\dfrac{\$651,969}{\$751,969}$
		= 90%	= 87%

As you can see, leverage is the mirror image of gearing.

4.4 Interest cover

The interest cover ratio shows whether a company is earning enough PBIT to pay its interest costs comfortably, or whether its interest costs are high in relation to the size of its profits, so that a fall in PBIT would then have a significant effect on profits available for ordinary shareholders.

FORMULA TO LEARN

Interest cover = $\dfrac{\text{Profit before interest and tax}}{\text{Interest charges}}$

An interest cover of two times or less would be low, and it should really exceed three times before the company's interest costs are to be considered within acceptable limits.

Consider the three companies below.

	Company A $'000	Company B $'000	Company C $'000
PBIT	40	40	40
Interest	10	25	30
Profit before tax	30	15	10
Taxation	9	5	3
Profit after tax	21	10	7

The interest cover for these companies is as follows.

Interest cover =	$\dfrac{\text{PBIT}}{\text{Interest payable}}$	=	$\dfrac{\$40,000}{\$10,000}$	$\dfrac{\$40,000}{\$25,000}$	$\dfrac{\$40,000}{\$30,000}$
			4 times	1.6 times	1.33 times

Both B and C have a low interest cover, which is a warning to ordinary shareholders that their profits are highly vulnerable, in percentage terms, to even small changes in PBIT.

EXAM FOCUS POINT

The ACCA examining team has indicated that interpretation questions are generally well answered. However, there was a question on interest cover in a past exam that was poorly answered. The question gave an extract from the financial statements and students should have calculated PBIT from that information. Many students used the figure for profit before tax and after interest instead.

QUESTION

Interest cover

Returning to the example of Furlong above, what is the company's interest cover?

ANSWER

Interest payments should be taken gross, from the note to the accounts, and not net of interest receipts as shown in the statement of profit or loss.

	20X8	20X7
$\dfrac{\text{PBIT}}{\text{Interest payable}}$ =	$\dfrac{\$360,245}{\$18,115}$	$\dfrac{\$247,011}{\$21,909}$
	= 20 times	= 11 times

Furlong has more than sufficient interest cover. In view of the company's low gearing, this is not too surprising and so we finally obtain a picture of Furlong as a company that does not seem to have a debt problem, in spite of its high (although declining) debt ratio.

4.5 Short-term solvency and liquidity

Profitability is of course an important aspect of a company's performance and gearing or leverage is another. Neither, however, addresses directly the key issue of **liquidity**.

Liquidity is the amount of cash a company can put its hands on quickly to settle its debts (and possibly to meet other unforeseen demands for cash payments too).

U 164 044
1 Ian Rush

Liquid funds consist of:

(a)   Cash

(b)   Short-term investments for which there is a ready market

(c)   Fixed-term deposits with a bank or other financial institution, for example, a six month high-interest deposit with a bank

(d)   Trade receivables (because they will pay what they owe within a reasonably short period of time)

In summary, **liquid assets are current asset items that will or could soon be converted into cash, and cash itself**. Two common definitions of liquid assets are:

(a)   All current assets without exception
(b)   All current assets with the exception of inventories

A company can obtain liquid assets from sources other than sales, such as the issue of shares for cash, a new loan and the sale of non-current assets. But a company cannot rely on these at all times and, in general, obtaining liquid funds depends on making sales and profits. Even so, profits do not always lead to increases in liquidity. This is mainly because funds generated from trading may be immediately invested in non-current assets or paid out as dividends. You should refer back to the chapter on statements of cash flow to examine this issue.

The reason why a company needs liquid assets is so that it can meet its debts when they fall due. Payments are continually made for operating expenses and other costs, and so there is a **cash cycle** from trading activities of cash coming in from sales and cash going out for expenses.

4.6 The cash cycle

To help you to understand liquidity ratios, it is useful to begin with a brief explanation of the cash cycle. The cash cycle describes **the flow of cash out of a business and back into it again as a result of normal trading operations**.

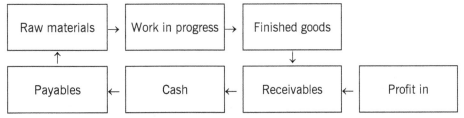

Cash goes out to pay for supplies, wages and salaries and other expenses, although payments can be delayed by taking some credit. A business might hold inventory for a while and then sell it. Cash will come back into the business from the sales, although customers might delay payment by themselves taking some credit.

The main points about the cash cycle are as follows.

(a)   The timing of cash flows in and out of a business does not coincide with the time when sales and costs of sales occur. **Cash flows out can be postponed by taking credit. Cash flows in can be delayed by having receivables.**

(b)   **The time between making a purchase and making a sale also affects cash flows**. If inventories are held for a long time, the delay between the cash payment for inventory and cash receipts from selling them will also be a long one.

(c)   **Holding inventories and having payables can therefore be seen as two reasons why cash receipts are delayed.** Another way of saying this is that if a company invests in working capital, its cash position will show a corresponding decrease.

(d)   Similarly, **taking credit from creditors can be seen as a reason why cash payments are delayed**. The company's liquidity position will worsen when it has to pay the suppliers, unless it can get more cash in from sales and receivables in the meantime.

The **liquidity ratios** and **working capital turnover ratios** are used to test a company's **liquidity, length of cash cycle** and **investment in working capital**.

4.7 Liquidity ratios: current ratio and quick ratio

The 'standard' test of liquidity is the **current ratio**. It can be obtained from the statement of financial position.

FORMULA TO LEARN

$$\text{Current ratio} = \frac{\text{Current assets}}{\text{Current liabilities}}$$

The idea behind this is that a company should have enough current assets that give a promise of 'cash to come' to meet its future commitments to pay off its current liabilities. A **current ratio in excess of 1 should be expected**. Otherwise, there would be the prospect that the company might be unable to pay its debts on time. In practice, a ratio comfortably in excess of 1 should be expected, but what is 'comfortable' varies between different types of businesses.

Companies are not able to convert all their current assets into cash very quickly. In particular, some manufacturing companies might hold large quantities of raw material stocks, which must be used in production to create finished goods inventory. These might be warehoused for a long time, or sold on lengthy credit. In such businesses, where inventory turnover is slow, most inventories are not very 'liquid' assets, because the cash cycle is so long. For these reasons, we calculate an additional liquidity ratio, known as the quick ratio or acid test ratio.

The **quick ratio**, or **acid test ratio**, is calculated as follows.

FORMULA TO LEARN

$$\text{Quick ratio} = \frac{\text{Current assets less inventory}}{\text{Current liabilities}}$$

The quick ratio should ideally be **at least 1** for companies with a slow inventory turnover. For companies with a fast inventory turnover, a quick ratio can be comfortably less than 1 without suggesting that the company should be in cash flow trouble.

Both the current ratio and the quick ratio offer an indication of the company's liquidity position, but the absolute figures **should not be interpreted too literally**. It is often theorised that an acceptable current ratio is 1.5 and an acceptable quick ratio is 0.8, but these should only be used as a guide. Different businesses operate in very different ways. A supermarket group, for example, might have a current ratio of 0.52 and a quick ratio of 0.17. Supermarkets have low receivables (people do not buy groceries on credit), low cash (good cash management), medium inventories (high inventories but quick turnover, particularly in view of perishability) and very high payables.

Compare this with a manufacturing and retail organisation, with a current ratio of 1.44 and a quick ratio of 1.03. Such businesses operate with liquidity ratios closer to the standard.

What is important is the **trend** of these ratios. From this, we can easily ascertain whether liquidity is improving or deteriorating. If a supermarket has traded for the last 10 years (very successfully) with current ratios of 0.52 and quick ratios of 0.17 then it should be supposed that the company can continue in business with those levels of liquidity. If in the following year the current ratio were to fall to 0.38 and the quick ratio to 0.09, then further investigation into the liquidity situation would be appropriate. It is the relative position that is far more important than the absolute figures.

Don't forget the other side of the coin either. A current ratio and a quick ratio can get **bigger than they need to be.** A company that has large volumes of inventories and receivables might be overinvesting in working capital, and so tying up more funds in the business than it needs to. This would suggest poor management of receivables (credit) or inventories by the company.

4.8 Efficiency ratios: control of receivables and inventories

A rough measure of the average length of time it takes for a company's customers to pay what they owe is the accounts receivable collection period.

FORMULA TO LEARN

The estimated average **receivables collection period** is calculated as:

$$\frac{\text{Trade receivables}}{\text{Credit sales}^*} \times 365 \text{ days}$$

* The revenue figure from the statement of profit or loss is often used instead of credit sales.

The estimate of the accounts receivable collection period is **only approximate**.

(a)   The value of receivables in the statement of financial position might be abnormally high or low compared with the 'normal' level the company usually has.

(b)   Revenue in the statement of profit or loss is exclusive of sales taxes, but receivables in the statement of financial position are inclusive of sales tax. We are not strictly comparing like with like.

Sales are usually made on 'normal credit terms' of payment within 30 days. A collection period significantly in excess of this might be representative of poor management of funds of a business. However, some companies must allow generous credit terms to win customers. Exporting companies in particular may have to carry large amounts of receivables, and so their average collection period might be well in excess of 30 days.

The **trend of the collection period over time** is probably the best guide. If the collection period is increasing year on year, this is indicative of a poorly managed credit control function (and potentially, therefore, a poorly managed company).

4.9 Receivables collection period: examples

Using the same types of company as examples, the collection period for each of the companies was as follows.

Company	Trade receivables revenue		Collection period (× 365)	Previous year		Collection period (× 365)
Supermarket	$\frac{\$5,016K}{\$284,986K}$	=	6.4 days	$\frac{\$3,977K}{\$290,668K}$	=	5.0 days
Manufacturer	$\frac{\$458.3m}{\$2,059.5m}$	=	81.2 days	$\frac{\$272.4m}{\$1,274.2m}$	=	78.0 days
Sugar refiner and seller	$\frac{\$304.4m}{\$3,817.3m}$	=	29.3 days	$\frac{\$287.0m}{\$3,366.3m}$	=	31.1 days

The differences in collection period reflect the differences between the types of business. Supermarkets have hardly any trade receivables at all, whereas the manufacturing companies have far more. The collection periods are fairly constant from the previous year for all three companies.

4.10 Inventory turnover period

Another ratio worth calculating is the inventory turnover period. This is another estimated figure, obtainable from published accounts, which indicates the average number of days that items of inventory are held for. As with the average receivable collection period, however, it is only an approximate estimated figure, but one which should be reliable enough for comparing changes year on year.

FORMULA TO LEARN

The **inventory turnover period** is calculated as:

$$\frac{\text{Inventory}}{\text{Cost of sales}} \times 365$$

This is another measure of how vigorously a business is trading. A lengthening inventory turnover period from one year to the next indicates one of two things.

(a)   A slowdown in trading

(b)   A build-up in inventory levels, perhaps suggesting that the investment in inventories is becoming excessive

Generally the **higher the inventory turnover is the better**, but several aspects of inventory-holding policy have to be balanced.

(a)   Lead times
(b)   Seasonal fluctuations in orders
(c)   Alternative uses of warehouse space
(d)   Bulk buying discounts
(e)   Likelihood of inventory perishing or becoming obsolete

Presumably if we add together the inventory turnover period and receivables collection period, this should give us an indication of how soon inventory is converted into cash. Both receivables collection period and inventory turnover period therefore give us a further indication of the company's liquidity.

4.11 Examples: inventory turnover period

The estimated inventory turnover periods for a supermarket are as follows.

Company	$\dfrac{\text{Inventory}}{\text{Cost of sales}}$	Inventory turnover period (days × 365)	Previous year
Supermarket	$\dfrac{\$15,554K}{\$254,571K}$	22.3 days	$\dfrac{\$14,094K}{\$261,368K} \times 365 = 19.7$ days

QUESTION

Liquidity ratios

Which of the following should the quick ratio include?

A   Inventory of finished goods
B   Raw materials and consumables
C   Long-term loans
D   Trade receivables

ANSWER

D   Quick ratio $= \dfrac{\text{Current assests} - \text{Inventory}}{\text{Current liabilities}}$

QUESTION

Calculate liquidity and working capital ratios from the accounts of the TEB Co, a business which provides service support (cleaning etc) for customers worldwide. Comment on the results of your calculations.

	20X7 $m	20X6 $m
Revenue	2,176.2	2,344.8
Cost of sales	1,659.0	1,731.5
Gross profit	517.2	613.3
Current assets		
Inventories	42.7	78.0
Receivables (Note 1)	378.9	431.4
Short-term deposits and cash	205.2	145.0
	626.8	654.4
Current liabilities		
Loans and overdrafts	32.4	81.1
Tax on profits	67.8	76.7
Dividend	11.7	17.2
Payables (Note 2)	487.2	467.2
	599.1	642.2
Net current assets	27.7	12.2

Notes

1	Trade receivables	295.2	335.5
2	Trade payables	190.8	188.1

ANSWER

	20X7		20X6	
Current ratio	$\dfrac{626.8}{599.1}$	= 1.05	$\dfrac{654.4}{642.2}$	= 1.02
Quick ratio	$\dfrac{584.1}{599.1}$	= 0.97	$\dfrac{576.4}{642.2}$	= 0.90
Accounts receivable collection period	$\dfrac{295.2}{2,176.2}$	× 365 = 49.5 days	$\dfrac{335.5}{2,344.8}$	× 365 = 52.2 days
Inventory turnover period	$\dfrac{42.7}{1,659.0}$	× 365 = 9.4 days	$\dfrac{78.0}{1,731.5}$	× 365 = 16.4 days
Accounts payable payment period	$\dfrac{190.8}{1,659.0}$	× 365 = 42.0 days	$\dfrac{188.1}{1,731.5}$	× 365 = 40.0 days

The company's current ratio is a little lower than average but its quick ratio is better than average and very little less than the current ratio. This suggests that inventory levels are strictly controlled, which is reinforced by the low inventory turnover period. It would seem that working capital is tightly managed, to avoid the poor liquidity which could be caused by a long receivables collection and comparatively high payables.

The company in the activity is a **service company** and therefore it would be expected to have very low inventory and a very short inventory turnover period. The similarity of receivables collection period and payables payment period means that the company is passing most of the delay in receiving payment on to its suppliers.

4.12 Payables payment period

FORMULA TO LEARN

Accounts payable payment period is ideally calculated by the formula:

$$\frac{\text{Trade accounts payable}}{\text{Purchases}} \times 365$$

It is rare to find purchases disclosed in published accounts and so **cost of sales serves as an approximation**. The payment period often helps to assess a company's liquidity. An increase is often a sign of lack of long-term finance or poor management of current assets, resulting in the use of extended credit from suppliers, increased bank overdraft and so on.

QUESTION

Operating cycle

(a)   Calculate the operating cycle for Moribund for 20X2 on the basis of the following information.

		$
Inventory:	raw materials	150,000
	work in progress	60,000
	finished goods	200,000
Purchases		500,000
Trade accounts receivable		230,000
Trade accounts payable		120,000
Sales		900,000
Cost of goods sold		750,000

Tip. You will need to calculate inventory turnover periods (total year-end inventory over cost of goods sold), receivables as daily sales, and payables in relation to purchases, all converted into 'days'.

(b)   List the steps which might be taken in order to improve the operating cycle.

ANSWER

(a)   The operating cycle can be found as follows.

Inventory turnover period: $\dfrac{\text{Total closing inventory} \times 365}{\text{Cost of goods sold}}$

plus

Accounts receivable collection period: $\dfrac{\text{Closing trade receivables} \times 365}{\text{Sales}}$

less

Accounts payable payment period: $\dfrac{\text{Closing trade payables} \times 365}{\text{Purchases}}$

	20X2
Total closing inventory ($)	410,000
Cost of goods sold ($)	750,000
Inventory turnover period	199.5 days
Closing receivables ($)	230,000
Sales ($)	900,000
Receivables collection period	93.3 days
Closing payables ($)	120,000
Purchases ($)	500,000
Payables payment period	(87.6 days)
Length of operating cycle (199.5 + 93.3 – 87.6)	205.2 days

(b)   The steps that could be taken to reduce the operating cycle include the following.

(i)   **Reducing the average raw material inventory turnover**

(ii)   **Reducing the time taken to produce goods**. However, the company must ensure that quality is not sacrificed as a result of speeding up the production process.

(iii)   **Increasing the period of credit taken from suppliers**. The credit period seems very long – the company is allowed three months' credit by its suppliers, and probably could not be increased. If the credit period is extended then the company may lose discounts for prompt payment.

(iv)   **Reducing the average finished goods inventory turnover**.

(v)   **Reducing the average receivables collection period**. The administrative costs of speeding up debt collection and the effect on sales of reducing the credit period allowed must be evaluated. However, the credit period does seem very long by the standards of most industries. It may be that generous terms have been allowed to secure large contracts and little will be able to be done about this in the short term.

5 Interpreting information

You **must** be able to interpret financial data as well as calculate ratios.

Examination questions may try to simulate a real-life situation. An extract from a set of accounts could be presented and you may be asked to calculate a specified ratio or you could be presented with certain ratios and asked to interpret them. The question may ask you to select a reason for a particular fluctuation or trend, or suggest a remedial action.

Try the following interpretation questions.

QUESTION

Interpreting information I

The following information for Hadrian is available.

	$'000
PBIT	370
Interest	6
Tax	80
Profit after tax	284
Share capital	2,000
Reserves	314
	2,314
Loan liability	100
	2,414
Industry average return on capital employed	10%

Hadrian purchased new non-current assets during the year.

Required

Calculate and comment on ROCE for Hadrian.

ANSWER

$$ROCE = \frac{PBIT}{Capital\ employed} \times 100\% = \frac{370}{2,414} \times 100\% = 15\%$$

ROCE, at 15% is better than the industry average of 10%. There could be a number of reasons for this. It may be that the company is exceptionally profitable, or it may be that its assets are undervalued. The first explanation is more likely, since new assets have been purchased, by definition at market value.

QUESTION

The statements of profit or loss for Egriff are given below.

	31 May 20X3		31 May 20X4	
	$'000	$'000	$'000	$'000
Revenue		20,000		26,000
Cost of sales		(15,400)		(21,050)
Gross profit		4,600		4,950
Expenses				
Administrative	800		900	
Selling and distribution	1,550		1,565	
Depreciation	110		200	
Loan note interest	–		105	
		(2,460)		(2,770)
Profit for the year		2,140		2,180

Egriff issued loan notes during the year to fund the expansion of the business. Non-current assets have increased from $3.8m in 20X3 to $4.6m in 20X4.

Required

(a) Calculate the following ratios for Egriff for both years.

(i) Gross profit percentage
(ii) Net profit percentage

(b) Comment on the success of the business expansion using the ratios you have calculated.

ANSWER

(a)

(i) Gross profit percentage $\dfrac{\text{Gross profit}}{\text{Sales}} \times 100$

20X3	20X4

$\dfrac{4,600}{20,000} \times 100 =$ 23.00% $\dfrac{4,950}{26,000} \times 100 =$ 19.04%

(ii) Net profit percentage $\dfrac{\text{Net profit}}{\text{Sales revenue}} \times 100$

20X3	20X4

$\dfrac{2,140}{20,000} \times 100 =$ 10.70% $\dfrac{2,180}{26,000} \times 100 =$ 8.38%

(b) The information given shows an expansion of the business in absolute terms; for example, revenue and non-current assets have increased. However, the profitability ratios have deteriorated. Both gross profit percentage and net profit percentage have gone down.

The deterioration in the gross profit percentage may have arisen because margins are being squeezed in order to boost revenue, which has indeed increased. Costs have also increased.

The decrease in net profit percentage arises partly because the gross profit percentage has decreased, but the main component of this is an increase in depreciation, as a result of the investment in non-current assets.

QUESTION

Which two of the following are valid reasons why the inventory turnover period of a company increases from one year to the next?

1 A slowdown in trading
2 A marketing decision to reduce selling prices
3 Seasonal fluctuations in orders
4 Obsolete goods

A 1 and 2
B 2 and 3
C 1 and 4
D 3 and 4

ANSWER

C A slowdown in trade increases the inventory turnover period. Assuming that inventory is still being ordered at the same rate, this can lead to a build up in inventory. Inventory levels also increase where there is no longer a demand for the product, for example due to obsolescence. Seasonal fluctuations in orders will affect the amount of inventory held at any one time, but they will not affect inventory turnover period year on year. A decision to reduce sales price would not directly affect either purchase price or level of inventory. If anything, it would be likely to reduce inventory holding period as the company moves to a low margin, fast turnover approach.

QUESTION

Information on Alpha for the previous two years is given below.

		20X1	20X2
Debt ratio =	$\dfrac{\text{Long-term debt}}{\text{Shareholders' equity}}$	45%	55%
Interest cover		4 times	2 times

Which of the following statements regarding Alpha is/are correct?

1 In 20X2, Alpha's profits more comfortably cover its interest payments compared to 20X1.
2 The debt position of Alpha has worsened since 20X1.
3 A rights issue of shares could help to reduce the debt ratio.

A 1 only
B 2 only
C 2 and 3 only
D 1 and 2 only

ANSWER

C The debt ratio has increased, which means that the proportion of debt to equity has increased and so Alpha's debt position has worsened. A rights issue of shares could help to reduce the debt ratio by raising additional equity. Interest cover is a measure of how many times PBIT covers the interest the business must pay. Because the interest cover has fallen, Alpha's profits less comfortably cover its interest payments in 20X2 compared to 20X1.

QUESTION

'The ratio has increased in 20X8 compared to 20X7 because we have increased the length of time allowed for customers to pay their invoices.'

A decrease in which ratio could be explained by the statement above?

A   The receivables collection period
B   The gearing ratio
C   Interest cover
D   The payables payment period

ANSWER

A   The receivables collection period measures the time taken for customers to pay their debts. If a company allows customers to take longer to pay their debts, then the receivables collection period will increase. The other ratios are unlikely to be affected by this change.

QUESTION

Information on Beta for the previous two years is given below.

	20X1	20X2
Quick ratio	1.5:1	1.5:1
Current ratio	1.8:1	3:1
Inventory turnover	15 days	27 days

Which of the following statements regarding Beta is/are correct?

1   Beta appears to have fewer inventories in 20X2 than in 20X1.
2   The debt position of Beta is worsening.
3   Stock obsolescence could be a problem for Beta.

A   1 only
B   1 and 3 only
C   3 only
D   2 and 3 only

ANSWER

C   The current ratio measures the ratio of current assets to current liabilities, whereas the quick ratio measures current assets less inventories compared to current liabilities. Because the quick ratio has stayed the same, the increase in the current ratio must have been caused by an **increase**, rather than a decrease, in the amount of inventories held. The significant increase in the inventory turnover period suggests that stock obsolescence could be an issue for Beta. This could also be the reason why the current ratio has increased. The information given does not allow any insight into the debt position of Beta.

QUESTION

ROCE has increased from 28% in 20X2 to 35% in 20X3.

Which of the following statements relating to this increase is/are correct?

1   An increase in profit margin in 20X3 could account for the increase in ROCE.

2   The increase suggests the company is more efficient in employing its resources in 20X3 compared to 20X2.

3   If profit margin has remained constant, the increase in ROCE suggests a decrease in asset turnover.

A   1 and 2 only
B   2 and 3 only
C   1 and 3 only
D   All three statements are correct

ANSWER

A   Remember that:

Profit margin × Asset turnover = ROCE

$$\therefore \quad \frac{PBIT}{Sales} \times \frac{Sales}{Capital\ employed} = \frac{PBIT}{Capital\ employed}$$

Therefore 1 is correct and 3 must be incorrect. ROCE measures how efficiently a company is employing its resources, therefore an increase in ROCE suggests that the efficiency of the company is improving.

6 Limitations of ratio analysis

Ratio analysis has limitations.

Ratio analysis is not foolproof. There are many problems in trying to identify trends and make comparisons. Below are just a few.

- **Information problems**

    – The base information is often out of date, so timeliness of information leads to problems of interpretation

    – Historical cost information may not be the most appropriate information for the decision for which the analysis is being undertaken

    – Information in published accounts is generally summarised information and detailed information may be needed

    – Analysis of accounting information only identifies symptoms, not causes, and is therefore of limited use

- **Comparison problems: trend analysis**

    – Effects of price changes make comparisons difficult unless adjustments are made

    – Impacts of changes in technology on the price of assets, the likely return and the future markets

    – Impacts of a changing environment on the results reflected in the accounting information

    – Potential effects of changes in accounting policies on the reported results

    – Problems associated with establishing a normal base year to compare other years with

- **Comparison problems: across companies**

    – Selection of industry norms and the usefulness of norms based on averages

    – Different firms having different financial and business risk profiles and the impact on analysis

    – Different firms using different accounting policies

    – Impacts of the size of the business and its comparators on risk, structure and returns

    – Impacts of different environments on results, eg different countries or home-based versus multinational firms

One of the PER objectives is PO8: Analyse and interpret financial reports. You can apply the knowledge you obtain from this chapter to help to achieve this objective.

CHAPTER ROUNDUP

- Users of financial statements can gain a better understanding of the **significance** of the information in financial statements by comparing it with other relevant information.

- Ratios provide information through **comparison**.

- **Profitability ratios** include:
    - Return on capital employed
    - Net profit as a percentage of sales
    - Asset turnover ratio
    - Gross profit as a percentage of sales

- **Liquidity and working capital ratios** include:
    - Current ratio
    - Quick ratio
    - Receivables collection period
    - Payables payment period
    - Inventory turnover period

- **Debt and gearing/leverage ratios** include:
    - Debt ratios
    - Gearing ratio/leverage
    - Interest cover

- You **must** be able to interpret financial data as well as calculate ratios.

- Ratio analysis has limitations.

QUICK QUIZ

1   Apart from ratio analysis, what other information might be helpful in interpreting a company's accounts?

2   What is the usual formula for ROCE?

3   ROCE can be calculated as the product of two other ratios. What are they?

4   Define the 'debt ratio'.

5   What is the relationship between 'gearing' and 'leverage'?

6   What are the formulae for:

    (a)   The current ratio?
    (b)   The quick ratio?
    (c)   The accounts receivable collection period?
    (d)   The inventory turnover period?

ANSWERS TO QUICK QUIZ

1   (a)   Commentary accompanying financial statements

    (b)   Age and nature of company's assets

    (c)   Future developments affecting the company

    (d)   Events after the reporting period, contingencies and other items disclosed in notes to the financial statements

2   $$\frac{\text{Profit before interest and tax}}{\text{Capital employed}}$$

3   $$\frac{\text{PBIT}}{\text{Sales}} \times \frac{\text{Sales}}{\text{Capital employed}}$$

4   Ratio of company's total debts to its total assets

5   $$\text{Gearing} = \frac{\text{Loan capital}}{\text{Total capital}}$$

    $$\text{Leverage} = \frac{\text{Equity capital}}{\text{Total capital}}$$

6   (a)   Current assets/current liabilities
    (b)   Current assets minus inventories/current liabilities
    (c)   Trade receivables/credit sales × 365
    (d)   Inventory/cost of sales × 365

Now try ...

Attempt the questions below from the **Practice Question Bank**

Number

Qs 98 – 100

Practice question and answer bank

1   **Which of the following are true of sole traders?**

1   A sole trader's financial statements are private; a company's financial statements are sent to shareholders and may be publicly filed

2   Only companies, and not sole traders, have capital invested into the business

3   A sole trader is fully and personally liable for any losses that the business might make; a company's shareholders are not personally liable for any losses that the company might make

A   1 and 2 only
B   2 and 3 only
C   1 and 3 only
D   1, 2 and 3

(2 marks)

2   **Who is responsible for the preparation of the financial statements of a company?**

1   The finance department
2   The board of directors
3   The external auditors

A   1 only
B   1 and 2 only
C   2 only
D   1, 2 and 3

(2 marks)

3   **Which TWO of the following are advantages of trading as a partnership?**

1   Additional capital can be raised because more people are investing in the business
2   A partnership has a separate legal identity from the individual partners
3   Partners have limited liability and are not personally liable for the debts of the partnership
4   A partnership is not required to make its financial accounts publicly available

A   1 and 2
B   1 and 4
C   2 and 4
D   2 and 3

(2 marks)

4   **Which TWO of the following are disadvantages of trading as a limited liability company?**

1   The shareholders of the company have limited liability for the debts of the company
2   A company must publish annual financial statements
3   Raising finance is easier as a company, as more shares can be issued
4   The financial statements of larger limited liability companies must be audited

A   1 and 2
B   1 and 4
C   2 and 3
D   2 and 4

(2 marks)

5   **What should be the main aim for a director of a company?**

A   To manage the affairs of the company in order to earn a good bonus

B   To manage the affairs of the company in order to create wealth for the shareholders

C   To manage the affairs of the company in order to generate the largest profits in the shortest time

D   To manage the affairs of the company in order to contribute to the general wellbeing of society

(2 marks)

6   **What is the role of the IFRS Interpretations Committee?**

A   To develop and issue a set of globally accepted International Financial Reporting Standards

B   To clarify issues in the application of IFRSs where unsatisfactory or conflicting interpretations have developed

C   To take account of the financial reporting needs of small and medium-sized entities

D   To provide a forum for the IASB to consult with the national accounting standard setters, academics and other interested parties

(2 marks)

7   **Which of the following is responsible for developing and issuing International Financial Reporting Standards (IFRSs)?**

A   IFRS Foundation
B   IFRS Interpretations Committee
C   International Accounting Standards Board (IASB)
D   IFRS Advisory Council

(2 marks)

8   The IASB's *Conceptual framework for financial reporting* gives four enhancing qualitative characteristics.

Which of the following are examples of those qualitative characteristics?

A   Faithful representation, neutrality and business entity concept
B   Verifiability, comparability and true and fair view
C   Comparability, timeliness and understandability
D   Relevance, accruals and going concern

(2 marks)

9   **Which of the following statements is/are correct?**

1   Materiality means that only items having a physical existence may be recognised as assets

2   The substance over form convention means that the legal form of a transaction must always be shown in financial statements even if this differs from the commercial effect

3   The accruals basis means that sales are recognised in the accounts as they occur and not when the cash is received

A   2 only
B   1, 2 and 3
C   1 only
D   3 only

(2 marks)

10   **Which TWO of the following are important fundamental assumptions for financial statements according to the IASB's *Conceptual framework for financial reporting*?**

1   Relevance
2   Going concern
3   Faithful representation
4   Accruals

A   1 and 2 only
B   2 and 3 only
C   3 and 4 only
D   1 and 3 only

(2 marks)

11   **Which of the following explains the imprest system of operating petty cash?**

A   Weekly expenditure cannot exceed a set amount
B   The exact amount of expenditure is reimbursed at intervals to maintain a fixed float
C   All expenditure out of the petty cash must be properly authorised
D   Regular equal amounts of cash are transferred into petty cash at intervals

(2 marks)

12   Petty cash is controlled under an imprest system. The imprest amount is $100. During a period, payments totalling $53 have been made.

How much needs to be reimbursed at the end of the period to restore petty cash to the imprest account?

A $100
B $53
C $47
D $50

(2 marks)

13   **Which of the following documents should accompany a payment made to a supplier?**

A   Supplier statement
B   Remittance advice
C   Purchase invoice
D   Purchase order

(2 marks)

14   **Which of the following are books of prime entry?**

1   Sales day book
2   Cash book
3   Supplier statements
4   Petty cash voucher

A   1 and 2 only
B   1, 2 and 4 only
C   1 only
D   All of them

(2 marks)

15   **In which book of prime entry will a business record credit notes received in respect of goods which the business has sent back to its suppliers?**

A   The sales returns day book
B   The cash book
C   The purchase returns day book
D   The purchase day book

(2 marks)

16   **The business entity concept requires that a business is treated as being separate from its owners.**

Is this statement true or false?

A   True
B   False

(1 mark)

17 A business sells $100 worth of goods to a customer, the customer pays $50 in cash immediately and will pay the remaining $50 in 30 days' time.

What is the double entry to record the sale?

A   Debit cash $50, credit receivables $50, credit sales $50
B   Debit receivables $50, debit cash $50, credit sales $100
C   Debit sales $100, credit receivables $50, credit cash $50
D   Debit sales $100, credit cash $100

(2 marks)

18 Chalk purchases $500 worth of cheese from Cheddar Co. Chalk agrees to pay Cheddar Co in 30 days' time. **What is the double entry to record the purchase in Cheddar Co's books?**

A   Debit sales $500, credit receivables $500
B   Debit purchases $500, credit payables $500
C   Debit receivables $500, credit sales $500
D   Debit payables $500, credit purchases $500

(2 marks)

19 **Which TWO of the following are credit entries?**

1   An increase in a liability
2   A decrease in a liability
3   An increase in income
4   A decrease in income

A   1 and 3
B   1 and 4
C   2 and 3
D   2 and 4

(2 marks)

20 **If the total debits exceed the total credits in a T-account, does the account have a debit or a credit balance?**

A   Credit balance
B   Debit balance

(1 mark)

21 **Does a debit balance brought down in the Cash T-account represent an asset or a liability?**

A   An asset
B   A liability

(1 mark)

22 A company's motor vehicles at cost account at 30 June 20X6 is as follows.

MOTOR VEHICLES – COST

	$		$
Balance b/d	35,800	Disposal	12,000
Additions	12,950	Balance c/d	36,750
	48,750		48,750

What opening balance should be included in the following period's trial balance for motor vehicles – cost at 1 July 20X6?

A $36,750 DR
B $48,750 DR
C $36,750 CR
D $48,750 CR

(2 marks)

23   A company's trade payables account at 30 September 20X1 is as follows.

TRADE PAYABLES ACCOUNT

	$		$
Cash at bank	21,600	Balance b/d	14,000
Balance c/d	11,900	Purchases	19,500
	33,500		33,500

What opening balance should be included in the following period's trial balance for payables at 1 October 20X1?

A $33,500 DR
B $11,900 DR
C $11,900 CR
D $33,500 CR

(2 marks)

24   An accountant has inserted all the relevant figures into the trade receivables account, but has not yet balanced off the account.

TRADE RECEIVABLES ACCOUNT

	$		$
Balance b/d	100,750	Cash at bank	250,225
Sales	325,010		

Assuming there are no other entries to be made, other than to balance off the account, what is the closing balance on the trade receivables account?

A $425,760 DR
B $175,535 DR
C $425,760 CR
D $175,535 CR

(2 marks)

25   Sales tax should be included in the statement of profit or loss of a registered trader.

Is this statement true or false?

A   True
B   False

(1 mark)

26   **Which of the following statements about sales tax is/are true?**

1   Sales tax charged on purchases is an expense to a business if the business is not sales tax registered.

2   Sales tax is charged by all businesses when they sell products.

A   1 only
B   2 only
C   Both 1 and 2
D   Neither 1 or 2

(2 marks)

27   A sales tax registered business in its first period of trading charges $8,000 of sales tax on its
     sales and suffers $6,750 of sales tax on its purchases which includes $1,250 irrecoverable sales
     tax on business entertaining.

     **How much sales tax is due to or receivable from the tax authorities at the end of the first
     period of trading?**

     A $2,500 due to the tax authorities
     B $2,500 receivable from the tax authorities
     C $1250 due to the tax authorities
     D   Nil due to or receivable from the tax authorities

                                                                                             (2 marks)

28   Michael, a sales tax registered trader, sells goods on credit to Darren for $880 plus sales tax.
     Darren is not registered for sales tax. Sales tax is charged at 20%.

     What are the entries in Michael's accounts for this sale?

	Sales account	*Sales tax account*	*Receivables account*
A	DR 880	nil	CR 880
B	DR 880	DR 176	CR 1,056
C	CR 880	nil	DR 880
D	CR 880	CR 176	DR 1,056

                                                                                             (2 marks)

29   **According to IAS 2 *Inventories*, which of the following costs should be included in valuing the
     inventories of a manufacturing company?**

     1   Carriage inwards
     2   Carriage outwards
     3   Depreciation of factory plant
     4   Storage costs of finished goods

     A   All four items
     B   1, 2 and 4 only
     C   2 and 3 only
     D   1 and 3 only

                                                                                             (2 marks)

30   A company values its inventory using the first in, first out (FIFO) method. At 1 January 20X5 the
     company had 800 widgets in inventory, valued at $75 each.

     During the year ended 31 December 20X5 the following transactions took place.

20X5			
1 February	Purchased	500 widgets	At $80 each
1 May	Sold	400 widgets	For $45,000
1 August	Purchased	450 widgets	At $69 each
15 November	Sold	450 widgets	For $28,750

     What is the value of the company's closing inventory of widgets at 31 December 20X5?

     A $8,000
     B $66,854
     C $67,050
     D $68,000

                                                                                             (2 marks)

31 **In times of rising prices, the FIFO method of inventory valuation, when compared with the average cost method of inventory valuation, will usually produce which of the following?**

A   A higher profit and a lower closing inventory value
B   A higher profit and a higher closing inventory value
C   A lower profit and a lower closing inventory value
D   A lower profit and a higher closing inventory value

(2 marks)

32 An organisation's inventory at 1 July is 15 units @ $3.00 each. The following movements occur.

- 3 July 20X6   5 units sold at $3.30 each
- 8 July 20X6   10 units bought at $3.50 each
- 12 July 20X6   8 units sold at $4.00 each

What would be the closing inventory at 31 July, using the FIFO method of inventory valuation?

A $31.50
B $36.00
C $39.00
D $41.00

(2 marks)

33 Your organisation uses the continuous weighted average cost method of valuing inventories. During August 20X1, the following inventory details were recorded.

Opening balance   30 units valued at $2 each
5 August   purchase of 50 units at $2.40 each
10 August   issue of 40 units
18 August   purchase of 60 units at $2.50 each
23 August   issue of 25 units

What is the value of the inventory at 31 August 20X1?

A $172.50
B $176.25
C $180.00
D $187.50

(2 marks)

34 **What is the correct double entry to record the depreciation charge for a period?**

A   DR   Depreciation expense
     CR   Accumulated depreciation

B   DR   Accumulated depreciation
     CR   Depreciation expense

(1 mark)

35 At 31 December 20X4 Q, a limited liability company, owned a building that it had purchased 10 years ago for $800,000. It was being depreciated at 2% per year on the straight line basis.

On 1 January 20X5 a revaluation to $1,000,000 was recognised. At this date the building had a remaining useful life of 40 years.

What is the depreciation charge for the year ended 31 December 20X5 and the revaluation surplus balance as at 1 January 20X5?

	Depreciation charge for year ended 31 December 20X5 $	Revaluation surplus as at 1 January 20X5 $
A	25,000	200,000
B	25,000	360,000
C	20,000	200,000
D	20,000	360,000

(2 marks)

36   An organisation's asset register shows a carrying value of $135,600. The non-current asset account in the nominal ledger shows a carrying value of $125,600.

Which of the following disposals, if not deducted from the asset register, could account for the difference?

A   Asset A with disposal proceeds of $15,000 and a profit on disposal of $5,000
B   Asset B with disposal proceeds of $15,000 and a carrying value of $5,000
C   Asset C with disposal proceeds of $15,000 and a loss on disposal of $5,000
D   Asset D with disposal proceeds of $5,000 and a carrying value of $5,000

(2 marks)

37   In the year to 31 December 20X9, Jason recorded some capital expenditure as revenue expenditure.

What is the effect on his profit for the year to 31 December 20X9 and his net assets at that date?

	Profit	Net assets
A	Overstated	Overstated
B	Overstated	Understated
C	Understated	Overstated
D	Understated	Understated

(2 marks)

38   **Which of the following are capital, as opposed to revenue, expenses?**

1   The repair of a machine currently used in the production process that has broken down

2   The cost of an extension to a factory building, which doubles the size of the production area

3   The cost of installing a new machine in a factory

A   2 only
B   1 and 2 only
C   2 and 3 only
D   1, 2 and 3

(2 marks)

39   The trucks account (at cost) of a business for the year ended 31 December 20X1 was as follows.

TRUCKS – COST

20X1	$	20X1	$
1 Jan balance	240,000	31 Mar disposal account	60,000
30 June cash – purchase of vans	160,000	31 Dec balance	340,000
	400,000		400,000

Brought forward accumulated depreciation at 1 January 20X1 was $115,000. The truck disposed of on 31 March had a carrying value of $20,000.

The company's policy is to charge depreciation at 20% per year on the reducing balance, and charges a full year's depreciation in the year of acquisition and none in the year of disposal.

What should be the depreciation charge for the year ended 31 December 20X1?

A $68,000
B $57,000
C $53,000
D $21,000

(2 marks)

40   **Which of the following statements about research and development expenditure are correct?**

1   Research expenditure, other than capital expenditure on research facilities, should be recognised as an expense as incurred.

2   In deciding whether development expenditure qualifies to be recognised as an asset, one of the factors it is necessary to consider is whether there will be adequate finance available to complete the project.

3   Development expenditure recognised as an asset must be amortised over a period not exceeding five years.

A   1, 2 and 3
B   1 and 2 only
C   1 and 3 only
D   2 and 3 only

(2 marks)

41   Bluebottle Co has incurred development expenditure of $500,000 and research expenditure of $400,000 in the year ended 31 December 20X1. The development expenditure has been capitalised in accordance with IAS 38. Bluebottle Co's policy is to amortise capitalised development expenditure over 25 years.

What balances relating to research and development would appear in the financial statements of Bluebottle for the year ended 31 December 20X1?

	Statement of financial position	Statement of profit or loss
A	$900,000	$nil
B	$500,000	$400,000
C	$864,000	$36,000
D	$480,000	$420,000

(2 marks)

42   Dodger Co's financial statements show a carrying value of $950,000 for capitalised development expenditure. Its policy is to amortise development expenditure on a straight line basis at 5% per annum. Accumulated amortisation brought forward is $50,000.

What is the charge in the statement of profit or loss for the year's amortisation?

A $43,500
B $47,500
C $45,000
D $50,000

(2 marks)

43   Ajeet prepared his draft end of year accounts. However, he has now realised that he did not adjust these for a prepayment of $2,100 and an accrual of $800.

How will Ajeet's profit and net assets be affected by including the prepayment and accrual?

	Profit for the year will:	Net assets will:
A	Increase by $2,900	Reduce by $2,900
B	Increase by $1,300	Increase by $1,300
C	Reduce by $1,300	Increase by $1,300
D	Reduce by $2,900	Reduce by $2,900

(2 marks)

44   Gamma Co prepares its financial statements for the year to 30 September each year. The company pays rent for its premises quarterly in advance on 1 February, 1 May, 1 August and 1 November each year. The annual rent was $120,000 per year until 30 April 20X8. It was increased from that date to $144,000 per year.

What balances were included in the statement of profit or loss and the statement of financial position for the year ended 30 September 20X8?

	Statement of profit or loss	Statement of financial position	
	Expense	Accrual	Prepayment
A	$130,000	nil	$12,000
B	$130,000	$24,000	nil
C	$132,000	nil	$12,000
D	$132,000	$24,000	nil

(2 marks)

45   A company receives rent from a large number of properties. The total received in the year ended 30 June 20X2 was $1,203,000.

The following were the amounts of rent in advance and in arrears at 30 June 20X1 and 20X2.

	30 June 20X1	30 June 20X2
	$	$
Rent received in advance	71,750	78,000
Rent in arrears (all subsequently received)	53,000	46,000

What amount of rental income should appear in the company's statement of profit or loss for the year ended 30 June 20X2?

A $1,152,250
B $1,189,750
C $1,216,250
D $1,253,750

(2 marks)

46   **Which of the following statements is/are true?**

1   Accrued expenses are expenses which relate to the current accounting period but have not been paid for. They are shown in the statement of profit or loss for the current period in accordance with the accruals concept.

2   Prepaid expenses are expenses which have already been paid in the current period but relate to a future accounting period. They are shown in the statement of profit or loss for the current period in accordance with the timeliness concept.

A   1 only
B   2 only
C   Both 1 and 2
D   Neither statement is true

(2 marks)

47   At 30 June 20X5 a company's allowance for receivables was $39,000. At 30 June 20X6 trade receivables totalled $517,000. It was decided to write off debts totalling $37,000 and the allowance for receivables was to be adjusted to the equivalent of 5% of the outstanding trade receivables.

What figure should appear in the statement of profit or loss for the year ended 30 June 20X6 for these items?

A $61,000
B $22,000
C $24,000
D $23,850

(2 marks)

48   **Which of the following statements is/are true?**

    1   An aged receivables analysis is a report used to help the business pay its suppliers on time.

    2   A credit limit is the minimum amount a customer must spend when purchasing goods on credit from a supplier.

    A   1 only
    B   2 only
    C   Both 1 and 2
    D   Neither 1 and 2

    (2 marks)

The following information relates to questions 49 and 50.

North Co has a receivables balance at 31 October 20X7 of $456,330. The accountant at North is preparing the financial statements for the year ended 31 October 20X7 and must account for the following.

    1   A balance owed by South Co of $780 is deemed irrecoverable and must be written off.

    2   The brought forward receivables allowance is $15,255. The allowance for receivables should be adjusted to the equivalent of 5% of the outstanding receivables balances.

    3   A payment of $450 from East Co has been received on 30 October. The payment relates to a balance that had previously been written off as irrecoverable by North Co.

49   **What value for receivables should appear in the statement of financial position of North Co at 31 October 20X7?**

    A $432,733.50
    B $432,772.50
    C $433,222.50
    D $433,513.50

    (2 marks)

50   **What is the total amount that should appear in the statement of profit or loss for irrecoverable debts expense at 31 October 20X7?**

    A $7,522.50
    B $7,852.50
    C $7,891.50
    D $8,302.50

    (2 marks)

51   **How should a contingent liability be included in a company's financial statements if the likelihood of a transfer of economic benefits to settle it is remote?**

    A   Disclosed by note with no provision being made
    B   No disclosure or provision is required

    (1 mark)

52   The following conditions exist.

    •   An event has occurred which means Booker Co has incurred a present obligation.
    •   It is probable that Booker Co will have to pay out cash in order to settle the obligation.
    •   A reliable estimate of the amount involved cannot be determined.

    What is the effect of the above on the financial statements of Booker Co?

    A   A provision should be created
    B   A contingent liability should be disclosed
    C   A contingent asset should be disclosed
    D   No effect

    (2 marks)

53 Raider Co has to include the following items in its financial statements.

1   Raider Co has been sued by Space Co for breach of trademark. Raider Co strongly disputes the claim and Raider Co's lawyers advise that the likelihood of having to pay any money to Space Co for the claim is remote.

2   Raider Co gives warranties on its products. Data from previous years show that about 15% of sales give rise to a warranty claim.

How should the items be reflected in the financial statements of Raider Co?

	Item 1	Item 2
A	create a provision	disclose by note only
B	disclose by note only	create a provision
C	disclose by note only	disclose by note only
D	no provision or disclosure required	create a provision

(2 marks)

54 Punt Co sells vacuum cleaners with a warranty. Customers are covered for the cost of repairs of any manufacturing defect that becomes apparent within the first year of purchase. The company's past experience and future expectations indicate the following pattern of likely repairs.

% of goods sold	Defects	Cost of repairs $'000
80	None	–
12	Minor	545
8	Major	800

The warranty provision brought forward is $99,750.

What amounts should be recognised in the financial statements of Punt Co relating to the warranty provision for the year to 20X3?

	Statement of profit or loss	Statement of financial position
A	$99,750 Cr	nil
B	$99,750 Dr	nil
C	$29,650 Dr	$129,400 Cr
D	$29,650 Cr	$129,400 Cr

(2 marks)

55 A company has a brought forward payables balance of $308,600 Cr. The following control account has been prepared by a trainee accountant.

PAYABLES LEDGER CONTROL ACCOUNT

	$		$
Opening balance	308,600	Credit purchases	337,200
Interest payable on overdue amounts	3,600	Cash purchases	55,670
Contras against credit balance in receivable ledger	1,400	Goods returned by customers	2,400
Cash paid	222,340	Discounts received	4,900
		Closing balance	135,770
	535,940		535,940

What should the closing balance be when all the errors made in preparing the payables ledger control account have been corrected?

A $202,440
B $420,760
C $470,430
D $472,830

(2 marks)

56   Claire is trying to reconcile the list of receivables balances with the balance on the receivables
      control account.

Which of the following would cause a difference between the total of the list of receivables balances and the balance on the receivables control account?

1   An invoice for $456 was entered as $546 in error in the sales day book

2   A credit note for $150 was omitted from the sales day book, but was credited to the customer's personal account in the receivables ledger

A   1 only
B   2 only
C   Both 1 and 2
D   Neither 1 or 2

                                                                                          (2 marks)

57   Roger has discounts allowed of $600 in his trial balance.

How should this amount be reported in his financial statements?

A $600 Cr to purchases
B $600 Dr to purchases
C $600 Dr to expenses
D $600 Dr to other income

                                                                                          (2 marks)

58   Angus received a statement of account from a supplier, Aberdeen, showing a balance to be paid of $14,560 at 31 August 20X1. Angus's payables ledger account for Aberdeen shows a balance due to Aberdeen of $12,160.

      Investigation reveals the following.

1   A credit note received by Angus for goods returned to Aberdeen has been incorrectly recorded in Angus's books as $4,200 instead of $2,400. The credit note is correctly recorded on the statement from Aberdeen.

2   Aberdeen has allowed Angus a cash discount of $150 which has not yet been recorded in Angus's ledger account.

What discrepancy remains between Angus's and Aberdeen's records after allowing for these items?

A $nil
B $150
C $750
D $4,350

                                                                                          (2 marks)

59   Mountain sells goods on credit to Hill. Hill receives a 10% trade discount from Mountain and a further 5% settlement discount if goods are paid for within 14 days. Hill bought goods with a list price of $200,000 from Mountain.

What amount should be included in Mountain's receivables ledger for this transaction?

A $180,000
B $190,000
C $171,500
D $171,000

                                                                                          (2 marks)

60 The following bank reconciliation statement has been prepared by a trainee accountant.

	$
Overdraft per bank statement	3,860
Less unpresented cheques	9,160
	5,300
Add deposits credited after date (outstanding lodgements)	16,690
Cash at bank as calculated above	21,990

What should be the correct balance per the cash book?

A $21,990 balance at bank as stated
B $3,670 balance at bank
C $11,390 balance at bank
D $3,670 overdrawn

(2 marks)

61 In preparing a company's bank reconciliation statement at 31 March 20X6, the following items are causing the difference between the cash book balance and the bank statement balance:

1   Bank charges $380
2   Error by bank $1,000 (cheque incorrectly debited to the account)
3   Lodgements not credited $4,580
4   Unpresented cheques $1,475
5   Direct debit $350
6   Cheque paid in by the company and dishonoured $400

Which of these items will require an entry in the cash book?

A   2, 4 and 6
B   1, 5 and 6
C   3, 4 and 5
D   1, 2 and 3

(2 marks)

62 **Which of the following items reconciling the balance on the bank ledger account to the balance shown on the bank statement are referred to as timing differences?**

1   Bank charges not recorded in the cash book
2   Interest charged not recorded in the cash book
3   Outstanding lodgements
4   Unpresented cheques

A   1 and 2
B   3 and 4
C   2 and 3
D   1 and 4

(2 marks)

63 Mauritz Co is preparing a bank reconciliation. The bank balance in the general ledger is $540 credit. There are two items that have not yet been dealt with.

1   A cheque for $620 was sent to a supplier but is not yet showing on the bank statement.
2   A bank charge of $28 was charged by the bank, but was not recorded by Mauritz Co.

What is the closing balance on Mauritz Co's bank statement?

A $1,132 overdrawn
B $1,188 overdrawn
C $52 cash at bank
D $108 cash at bank

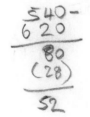

(2 marks)

64   The debit side of a company's trial balance totals $800 more than the credit side.

Which one of the following errors would fully account for the difference?

A $400 paid for plant maintenance has been correctly entered in the cash book and credited to the plant asset account

B   Discount received $400 has been debited to discount allowed account

C   A receipt of $800 for commission receivable has been omitted from the records

D   The petty cash balance of $800 has been omitted from the trial balance

(2 marks)

65   A suspense account was opened when a trial balance failed to agree. The following errors were later discovered.

- A gas bill of $420 had been recorded in the gas account as $240
- A discount of $50 given to a customer had been credited to discounts received
- Interest received of $70 had been entered in the bank account only

What was the original balance on the suspense account?

A   DEBIT $210
B   CREDIT $210
C   DEBIT $160
D   CREDIT $160

Suspense A/c

Int	70	Gas bill (420-240)	180
Bal	210	asc. (2×50)	100
	280	bck. 210	280

(2 marks)

66   The bookkeeper of Field made the following mistakes: Discounts allowed $3,840 was credited to the discounts received account. Discounts received $2,960 was debited to the discounts allowed account.

Which journal entry will correct the errors?

2× 3,840 = 7,680
2× 2960 = 5,920
1,760

		Dr	Cr
A	Discounts allowed	$7,680	
	Discounts received		$5,920
	Suspense account		$1,760
B	Discounts allowed	$880	
	Discounts received	$880	
	Suspense account		$1,760
C	Discounts allowed	$6,800	
	Discounts received		$6,800
D	Discounts allowed	$3,840	
	Discounts received		$2,960
	Suspense account		$880

(2 marks)

67   Marcia Blane, a sole trader, extracted the following trial balance on 31 December 20X2.

TRIAL BALANCE AS AT 31 DECEMBER 20X2

	Debit $	Credit $
Capital at 1 January 20X2		26,100
Receivables	41,000	
Cash in hand	1,500	
Payables		34,500
Fixtures and fittings at cost	42,200	
Discounts allowed	1,302	
Discounts received		1,200
Inventory at 1 January 20X2	18,460	
Sales		487,550
Purchases	379,590	
Motor vehicles at cost	45,730	
Lighting and heating	6,100	
Motor expenses	3,250	
Rent	10,750	
General expenses	9,475	
Bank overdraft		20,100
Provision for depreciation		
Fixtures and fittings		2,200
Motor vehicles		15,292
Drawings	27,585	
	586,942	586,942

The following information as at 31 December is also available.

(a) $520 is owing for motor expenses

(b) $450 has been prepaid for rent

(c)   Depreciation is to be provided for the year as follows:

Motor vehicles: 20% on cost
Fixtures and fittings: 10% reducing balance method

(d)   Inventory at the close of business was valued at $20,250

(e)   Marcia took some goods costing $800 from inventory for her own use. The normal selling price of the goods is $1,600

Required

(a)   What is the net effect on profit of the adjustments in notes (a) to (c) above?   **(6 marks)**

(b)   Which of the following journal entries would correctly record the transaction in note (e)?

		Dr $	Cr $
A	Drawings account	800	
	Inventory account		800
B	Drawings account	800	
	Purchases account		800
C	Sales account	1,600	
	Drawings account		1,600
D	Inventory account		1,600
	Drawings account	1,600	

(2 marks)

(c)   Prepare Marcia's statement of financial position as at 31 December 20X2.   **(7 marks)**

Total marks for the question   **(15 marks)**

68   **Which of the following calculates a sole trader's closing net assets?**

A   Opening net assets – drawings + capital introduced + profit
B   Opening net assets + drawings + capital introduced + profit
C   Opening net assets + drawings – capital introduced – profit
D   Opening net assets – drawings – capital introduced + profit

(2 marks)

69   A fire on 30 September destroyed some of a company's inventory and its inventory records. The following information is available.

	$
Inventory at 1 September	318,000
Sales for September	612,000
Purchases for September	412,000
Inventory in good condition at 30 September	214,000

Standard gross profit percentage on sales is 25%.

Based on this information, what is the value of the inventory lost?

A $96,000
B $271,000
C $26,400
D $57,000

(2 marks)

70   Bob is a sole trader. He has calculated a cost of sales figure for the year, which is $342,000. Bob received a payment of $8,030 into the business bank account for goods sold on a special deal to Harry and this amount has been included within sales. The figure of $8,030 was calculated by adding a mark-up of 10% to the cost of the goods. His gross profit percentage on all other goods sold was 20% of sales.

What is the total figure of sales for the year?

A $401,640
B $402,370
C $418,375
D $426,405

(2 marks)

71   Ossie does not keep full accounting records. The last accounts drawn up show that his capital balance was $51,980. At the year end he calculated that his assets and liabilities at 30 June 20X0 were:

	$
Non-current assets	51,300
Inventory	7,770
Receivables	5,565
Payables	3,994
Bank overdraft	3,537

On reviewing his calculations, you note that there were no entries made in relation to rent for June 20X0 because the rent for June 20X0 was paid on 1 July 20X0. Rent is $500 per month.

What is the value of Ossie's closing capital?

A $51,980
B $56,604
C $57,604
D $63,678

(2 marks)

72 Patience is trying to work out her cost of sales for the year ended 31 December 20X9.

She has the following details for supplier and inventory balances.

	At 1 January 20X9	At 31 December 20X9
Suppliers	$15,264	$16,812
Inventory	$6,359	$4,919

In the year to 31 December 20X9, Patience's payments to suppliers totalled $141,324.

What was Patience's cost of sales for the year to 31 December 20X9?

A $149,231
B $144,312
C $142,872
D $141,432

(2 marks)

73 **Should dividends paid appear on the face of a company's statement of profit or loss?**

A Yes
B No

(1 mark)

74 **Which of the following journal entries are correct, according to their narratives?**

		Dr $	Cr $
1	Suspense account	18,000	
	Rent received account		18,000
	Correction of error in posting $24,000 cash received for rent to the rent received amount as $42,000		
2	Share premium account	400,000	
	Share capital account		400,000
	1 for 3 bonus issue on share capital of 1,200,000 50c shares		
3	Trade investment in X	750,000	
	Share capital account		250,000
	Share premium account		500,000
	500,000 50c shares issued at $1.50 per share in exchange for shares in X		

A 1 and 2
B 2 and 3
C 1 only
D 3 only

(2 marks)

75 **Which of the following should appear in a company's statement of changes in equity?**

1 Profit for the financial year
2 Dividends proposed during the year
3 Surplus on revaluation of non-current assets

A All three items
B 2 and 3 only
C 1 and 3 only
D 1 and 2 only

(2 marks)

76   Lorel Co, a limited liability company, has the following capital structure.

		$'000
Share capital		
50c ordinary shares		45,000
Share premium		60,000
		105,000

The company made a bonus issue of two shares for every three shares held, using the share premium account for the purpose.

What was the company's capital structure after the bonus issue?

	Ordinary share capital	*Share premium account*
	$	$
A	60,000	45,000
B	75,000	30,000
C	105,000	nil
D	112,500	(7,500)

(2 marks)

77   **Which of the following statements is/are correct?**

1   IAS 1 requires that some items must appear on the face of the statement of financial position.

2   IAS 1 requires that a company must present a combined statement of profit or loss and other comprehensive income.

A   1 only
B   2 only
C   Both 1 and 2
D   Neither 1 or 2

(2 marks)

78   **Where are the following items shown in a company's financial statements?**

1   Gains on property revaluations
2   Dividends paid
3   Bonus issue of shares

	Statement of profit or loss and other comprehensive income	*Statement of changes in equity*
A	1 and 2 only	2 and 3 only
B	1 and 3 only	1 and 2 only
C	1 only	1, 2 and 3
D	1 only	2 and 3 only

(2 marks)

79   **Which of the following is/are required for disclosure of revalued assets in a company's financial statements?**

1   The methods and significant assumptions applied in estimating the value
2   Whether an independent valuer was involved in the valuation
3   How certain the directors are that the valuation will not change in the next five years

A   1 only
B   1 and 2 only
C   2 only
D   All three are required

(2 marks)

80   The following trial balance for ABC Ltd is extracted at 31 December 20X1.

	Dr	Cr
Sales		341,726
Purchases	202,419	
Carriage inwards	376	
Carriage outwards	729	
Wages and salaries	54,210	
Rent and rates	12,466	
Heat and light	4,757	
Inventory at 1 January 20X1	14,310	
Dividends paid	28,500	
Receivables	49,633	
Payables		32,792
Bank		3,295
Sundry expenses	18,526	
Cash	20,877	
Share capital		20,000
Reserves		8,990
	406,803	406,803

Closing inventory is 15,327.

(a)   Gross profit for the year is $ _____   **(3 marks)**

(b)   Profit before tax for the year is $ _____   **(4 marks)**

(c)   Net assets are $ _____   **(2 marks)**

(d)   The directors of ABC Ltd are considering refinancing. **Where should the following be classified in a company's statement of financial position at 31 December 20X1?**

   1   An overdraft balance of £55,000

   2   A loan from a bank due for repayment in full in July 20X3

	Current liabilities	Current assets	Non-current liabilities
A	(1)	–	(2)
B	(1) and (2)	–	–
C	(2)	(1)	–
D	–	–	(1) and (2) **(2 marks)**

(e)   Which of these transactions would **not** increase a company's retained earnings for the year?

   A   Revaluation of a freehold factory from $140,000 to $250,000

   B   Receipt of $5,000 from a receivable previously written off

   C   Receive discounts of $1,000 from a supplier

   D   Sell a car for $6,000 which cost $10,000 and has been depreciated by $4,500

                                                                    (2 marks)

(f)   ABC's tax charge for the year is $5,000 and $10,000 is to be transferred to a non-current asset reserve. A final dividend of 5c per ordinary share is proposed.

   The retained earnings for the year is $_____.   **(2 marks)**

   Total marks for the question   **(15 marks)**

81 **Which material events after the reporting period should be disclosed in the notes to financial statements according to IAS 10 *Events after the reporting period*?**

A   Adjusting events
B   Non-adjusting events

(1 mark)

82   H has prepared its financial statements for the year ending 30 June 20X8. On 15 July a major fraud was uncovered which had taken place during the year to 30 June. On 31 July the company made a bonus issue of shares that significantly increased the number of shares in issue.

In accordance with IAS 10 *Events after the reporting period*, how should the two events be treated in the financial statements?

	Fraud	*Bonus share issue*
A	Accrued in accounts	Disclosed in notes
B	Accrued in accounts	Accrued in accounts
C	Disclosed in notes	Disclosed in notes
D	Disclosed in notes	Accrued in accounts

(2 marks)

83   The following material events take place after the reporting date of 31 December 20X1 and before the financial statements for Tapenade Co are approved.

1   Barroles Co, a major customer of Tapenade Co, went into liquidation. Tapenade Co has been advised that it is highly unlikely to receive any of the outstanding debt of $150,000 owed by Barroles at the year end.

2   A fire occurred in the warehouse of Tapenade Co and stock costing $75,000 was destroyed.

Adjustments are made in the financial statements as required by IAS 10 *Events after the reporting date*.

What is the effect on profit for the year in the financial statements at 31 December 20X1 of making the required adjustments?

A   Reduction of $150,000
B   Reduction of $75,000
C   Reduction of $225,000
D   No effect on profit

(2 marks)

84   Part of a company's statement of cash flows is shown below.

	$'000
Operating profit	8,640
Depreciation charges	(2,160)
Increase in inventory	(330)
Increase in accounts payable	440

The following criticisms of the extract have been made.

1   Depreciation charges should have been added, not deducted
2   Increase in inventory should have been added, not deducted
3   Increase in accounts payable should have been deducted, not added

Which of the criticisms are valid?

A   2 and 3 only
B   1 only
C   1 and 3 only
D   2 only

(2 marks)

85 Flail Co commenced trading on 1 January 20X1 with a medium-term loan of $21,000 and a share issue which raised $35,000. The company purchased non-current assets for $21,000 cash and during the year to 31 December 20X1 entered into the following transactions.

(i) Purchases from suppliers were $19,500, of which $2,550 was unpaid at the year end.

(ii) Wages and salaries amounted to $10,500, of which $750 was unpaid at the year end.

(iii) Interest on the loan of $2,100 was fully paid in the year and a repayment of $5,250 was made.

(iv) Sales turnover was $29,400, including $900 receivables at the year end.

(v) Interest on cash deposits at the bank amounted to $75.

(vi) A dividend of $4,000 was proposed as at 31 December 20X1.

(a) **You are required to prepare Flail Co's statement of cash flows for the year ended 31 December 20X1.** **(13 marks)**

(b) **Which of the following items could appear in Flail Co's statement of cash flows?**

  1 Surplus on revaluation of non-current assets
  2 Proceeds of issue of shares
  3 Proposed dividend
  4 Dividends received

  A 1 and 2
  B 3 and 4
  C 1 and 3
  D 2 and 4 **(2 marks)**

  Total marks for the question **(15 marks)**

86 **Which of the following statements is/are correct?**

  1 An increase in a loan made to another company will be classified under investing cash flows.

  2 An increase in a loan from a bank will be classified under investing cash flows.

  3 Bonus issues of shares do not feature in statements of cash flows.

  4 A loss on the sale of a non-current asset will be deducted from net profit in order to calculate operating cash flows using the indirect method.

  A 1 and 2
  B 1 and 3
  C 3 only
  D 1 and 4

  (2 marks)

87 **How should the following investments be accounted for in the consolidated financial statements of Barracuda Inc?**

  1 Investment of 30,000 ordinary shares in Minnow Inc. Minnow has a total of 45,000 ordinary shares.

  2 Investment of 21% of the ordinary shares in Major Inc. Barracuda Inc has the right to appoint 4 out of 6 of the board of directors of Major Inc.

	Subsidiary	*Associate*
A	1	2
B	1, 2	–
C	–	1, 2
D	2	1

  (2 marks)

88   **Which of the following statements is/are correct?**

1   If a company owns more than 50% of the ordinary shares of another company, the investment will always be classified as a subsidiary.

2   Consolidated accounts are required for a group of companies in order to represent the legal form, rather than the substance, of the relationship between the parent and its subsidiaries.

3   An trade investment is an entity in which an investor has significant influence, which is neither a subsidiary or a joint venture of the investor.

A   1 and 2 only
B   1 only
C   All three statements are correct
D   None of the statements are correct

(2 marks)

89   Alpha is an associate of Delta.

How should profits generated by Alpha be shown in the consolidated accounts of Delta?

A   All the profits after tax generated by Alpha are included by consolidating the revenue and expenses of Alpha on a line by line basis from revenue down to profit for the year.

B   Delta's share of Alpha's profit after tax is included by the payment of a dividend from Alpha to Delta, which is shown in the consolidated statement of profit or loss of Delta.

C   Delta's share of Alpha's profit after tax is included in the consolidated statement of profit or loss of Delta as a single amount.

D   All the profits after tax generated by Alpha are included in the consolidated statement of profit or loss of Delta as a single amount.

(2 marks)

90   Martin Co owns 100% of Kyle Co. The following information has been extracted from the individual company statements of financial position as at 31 December 20X8.

	Martin Co	Kyle Co
	$	$
Current assets	250,000	100,000
Current liabilities	110,000	45,000

Included in the receivables of Martin Co and the payables of Kyle Co is an amount of $6,000 owed to Martin Co by Kyle Co.

If there are no other intra-group balances, what amount would be shown for consolidated current assets?

A $149,000
B $350,000
C $344,000
D $356,000

(2 marks)

91 Holder Inc acquired 150,000 $1 ordinary shares in Sub Inc on 1 July 20X6 at a cost of $300,000. Sub Inc's reserves at 1 July 20X6 were $36,000 and its issued ordinary share capital was $200,000. The fair value of the non-controlling interest at acquisition was $100,000.

At 30 June 20X9 Sub Inc's reserves were $16,000.

What is the goodwill arising on consolidation?

A $64,000
B $123,000
C $164,000
D $184,000

(2 marks)

92 Alpha Co acquired 80% of all the share capital of Beta Co on 1 January 20X1. The consideration given was $500,000. On 1 January the fair value of Beta Co's net tangible assets was $450,000 and the fair value of the non-controlling interest was $125,000.

At 31 December 20X1 the fair value of the net tangible assets of Beta Co is $600,000.

What is the amount of goodwill to be entered in the consolidated accounts?

A $25,000
B $50,000
C $175,000
D $265,000

(2 marks)

93 Vaynor Co acquired 100% of the ordinary shares in Weeton Co and Yarlet Co some years ago. Extracts from the statements of financial position of the 3 companies as on 30 September 20X7 were as follows.

	Vaynor Co $'000	Weeton Co $'000	Yarlet Co $'000
Retained earnings	90	40	70

At acquisition Weeton Co had retained losses of $10,000 and Yarlet Co had retained earnings of $30,000.

What are the consolidated retained earnings of Vaynor Co on 30 September 20X7?

A $160,000
B $180,000
C 200,000
D $220,000

(2 marks)

94 Spring Co has held 75% of the equity share capital of Summer Co for many years. Cost of sales for each entity for the year ended 31 December 20X8 was as follows.

	$
Spring Co	200,000
Summer Co	160,000

During the year Spring Co sold goods costing $10,000 to Summer Co for $16,000. At the year end, all these goods remained in inventory.

What figure should be shown as cost of sales in the consolidated statement of profit or loss of the Spring Group for the year ended 31 December 20X8?

A $344,000
B $350,000
C $360,000
D $370,000

(2 marks)

The following information relates to questions 95 and 96.

Patience Co has a subsidiary, Bunthorne Co. During 20X1 Bunthorne Co sold goods to Patience Co for $40,000 which was cost plus 25%. At 31 December 20X1 $20,000 of these goods remained unsold.

95   **What will revenue will be reduced by in the consolidated statement of profit or loss for the year ended 31 December 20X1?**

    A $20,000
    B $30,000
    C $32,000
    D $40,000

(2 marks)

96   **What will profit be reduced by in the consolidated statement of profit or loss for the year ended 31 December 20X1?**

    A $4,000
    B $6,000
    C $8,000
    D $10,000

(2 marks)

97   The following figures related to Sanderstead Co and its subsidiary Croydon Co for the year ended 31 December 20X9.

	Sanderstead Co	Croydon Co
	$	$
Revenue	600,000	300,000
Cost of sales	(400,000)	(200,000)
Gross profit	200,000	100,000

During the year Sanderstead Co sold goods to Croydon Co for $20,000, making a profit of $5,000.

These goods were all sold by Croydon Co before the year end.

What are the amounts for total revenue and gross profit in the consolidated statement of profit or loss of Sanderstead Co for the year ended 31 December 20X9?

	Revenue	Gross profit
A	$900,000	$300,000
B	$900,000	$295,000
C	$880,000	$300,000
D	$880,000	$295,000

(2 marks)

98   Z has a current ratio of 1.5, a quick ratio of 0.4 and a positive cash balance. **If it purchases inventory on credit, what is the effect on these ratios?**

	Current ratio	Quick ratio
A	Decrease	Decrease
B	Decrease	Increase
C	Increase	Decrease
D	Increase	Increase

(2 marks)

99   HJ has an asset turnover of 2.0 and an operating profit margin of 10%. The entity is about to
      launch a new product which is expected to generate additional sales of $1.6m and additional
      profit of $120,000 in its first year. To manufacture the new product HJ will need to purchase
      additional assets of $500,000.

      What will be the effect of the new product on the following ratios of HJ?

	Operating profit margin	Return on capital employed
A	Decrease	Decrease
B	Decrease	Increase
C	Increase	Decrease
D	Increase	Increase

      (2 marks)

100   Jessica Co acquired 75% of the share capital of Patpost Co on 1 January 20X7. The draft
      statements of profit or loss for the two companies for the year ended 31 December 20X7 are
      shown below.

	Jessica Co $m	Patpost Co $m
Revenue	7,500	3,000
Cost of sales	4,000	1,600
	3,500	1,400
Operating expenses	2,000	500
Profit before tax	1,500	900
Tax	300	120
Profit for the year	1,200	780

      During the year, Jessica Co sold goods costing $3m to Patpost Co for $5m. At the year end,
      50% of these goods remained in Patpost's inventory.

      (a)   Prepare the Jessica Group's statement of profit or loss for the year ended 31 December
            20X7.   **(8 marks)**

      (b)   The profit attributable to the equity owners of Jessica amounted to $ [   ] **(3 marks)**

      (c)   Jessica's current ratio increased from 0.7 at 31 December 20X6 to 1.5 at 31 December
            20X7. The company sells goods at a mark-up of 25% on cost.

      Which of the following statements concerning this increase is/are correct?

      1   The increase in the current ratio could indicate that the company is less likely to be able
            to pay its debts on time.

      2   The increase in the current ratio could have been caused by an increase in revenue
            generated by increased credit sales prices, while supplier costs remained the same.

      3   The increase in the current ratio could have been caused by an increase in costs charged
            by suppliers, while the selling price of goods remained the same.

      A   1 only
      B   2 only
      C   2 and 3 only
      D   1 and 3 only

      (2 marks)

      (d)   Which of the following factors need to be taken into account when deciding if a parent-
            subsidiary relationship exists?

      A   Control
      B   Greater than 50% of the preference shares held by an investor
      C   Significant influence
      D   50% of all shares held by an investor   **(2 marks)**

      Total marks for the question   **(15 marks)**

1	C	A sole trader also invests capital in their business.
2	C	The board of directors are **responsible** for the preparation of financial statements. Even though the financial statements may be physically prepared by the finance department, the board of directors still has responsibility for them. The auditors are not responsible for the financial statements; they are responsible for the annual audit and producing an audit report.
3	B	A company has a separate legal identity to its owners. Unless the partners have formed a limited liability partnership, the partners are jointly liable for the debts of the business.
4	D	1 and 3 are **advantages** of trading as a limited liability company. Publishing annual financial statements and the requirement for an audit are **disadvantages** of trading as a limited liability company.
5	B	A director's main aim should be to create wealth for the shareholders of the company. The shareholders are the owners of the company and the directors are managing the affairs of the company on their behalf. This can lead to a conflict of interest and short-termism where the directors put their own interests (ie short-term profits and earning bonuses) ahead of the interests of the shareholders. Every company should consider its contribution to society; this is known as corporate social responsibility. However, this is not the main aim of a director.
6	B	The IASB is responsible for developing and issuing IFRSs. An objective of the IFRS Foundation is to take account of the financial reporting needs of small and medium-sized entities. The IFRS Advisory Council provides a forum for the IASB to consult with the national accounting standard setters, academics and other interested parties.
7	C	The IASB is responsible for developing and issuing IFRSs.
8	C	The fourth enhancing qualitative characteristic is verifiability.
9	D	Information is **material** if its omission or misstatement could affect the decisions of the users of accounts. The substance over form convention means that transactions are accounted for in accordance with their substance and not merely their legal form.
10	D	The fundamental qualitative characteristics are relevance and faithful representation.
11	B	
12	B	Under the imprest system, a reimbursement is made of the amount of the vouchers (or payments made) for the period.
13	B	A remittance advice gives details of the invoices covered by the payment.
14	A	Supplier statements are statements sent out by suppliers listing all the transactions on a customer's account. Petty cash vouchers are vouchers issued in the petty cash imprest system for payments made from petty cash.
15	C	Credit notes received from suppliers are recorded in the purchase returns day book.
16	A	
17	B	A is incorrect as the debits and credits don't equal each other, C is incorrect as the debits and credits are the wrong way round and D is incorrect as the debits and credits are the wrong way round and the credit sale has been ignored.
18	C	You are recording the transaction in Cheddar's books – Cheddar is the seller, so the double entry is Dr receivables, Cr sales $500.
19	A	A credit increases a liability, increases income or decreases an asset.
20	B	The account has a debit balance.
21	A	A debit balance brought down on the cash T-account represents an asset.
22	A	Balance carried down from the previous period shows debits exceed credits and so it is a debit balance brought down for the new period.

23 C Balance carried down from the previous period shows credits exceed debits and so it is a credit balance brought down for the new period.

24 B

TRADE RECEIVABLES ACCOUNT

	$		$
Balance b/d	100,750	Cash at bank	250,225
Sales	325,010	Balance c/d	175,535
	425,760		425,760

25 B False. Sales tax for a registered trader is removed from income and expenses.

26 A Sales tax can only be charged and reclaimed by businesses if they are registered for sales tax. If a business is not registered for sales tax, the sales tax incurred on purchases will be charged to the statement of profit or loss as an expense.

27 A

SALES TAX CONTROL ACCOUNT

	$		$
Payables (6,750 – 1,250)	5,500	Receivables	8,000
Balance c/d (owed to tax authorities)	2,500		
	8,000		8,000
		Balance b/d	2,550

28 D The entries required are   DR Receivables $1,056
                                CR Sales $880
                                  CR Sales tax $176

Michael is registered for sales tax, so he can charge sales tax and recover the balance from the tax authorities.

29 D Carriage outwards is a selling expense.

30 C (450 @ 80) + (450 @ 69) = $67,050

A is incorrect, as it does not include the inventory on hand at the beginning of the period. B is incorrect, as it uses the average cost method. D is incorrect, as it uses the LIFO method.

31 B According to FIFO, the first items of inventory to be sold would be included as expenses in the statement of profit or loss at the cost of the first items purchased. This cost will be lower than the average over the whole period (because of rising prices), so the expense in the statement of profit or loss will be lower than average and profit will be higher.

Likewise closing inventory value: as prices are rising, the items still left in inventory will be valued at the higher, later price, which means that inventory value will be higher than the average value in the period.

32 D 2 @ $3.00 + 10 @ $3.50 = $41.00

33 C

	Units	Unit cost $	Total $	Average $
Opening inventory	30	2	60	
5 August purchase	50	2.40	120	
	80		180	2.25
10 August issue	(40)	2.25	(90)	
	40		90	
18 August purchase	60	2.50	150	
	100		240	2.40
23 August issue	(25)	2.40	(60)	
	75		180	

34   A

35   B   1,000,000/40 years = 25,000; 1,000,000 − (800,000 − (800,000 × 2% × 10 years)) = 360,000

36   A   If disposal proceeds were $15,000 and profit on disposal is $5,000, then carrying value must be $10,000, the difference between the asset register figure and the non-current asset account in the nominal ledger.

37   D   Non-current assets will be understated, leading to a lower net assets position. Additionally, too much will have been charged in the statement of profit or loss, resulting in an understatement of profit.

38   C   Repair and maintenance of machinery is revenue expenditure. The cost of installing new machinery can be added to the cost of the machine and capitalised, therefore it is capital expenditure. An extension to a factory building is capital expenditure, as it enhances the existing factory.

39   C

		$'000	Charge for year $'000
Trucks at 1 Jan			
Cost	(240 − 60)	180,000	
Acc dep'n	(115 − (60 − 20))	75,000	
Carrying value		105,000	
Dep'n charge @ 20%		21,000	21,000
Purchased truck			
Dep'n charge @ 20%	160 @ 20%	32,000	32,000
			53,000

40   B   There is no requirement that development expenditure should be amortised over a period not exceeding five years.

41   D   The development expenditure should be capitalised and amortised over 25 years, giving the statement of financial position balance as 500,000 − 500,000/25 = $480,000, and $20,000 charged to the statement of profit or loss.

The research expenditure should be charged to the statement of profit or loss in full, therefore the total charge to the statement of profit or loss is $420,000.

42   D   Amortisation for the year = $1,000,000* × 5% = $50,000.

* Cost = carrying value ($950,000) + accumulated amortisation ($50,000)

43   B   The prepayment will add $2,100 to profit and net assets.

The accrual will reduce profit and net assets by $800.

The net effect will be to increase both by $1,300.

44   A   (120,000 × 7/12) + (144,000 × 5/12) = 130,000; rent is payable in advance, therefore the rent for October has been prepaid at 30 September 20X8: 144,000 × 1/12 = 12,000

45   B

RENT RECEIVABLE

	$		$
Balance b/d	53,000	Balance b/d	71,750
Statement of profit or loss	1,189,750	Cash received	1,203,000
Balance c/d	78,000	Balance c/d	46,000
	1,320,750		1,320,750

46   A   Prepaid expenses are not included in the statement of profit or loss for the current period, as they do not relate to that period. The expenses are instead shown in the period to which they relate, in accordance with the accruals concept.

47   B   37,000 + ((517,000 – 37,000) × 5%) – 39,000) = 22,000. New allowance required
         is $24,000, so the allowance is reduced by $15,000.

48   D   Neither statement is true.

         An aged receivables analysis is a report used to help the business monitor its receivables
         balances and identify which receivables balances are overdue. A credit limit is the
         maximum amount a customer can owe to a business at any one time. If an order is placed
         by a customer that would take the customer's account over its credit limit, the order will
         not be filled until a payment is received to reduce the balance on the customer's account.

49   B

	$
Receivables balance before adjustments	456,330.0
Less irrecoverable debts written off	(780.0)
	455,550.0
Receivables allowance $455,550 @ 5%	(22,777.5)
Receivables balance for statement of financial position	432,772.5

50   B

	$
Irrecoverable debts expense	
Increase in allowance (22,777.5 – 15,255)	7,522.5
Add irrecoverable debts written off	780.0
	8,302.5
Less cash recovered from previously written off debt	(450.0)
Irrecoverable debt expense	7,852.5

51   B

52   B   Booker should disclose a contingent liability in the financial statements because the
         amount cannot be reliably estimated. If the amount could be reliably estimated, then a
         provision would be recognised.

53   D   As the likelihood of paying any cash to Space Co for the claim is remote, there is nothing
         to disclose in the accounts regarding this claim. A provision should be created for the
         warranties, as the conditions for recognising a provision are met – present obligation,
         probably outflow of cash, reliable estimate of amount.

54   C   The 20X3 provision is calculated using expected cost:

         (80% × 0) + (12% × 545,000) + (8% × 800,000) = $129,400

         The increase in the provision is therefore 129,400 – 99,750 = $29,650. This is a debit
         to the statement of profit or loss.

55   B   PAYABLES LEDGER CONTROL ACCOUNT

	$		$
Cash paid	222,340	Opening balance	308,600
Discounts received	4,900	Credit purchases	337,200
Contras against credit balance in receivable ledger	1,400	Interest payable on overdue amounts	3,600
Closing balance	420,760		
	649,400		649,400

56   B   Because the credit note was not entered in the sales day book, it would not be included in
         the total that is entered into the receivables control account. Therefore the total of the list
         of balances would be $150 less than the receivables control account balance. The invoice
         entered incorrectly in the sales day book would cause both the list of balances and the
         receivables control account to be overstated by $90.

57   C   Discounts allowed relate to sales and are an expense of the business.

58   C   (12,160 + 1,800 – 150) – (14,560) = 750

			$
59	A	List price	200,000
		Trade discount	(20,000)
			180,000

60 B − 3,860 − 9,160 + 16,690 = 3,670. Remember that the opening bank balance is overdrawn.

61 B Items 2 to 4 are adjustments to the bank balance per the statement.

62 B Outstanding lodgements and unpresented cheques are timing differences.

63 C The ledger balance of $540 credit should be adjusted by a credit entry of $28 for bank charges. Therefore the corrected ledger balance is $568 credit. The bank statement balance is then $(568) + $620 cheques not yet on bank statement, ie $52 cash at bank.

64 B

65 A

SUSPENSE ACCOUNT

	$		$
Balance b/d	210	Gas bill (420 − 240)	180
Interest	70	Discount (2 × 50)	100
	280		280

66 B

67 (a) The effects are as follows.

    (a) Motor expenses accrual – $520 additional expense, so reduction in profit.

    (b) Rent prepayment – $450 reduction in expense, so increase in profit.

    (c) Depreciation – total charge $13,146 additional expense, so reduction in profit.

        Total effect on net profit   = − 520 + 450 − 13,146

                            = 13,216 reduction

Working: Depreciation charge

Motor vehicles: $45,730 × 20% = $9,146
Fixtures and fittings: 10% × $(42,200 − 2,200) = $4,000
Total: $4,000 + $9,146 = $13,146

(b) B The inventory account is only changed at the end of the accounting period.

(c) MARCIA BLANE
STATEMENT OF FINANCIAL POSITION AS AT 31 DECEMBER 20X2

	Cost	Depreciation	Carrying value
	$	$	$
Non-current assets			
Fixtures and fittings	42,200	6,200	36,000
Motor vehicles	45,730	24,438	21,292
	87,930	30,638	57,292
Current assets			
Inventory		20,250	
Receivables		41,000	
Prepayments		450	
Cash in hand		1,500	
			63,200
			120,492

BPP
LEARNING MEDIA

Capital

Balance b/f	26,100
Profit for year (balancing figure)	67,657
	93,757
Less drawings (27,585 + 800)	28,385
	65,372

Current liabilities

Payables	34,500	
Accruals	520	
Bank overdraft	20,100	
		55,120
		120,492

Proof of profit for the year figure

Revenue	487,550
Cost of sales (18,460 + 379,590 – 800 – 20,250)	377,000
	110,500
Discounts received	1,200
Expenses (1,302 + 6,100 + 3,250 +10,750 +9,475 + 520 – 450 + 13,146)	44,093
Profit for the year	67,657

68 A Remember the business equation: $P = I + D - C_i$.

69 D (318,000 + 412,000 – 214,000) – (612,000 × 75%) = 57,000

70 D

	Total sales $	Ordinary sales $	Sales to Harry $
Cost of sales	342,000	334,700	7,300
Mark-up:			
10% on cost	730	–	730
20% on sales (= 25% on cost)	83,675	83,675	
Sales	426,405	418,375	8,030

71 B

	$	$
Non-current assets		51,300
Inventory		7,770
Receivables		5,565
		64,635
Less		
Payables	3,994	
Overdraft	3,537	
Rent accrual	500	
		(8,031)
Closing capital		56,604

72 B Purchases were payments made plus increase in suppliers' balances

ie $141,324 + ($16,812 – $15,264) = $142,872

		$
Thus cost of sales	Opening inventory	6,359
	Purchases	142,872
		149,231
	Less closing inventory	(4,919)
		144,312

73 B Dividends appear in the statement of changes in equity.

74 D

75	C	Dividends are not included the statement of changes in equity until they are declared.

76 B Number of shares = 45,000/0.5   = 90,000

Number of bonus shares issued   = 90,000/3 × 2 = 60,000

Nominal value of bonus shares issued   = 60,000 × 0.5 = 30,000

Therefore: Share capital = 45 + 30   = $75,000

Share premium = 60 – 30 = $30,000

77 A IAS 1 does require that some items must appear on the face of the statement of financial position; however, it allows companies to choose whether they present a combined statement of profit or loss and other comprehensive income or separate statement of profit or loss and statement of other comprehensive income.

78 C Gains on property revaluations are shown in the 'other comprehensive income' section of the statement of profit or loss and other comprehensive income. They are also shown in the statement of changes in equity as the movement on the revaluation surplus. Dividends paid and a bonus issue of shares are shown in the statement of changes in equity.

79 B There is no requirement in IAS 16 for the directors to disclose how certain they are that the valuation won't change in the next five years.

80 (a) $139,948

(b) $49,260

(c) $49,750

(d) A

The overdraft is a current liability and must not be deducted from any cash balances; the bank loan is a non-current liability as it is not due for payment for more than 12 months from the reporting date.

(e) A.

'Profit' on revaluation must be credited to a revaluation surplus, not to retained earnings for the year.

(f) $44,260

	$
Profit before tax	49,260
Tax	(5,000)
Retained earnings for the year	44,260

Remember that dividends and transfers to reserves are part of the statement of changes in equity.

81 B

82 A The fraud is an adjusting event, as it took place during the year to 30 June, although it was not discovered until after the year end. The loan stock issue is a non-adjusting event but due to its materiality should be disclosed in the notes.

83 A 1 is an adjusting event, as it provides evidence of a condition that existed at the reporting date – ie that the customer's debt was irrecoverable. The debt should be written off, and therefore net profit is reduced by $150,000. (2) is non-adjusting, as it does not affect the situation at the reporting date and therefore has no impact on profit at the reporting date. This event should simply be disclosed in the financial statements.

84 B

85

(a) FLAIL CO
STATEMENT OF CASH FLOWS FOR THE YEAR ENDED 31 DECEMBER 20X1

	$	$
Cash flows from operating activities		
Cash received from customers ($29,400 – $900)	28,500	
Cash paid to suppliers ($19,500 – $2,550)	(16,950)	
Cash paid to and on behalf of employees ($10,500 – $750)	(9,750)	
Interest paid	(2,100)	
Interest received	75	
Net cash flows from operating activities		(225)
Investing activities		
Purchase of non-current assets		(21,000)

	$	$
Financing activities		
Issue of shares	35,000	
Proceeds from medium-term loan	21,000	
Repayment of medium-term loan	(5,250)	
Net cash flows from financing activities		50,750
Net increase in cash and cash equivalents		29,525
Cash and cash equivalents at 1 January 20X1		–
Cash and cash equivalents at 31 December 20X1		29,525

Note that the dividend is only proposed and so there is no related cash flow in 20X1.

(b) D   Items 1 and 3 do not involve movements of cash.

86 B   An increase in a bank loan will be classified under financing cash flows. A loss on the sale of a non-current asset will be added back to net profit to calculate operating cash flows using the indirect method.

87 B   Both investments are subsidiaries. In 1, Barracuda has more than 50% of the voting rights, as it owns more than 50% of the ordinary shares. In 2, Barracuda has the ability to control Major, as it can appoint more than half the board of directors of Major Inc.

88 D   None of the statements are correct. A 50% investment will usually mean that an investment is a subsidiary, however, if it can be shown that the investor does not have control over the investee company, it will not be classified as a subsidiary. Consolidated accounts are prepared to represent the substance and not the legal form of the relationship between parent and subsidiary. An associate is an entity in which an investor has significant influence.

89 C   Delta's share of profit after tax should be included as a single amount in the consolidated statement of profit or loss.

90 C

Current assets (250 +100 – 6)	344

91 C

	$'000
Consideration transferred	300
Fair value of non-controlling interest at acquisition	100
	400
Less net assets acquired (200 + 36)	(236)
	164

92 C

	$'000
Consideration transferred	500
Fair value of non-controlling interest	125
	625
Less net assets acquired	(450)
	175

93 B

	$'000
Vaynor Co	90
Weeton Co (40 + 10)	50
Yarlet Co (70 – 30)	40
	180

94 B

	$'000
Spring	200,000
Summer	160,000
	360,000
Less intra-group sales	(16,000)
Add provision for unrealised profit (16,000 – 10,000)	6,000
	350,000

95 D Reduce revenue by intra-group sales of $40,000.

96 A Reduce consolidated profit by provision for unrealised profit.

$$20,000 \times \frac{25}{125} = \$4,000$$

97 C

	Sanderstead Co $	Croydon Co $	Adj $	Consol $
Revenue	600,000	300,000	(20,000)	880,000
Cost of sales	(400,000)	(200,000)	20,000	(580,000)
Gross profit				300,000

98 A Example: suppose the entity purchases inventory worth $300,000:

	Current ratio		Quick ratio	
Before	$\frac{1,500}{1,000}$	= 1.5	$\frac{400}{1,000}$	= 0.4
After	$\frac{1,800}{1,300}$	= 1.4	$\frac{400}{1,300}$	= 0.3

99 B Calculate the ratios relating to the new product:

Operating profit margin: $\frac{120}{1,600}$ = 7.5% (less than existing margin of 10%)

ROCE: $\frac{120}{500}$ = 24% (greater than existing ROCE of 20%)

Existing ROCE is 10% × 2 = 20%.

100

(a) JESSICA GROUP
CONSOLIDATED STATEMENT OF PROFIT OR LOSS
FOR THE YEAR ENDED 31 DECEMBER 20X7

	$m
Revenue (7,500 + 3,000 – 5)	10,495
Cost of sales (4,000 + 1,600 – 5 + 1)	5,596
Gross profit	4,899
Operating expenses (2,000 + 500)	2,500
Profit before taxation	2,399
Income taxes (300 + 120)	420
Profit for the year	1,979

Intra-group trading

Selling price	5
Cost	3
Profit	2

Unrealised 50% × 2m = 1m

NCI share = 25% × 1m = 0.25m

(b) Profit attributable to:

Owners of the parent (bal. fig.)	1,484.5
Non-controlling interest ((25% × 1979) – 0.25)	494.5
	1,979.0

(c) B Current ratio = current assets/current liabilities. If the ratio is less than 1, it could mean that the company is unable to pay its debts on time.

Therefore 1 is incorrect, because the ratio has gone up and is now above 1, it means the company is **more likely** to be able to pay its debts on time compared with before when the ratio was less than 1. 2 is correct, as an increase in revenue caused by an increase in price (as opposed to a change in volume) will lead to a larger receivables balance, hence a larger current assets balance compared to current liabilities. 3 is incorrect, as a higher supplier costs will result in a larger current liabilities balance, while current assets remain the same.

(d) A Control is the main factor to be taken into account when considering a parent-subsidiary relationship. Control is deemed to exist if an investor owns more than 50% of the ordinary shares. Significant influence is used to decide whether an investment is an associate.

Index

Depreciation   141, 161
        reducing   144
        Straight   143
        Methods   142

Depreciable amounts
        of assets   141, 172

Review form

Name: _____   Address: _____

_____

_____

How have you used this Interactive Text?
(Tick one box only)

☐ Home study (book only)

☐ On a BPP in-centre course _____

☐ On a BPP online course

☐ On a course with another college

☐ Other _____

Why did you decide to purchase this Interactive Text? *(Tick one box only)*

☐ Have used BPP Texts in the past

☐ Recommendation by friend/colleague

☐ Recommendation by a lecturer at college

☐ Saw advertising

☐ Other _____

Which BPP products have you used?

☑ Text   ☐ Kit   ☐ i-Pass   ☐ Passcards

During the past six months do you recall seeing/receiving any of the following?
(Tick as many boxes as are relevant)

☐ Our advertisement in *ACCA Student Accountant*

☐ Our advertisement in *Teach Accounting*

☐ Other advertisement _____

☐ Our brochure with a letter through the post

☐ ACCA E-Gain email

☐ BPP email

☐ Our website www.bpp.com

Which (if any) aspects of our advertising do you find useful?
(Tick as many boxes as are relevant)

☐ Prices and publication dates of new editions

☐ Information on Interactive Text content

☐ Facility to order books

☐ None of the above

Your ratings, comments and suggestions would be appreciated on the following areas

	Very useful	Useful	Not useful
Introductory section (How to use this Interactive Text)	☐	☐	☐
Key terms	☐	☐	☐
Examples	☐	☐	☐
Questions and answers	☐	☐	☐
Fast forwards	☐	☐	☐
Quick quizzes	☐	☐	☐
Exam alerts	☐	☐	☐
Practice Question Bank	☐	☐	☐
Practice Answer Bank	☐	☐	☐
Index	☐	☐	☐
Structure and presentation	☐	☐	☐
Icons	☐	☐	☐

	Excellent	Good	Adequate	Poor
Overall opinion of this Interactive Text	☐	☐	☐	☐

Do you intend to continue using BPP products?   ☐ Yes   ☐ No

Please note any further comments and suggestions/errors on the reverse of this page.

The author of this edition can be emailed at: accaqueries@bpp.com

Please return this form to: Head of ACCA & Foundations in Accountancy Programmes, BPP Learning Media Ltd, FREEPOST, London, W12 8AA

Review form (continued)

Please note any further comments and suggestions/errors below